A+ Complete

Exam Notes

A+® Complete

Exam Notes™

David Groth
Dan Newland
Todd Halpin

San Francisco • Paris • Düsseldorf • Soest • London

SYBEX

Associate Publisher: Neil Edde
Contracts and Licensing Manager: Kristine O'Callaghan
Acquisitions and Developmental Editor: Elizabeth Hurley
Editor: Linda Recktenwald
Production Editor: Shannon Murphy
Technical Editor: André Paree-Huff
Book Designer: Bill Gibson
Graphic Illustrators: Duane Bibby, Tony Jonick
Electronic Publishing Specialist: Judy Fung
Proofreaders: Jennifer Campbell, Leslie Higbee Light, Laurie O'Connell, Yariv Rabinovitch, Nancy Riddiough
Indexer: Marilyn Smith
Cover Designer: Archer Design
Cover Illustrator/Photographer: Tony Stone Images

Library of Congress Card Number: 2001087092
ISBN: 0-7821-2803-3

Manufactured in the United States of America

10 9 8 7 6 5 4 3 2 1

Acknowledgments

The staff at Sybex are wonderfully professional and easy to work with. Linda Recktenwald did a great job of turning my misplaced "which"es into "that"s and made everything about this manuscript better. Elizabeth Hurley and Shannon Murphy were great (as usual!) at getting the project going and keeping it on track. Special thanks as well to Senoria Bilbo-Brown for all her help in the confusing world of contracts. Judy Fung did a lovely job turning the manuscript into the beautiful book you are now holding, and Jennifer Campbell, Leslie Higbee Light, Laurie O'Connell, Yariv Rabinovitch, and Nancy Riddiough caught all my typos. Thanks for all the terrific work! On the home front, I am in debt to Steph for putting up with me during the writing process, to our Blue Heeler Rudi for always listening, and to my Bunn coffee machine, without which my work on this book would not have been possible.

—Dan Newland

While writing this book, several people provided me with support and helped ease the strain on my time: Tonya McGuire, Linda Ogura, and Dave Thomas at Eye-Mart; Scott Hess of Acute Network Technologies, who happens to sell one heck of a thin client; and Karla Weiss of CDW. Karla makes sure I keep on top of orders and is the most thorough sales associate/coordinator I have ever dealt with.

I would like to say hello to Dr. David Ogle, Dr. Tony Klein, Dr. Bradley Bath, Julie Bath, Dr. Chad Ashley, Dr. William Rousch, Jarrett Buse, Jeff, Wayne, Crystal, Tabby and everyone at ESB, Mark Chapman, Glen Ogle, Irvin, Phyllis, Sherry, Cameron, Ben, Daniel and Lehman Smith, my step-father Retired Air Force Colonel Reverend William J. Wade, my sister Jenifer, her husband "Wayner," my nephew Bradley and niece Lauren, all of my recess buddies at Harper Elementary, Kris "Jr." Miller, and Robert Kessinger and Steve Wulf, two better friends than I deserve.

A special thanks to Jeff Gray. As my mentor, he chose to give me just enough information to get me started and made me sweat the details. I'm not sure whether to thank him or break his legs.

The person who gave the most is my wonderful six-year-old daughter, Jordan. People don't quite understand what a project like this does to your personal life. This incredibly special girl gave up a lot of clowning-around time with Daddy so he could "work on the stupid book," as she says. I love you and cherish each day I can watch you grow.

I would also like to thank my ex-wife. Despite our differences, I value her as a co-parent and look forward to raising our baby the best way we know how.

This year one of the most inspiring athletes in history proved that his amazing win last year was no accident. Anyone who rides knows the courage it takes just to enter a race; now consider winning, and then consider twice winning after battling cancer. GO, LANCE ARMSTRONG! Lance has a foundation that provides funding for cancer research and a wonderful book, *It's Not About the Bike* (ISBN 0-399-14611-3).

Another person I should mention is my fiancée, Michele. She is a former swimsuit model who destroys men on the golf course and the keyboard. Every day, she fights the stereotypes given to beautiful women. She doesn't get mad; she gets even. When we go to purchase components at computer shops, she walks in and jaws drop, and then when she asks for a component, they look at me like, "Are you going to put this in?" She runs them around for a while until they know whom they are dealing with—a highly educated, incredibly technical, driven network administrator who just happens to have been on a few posters and billboards. If the people at a certain beer company only knew how sharp her mind was, they would have had her running the company instead of wearing the label. Thank you for loving me, dear; a more perfect fit in this world does not exist.

Finally I want to add a little note. I am dyslexic, and so are my daughter and my fiancée. I am not ashamed of it; rather, I take pride in my accomplishments. In grade school, I was sent to special education centers and was considered "handicapped." Back in the late seventies and early eighties, little was known about what this "gift" was or how to help a child develop and utilize his or her overactive mind. I am positive that this incredible gift has made me as successful as I am today. For those who wrote me off as a child, I want you to know that this is my second published book, and I hold several very respectable certifications.

You don't treat dyslexia, you enhance it. There are now techniques that can help a dyslexic child cope with the near-impossible things that most people take for granted. If your child has been diagnosed with attention deficit disorder or dyslexia, I encourage you to purchase a copy of *Brilliant Idiot*, by Dr. Abraham Schmitt (ISBN 1-56148-108-4). Educate yourself—don't medicate the child!

Finally, a special thanks to everyone at Sybex for making this project flow quickly and easily. Although this was only my second book, I was very pleased that their dedication to achieve the best content was not overshadowed by an accelerated timetable. Everyone from acquisitions to the editors was extremely helpful, and their efforts were greatly appreciated.

—*Todd Halpin*

Contents

Introduction

The A+ certification program was developed by the Computer Technology Industry Association (CompTIA) to provide an industry-wide means of certifying the competency of computer service technicians. The A+ certification, which is granted to those who have attained the level of knowledge and troubleshooting skills that are needed to provide capable support in the field of personal computers, is similar to other certifications in the computer industry. For example, Novell offers the Certified NetWare Engineer (CNE) program to provide the same recognition for network professionals who deal with its NetWare products, and Microsoft has its Microsoft Certified Systems Engineer (MCSE) program. The theory behind these certifications is that if you need to have service performed on any of their products, you would sooner call a technician who has been certified in one of the appropriate programs than you would just call the first so-called expert in the phone book.

In order for this certification to maintain its relevance, though, occasional updates must be made. Sometimes, those updates are quite significant, and so it is with this one. After years of focusing on Microsoft's DOS operating system, CompTIA has revamped its A+ exams to focus on the new hardware and software that have been coming out over the past few years. Therefore, this exam guide focuses on Windows 98 and 2000, which were not even mentioned in the previous exams, and looks at hardware such as Pentium II and III processors, which were similarly not dealt with before.

This book and the Sybex *A+ Complete Study Guide* are tools to help you prepare for this new exam—and for the new focuses of a modern computer technician's job.

What Is A+ Certification?

The A+ certification program was created to offer a wide-ranging certification, in the sense that it is intended to certify competence with personal computers from many different makers/vendors. There are two tests required to become A+ certified. You must pass the A+ Core Hardware Service Technician exam, which covers basic computer concepts, hardware troubleshooting, customer service, and hardware upgrading. You must also pass the A+ Operating System Technologies exam (formerly known as the A+ DOS/Windows exam), which covers the DOS and Windows operating system environments. You don't have to take the Core Hardware and the Operating System Technologies exams at the same time; you have 90 days from the time you pass one test to pass the second test. The A+ certified "diploma" is not awarded until you've passed both tests.

Why Become A+ Certified?

There are several good reasons to get your A+ certification. The CompTIA Candidate's Information Packet lists five major benefits of certification:

- It demonstrates proof of professional achievement.

- It increases your marketability.

- It provides greater opportunity for advancement in your field.

- It is increasingly found as a requirement for some types of advanced training.

- It raises customer confidence in you and your company's services.

Provides Proof of Professional Achievement

The A+ certification is quickly becoming a status symbol in the computer service industry. Organizations whose membership includes computer service industry technicians are recognizing the benefits of A+ certification and are pushing for their members to become certified. And more people every day are putting the "A+ Certified Technician" emblem on their business cards.

Increases Your Marketability

A+ certification makes individuals more marketable to potential employers. Also, A+ certified employees may receive a higher base salary, because employers won't have to spend as much money on vendor-specific training.

What Is an AASC?

More service companies are becoming A+ Authorized Service Centers (AASCs). This means that over 50 percent of the technicians employed by that service center are A+ certified. At the time of the writing of this book, there are over 1,400 A+ Authorized Service Centers in the world. Customers and vendors alike recognize that AASCs employ the most qualified service technicians. Because of this, an AASC will get more business than a non-authorized service center. Also, because more service centers want to reach the AASC level, they will give preference in hiring to a candidate who is A+ certified over one who is not.

Provides Opportunity for Advancement

Most raises and advancements are based on performance. A+ certified employees work faster and more efficiently, thus making them more productive. The more productive employees are, the more money they will make for their company. And, of course, the more money they make for the company, the more valuable they will be to the company. So if an employee is A+ certified, their chances of getting promoted will be greater.

Fulfills Training Requirements

A+ certification is recognized by most major computer hardware vendors, including (but not limited to) IBM, Hewlett-Packard, Apple, and Compaq. Some of these vendors will apply A+ certification toward prerequisites in their own respective certification programs. For example, an A+ certified technician is automatically given credit toward HP laser printer certification without having to take prerequisite classes and tests. This has the side benefit of reducing training costs for employers.

Raises Customer Confidence

As the A+ certified technician moniker becomes better known among computer owners, more of them will realize that the A+ technician is more qualified to work on their computer equipment than a non-certified technician is.

Is This Book for You?

A+ Complete Exam Notes is designed to be a succinct, portable exam review guide that can be used either in conjunction with a more complete study program (book, CBT courseware, classroom/lab environment) or as an exam review for those who don't feel the need for more extensive test preparation. It isn't our goal to "give the answers away," but rather to identify those topics on which you can expect to be tested and to provide sufficient coverage of these topics.

Perhaps you've been working with information technologies for years now. The thought of paying lots of money for a specialized IT exam-preparation course probably doesn't sound too appealing. What can they teach you that you don't already know, right? Be careful, though. Many experienced network administrators have walked confidently into the test center only to walk sheepishly out of it after failing an IT exam. After you've finished reading through this book, you should have a clear idea of how your understanding of the technologies involved matches up with the expectations of the A+ test makers.

Or perhaps you're relatively new to the world of IT, drawn to it by the promise of challenging work and higher salaries. You've just waded through an 800-page study guide or taken a class at a local training center. Lots of information to keep track of, isn't it? Well, by organizing the *Exam Notes* book according to CompTIA's exam objectives, and by breaking up the information into concise, manageable pieces, we've created what we think is the handiest exam review guide available. Throw it in your briefcase and carry it to work with you. As you read through the book, you'll be able to quickly identify those areas you know best and those that will require a more in-depth review.

NOTE   The goal of the Exam Notes series is to help A+ candidates familiarize themselves with the subjects on which they can expect to be tested in the A+ exams. For complete in-depth coverage of the technologies and topics involved, we recommend the *A+ Complete Study Guide* from Sybex.

How Is This Book Organized?

This book is organized according to the official objectives list prepared by CompTIA for the A+ exam. The chapters correspond with the broad objective groupings, such as Installation and Upgrading, Networks, Configuration, and Diagnosing and Troubleshooting.

Within each chapter, the individual exam objectives are addressed in turn. Each objectives section is further divided into Critical Information, Exam Essentials, Necessary Procedures, and Key Terms and Concepts, according to the type of information required.

Critical Information

The Critical Information section presents the greatest level of detail on information that is relevant to the objective. This is the place to start if you're unfamiliar with or uncertain about the technical issues related to the objective.

Exam Essentials

Here you will be given a short list of topics that you will want to explore fully before taking the test. Included in the Exam Essentials areas are notations of the key information that you should have taken out of the *A+ Complete Study Guide* or the Critical Information section.

Necessary Procedures

Here you'll find instructions for procedures that require a lab computer for their completion. From installing operating systems to modifying configuration defaults, the information in these sections addresses the hands-on requirements for the A+ exams.

NOTE Not every objective has procedures associated with it. For such objectives, the Necessary Procedures section has been omitted.

Key Terms and Concepts

Here we've compiled a mini-glossary of the most important terms and concepts related to the specific objective. You'll need to understand what all those technical words mean within the context of the related subject matter.

How Do You Become A+ Certified?

A+ certification is available to anyone who passes the tests. You don't have to work for any particular company. It's not a secret society. It is, however, an elite group. In order to become A+ certified, you must do two things:

- Pass the A+ Core Hardware Service Technician exam.

- Pass the A+ Operating System Technologies exam (formerly the DOS/Windows exam).

Note, you don't have to take both exams at the same time; you have 90 days from the time you pass one test to pass the other test.

To register for the tests, call Prometric at (800) 77-MICRO (776-4276). You'll be asked for your name, Social Security number (an optional number may be assigned if you don't wish to provide your Social Security number), mailing address, phone number, employer, when and where (i.e., which Prometric testing center) you want to take the test, and your credit card number. Arrangement for payment must be made at the time of registration. If you have to take a test more than once in order to get a passing grade, you have to pay each time.

Where Do You Take the Exam?

The exams are administered by Prometric and can be taken at any Prometric Testing Center. If you pass both exams, you will get a certificate in the mail from CompTIA saying that you have passed, and you will also receive a lapel pin and business card. To find the Prometric training center nearest you, call (800) 755-EXAM (755-3926). You can also find this information on their Web site: www.2test.com.

What the A+ Exams Measure

Behind every computer industry exam, you can be sure to find exam objectives—the broad topics in which the exam developers want to ensure your competency. The official CompTIA exam objectives are listed in the following sections.

The A+ Core Hardware Service Technician Exam Objectives

The following are the areas (or "domains" according to CompTIA) in which you must be proficient in order to pass the A+ Core Hardware Service Technician exam.

Domain 1.0: Installation, Configuration, and Upgrading

This content area deals with the installation, configuration, and upgrading of common computer Field Replaceable Units (FRUs). Most technicians spend a lot of time performing these operations. To that end, CompTIA has made sure that questions from this content area will make up 30 percent of the exam.

Domain 2.0: Diagnosing and Troubleshooting

Before a technician can install or upgrade a component, he or she must determine which component needs to be replaced. A technician will normally use the skills addressed by the diagnosing and troubleshooting content areas to make that determination. Questions about these two topics together make up 30 percent of the exam.

Domain 3.0: Preventive Maintenance

Most people don't think of computer service as a dangerous job. Most often, safety precautions are taken to prevent damage to the components. In actuality, there are a few components that can cause severe injury if improperly handled. This topic also covers maintaining and cleaning computer components. Questions about these topics constitute 5 percent of the exam.

Domain 4.0: Motherboards, Processors, and Memory

Several of the items in this content area give people the most problems (for example, learning the differences between the various types of processors). This content area makes up 15 percent of the exam.

Domain 5.0: Printers

Although there are only two objectives here and the questions on printers make up 10 percent of the test, printer problems are extremely common and can cause no end of trouble. Therefore, you will want to be prepared on how to deal with all facets of troubleshooting printer hardware. Printer software issues are dealt with in the OS exam.

Domain 6.0: Basic Networking

With the explosion of the Internet into the service world, the line between a service technician and networking technician has blurred. Frequently, computers that are brought in for service have problems that are related to their networking hardware. An A+ certified technician should know how both the hardware and software components of networking can affect the operation of the computer. CompTIA has put basic networking concepts on the A+ Core Hardware exam, and they make up 10 percent of the total exam questions.

Operating System Technologies Exam Objectives

The following are the areas in which you must be proficient in order to pass the A+ Operating System Technologies exam.

Domain 1.0: Operating System Fundamentals

This domain requires knowledge of Windows 95/98, Windows NT, and Windows 2000 operating systems. You will need to know how they work, as well as the components that compose them. You will also need to know topics relating to navigating the operating systems and, in general, how to use them. Operating system fundamentals make up 30 percent of the exam.

Domain 2.0: Installation, Configuration, and Upgrading

This domain basically tests your knowledge of the day-to-day servicing of operating systems. This includes topics such as installing, configuring, and upgrading the various operating systems (Windows 9*x*, NT, and 2000). You will also be expected to know system boot sequences. These topics make up 15 percent of the exam.

Domain 3.0: Diagnosing and Troubleshooting

Questions in this domain test your ability to diagnose and troubleshoot Windows 9*x*, NT, and 2000 systems and make up a whopping 40 percent of the test.

Domain 4.0: Networks

This domain requires knowledge of the network capabilities of Windows 9*x* and 2000 and how to connect to networks. It includes the Internet, its capabilities, basic concepts relating to Internet access, and generic procedures for system setup. Network questions make up 15 percent of the exam.

Tips for Taking the A+ Exam

Here are some general tips for taking your exam successfully:

- Bring two forms of ID with you. One must be a photo ID, such as a driver's license. The other can be a major credit card or a passport. Both forms must bear your signature.

- Arrive early at the exam center so you can relax and review your study materials, particularly tables and lists of exam-related information.

- Read the questions carefully. Don't be tempted to jump to an early conclusion. Make sure you know exactly what the question is asking.

- Don't leave any unanswered questions. Unanswered questions are scored against you.

- There will be questions with multiple correct responses. When there is more than one correct answer, a message at the bottom of the screen will prompt you to "Choose all that apply." Be sure to read the messages displayed.

- When answering multiple-choice questions you're not sure about, use a process of elimination to get rid of the obviously incorrect options first. This will improve your odds if you need to make an educated guess.

- On form-based tests, because the hard questions will eat up the most time, save them for last. You can move forward and backward through the exam. When the exam becomes adaptive, this tip will not work.

Contact Information

For the latest pricing on the exams and updates to the registration procedures, call Prometric at (866) Prometric (776-6387) or (800) 77-MICRO (776-4276). You can also go to either www.2test.com or www.prometric.com for additional information or to register online. If you have further questions about the scope of the exams or related CompTIA programs, refer to the CompTIA Web site at www.comptia.org/.

How to Contact the Publisher

Sybex welcomes feedback on all of their titles. Visit the Sybex Web site at www.sybex.com for book updates and additional certification information. You'll also find forms you can use to submit comments or suggestions regarding this or any other Sybex title.

A+: Core Hardware Service Technician Exam

Chapter

1

Domain 1.0 Installation, Configuration, and Upgrading

COMPTIA A+ EXAM OBJECTIVES COVERED IN THIS CHAPTER:

▶ **1.1 Identify basic terms, concepts, and functions of system modules, including how each module should work during normal operation and during the boot process.** *(pages 7 – 29)*

- System board
- Power supply
- Processor/CPU
- Memory
- Storage devices
- Monitor
- Modem
- Firmware
- BIOS
- CMOS
- LCD (portable systems)
- Ports
- PDA (Personal Digital Assistant)

▶ **1.2 Identify basic procedures for adding and removing field-replaceable modules for both desktop and portable systems.** *(pages 29 – 39)*

- System board
- Storage device
- Power supply
- Processor/CPU
- Memory
- Input devices
- Hard drive

- Keyboard
- Video board
- Mouse
- Network interface card (NIC)
- AC adapters
- DC controllers
- LCD panel
- PC card
- Pointing devices

1.3 Identify available IRQs, DMAs, and I/O addresses and procedures for configuring them for device installation and configuration. *(pages 39 – 47)*

- Standard IRQ settings
- Modems
- Floppy drive controllers
- Hard drive controllers
- USB port
- Infrared ports
- Hexadecimal/Addresses

1.4 Identify common peripheral ports, associated cabling, and their connectors. *(pages 47 – 52)*

- Cable types
- Cable orientation
- Serial versus parallel
- Pin connections
- DB-9
- DB-25
- RJ-11
- RJ-45
- BNC
- PS2/Mini-DIN
- USB
- IEEE-1394

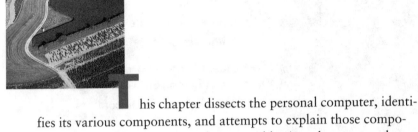

his chapter dissects the personal computer, identifies its various components, and attempts to explain those components as succinctly and precisely as possible. As a doctor must be intimately acquainted with human anatomy, so a computer technician must also understand the physical and functional structure of a personal computer.

Any PC is a complex machine. It could be described as a bit of a "melting pot" of various technologies and products, manufactured by a host of companies in many different countries. This diversity is also a great advantage because it gives the PC all of its versatility. However, these components don't always "melt" together into a unified whole without the help of a technician. These different products—whether they are hard disks, modems, sound cards, or memory boards—must share one processor and one motherboard and therefore must be designed to work in harmony. For this reason, configuration of the computer components is especially emphasized on the A+ Core Hardware exam, and nearly one-third of the exam's question pool pertains to the objectives reviewed in this chapter.

Before sitting for the exam, you will need to have a working knowledge of the components that make up a computer and their function within the system as a whole. The exam will test your knowledge of the types of components and their functions. The objective of this chapter is to review and identify the main components and their functions.

To pass the exam, you must be able to recognize these components and understand their relationship to one another. Figure 1.1 shows a typical PC, its components, and their locations.

FIGURE 1.1: Typical PC components

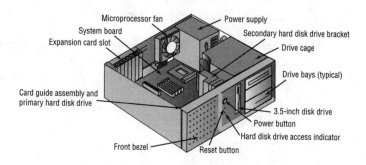

1.1 Identify basic terms, concepts, and functions of system modules, including how each module should work during normal operation and during the boot process.

- **System board**
- **Power supply**
- **Processor/CPU**
- **Memory**
- **Storage devices**
- **Monitor**
- **Modem**
- **Firmware**
- **BIOS**
- **CMOS**
- **LCD (portable systems)**
- **Ports**
- **PDA (Personal Digital Assistant)**

The function of each of these components is critical to the operation of the computer. The knowledge needed to effectively describe each of these components and their operation is not only key to passing the exam, but is necessary to productively troubleshoot issues that arise in daily PC break-fix repair environments.

The exam will test you on your knowledge of these components and demonstrate to employers and customers that you have the needed skills to succeed in this exciting and challenging field. This is normally the first step to becoming more than just one of the masses who consider themselves computer geeks.

Pay close attention to the critical information in this chapter; the information about the major components of the PC will be one of the more important topics on this test.

Critical Information

The system modules described in this section are either essential computer components or available on the market as optional equipment. Each has a distinct and very practical function.

Concepts and Modules

To troubleshoot and repair computers, you must be familiar with the components and their function when operating. Each component provides a specific function to the operation of the computer.

System Board

The spine of the computer is the *system board*, or *motherboard*. This component is made of green or brown fiberglass and is placed in the bottom or side of the case. It is the most important component in the computer because it connects all the other components of a PC together. Figure 1.2 shows a typical PC system board, as seen from above. On the system board you will find the CPU, underlying circuitry, expansion slots, video components, RAM slots, and a variety of other chips.

FIGURE 1.2: A typical system board

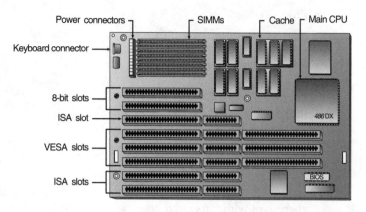

TYPES OF SYSTEM BOARDS

There are two major types of system boards: integrated and nonintegrated. Both of these types relate to the services provided by the board itself without the addition of other components.

Nonintegrated system boards require video, audio, or network devices to be added to the system with the expansion slots. This requirement mandates a greater assembly time for the computer and in some cases reduces the reliability of the system in transport.

Integrated system boards are called that because most of the components that would otherwise be installed as expansion cards are integrated into the motherboard circuitry. This reduces assembly time and ensures greater reliability of the system in transport, but it also prevents the individual replacement of a failed component.

SYSTEM BOARD COMPONENTS

Motherboards include components that provide basic functionality to the computer. The following components are found on a typical motherboard:

- Expansion slots
- Memory slots

- Processor slots or sockets
- Power connectors
- On-board disk drive connectors
- Keyboard connector
- Peripheral port connectors
- BIOS chip
- CMOS battery
- Jumpers and DIP switches

As we mentioned earlier, these may not be the only components on the motherboard with integrated systems. However, both integrated and nonintegrated systems contain most of these components. Figure 1.3 illustrates many of the components found on a typical motherboard.

FIGURE 1.3: Components on a motherboard

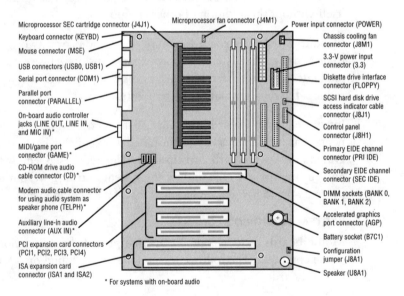

Microprocessor SEC cartridge connector (J4J1)
Keyboard connector (KEYBD)
Mouse connector (MSE)
USB connectors (USB0, USB1)
Serial port connector (COM1)
Parallel port connector (PARALLEL)
On-board audio controller jacks (LINE OUT, LINE IN, and MIC IN)*
MIDI/game port connector (GAME)*
CD-ROM drive audio cable connector (CD)*
Modem audio cable connector for using audio system as speaker phone (TELPH)*
Auxiliary line-in audio connector (AUX IN)*
PCI expansion card connectors (PCI1, PCI2, PCI3, PCI4)
ISA expansion card connector (ISA1 and ISA2)

Microprocessor fan connector (J4M1)

Power input connector (POWER)
Chassis cooling fan connector (J8M1)
3.3-V power input connector (3.3)
Diskette drive interface connector (FLOPPY)
SCSI hard disk drive access indicator cable connector (J8J1)
Control panel connector (J8H1)
Primary EIDE channel connector (PRI IDE)
Secondary EIDE channel connector (SEC IDE)
DIMM sockets (BANK 0, BANK 1, BANK 2)
Accelerated graphics port connector (AGP)
Battery socket (B7C1)
Configuration jumper (J8A1)
Speaker (U8A1)

* For systems with on-board audio

Expansion slots Expansion slots are used to install various devices in the computer to expand its capabilities. Some expansion devices that might be installed in these slots include video, network, sound, and disk interface cards.

Expansion slots come in three main types: ISA, PCI, and AGP. Each type is different in appearance and function, which you'll learn more about in future chapters. This chapter shows how to visually identify the different expansion slots on the motherboard.

ISA expansion slots If you are repairing a computer made before 1997, chances are the motherboard in your computer has a few Industry Standard Architecture (ISA) slots. These slots are usually brown and are separated into two unequal lengths. Computers made after 1997 generally include a few ISA slots for backward compatibility with old expansion cards.

PCI expansion slots Most computers made today contain primarily Peripheral Component Interconnect (PCI) slots. They are easily recognizable as they are short (around 3 inches long) and are usually white. PCI slots can usually be found in any computer that has a Pentium-class processor or higher.

AGP expansion slots Accelerated Graphics Port (AGP) slots are becoming more popular. In the past, if you wanted to use a high-speed, accelerated 3-D graphics video card, you had to install the card into an existing PCI or ISA slot. AGP slots were designed to be a direct connection between the video circuitry and the PC's memory. They are also easily recognizable because they are usually brown, located right next to the PCI slots on the motherboard. Figure 1.4 shows an example of an AGP slot, along with a PCI slot, for comparison. Notice the difference in length between the two.

FIGURE 1.4: An AGP slot compared to a PCI slot

MEMORY SLOTS

Memory, or random access memory (RAM), slots contain the actual memory chips. There are many and varied types of memory for PCs today. We'll further discuss the memory itself later in this chapter. PCs use memory chips arranged on a small circuit board. These circuit boards are called *Single Inline Memory Modules (SIMMs)* or *Dual Inline Memory Modules (DIMMs)*. DIMMs utilize memory chips on both sides of the circuit board while SIMMs utilize memory chips on a single side. Along with chip placement, memory modules also differ in the number of conductors, or pins, that the particular module uses. The number of pins used directly affects the overall size of the memory slot. Slot sizes include 30-pin, 72-pin, and168-pin. Laptop memory comes in smaller form factors known as *Small Outline DIMMs (SODIMMs)*. Figure 1.5 shows the popular form factors for the most popular memory chips. Notice how they basically look the same, but the memory module sizes are different.

FIGURE 1.5: Various memory module form factors

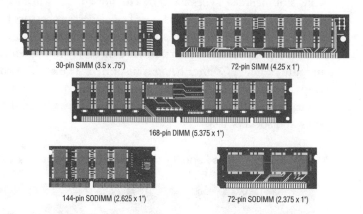

30-pin SIMM (3.5 x .75")   72-pin SIMM (4.25 x 1")

168-pin DIMM (5.375 x 1")

144-pin SODIMM (2.625 x 1")   72-pin SODIMM (2.375 x 1")

Memory slots are easy to identify on a motherboard. They are usually white and placed very close together. The number of memory slots varies from motherboard to motherboard, but the appearance of the different slots is very similar. There are metal pins in the bottom to make contact with the soldered tabs on each memory module. There are also small metal or plastic tabs on each side of the slot that are used to keep the memory module securely in its slot.

CENTRAL PROCESSING UNIT (CPU) AND PROCESSOR SLOTS

The CPU slot permits the attachment of the CPU to the motherboard, allowing the CPU to use the other components of the system. There are many different types of processors, which means many types of CPU slots. We'll expand upon the different types of processors in Chapter 4, "Motherboard/Processors/Memory"; for now we will discuss only its interface with the motherboard.

The CPU slot can take on several different forms. In the past, the CPU slot was a rectangular box with many small holes to accommodate the pins on the bottom of the chip. With the release of new and more powerful chips, additional holes were added, changing the configuration of the slot and its designator or number. Pre-PII chips include sockets 1–8.

With the release of the Pentium II, the architecture of the slot went from a rectangle to more of an expansion-slot style of interface. This style of CPU slot includes Types I and II. The slot change was facilitated by Intel and is now being phased out. The newest processors by Intel and AMD are returning to a flat style of chip similar to the pre-PII chips. According to industry leaders, this is a direct result of an increased failure rate of new PCs after being transported. The bulky Type I and II chips had a habit of dislodging during transport, which rendered the PC useless upon delivery. Figure 1.6 shows Types I and II processor slots and sockets 1–8.

FIGURE 1.6: Types I and II processor slots and sockets 1–8

To see which socket type is used for which processors, examine Table 1.1.

TABLE 1.1: Socket Types and the Processors They Support

Connector Type	Processor
Socket 1	486 SX/SX2, 486 DX/DX2, 486 DX4 Overdrive
Socket 2	486 SX/SX2, 486 DX/DX2, 486 DX4 Overdrive, 486 Pentium OverDrive
Socket 3	486 SX/SX2, 486 DX/DX2, 486 DX4 486 Pentium Overdrive
Socket 4	Pentium 60/66, Pentium 60/66 Overdrive
Socket 5	Pentium 75-133, Pentium 75+ Overdrive
Socket 6*	DX4, 486 Pentium Overdrive
Socket 7	Pentium 75-200, Pentium 75+ Overdrive
Socket 8	Pentium Pro
SECC (Type I)	Pentium II
SECC (Type II)	Pentium III

POWER CONNECTORS

A power connector (shown in Figure 1.7) allows the motherboard to be connected to the power supply. Normally, there are one or two plugs that connect to the power connector. If there are two connectors, they are normally keyed to prevent the technician from improperly attaching them and destroying the motherboard.

FIGURE 1.7: A power connector on a motherboard

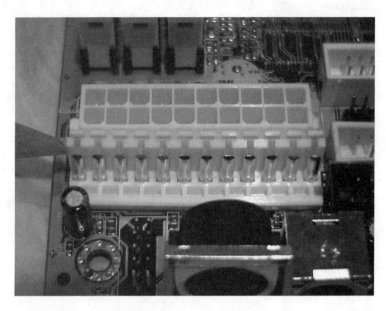

"ON BOARD" FLOPPY AND HARD DISK CONNECTORS

With the exception of diskless workstations, every PC made today uses some type of disk drive to store data and programs until they are needed. Disk drives need a connection to the motherboard in order for the computer to utilize the disk drive. These connections are known as *drive interfaces*. There are two primary types: *floppy drive interfaces* and *hard disk interfaces*. Floppy disk interfaces allow floppy disk drives to be connected to the motherboard and, similarly, hard disk interfaces do the same for hard disks. When you see them on the motherboard, these interfaces are said to be "on board," as opposed to being on an expansion card, known as "off board." The interfaces consist of circuitry and a port.

KEYBOARD CONNECTORS

Keyboard connectors allow for the direct connection of the keyboard to the motherboard. There are two keyboard connector types, AT and PS2.

AT connectors are round, about ½-inch in diameter, and have five sockets in the DIN-5 configuration. The second style, PS/2 connectors, is smaller and more common than the AT connectors. Most new PCs today contain a PS/2 keyboard connector on the motherboard.

PERIPHERAL PORTS AND CONNECTORS

PCs were developed to perform calculations on data. In order for the PC to be useful, there must be a way of getting the data into and out of the computer. To accomplish this, several ports are available. The four most common types of ports are the serial, parallel, Universal Serial Bus (USB), and game ports. Figure 1.8 shows examples of 9-pin and 25-pin serial ports. Figure 1.9 shows a typical parallel port (commonly referred to as a *printer port*), Universal Serial Bus (USB) ports, and a game port.

FIGURE 1.8: Typical 9-pin and 25-pin serial ports

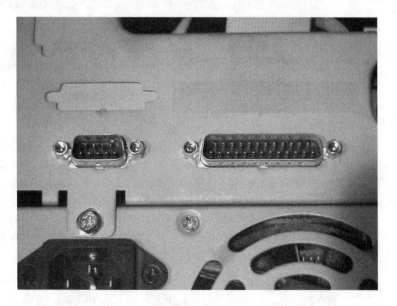

FIGURE 1.9: A typical parallel port

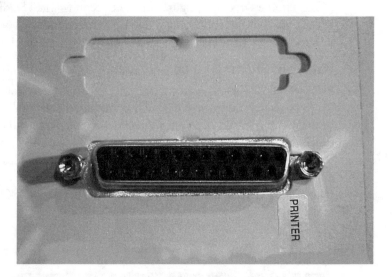

These ports are connected to the motherboard using a dongle connection or by the direct solder method. Most manufacturers utilize integrated motherboards or proprietary motherboards, which utilize the direct solder method.

BIOS CHIP

This chip is a special memory chip that contains the BIOS software that tells the processor how to interact with the hardware in the computer. The BIOS chip is easily identified. If you have a "branded" computer (e.g., Compaq, IBM, HP), this chip will have the name of the manufacturer and usually the word *BIOS*. Clones will usually have a sticker or printing on them from one of the three major BIOS manufacturers (AMI, Phoenix, and Award).

NOTE If you can't find the BIOS chip with these guidelines, look for a fairly large chip close to the CPU.

CMOS BATTERY

Your PC has to keep certain settings when it's turned off and its power cord is unplugged. These settings include date, time, hard drive configuration, and memory.

Your PC stores the settings in a special memory chip called the Complementary Metallic Oxide Semiconductor (CMOS) chip. To retain these settings, the CMOS chip requires power constantly. To prevent the CMOS chip from losing its charge, a small battery is located on the motherboard. This battery is called the CMOS battery.

JUMPERS AND DIP SWITCHES

Jumpers and DIP (Dual Inline Package) switches are used to configure various hardware options on the motherboard. Processors use different voltages and multipliers to achieve their target voltage and frequency. You must set these parameters on the motherboard by changing the jumper or DIP switch settings. Figure 1.10 shows both a jumper set and a DIP switch. Motherboards often have either several jumpers or one bank of DIP switches. Individual jumpers are often labeled with the moniker "JPx" (where x is the number of the jumper).

FIGURE 1.10: A jumper set and DIP switch

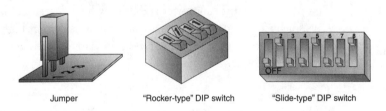

Jumper   "Rocker-type" DIP switch   "Slide-type" DIP switch

Power Supply

The device in the computer that provides the power is the power supply. A power supply converts 110-volt AC current into the four voltages that a computer needs to operate. These are +5 volts DC, –5 volts DC (ground), +12 volts DC, and –12 volts DC (ground).

Power supplies contain transformers and capacitors that carry *lethal* amounts of current. They are not meant to be serviced. *Do not* attempt to open them or do any work on them. Figure 1.11 shows a generic power supply.

FIGURE 1.11: A power supply

The CPU

The *CPU*, or *central processing unit*, controls all activities of the computer using both external and internal buses. It is a processor chip consisting of an array of millions of transistors.

The shape and architecture of CPUs range from a rectangle to a long circuit board with transistors. Normally, any Pentium class or higher chip has a heat sink or cooling fan attached. One reason why Pentium class or higher chips run hotter is that they have increased data pathways, or buses. Another reason is that they pass data at higher rates, which is referred to as the *MHz* of the chip. This causes a heavier load on the buses, which creates heat.

NOTE The best way to determine which CPU your computer is using is to open the case and view the numbers stamped on the CPU. Another way to determine a computer's CPU is to save your work, exit any open programs, and restart the computer. Watch closely as the computer returns to its normal state. You should see a notation that tells you what chip you are using. If you are using MS-DOS, you can also run Microsoft Diagnostics to view the processor type (that is, unless your computer has a Pentium, in which case it will report a very fast 486).

CLOCK SPEED

The *clock speed* is the frequency with which a processor executes instructions. This frequency is measured in millions of cycles per second, or megahertz (MHz). This clock signal is generated by a quartz crystal, which vibrates as electricity passes through it, thereby generating a steady pulse to every component synchronized with the signal. A system cycle is generated by this pulse (called a clock *tick*), which sends a signal through the processor telling it to perform another operation. In most cases, the higher the MHz value, the faster the PC will be.

CACHE MEMORY

Cache memory is a storage area for frequently used data and instructions. It requires a small amount of physical RAM that can keep up with the processor. The processor contains an internal cache controller that integrates the cache with the CPU. The controller stores frequently accessed RAM locations to provide faster execution of data and instructions. This type of cache is known as a *Level 1 Cache*. It is also possible to have a cache external to the CPU, called a *Level 2 Cache*. This type of cache performs the same functions as a Level 1 Cache and can speed up the perceived performance. Basically, a larger cache leads to the perception of a faster CPU.

THE BUS

The processor's ability to communicate with the rest of the system's components relies on the supporting circuitry. The system board's underlying circuitry is called the *bus*. The computer's bus moves information into and out of the processor and other devices. A bus allows all devices to communicate with each other.

Memory

As the computer's CPU works, it stores information in the computer's memory. The rule of thumb is that the more memory a computer has, the faster it will operate. Let's briefly look at the four major types of computer memory.

DRAM DRAM is Dynamic Random Access Memory. This is actually the "RAM" that most people are talking about when they mention RAM. "Dynamic" refers to the chips' need for a constant update signal (also called a *refresh* signal) in order to keep the information that is written there.

SRAM   The *S* in SRAM stands for Static. Static Random Access Memory doesn't require the refresh signal that DRAM does. The chips are more complex and are thus more expensive. However, they are faster. DRAM access times come in at 80 nanoseconds (ns) or more; SRAM has access times of 15 to 20 ns. SRAM is often used for cache memory.

ROM   ROM stands for Read-Only Memory. It is called *read-only* because it can't be written to. Once the information has been written to the ROM, it can't be changed. ROM is normally used to store the computer's BIOS. The system ROM enables the computer to "pull itself up by its bootstraps," or *boot* (start the operating system).

CMOS   CMOS is a special kind of memory that holds the BIOS configuration settings. CMOS memory is powered by a small battery so that the settings are retained when the computer is shut off.

Storage Devices

Storage media hold the data being accessed, as well as the files the system needs to operate and data that needs to be saved. The various types of storage differ in terms of capacity, access time, and the physical type of media being used.

HARD DISK SYSTEMS

Hard disks reside inside the computer and can hold more information than other forms of storage. The hard disk system contains three critical components: the controller, the hard disk, and the host adapter. The controller controls the drive, the hard disk provides a physical medium to store the data, and the host adapter is the translator.

FLOPPY DRIVES

A floppy disk drive is a magnetic storage medium that uses a floppy disk made of thin plastic enclosed in a protective casing. The floppy disk itself (or *floppy*, as it is often called) enables the information to be transported from one computer to another very easily. The downside of a floppy disk drive is its limited storage capacity. Floppy disks are limited to a maximum capacity of 2.88 MB. Table 1.2 lists the various floppy disks and their capacity.

TABLE 1.2: Floppy Disk Capacities

Floppy Drive Size	Number of Tracks	Capacity
5¼"	40	360KB
5¼"	80	1.2MB
3½"	80	720KB
3½"	80	1.44MB
3½"	80	2.88MB

CD-ROM DRIVES

CD-ROM stands for Compact Disc Read-Only Memory. The CD-ROM is used for long-term storage of data. CD-ROMs are read-only, meaning that once information is written to a CD, it can't be erased or changed. Access time for CD-ROMs is considerably slower than for a hard drive. CDs normally hold 650MB of data and use the ISO 9660 standard, which allows them to be used in multiple platforms.

DVD-ROM DRIVES

Because DVD-ROMs use slightly different technology than CD-ROMs, they can store up to 1.6GB of data. This makes them a better choice for distributing large software bundles. Many software packages today are so huge that they take multiple CD-ROMs to hold all the installation and reference files. A single DVD-ROM, in a double-sided, double-layered configuration, can hold as much as 17GB (as much as 26 regular CD-ROMs).

OTHER STORAGE MEDIA

Many additional types of storage are available for PCs today. However, most of them are not covered on the A+ exam, so we'll just discuss them briefly here. Among the other types of storage are Zip drives, tape backup devices, and optical drives.

Zip drives and Jaz drives Iomega's Zip and Jaz drives are detachable, external hard disks that are used to store a large volume (around 100MB for the Zip, 1GB and 2GB for the Jaz) of data on a single, floppy-sized disk. The drives connect to either a parallel port or a special interface card. The major use of Zip and Jaz drives is for transporting large amounts of data from place to place. This used to be accomplished with several floppies.

Tape backup devices Another form of storage device is the tape backup. Tape backup devices can be installed internally or externally and use a magnetic tape medium instead of disks for storage. They hold much more data than any other medium but are also much slower. They are primarily used for archival storage.

Optical drives The final type of storage is the optical drive. Optical drives work by using a laser rather than magnetism to change the characteristics of the storage medium.

Monitors

Display systems convert computer signals into text and pictures and display them on a television-like screen. There are several different types of computer displays in use today, including the TV. All of them use either the same *cathode ray tube* (*CRT*) technology found in television sets or the *liquid crystal display* (*LCD*) technology found on all laptop, notebook, and palmtop computers.

As we have already mentioned, a monitor contains a CRT. But how does it work? Basically, a device called an *electron gun* shoots electrons toward the back of the monitor screen (see Figure 1.12). The back of the screen is coated with special chemicals (called *phosphors*) that glow when electrons strike them. This beam of electrons scans the monitor from left to right and top to bottom to create the image.

FIGURE 1.12: How a monitor works

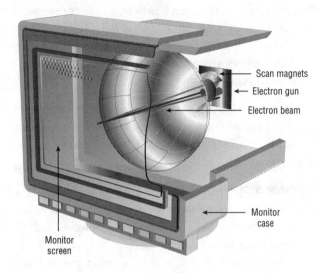

There are two ways of measuring a monitor's quality of image: dot pitch and refresh (scan) rate. A monitor's *dot pitch* is the shortest distance between two dots of the same color on the monitor. Usually given in fractions of a millimeter (mm), it tells how "sharp" the picture is. The lower the number, the closer together the pixels are, and thus the sharper the image. An average dot pitch is 0.28mm. Anything smaller than 0.28mm is considered great.

A monitor's *refresh rate* specifies how many times in one second the scanning beam of electrons redraws the screen. The phosphors stay bright only for a fraction of a second, so they must constantly be hit with electrons to stay lit. Given in draws per second, or Hertz, the refresh rate specifies how much energy is being put into keeping the screen lit. The standard refresh rate is 60Hz for VGA.

Liquid Crystal Displays

Two major types of LCDs are in use in laptops today: *active matrix* screen and *passive matrix* screen. Their main differences lie in the quality of the image. Both types use some kind of lighting behind the LCD panel to make the screen easier to view.

ACTIVE MATRIX

An active matrix screen works in a similar manner to an LCD watch. The screen is made up of several individual LCD pixels. A transistor behind each pixel, when switched on, activates two electrodes that align the crystals and turn the pixel dark. This type of display is very crisp and easy to look at.

The major disadvantage of an active matrix screen is that it requires large amounts of power to operate all the transistors. Even with the backlight turned off, the screen can still consume battery power at an alarming rate.

PASSIVE MATRIX

The main difference between active matrix and passive matrix is image quality. Because the computer takes a millisecond or two to light the coordinates for a pixel in passive matrix displays, the response of the screen to rapid changes is poor, causing an effect known as *submarining*. If, on a computer with a passive matrix display, you move the mouse rapidly from one location to another, it will disappear from the first location and reappear in the new location without appearing anywhere in between.

In order to keep the quality of the image on an LCD optimal, the screen must be cleaned often. Liquid crystal displays are typically coated with a clear, plastic covering. This covering commonly gets covered with fingerprints as well as a generous coating of dust. The best way to clean the LCD lens coating is to wipe it off occasionally with a damp cloth. This will ensure that the images stay crisp and clear.

Portable Computer Systems

A *portable computer* is any computer that contains all the functionality of a desktop computer system but is portable. Most portable computers fall into one of three categories: "luggable," laptop, or PDA. Luggable computers were the first truly portable computers, although some of their owners would beg to differ with me. Compaq made some of the first luggable computers.

Laptop computers were the next type of portable computer. They contain a built-in keyboard, pointing device, and LCD screen in a clamshell design. They are also called *notebook* computers because they resemble large notebooks. Most portable computers in use today are laptop computers.

The final type of portable computer, and one that has really taken off recently, is the palmtop computer (also known as a Personal Digital Assistant, or PDA). These computers are designed to keep the information you need close by so that you have access to it whenever you need it.

PORTABLE COMPUTER ACCESSORIES

Since portable computers have unique characteristics as a result of their portability, they have unique accessories as well. First of all, portable computers use either of two power sources: batteries or AC power. There are many different sizes and shapes of batteries, but most of them are Nickel-Cadmium (NiCad), Lithium Ion, or Nickel Metal Hydride (NiMH). All of these perform equally well as batteries, but NiCad batteries can be recharged only a finite number of times.

Most notebook computers are also able to use AC power with a special adapter that converts AC power into DC power (called an AC adapter). These can be integrated into the notebook (as on some Compaq models) or as a separate "brick" with a cord that plugs into the back of the laptop.

The final accessory that is unique to portable computers is the docking station. A docking station allows a portable computer to function as a desktop computer when it is attached to it (or *docked*). The docking station usually contains interfaces and expansion ports and bays that the laptop can use only when it is docked.

PDA

Mobile computing is becoming more and more flexible every day. PDAs (Personal Digital Assistants) or palmtop computers are capable of connecting though an external interface with a PC to synchronize mail, contact, and money management databases. Some high-end PDAs also have wireless e-mail and Web service that allows people to send and receive e-mail and browse the Web from virtually anywhere.

PDAs are called *palmtop* computers because of their size. The majority of these computers are the size of a large handheld calculator and utilize an LCD screen to view data. The data entry is accomplished with command buttons, a micro-sized keyboard, or, most commonly, a special magnetic pen. This special pen acts as a pointing device that sends signals to the palmtop for selecting items. Though different in appearance, its function is similar to a mouse or graphics pad.

Most of these computers also have their own shorthand language that the palmtop can recognize when the user draws on the pad. Because of their broad uses, the popularity of these devices will continue to grow.

Exam Essentials

Know what the BIOS does.   This is a special memory chip that contains the BIOS software that tells the processor how to interact with the hardware in the computer. The BIOS chip is easily identified. In some brands of computers, this chip has the name of the manufacturer and the word *BIOS* printed on the chip.

Know the different types of memory.   DRAM is Dynamic Random Access Memory. SRAM is Static Random Access Memory. ROM stands for Read-Only Memory, and it is normally used to store the computer's BIOS. CMOS is a special kind of memory that holds the BIOS configuration settings.

Key Terms and Concepts

System board   The spine of the computer is the system board, or motherboard. This component is made of green or brown fiberglass and is placed in the bottom or side of the case.

Memory slots   Memory slots hold the actual memory chips.

Processor slot   The CPU slot permits the attachment of the CPU to the motherboard, allowing the CPU to use the other components of the system.

BIOS chip   This is a special memory chip that contains the BIOS software that tells the processor how to interact with the hardware in the computer.

CMOS battery   A PC must retain certain settings when it's turned off and its power cord is unplugged. The CMOS battery provides power to the portion of the BIOS that stores CMOS settings.

Jumpers and DIP switches   Jumpers and DIP switches are used to configure various hardware options on the motherboard.

Cache memory   Cache memory is a storage area for frequently used data and instructions.

1.2 Identify basic procedures for adding and removing field-replaceable modules for both desktop and portable systems.

- **System board**
- **Storage device**
- **Power supply**
- **Processor/CPU**
- **Memory**
- **Input devices**
- **Hard drive**
- **Keyboard**
- **Video board**
- **Mouse**

- **Network interface card (NIC)**
- **AC adapters**
- **DC controllers**
- **LCD panel**
- **PC card**
- **Pointing devices**

At some point, every computer will need to be upgraded. Upgrading usually means one of two things: replacing old technology with new technology or adding functionality to an existing system. An example of upgrading old technology would be replacing a slower, older modem with a faster, newer one. An example of adding functionality to an existing system would be adding more RAM to increase performance. In either case, upgrading usually involves adding a new component. This process consists of several basic steps, each of which must be carefully followed. In this section, we will cover the following steps:

- Disassembly

- Inspection

- Installation and upgrades

- Reassembly

Critical Information

When you choose an area in which to work on a computer, pick a workspace that is sturdy enough to support the weight of a computer and any peripherals you are adding to your system. The area must also be well lit, clean, and large enough to hold all of the pieces and necessary tools.

Disassembling the Computer

Several steps need to be followed during the disassembly in order for the reassembly to be successful. People who take shortcuts through these steps often find themselves with "extra" parts and a computer that no longer functions.

Preparing Your Work Area

For any work you do on a computer, you must have an adequate workspace. This could mean any number of things. First, the work area must be flat. Second, the area must be sturdy. Make sure the work surface you are using can support the weight of the components. Third, the area must be well lit, clean, and large enough to hold all pieces (assembled and disassembled) and all necessary tools.

Before you begin, make sure all necessary tools are available and in working order. Also make sure that the documentation for the system you are working on is available (including owner's manuals, service manuals, and Internet resources).

The final guideline to preparing your work area is to set aside plenty of time to complete the task. Estimate the time required to complete the entire task (disassembly, installation, reassembly, and testing). Once you've prepared your work area and gathered your tools, you're ready to begin the actual disassembly of the computer. The steps are basically the same for all brands and types of computers.

Disassembly Prerequisites

There are several things you need to do before you even move the computer to your work area:

1. Shut down any running programs and turn the computer off.

2. Remove all cables that are attached to the computer.

3. Remove any floppy disks from their drives.

4. Check to see that all the prerequisites have been met, and move the computer to the work surface.

Removing the Case Cover

Now you are going to remove the computer's cover by removing the retaining screws at the back of the computer. *Slowly* remove the computer's cover by pulling it toward the rear and then lifting upward, as shown in Figure 1.13.

Don't remove *all* the screws at the back of the computer! Some of these screws hold vital components (such as the power supply) to the case, and removing them will cause those components to drop into the computer. Many of today's PCs can be completely disassembled without a single tool.

FIGURE 1.13: Removing the case cover

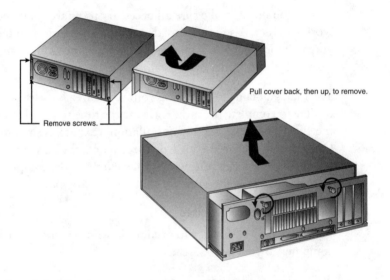

Pull cover back, then up, to remove.

Remove screws.

Removing the Expansion Cards

The next step in disassembly is to put on an antistatic wrist strap, plugging one end into the ground plug of an outlet. Then you can start to remove any *expansion cards*. There are four major steps in removing the expansion cards, as shown in Figure 1.14:

1. Remove any internal or external cables or connectors.

2. Remove any mounting screws that are holding the boards in place, and place the screws somewhere where they won't be lost.

3. Grasp the board by the top edge with both hands and gently rock it front to back (not side to side).

4. Finally, once the board is out, place it in an antistatic bag to help prevent ESD damage while the board is out of the computer.

Duplicate this procedure for each card.

NOTE   Be sure to note the slot each card is removed from, since some bus types (EISA, MCA, and PCI) keep track of which slots the expansion boards are installed in.

FIGURE 1.14: Removing an expansion board

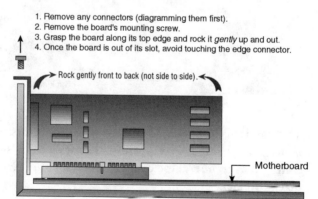

1. Remove any connectors (diagramming them first).
2. Remove the board's mounting screw.
3. Grasp the board along its top edge and rock it *gently* up and out.
4. Once the board is out of its slot, avoid touching the edge connector.

Rock gently front to back (not side to side).

Motherboard

Removing Input Devices

Input devices such as the keyboard and mouse should be removed before you open the case. With most of today's machines, the ports that the devices attach to are a physical part of the motherboard. If the devices are not removed before you take off the case, you are likely to damage the motherboard.

Removing the Power Supply

Before you remove the power supply from the computer, you must do two things: Disconnect the power supply connectors from the internal devices, and remove the mounting hardware for the power supply, as shown in Figure 1.15.

Grasp the connector (*not* the wires) and gently wiggle it out of its receptacle. Then, proceed to the next connector. The system board and disk drives both use power connectors. Make sure all of them are removed. AT cases have power leads connected to a switch at the front of the case that will also need to be removed.

FIGURE 1.15: Removing power supply connectors

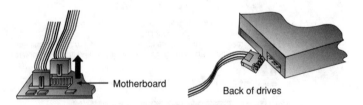

Motherboard

Back of drives

The standard PC power supply has two connectors to the motherboard. These plug into receptacles that are side by side. If you get confused as to how these connectors attach, the general rule is black-to-black.

Once all the power supply connectors are disconnected from their devices, you can remove the mounting hardware. You can usually detach the power supply from the case by removing four screws.

Some power supplies don't need to have screws removed; instead, they are installed on tracks or into slots in the case and need only to be slid out or lifted out.

Removing the Disk Drives

Most disk drives are installed in IBM-compatible computers with rails that are attached to the drives with screws. These rails allow the drive to be slid into the computer's drive bays like a drawer. The drives are then secured with at least two screws on the sides (see Figure 1.16).

FIGURE 1.16: Removing the hard drive

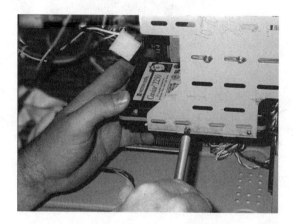

Many desktop computers use a special drive carrier that holds the drive in place and can be easily removed without tools. With most drives, however, you can just remove the mounting screws and slide the drive out. High-end desktops and most servers have hot-pluggable drives, which means that they can be added or removed while the computer is running. You remove them by depressing a retaining clip or button. You will need to consult the documentation that was provided with the machine or drives for the exact details.

Removing the Motherboard

The motherboard is held away from the metal case using spacers and is secured and grounded using mounting screws. To remove the motherboard, you must remove the screws holding the motherboard to the mounting brackets. Then you must slide the motherboard to the side to release the spacers from their mounting holes in the case (see Figure 1.17).

FIGURE 1.17: Removing the motherboard

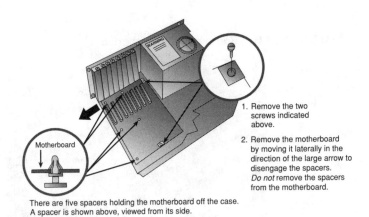

1. Remove the two screws indicated above.

2. Remove the motherboard by moving it laterally in the direction of the large arrow to disengage the spacers. *Do not* remove the spacers from the motherboard.

Motherboard

There are five spacers holding the motherboard off the case. A spacer is shown above, viewed from its side.

Removing the Memory

Memory is held in place by retaining clips at both ends of the module. To remove memory, simply depress the retaining clips and pull the module from its slot. Place the removed memory in an antistatic bag to prevent damage.

Inspecting the Computer

Inspecting the computer is an important step in the disassembly and reassembly of the system. You should check the components for any damage and gather any documentation. Damage is sometimes visible on motherboards. Discolored areas on the board are often caused by power surges.

After a component is removed, it is a good idea to create a parts list on a notepad and make sure that you have all of the supporting documentation and device drivers. If you do not have the supporting documentation and drivers, then it is good practice to download them from the manufacturer's Web site or from a multi-vendor information site such as Driver Guide.

Reassembly

The reassembly of the machine is almost an exact reversal of its disassembly. Once you have all of the necessary documentation and device drivers, the process is quite simple. You reassemble the computer by replacing the hard-to-reach items first and then attaching the supporting devices.

Installing the System Board

The motherboard attaches to the case by the spacers that hold it away from the metal case. Before you reattach the motherboard, it is best to make sure that the memory and the processor are properly secured and seated in the slots. This will help prevent damage to the chips and protect your hand from cuts, since installing them after the board is secured will leave you with limited space. After you have snapped the board onto its spacers, there are normally one or two retaining screws that need to be attached. When attaching these screws, be sure not to over-tighten them and damage the board.

Installing the Power Supply

The power supply should be installed next. Attach the power supply with the screws that were removed during its disassembly. After it is secure, reattach the power leads to their respective connectors on the motherboard.

Installing Drives

The drives are the next components you attach. The first drive you should attach is the floppy drive. The ribbon cable and the power connector connect to the back of the drive as they were removed. Be sure to check the ribbon cable's attachment, as it is the most commonly reversed item on the PC. The pin faces the opposite direction than the hard drive ribbon cable faces on the back of the drive; however, in most cases the number-one pin is always closest to the power connecter.

Once the floppy drive has been attached, it is a good practice to attach all of the IDE hard drives, followed by the CD-ROM drive. By using this order of assembly, you will limit the number of bleeding knuckles.

Installing PCI, ISA, and AGP Devices

After the drives are attached, add any PCI, ISA, and AGP devices that the system uses. With most integrated motherboards, the majority of the devices that would occupy these slots are built into the motherboard components.

Closing the Case

After installing all of the components, slide the cover over the metal frame of the case. This may be a challenging part of the repair. Cases are generally designed to be the most inexpensive part of the PC. They are disassembled much more easily than they are reassembled. Tighten the screws on the outside of the case or make sure that the case has snapped into the proper position.

Attaching Input Devices

Input devices such as the keyboard and mouse should be attached in the same ports from which they were removed. Be sure that the keyboard and mouse are plugged into the correct ports if they both use a PS2 connector. A good rule of thumb is that the keyboard attaches to the port closest to the outside of the machine.

Exam Essentials

Know when to attach an antistatic wrist strap   One thing from this chapter that will be on the test will be attaching an antistatic wrist strap. You should attach one of these to a ground mat every time you open a computer. More components are damaged from static discharge than from anything else.

Key Terms and Concepts

Antistatic wrist strap   Attaching this device to a grounding mat will protect the computer system's components from accidental damage.

1.3 Identify available IRQs, DMAs, and I/O addresses and procedures for configuring them for device installation and configuration.

- **Standard IRQ settings**
- **Modems**
- **Floppy drive controllers**
- **Hard drive controllers**
- **USB port**
- **Infrared ports**
- **Hexadecimal/Addresses**

Interrupt request lines, direct memory access channels, and input/output addresses are configurable aspects of the communication between the devices inside a PC. *Interrupt request lines,* or *IRQs,* are used to signal that an event has taken place that requires the attention of the CPU. *Input/output addresses,* or *I/O addresses,* refer to the hardware communication lines that carry data between the CPU and the bus slots of the PC. *Direct memory access channels,* or *DMA channels,* allow a storage device or adapter card to send information directly into memory without passing through the CPU, which results in a faster data transfer rate.

Whenever a new component is installed into a PC, its IRQs, I/O addresses, and DMA channels must be correctly configured or the device will not function correctly. This is the most common problem when installing new circuit boards. For this reason, the A+ Core Hardware exam includes several questions pertaining to the determination and configuration of these resources.

Critical Information

At some point, every computer will require the installation of a new component, whether it's a new sound card, a memory upgrade, or the replacement of a failed device. As a technician, you will be required to perform this task time and time again. You should be well versed in determining the installation configuration and resources.

Determining Available Resources

The best way to determine the PC's available resources is by using hardware-configuration-discovery utilities. These software programs talk to the PC's BIOS as well as the various pieces of hardware in the computer and display which IRQ, DMA, and memory addresses are being used. Most operating systems include some way of determining this information. MS-DOS, Windows 3.*x*, and Windows 95 included a tool named MSD.EXE. Windows 98 and Windows 2000 have a graphical utility called Device Manager. Windows NT includes a program known as NT Diagnostics. Since all of these tools report the same type of information, we'll use MSD.EXE as our example. One advantage of MSD.EXE over the other programs listed is that it can be included on a boot floppy. In the event that a resource conflict is preventing your system from booting properly, you can boot to the DOS floppy and troubleshoot your problem.

When you run MSD.EXE, it displays information about the computer's memory, I/O ports, IRQs that are being used, and many other PC resources that you want to see. Figure 1.18 shows the main menu that appears when you first run the program.

FIGURE 1.18: The main menu of MSD.EXE

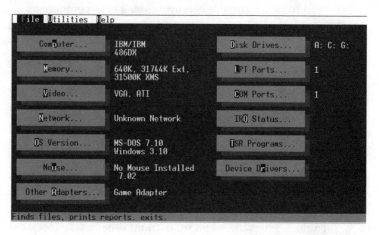

From the main menu, you can use the menu options to display detailed information about the various resources. Don't rely completely on the report you get from MSD if you're running it under Windows 3.x (or Windows 95). In that situation, MSD simply gives the information that it gets from Windows. This may be incorrect and could prove to be a problem.

Besides addressing resources, there is one other resource you need to make sure is available: physical space. There must be adequate space in the computer for the device you are installing. For example, if you are installing a disk drive, an open disk bay must be available.

Understanding Computer Resources

The various tools that you can use to discover the available resources on a PC can make installing new hardware a lot easier. Unfortunately, the tools are of little use unless you understand the information that they present. In this section, we discuss the various resources that might be used by PC components (including that new sound card you are installing) and how those resources are used.

In general, there are four main types of PC resources that you might need to be aware of when installing a new component: interrupt request (IRQ) lines, memory addresses, direct memory access (DMA) channels, and I/O addresses.

Interrupt Request Lines

IRQs are appropriately named. Interrupts are used by peripherals to interrupt, or stop, the CPU and demand attention. When the CPU receives an interrupt alert, it stops whatever it is doing and handles the request.

Each device is given its own interrupt to use when alerting the CPU. AT-based PCs have 16 interrupts available. Given the limited number of available interrupts, it is critical that you assign them wisely! Table 1.3 lists the standard use and other uses associated with each interrupt available on an AT PC.

TABLE 1.3: AT Interrupts

Interrupt	Most Common Use	Other Common Uses
0	System timer	Nothing else uses (or should use) interrupt 0.
1	Keyboard	Nothing else uses (or should use) interrupt 1.
2	None. This interrupt is used to cascade to the higher eight interrupts (see note following this table).	Modems; COM 3, COM 4.
3	COM 2	COM 4, network interface cards, sound cards, and just about anything else.

TABLE 1.3: AT Interrupts *(continued)*

Interrupt	Most Common Use	Other Common Uses
4	COM 1	COM 3, network interface cards, sound cards, and just about anything else.
5	Sound card	LPT2, LPT3, COM 3, COM 4, and disk controllers on older XT-based computers.
6	Floppy disk controller	Tape controllers.
7	LPT1	LPT2, COM 3, COM 4, network interface cards, sound cards, and just about anything else.
8	Real time clock	Nothing else uses (or should use) interrupt 8.
9		SCSI controllers, PCI cards, and just about anything else.
10		Secondary IDE channel, SCSI controllers, PCI cards, and just about anything else.
11		Third or fourth IDE channel, SCSI controllers, PCI cards, and just about anything else.
12	PS/2-style mouse	Just about anything.
13	Floating-point coprocessor	None.
14	Primary IDE channel	SCSI controllers.
15	Secondary IDE channel	SCSI controllers and network adapters.

> **NOTE** Interrupt 2 is a special case. In earlier (XT-based) PCs, there were only eight interrupts because those computers used an 8-bit bus. With the development of the AT, eight more interrupts were created (to match the 16-bit bus), but no mechanism was available to use them. Rather than redesign the entire interrupt process, AT designers decided to use interrupt 2 as a gateway, or cascade, to interrupts 9–15. In reality, interrupt 2 is the same as interrupt 9. You should never configure your system so that both interrupt 2 and 9 are used.

Configuring interrupts is so common that most experienced field technicians have the standards (as listed in Table 1.3) memorized.

Memory Addresses

Many components use blocks of memory as part of their normal functioning. Network interface cards often buffer incoming data in a block of memory until it can be processed. This prevents the card from being overloaded if a burst of data is received from the network.

When the device driver loads, it lets the CPU know which block of memory should be set aside for the exclusive use of the component. This prevents other devices from overwriting the information stored there. Certain system components also need a memory address. Some of the more common default assignments are listed in Table 1.4.

TABLE 1.4: Common Memory Address Assignments

Address	Assignment
F0000–FFFFF	System BIOS
E0000–EFFFF	In use on true IBM compatibles
CA000–DFFFF	Available on most PCs
C8000–C87FF	Hard disk controller on an XT system

TABLE 1.4: Common Memory Address Assignments *(continued)*

Address	Assignment
C0000–C7FFF	EGA/VGA display
B8000–BFFFF	CGA/EGA/VGA display
B0000–B7FFF	Monochrome display
A0000–AFFFF	EGA/VGA display
00000–9FFFF	System memory

Direct Memory Access

Direct memory access (DMA) is a method used by peripherals to place data in memory without utilizing CPU resources. As an example, a sound card can buffer music in memory while the CPU is busy recalculating a spreadsheet. The DMA peripheral has its own processor to move the data. It uses dead time on the ISA bus to perform the transfer. At the hardware level, DMA is quite complex, but the important feature to remember is that the transfer of data is accomplished without intervention from the CPU.

All DMA transfers use a special area of memory set aside to receive data from the expansion card (or CPU if the transfer is going the other direction) known as a *buffer*. The basic architecture of the PC DMA buffers is limited in size and memory location.

No DMA channel can be used by more than one device. If you accidentally choose a DMA channel that another card is using, the usual symptom is that no DMA transfers will occur and the device is unavailable.

Certain DMA channels are assigned to standard AT devices. Table 1.5 lists the eight DMA channels and their default assignments.

TABLE 1.5: DMA Assignments

DMA Channel	Default Assignment
0	Dynamic RAM refresh
1	Hard disk controller
2	Floppy disk controller
3	Available on all PCs
4–7	Available on AT and Micro Channel PS/2 computers

I/O Addresses

I/O (input/output) addresses, also known as *port addresses*, are a specific area of memory that a component uses to communicate with the system. While they sound quite a bit like memory addresses, the major difference is that memory addresses are used to store information that will be used by the device itself. I/O addresses are used to store information that will be used by the system.

A perfect example of how I/O addresses are used is the keyboard. When you type, the keystrokes are stored in a specific area of memory. The CPU looks at this address to find information from the keyboard. Each I/O address acts as stop for information being exchanged between the CPU and a device.

Exam Essentials

Know the default IRQs for COM ports and common devices. Know the default IRQs for COM ports and common devices such as modems, sound cards, disk drives, etc.

Be familiar with MSD.EXE. MSD.EXE can display information about the computer's memory, I/O ports, IRQs being used, and many other PC resources that you want to see.

Key Terms and Concepts

Interrupt request (IRQ) lines   IRQs are appropriately named. Interrupts are used by peripherals to interrupt or stop the CPU and demand attention.

MSD.EXE   MSD.EXE can display information about the computer's memory, I/O ports, IRQs being used, and many other PC resources.

Memory addresses   Many components use blocks of memory as part of their normal functioning. Expansion cards often buffer incoming data in a block of memory until it can be processed.

Direct memory access (DMA)   Direct memory access is a method used by peripherals to place data in memory without utilizing CPU resources.

▶ 1.4 Identify common peripheral ports, associated cabling, and their connectors.

- **Cable types**
- **Cable orientation**
- **Serial versus parallel**
- **Pin connections**
- **DB-9**
- **DB-25**
- **RJ-11**
- **RJ-45**
- **BNC**
- **PS2/Mini-DIN**
- **USB**
- **IEEE-1394**

The peripheral ports of a computer are the physical connectors found outside the computer. Cables of various types are designed to plug into these ports and create a connection between the PC and the external devices that may be attached to it. A successful IT technician should have an in-depth knowledge of ports and cables.

Critical Information

Because the peripheral components need to be upgraded frequently, either to keep pace with technological change or simply to replace broken devices, the test requires a well-rounded familiarity with the ports and their associated cabling.

Peripheral Ports

Unless a peripheral device connects directly to the motherboard using a SCSI or IDE connection, it must use a port. The speed that the device requires dictates the type of port to use. At the time that this book is being written, the most commonly used ports are still parallel and serial ports; however, USB is now gaining ground at an extremely fast pace due to its throughput speed.

Cabling

Cables are used to connect two or more entities together. They are usually constructed of several wires encased in a rubberized outer coating. The wires are soldered to modular connectors at both ends. These connectors allow the cables to be quickly attached to the devices they connect. A list of common cable types used in PCs, their descriptions, their maximum effective lengths, and their most common uses is given in Table 1.6.

TABLE 1.6: Common PC Cable Descriptions

Application	1st Connector	2nd Connector	Max. Length
Null modem	DB-9F	DB-9F	25 feet
Null modem	DB-25F	DB-25F	25 feet
RS-232 (modem cable)	DB-9F	DB-25M	25 feet
RS-232 (modem cable)	DB-25F	DB-25M	25 feet

TABLE 1.6: Common PC Cable Descriptions *(continued)*

Application	1st Connector	2nd Connector	Max. Length
Parallel printer	DB-25M	Centronics 36M	10 feet
External SCSI cable	Centronics 50M	Centronics 50M	10 feet (total SCSI bus length)
VGA extension cable	DB-15M	DB-15M	3 feet
UTP Ethernet cable	RJ-45M	RJ-45M	100 meters
Thinnet Ethernet cable	BNCM	BNCM	100 meters
Telephone wall cable	RJ-11M	RJ-11M	N/A

One cable that deserves special mention is the null modem cable. It allows two computers to communicate with each other without using a modem. This cable has its transmit and receive wires crossed at both ends, so when one entity transmits on its TD line, the other entity is receiving it on its RD line.

Connectors

Computers connect to many different types of devices. The wide variety of devices requires equally diverse connectors. The following section lists the types of connectors and some of their uses.

DB-9

The DB-9 connector is generally used for serial ports. Serial ports are used for devices that require a moderate speed from the interface. Serial ports support an 8-bit transfer but only one bit at a time. The easiest way to picture this is to imagine a group of eight children waiting to go down a slide. Each child represents one bit sliding down in a single-file line.

The most common peripheral that uses the DB-9 connector is the external modem. An external modem uses a modem cable to attach to a serial port, which is normally located on the back of the PC. A modem cable is nothing more than a cable with a male and female DB-9 connector on each end.

The male end of the connector attaches to the female end of the modem, and the female end of the connector attaches to the male end on the back of the PC. Other than connecting the modem's power supply and adding the modem's driver to the operating system, there are no other installation or configuration issues.

DB-25

The DB-25 connector is used for either a serial or parallel port. It is easy to tell the application of the connector by its type (male or female) on the back of the computer. Serial ports using a DB-25 are always male on the back of the PC, and parallel or printer ports are always female on the back of the PC.

If the connector is being used as a parallel interface, the speed will be faster than for a serial port. Let's again imagine our group of children, only now we have a larger slide that allows eight of them to slide down at the same time in parallel.

RJ-11

The RJ-11 connector is used to connect a 2-pair wire to a receiving jack. The most common example of the RJ-11 connector is a telephone cord. The clear plastic connector on the end of the cord that you plug into the telephone set or into your modem is an RJ-11 connector.

With the increase in popularity of home networking, some manufacturers have developed a home networking kit that uses the existing telephone wiring in the home to connect the network cards. This system is considerably slower than most networking done in businesses and is best used for sharing Internet connections.

RJ-45

The RJ-45 connector is the industry standard for Ethernet or Fast Ethernet networking. This 4-pair connector allows a short network cable, known as a *patch cable*, to attach the computer to the wall jack. This connector is found in 80 percent of networked businesses.

The connector and cabling currently allow for transfer rates of up to 100MB. Since this is the most common type of connector used by networked businesses today, you should make sure that you are familiar with its appearance. The connector and jack resemble the RJ-11 connector, or phone connector, but they are twice its size. The standard phone connector holds four strands of jacketed copper wire while the RJ-45 accepts eight strands of jacketed copper wire.

BNC

BNC connectors are becoming less prevalent in today's networked businesses. In the past, this connector was a standard in small networked businesses, but with the introduction of Fast Ethernet a few years ago and the use of networking products required by twisted-pair cabling, this type of network is disappearing quickly because of speed and reliability concerns.

The BNC connector looks like a barrel, which led to its nickname as the "barrel connector." BNC connectors are normally attached to a T connector at the workstation. The T connector allows the PC to be attached to the network.

PS2/MINI-DIN

The PS2/Mini-DIN connector is most commonly used to connect keyboards and mice to the back of the PC. The Mini-DIN is the most common type of peripheral connector used. You can count on having two of these on the back of the PC.

USB

USB is the fastest growing interface type at this time. The flexibility of the device's architecture is providing manufacturers with a high-speed chainable port system that is easy to configure.

USB devices can be chained with the use of hubs, allowing up to 32 devices to be connected to one port. The transfer rate is also very good, with a maximum throughput of 4Mbps.

Exam Essentials

Know what RJ-45 connectors are used for.   You are likely to be asked what type of connector would be used to attach a network connector to a wall jack.

Know what PS2/Mini-DIN connectors are used for.   You are likely to be asked what type of connector would be used to connect a keyboard or mouse to the back of a PC.

Know what RJ-11 connectors are used for.   You are likely to be asked what type of connector would be used to connect a modem to a wall jack.

Key Terms and Concepts

RJ-11   The RJ-11 connector is used to connect a 2-pair wire to a receiving jack. The most common example of the RJ-11 connector is a standard telephone cord.

RJ-45   The RJ-45 connector is the industry standard for Ethernet or Fast Ethernet networking. This 4-pair connector allows a short network cable, known as a patch cable, to attach the computer to the wall jack.

USB   USB is the fastest growing interface type at this time. The flexibility of the device architecture provides manufacturers with a high-speed chainable port system that is easy to configure.

USB devices can be chained with the use of hubs, allowing up to 32 devices to be connected to one port. The transfer rate is also very good, with a maximum throughput of 4Mbps.

1.5 Identify proper procedures for installing and configuring IDE/EIDE devices.

- Master/slave
- Devices per channel
- Primary/secondary

The most popular hard disk types are the Integrated Drive Electronics (IDE) and the Enhanced IDE (EIDE) disk drives. The major feature of an IDE/EIDE system is a controller card located on the drive itself, using a relatively short cable to connect the drive/controller to the system. This design offers the benefits of decreasing signal loss (thus increasing reliability) and making the drive easier to install.

Critical Information

IDE drives, in addition to being relatively simple to install, can support drives of up to 528MB. Enhanced IDE, a technology developed in the last few years, can support drives of several gigabytes. These newer drives have data transfer rates greater than 10Mbps.

IDE Disk Systems

IDE drives are the most prevalent in the industry today. IDE drives are easy to install and configure, and they provide acceptable performance for most applications. Their ease of use relates to their most identifiable feature—the controller is located on the drive itself.

IDE Technologies

The design of the IDE is simple: Put the controller right on the drive itself and use a relatively short cable to connect the drive/controller to the system, as shown in Figure 1.19. This offers the benefits of decreasing signal loss (thus increasing reliability) and making the drive easier to install.

FIGURE 1.19: An IDE drive and interface

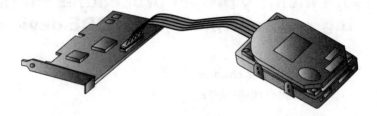

In addition, because the controller is integrated into the same assembly as the drive, the only board that needs to be installed in the computer is an adapter that converts signals between the motherboard and the drive/controller.

The original IDE specification, in addition to being relatively simple to install, could support drives of up to 528MB and speeds of 3.3Mbps. To overcome limitations, a new technology was developed that could support drives of several gigabytes. This technology is *ATA version 2 (ATA-2)*. These newer drives have data transfer rates of 11.1Mbps. This general category of ATA-2 drives is known as Enhanced IDE, or EIDE.

The main limitation to IDE technologies is that they support only two drives (or four if you're using ATA-2). In order to add more drives, you must use a different technology, such as SCSI. In addition, you are limited to hard disks. To overcome this limitation, an extension to ATA-2 was developed, called the *ATA Packet Interface (ATAPI)*. ATAPI allows other non-hard-disk devices (such as tape drives and CD-ROMs) to be attached to an ATA interface and coexist with hard disks.

Another update to the ATA standard is ATA version 4 (ATA-4), also known as *Ultra DMA IDE*. It can transfer data at 33Mbps, so it is also commonly seen in motherboard specifications as Ultra DMA/33, or UDMA.

Installation and Configuration

The basic steps for installing an IDE drive are simple: Mount the drive in the carrier, connect the cable to the drive, install the drive in the computer, and configure the drive. However, IDE's cabling and configuration issues are more complex. For example, you only have a single, 40-pin cable to connect the drives to the computer. Cabling is just a matter of connecting the drive(s) to the cable and plugging the cable into the motherboard. This is made easier because the majority of the IDE cables today are keyed so that they plug in only one way. If you happen to get one of the cables that isn't keyed, make sure that the red lead of the cable is closest to the power connector.

The one situation that does complicate matters is when you have two (or more) drives in an IDE/EIDE system. Remember that an IDE drive has the controller *mounted on the drive*. If you had two drives connected, which controller would be talking to the computer and sending data back and forth? The answer is "only one of them." When you install a second drive, you need to configure it so that the controller on one drive is active and the other drives use the controller on this drive for their instructions. You do this by setting the first drive to be the *master drive* and the others to be *slave drives*. As you might suspect, the master is the drive whose controller is used by the other drives (the slaves).

You implement the master/slave setting by jumping a set of pins. There are several different configurations of these pins, so we'll just examine the most common ones. As always, check your documentation to determine which method your drive uses.

The first type is the simplest. There are two sets of pins, one labeled "master/single," the other labeled "slave," as shown in Figure 1.20. If you have one drive, you jumper the master side and leave the slave side jumper off. If you have two drives, you jumper the master side only on the first drive (at the end of the cable) and jumper the slave side only on the other drive(s). A variant of this type uses no jumpers on either side to indicate just one drive in the system.

FIGURE 1.20: Master/slave jumpers

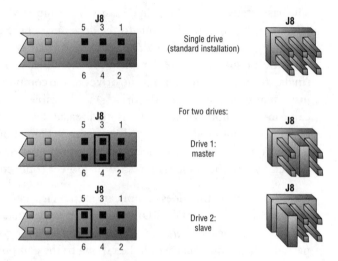

The other type commonly in use has three sets of pins labeled 1 through 6. These six pins are arranged in three rows of two, with one set labeled "master," another set labeled "slave," and the third set with no label. With one drive installed, you leave all jumpers off. With two drives installed, you set the first drive (usually located at the end of the cable) to master by jumping the two pins labeled "master," then set the second drive to slave by jumping the two pins labeled "slave."

WARNING If you have two drives in your system and both are set to master or both are set to slave, neither drive will work. However, if you have an EIDE interface system, you can have two masters as long as the drives are on two separate IDE buses.

Once you have the cable installed and the drives configured as either master or slave, you must tell the computer that the drives exist and what their drive geometry is. You do this by entering the BIOS's CMOS setup program (or the disk-based BIOS setup program for older computers). This setup program modifies the computer's settings in the CMOS memory that stores the configuration information for the computer.

Now that your drive is installed, you can proceed to format it for the operating system you have chosen. Then, finally, you can install your operating system of choice.

NOTE   IDE was such a popular hard disk interface that some people have adapted CD-ROM and tape devices to operate on IDE-type interfaces as well. Granted, an "IDE" CD-ROM may or may not coexist peacefully with an IDE hard disk.

Exam Essentials

Know how many pins an IDE cable has.   An IDE cable has 40 pins. You are likely to be asked to choose a cable in a scenario question simply by knowing how many pins the drive requires.

Know how a controller works in a master/slave environment. When you have a master and a slave, only one of the two controllers controls data transfers. You are likely to be asked a scenario question that relates to this environment.

Know what other devices besides hard drives use IDE interfaces. With the popularity of IDE technology, manufacturers have introduced tape drives and CD-ROMs that use IDE interfaces.

Key Terms and Concepts

Master   The IDE drive that is configured as the master is responsible for managing the data transfers for itself and the slave drive.

Slave   The slave drive shares the channel with the master and does not manage the data transfers. It is totally reliant on the master drive for communication.

ATAPI   ATAPI allows other non-hard-disk devices (such as tape drives and CD-ROMs) to be attached to an ATA interface and coexist with hard disks.

1.6 Identify proper procedures for installing and configuring SCSI devices.

- Address/termination conflicts
- Cabling
- Types (example: regular, wide, ultra-wide)
- Internal versus external
- Jumper block settings (binary equivalents)

The *small computer systems interface (SCSI)* is a type of subsystem that is both highly flexible and robust. The range of devices that can use SCSI technology includes hard disk drives, scanners, tape drives, and CD-ROM drives. This is why it's so flexible. Conversely, it's probably the most complex. In this section, we will review the different types of SCSI, and we'll discuss configuration and installation issues.

Critical Information

SCSI (pronounced "scuzzy") is a technology developed and standardized by the American National Standards Institute (ANSI). The standard specifies a universal, parallel, system-level interface for connecting up to eight devices (including the controller) on a single shared cable, called the *SCSI bus*. One of the many benefits of SCSI is that it is a very fast, flexible interface. You can buy a SCSI disk and install it in a Mac, a PC, or virtually any computer if a SCSI adapter is available.

Small Computer Systems Interface

SCSI devices can be either internal or external to the computer. If they are internal, they use a 50-pin ribbon cable (similar to the 40-pin IDE drive cable). If the devices are external, they use a thick, shielded cable with Centronics-50 or male DB-25 connectors on it. These devices aren't always disk drives. Scanners and some printers also use SCSI because it has a very high data throughput.

To configure SCSI, you must assign a unique device number (often called a *SCSI address*) to each device on the SCSI bus. These numbers are configured through either jumpers or DIP switches. When the computer needs to send data to the device, it sends a signal on the wire "addressed" to that number. A device called a *terminator* (technically a *terminating resistor pack*) must be installed at both ends of the bus to keep the signals "on the bus." The device then responds with a signal that contains the device number that sent the information and the data itself.

Types of SCSI

The original implementation of SCSI was just called "SCSI" at its inception. However, as new implementations came out, the original was referred to as *SCSI-1*. This implementation is characterized by its 5Mbps transfer rate, its Centronics 50 or DB-25 female connectors, and its 8-bit bus width. SCSI-1 had some problems, however. Some devices wouldn't operate correctly when they were on the same SCSI bus as other devices. The problem here was mainly that the ANSI SCSI standard was so new that vendors chose to implement it differently. These differences were the primary source of conflicts.

The first improvement that was designed into *SCSI-2* was a wider bus. The new specification specified both 8-bit and 16-bit buses. The larger of the two specifications is known as *Wide SCSI-2*. It improved data throughput for large data transfers. Another important change was to improve upon the now-limiting 5Mbps transfer rate. The *Fast SCSI-2* specification allowed for a 10Mbps transfer rate, thus allowing transfers twice as fast as SCSI-1. So, Wide SCSI-2 transfers data 16 bits at a time, and Fast SCSI transfers data 8 bits at a time but twice as fast (at 10Mbps).

Finally, there is a new SCSI standard, *SCSI-3*. One of the feature sets is known as *Fast-20 SCSI* (also known to some as *Ultra SCSI*). Basically, this is a faster version of Fast SCSI-2 operating at 20Mbps for narrow SCSI and 40Mbps for Wide SCSI. Another feature set is the *Ultra2 Low Voltage Differential* (*LVD*), which increases the maximum SCSI bus length to 25 meters (82 feet) and increases the maximum possible throughput to 160Mbps (on Ultra2 Wide LVD).

There are other proposed SCSI implementations, such as Apple's FireWire, Fiber Channel, and IBM's SSA, all offering speeds in the hundreds of megabytes-per-second range.

SCSI Device Installation and Configuration

Installing SCSI devices is more complex than installing an IDE drive. The main issues with installing SCSI devices are cabling, termination, and addressing.

We'll discuss termination and cabling together because they are very closely tied. There are two types of cabling:

- Internal cabling uses a 50-wire ribbon cable with several keyed connectors on them. These connectors are attached to the devices in the computer (the order is unimportant), with one connector connecting to the adapter.

- External cabling uses thick, shielded cables run from adapter to device to device in a fashion known as *daisy-chaining*. Each device has two ports on it (most of the time). When hooking up external SCSI devices, you run a cable from the adapter to the first device. Then you run a cable from the first device to the second device, from the second to the third, and so on.

Because there are two types of cabling devices, you have three ways of connecting them. The methods differ by where the devices are located and whether or not the adapter has the terminator installed.

The guide to remember here is that *both ends* of the bus must be terminated. Let's look briefly at the three connection methods:

Internal devices only   When you have only internal SCSI devices, you connect the cable to the adapter and to every SCSI device in the computer. You then install the terminating resistors on the adapter and on the last drive in the chain. All other terminating resistors are removed. This is demonstrated in Figure 1.21.

FIGURE 1.21: Cabling internal SCSI devices only

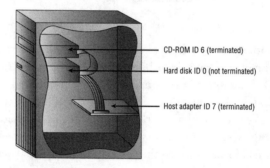

CD-ROM ID 6 (terminated)

Hard disk ID 0 (not terminated)

Host adapter ID 7 (terminated)

NOTE   Some devices and adapters don't use terminating resistor packs; instead you use a jumper or DIP switch to activate or deactivate SCSI termination on such devices. (Where do you find out what type your device uses? In the documentation, of course.)

External devices only   In the next situation, you have external devices only, as shown in Figure 1.22. By external devices, we mean that each has its own power supply. You connect the devices in the same manner in which you connected internal devices, but in this method you use several very short (less than 0.5 meters) "stub" cables to run between the devices in a daisy chain (rather than one long cable with several connectors). The effect is the same. The adapter and the last device in the chain (the one with only one stub cable attached to it) must be terminated.

FIGURE 1.22: Cabling external SCSI devices only

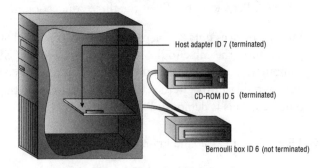

Host adapter ID 7 (terminated)

CD-ROM ID 5 (terminated)

Bernoulli box ID 6 (not terminated)

Both internal and external devices Finally, there's the hybrid situation in which you have both internal and external devices (Figure 1.23). Most adapters have connectors for both internal and external SCSI devices—if yours doesn't have both, you'll need to see if anybody makes one that will work with your devices. For adapters that do have both types of connectors, you connect your internal devices to the ribbon cable and attach the cable to the adapter. Then, you daisy-chain your external devices off the external port. Finally, you terminate the last device on each chain, leaving the adapter unterminated.

FIGURE 1.23: Cabling internal and external SCSI devices together

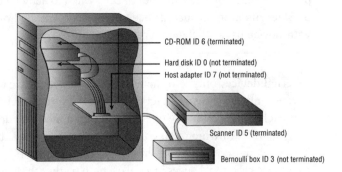

CD-ROM ID 6 (terminated)

Hard disk ID 0 (not terminated)
Host adapter ID 7 (not terminated)

Scanner ID 5 (terminated)

Bernoulli box ID 3 (not terminated)

NOTE   Even though the third technique described is the technically correct way to install termination for the hybrid situation (in which you have both internal and external devices), some adapter cards still need to have terminators installed.

Once all the devices are correctly connected, you need to assign each device a unique SCSI ID number. This number can be assigned by the jumper (with internal devices) or with a rotary switch (on external devices). You start by assigning your adapter an address. This number can be any number from 0 to 7 on an 8-bit bus, 0 to 15 on a 16-bit bus, and 0 to 31 on a 32-bit bus, as long as no other device is using that ID.

Here are some recommendations that are commonly accepted by the PC community. Remember that these are guidelines, not rules:

- Generally speaking, give slower devices higher priority so they can access the bus whenever they need it.

- Set the bootable (or first) hard disk to ID 0.

- Set the CD-ROM to ID 3.

After the devices are cabled and terminated, you have to get the PC to recognize the SCSI adapter and its devices. Because SCSI devices are intelligent, you tell the PC that there is no disk installed and let the adapter control the devices. You have two other ways of getting the PC to recognize the SCSI devices:

- If the device is bootable, then you must set the card to be BIOS-enabled, meaning that the card has its own BIOS extension that will allow the PC to recognize the device without a software driver.

- The other method is to load into the operating system a driver for the adapter. This method works only if you are booting from some other non-SCSI device. This method is commonly used when the only SCSI device attached to the computer is a scanner or CD-ROM drive.

Once the drive is installed and talking to the computer, you can high-level format the media and install the operating system.

TIP If there are problems, double-check the termination and ID numbers. If everything looks correct, try changing the ID numbers one at a time. SCSI addressing is gray area where many problems arise.

Exam Essentials

Know the transfer rates of the different types of SCSI architectures. The different types of SCSI controllers and their supporting devices support throughput ranging from 5Mbps to 160Mbps. You should be familiar with these types and their throughput.

Understand SCSI IDs. SCSI IDs are a critical concept to understand. This information is not only necessary for the exam, but you must be able configure SCSI ID numbers in order to install a SCSI device.

Understand termination. You must not only understand what termination does, but also know how to implement it for the exam and to install a SCSI device.

Key Terms and Concepts

SCSI Small computer systems interface (SCSI) that supports data throughput up to 5Mbps.

SCSI-2 Small computer systems interface (SCSI) that supports data throughput up to 10Mbps.

SCSI-3 Small computer systems interface (SCSI) that supports data throughput up to 20Mbps.

Wide SCSI-2   A version of SCSI-2 that doubles the bus from 8-bit to 16-bit, increasing data throughput to 20Mbps.

Wide SCSI-3   A version of SCSI-3 that doubles the bus from 8-bit to 16-bit, increasing data throughput to 40Mbps.

Terminator   A terminator is placed at each end of the chain of devices. This tells the controller that there are no other devices on the chain by creating an electrical short.

1.7 Identify proper procedures for installing and configuring peripheral devices.

- **Monitor/video card**
- **Modem**
- **USB peripherals and hubs**
- **IEEE-1284**
- **IEEE-1394**
- **External storage**
- **Docking stations**
- **PC cards**
- **Port replicators**
- **Infrared devices**

Two of the more common (and complicated) peripheral devices are monitors and modems. A *monitor* is the user interface that allows you to see not only what you're doing, but also the results of the computer's computations. Modems have also become a fairly standard fixture for all PCs. Both of these devices are described and reviewed in detail in this section.

Critical Information

A PC technician must know how peripheral devices work, how to install them, and how to configure them. These devices are the focus of several test questions.

Procedures for Installing and Configuring Peripherals

For devices to be added to a computer, they must be physically installed on the machine. This section will outline the procedures for adding devices to a computer.

Video Adapters

Video adapters have undergone a large number of improvements since the first PCs were released. The first display adapters were capable of only two-color, text-based graphics. Now PCs are used for 3-D modeling with millions of colors. Table 1.7 lists the enhancements that have been made to display adapters since their introduction.

TABLE 1.7: Video Display Adapter Comparison

Name	Resolutions	Colors
Monochrome Display Adapter (MDA)	720 × 350	Mono (text only)
Hercules Graphics Card (HGC)	720 × 350	Mono (text and graphics)
Enhanced Graphics Adapter (EGA)	640 × 350	16
Video Graphics Array (VGA)	640 × 480 320 × 200	16 256
SuperVGA (SVGA)	800 × 600 1024 × 768	256 16
Extended Graphics Array (XGA)	800 × 600 1024 × 768	65,536 256

INSTALLING A VIDEO CARD

Video cards are either built into the motherboard's components or occupy an expansion slot. The expansion card can occupy an ISA,

PCI, or AGP slot in the computer. Installing a video card is a simple process that requires these few steps:

- Remove the cover after attaching your antistatic wrist strap to your arm and the grounding mat.

- Install the card into the correct slot on the PC's motherboard.

- Boot the machine and install the driver into the computer's operating system.

These steps consider that you are following the standard practices for adding and removing field-replaceable modules as described earlier in this chapter.

Monitors

Display systems convert computer signals into text and pictures and display them on a TV-like screen. As a matter of fact, the first personal computers actually used television screens because it was simpler to use an existing display technology rather than develop a new one. There are several different types of computer displays in use today, including the TV. All of them use either the same cathode ray tube (CRT) technology found in television sets (almost every desktop monitor uses this technology) or the liquid crystal display (LCD) technology found on all laptop, notebook, and palmtop computers.

One note about monitors that may seem rather obvious: You must use a video card that supports the type of monitor you are using. For example, you can't use a CGA monitor on a VGA adapter.

NOTE   To use a 72Hz monitor, your video card must also support the 72Hz refresh rate. Most video cards sold today support this faster 72Hz refresh rate but are configured as 60Hz out of the box. If you intend to use the 72Hz rate, you must configure the card to do so. Check the documentation that came with the card for details on how to configure it.

INSTALLING A MONITOR

Monitors are extremely easy to install. You simply connect the monitor's connector to the video card, attach its power cord to a power source, and turn it on. Some monitors have additional features that may require the addition of special drivers into the operating system.

Modems

There are two types of modems: internal and external. Internal modems are installed as expansion cards inside a computer. External modems have their own power supplies and connect to an external COM port with an RS-232 cable. There are advantages and disadvantages to each.

Internal modems are usually smaller and cheaper than their external counterparts. However, they are more difficult to configure. You need to configure them to use an unused COM port. Table 1.8 lists the IRQ and I/O port addresses of the standard COM ports installed.

TABLE 1.8: Standard COM Port and IRQ Addresses

COM Port	IRQ Address	I/O Address
COM1	4	3F8–3FF
COM2	3	2F8–2FF
COM3	4	3E8–3EF
COM4	3	2E8–2EF

External modems use an existing serial port, so they don't have the configuration problem with IRQs and I/O addresses. However, they don't interface directly with the computer's expansion bus, so data transfers may be slow (especially if the modem is faster than 9600bps). If this is the case, the serial port must use a higher-speed UART (Universal Asynchronous Receiver/Transmitter). The UART is the chip that manages the serial data that's moving in and out the serial port. If the modem is 9600bps or faster, you need to use a 16-bit UART (for example, the 16450 or 16550 model). Most computers come with 16550 UARTs, so you shouldn't have to worry about this. However, some older computers came with the 8-bit 8550 UART and may need to be upgraded.

INSTALLING A MODEM

The installation of a modem depends on whether it is an internal or external modem. Before installing a modem, be sure to us the information in the "Determining Available Resources" section of this chapter.

Internal modems   Internal modems are harder to install than external modems. First you must determine the available resources for the modem that you will be installing. You can then configure any settings on the modem card by using jumpers or DIP switches and continue by following these steps:

1. Remove the cover after attaching your antistatic wrist strap to you arm and the grounding mat.

2. Install the card into the correct slot on the PC's motherboard.

3. Reattach the cover and tighten any screws.

4. Boot the machine and install the driver into the computer's operating system.

NOTE   This is a generalized process, so you should consult the documentation provided with the device before beginning to install it.

External modems   External modems do not require you to configure COM port or IRQ settings because you connect the modem to an empty COM port on the back of the PC. This means that the modem does not use up additional resources on your PC (except for the empty COM port). To install an external modem, simply follow these steps:

1. Attach the modem to an empty serial or parallel port on the back of your computer.

2. Connect any power supply required by your modem to a power source.

3. Boot the computer and install the driver from within the operating system.

NOTE Again, this is a generalized process, so you should consult the documentation provided with the device before beginning to install it.

USB Devices

The USB controller manages USB devices, which are connected to the USB port that is located either on the motherboard or in an expansion slot. Because the controller manages the device, only the controller uses the resources. This allows you to add multiple devices without worrying about available resources.

INSTALLING A USB DEVICE

To install USB device, simply follow these steps:

1. Install the software provided by the computer manufacturer.

2. Shut down the PC.

3. Connect the USB device to the USB port or hub, and attach any power supply required by the device to a power source.

4. Boot the computer and finish any device-specific configuration.

NOTE This is a generalized process, so you should consult the documentation provided with the device before beginning to install it.

Exam Essentials

Most of the information in this section seems very basic. Remember to use the principles set forth in domain 1.2, "Identify basic procedures for adding and removing field-replaceable modules for both desktop and portable systems," earlier in this chapter.

Know the basic procedure for installing a video card. You will need to know how to install a video card to be a computer technician.

Know the basic procedure for installing a modem. You will need to know how to install a modem to be a computer technician.

Know the basic procedure for installing a USB device. You will need to know how to install a USB device to be a computer technician.

Key Terms and Concepts

Display system A device that converts computer signals into text and pictures and displays them on a TV-like screen.

External modems Modems that are contained in a separate box connected to your computer by a cable. They do not require COM port configuration or IRQ settings.

Internal modems Modems that are implemented on a card and plugged into your computer. They are generally harder to install than external modems because you must first determine the available resources. Any settings on the modem card can be configured by using jumpers or DIP switches.

USB devices The Universal Serial Bus can be used to connect any type of device (mouse, keyboard, scanner, printer) into a hub or PC. USB software automatically configures resource settings, such as IRQs.

1.8 Identify hardware methods of upgrading system performance, procedures for replacing basic subsystem components, and unique components and when to use them.

- Memory
- Hard drives
- CPU
- Upgrading BIOS
- When to upgrade BIOS

- **Battery**
- **Types I, II, III cards**

Upgrades are a part of any technician's job description. Upgrades present their own set of challenges that can range from compatibility to space requirements. This section describes some hardware upgrades that can enhance system performance.

Critical Information

The most common need for an upgrade is to increase system performance. Over time, a computer's performance will decrease as newer software is added. In most cases, newer versions of software require additional resources that are not available. The PC was originally configured to run at certain performance levels that considered the applications and peripherals that were available when it was produced. Upgrades will increase the system's performance to accommodate newer software and peripheral devices.

Upgrading System Performance

Toward the end of the life expectancy of the system, it may become necessary to upgrade the system for required programs or for new hardware to function. If the system is too antiquated, it may be more cost efficient to replace the entire computer. However, in many cases, the system's performance can be enhanced to acceptable levels by adding resources.

Memory

Increasing the amount of memory or RAM that a system has will increase the speed at which data can be processed. As mentioned earlier in this chapter, RAM is used to store data. The operating system and applications utilize RAM, so if the amount of available RAM is insufficient, the operating system will utilize hard disk space to store some of the data. Since the speed at which the data stored on a hard drive is considerably lower than the speed at which data can be accessed in RAM, the performance of the system will degrade as more and more information is stored on the hard drive.

In such a case, adding RAM can have a significant effect on the system's performance. To fully understand the effect that the amount of RAM can have on a system, consider the memory requirements of past and present operating systems.

When Windows 3.1 was introduced, a computer would operate very well with 8MB of RAM. When Windows 95 was released, 16MB was recommended, and the machine operated much better with 32MB. With the release of Windows 98, 32MB of RAM was specified as a minimum requirement and 64MB was recommended. Windows Me and Windows 2000 Professional both require a minimum of 64MB of RAM to install. Although Windows 2000 Server will install with 64MB of RAM, the recommended is 128MB; in the real world, most companies use 512MB to 1GB of RAM.

Hard Drives

Hard drives are most commonly replaced because the system runs out of space to store data and program files. Throughout the lifecycle of a computer, data will be stored or programs added to the hard drive. Software is replaced with newer versions to increase stability or, more commonly, to increase the capabilities or ease of use. It stands to reason that these newer versions require additional space to store their files.

When you store data files on the hard drive, they utilize space. The requirements of most files are much lower than for program files, but they also require space on the hard drive. The data files stored by graphically intense programs like AutoCAD or multimedia-generation applications can be very large. Multimedia files that contain audio and video are without a doubt the largest found on computers. These files can consume space by the gigabyte.

Another reason to upgrade a hard drive is to increase the speed at which data can be written to or read from the drive. In some cases, it may become necessary to change the disk architecture altogether to achieve higher read/write speeds. An example of this would be the addition of a SCSI controller and hard disk to a machine that was using EIDE. The upgrade will increase the speed at which the system can operate, but keep in mind that increasing the amount of RAM or processor speed will have the most noticeable effect.

There are two common ways to replace a disk drive in a computer: adding a drive or completely replacing the disk. Each has its own benefits and drawbacks.

COMPLETE REPLACEMENT

If you need additional hard disk capacity and do not have the physical room inside of the computer's case, or you do not want to manage two drives, complete replacement is necessary. Complete replacement requires reinstalling or restoring the operating system, program files, and data on the new drive. Since this is a considerable undertaking, drive-image tools have been developed to aid in this process. A drive-image tool takes a snapshot of the drive and allows you to create an image that can be expanded on the larger drive, avoiding reinstallation.

These images are normally compressed and require less space than the actual contents of the drive, allowing the images to be placed on a CD-ROM or other storage media. Some examples of this type of data transfer programs are Norton Ghost and Seagate Power Quest Drive Image. Larger corporations use these tools to create a basic image of the operating system and commonly used programs to decrease downtime and lower upgrade and repair costs.

ADDING DRIVES

The simplest way to increase hard drive capacity is to add another drive. Most desktop PCs have IDE controllers built into the motherboard. These controllers allow for two devices to be connected to both the primary and secondary controller. With this type of architecture, four IDE devices can be installed in a PC if space permits.

After adding the drive, you can place data and programs on it. This type of installation does not require the reinstallation or restore of the operating system and program files on the new drive.

CPU

The frequency at which the processor operates, or MHz, determines the speed at which data passes through the processor. Upgrading the processor to a higher frequency will provide a dramatic improvement in the system's overall performance.

It is important to remember that replacing a processor requires some research. Most motherboards support a certain class of processor; they do not have the capacity to upgrade to a different class of chip. For example, it is not possible to upgrade a Pentium-class chip to a Pentium II–class chip. This relates not only to the processor slots, but also to the power requirements of the chip. You must consider the additional cooling requirements of the new chip as well. In most cases, processor upgrades are accomplished by replacing the motherboard and processor by using a special overdrive chip. Overdrive chips will be discussed further in Chapter 4.

Upgrading the BIOS

When the BIOS no longer supports all of the devices that need to be connected to the PC, an upgrade is needed. There are two ways to upgrade the BIOS chip: by manually replacing the chip or by using special flash software.

MANUAL CHIP REPLACEMENT

Manual chip replacement requires a technician to remove the old chip and replace it with a new chip provided by the motherboard manufacturer. Manual replacement is not an option in today's PCs.

FLASH BIOS REPLACEMENT

Flash BIOS is the modern way of upgrading a computer's BIOS. By placing the flash disk in the floppy drive and booting the machine, a technician can reprogram the system's BIOS to handle new hardware devices that the manufacturer has included.

Manufacturers periodically post the flash upgrades on their Web sites for technicians to download. Be aware that you must take care in this process because the BIOS could be disabled and require the motherboard to be shipped back to the manufacturer. In most cases, the flash program will give the technician the opportunity to save the current software and settings to a restore disk that can reverse the changes if necessary.

Portables

You can upgrade portable systems to increase system performance just like you can desktop PCs. However, because of the proprietary nature of portable systems and their space limitations, any upgrade part should be purchased only from the manufacturer.

Unless you are working at an authorized repair facility and have been certified by the manufacturer to work on the specific model, any work you do might void the warranty. Another factor to consider is that most of the portable system manufacturers will not sell the upgrade part unless the technician performing the work is certified to work on the specific model. Compaq and HP both strictly adhere to this policy.

One upgrade that can be performed on a portable is the battery. Aftermarket battery manufacturers make replacement batteries that have a longer battery life. The increased battery life will allow the user to accomplish more work between charging periods.

Replacing Basic Subsystem Components

If manufacturers produce an improved replacement or upgrade part for a subsystem component, technicians can increase a system's performance by replacing it. In the past, the most common modification was to support new IDE variants and increase data throughput.

By adding an improved IDE architecture expansion card, it's possible to add larger or faster hard drives to a system. In most cases, though, to fully utilize this new architecture, all of the supporting subsystems such as bus speed need to be upgraded as well. This requires the replacement of the motherboard.

Working with Unique Components

The most important requirement when working with unique components is having information about the device. Most large manufacturers, such as Compaq, HP, Dell, and Gateway, have their own particular take on what components can and cannot be upgraded. They sometimes design in options that can be upgraded in order to increase the system performance of a particular model.

To accomplish any such upgrade, you must first know what you are looking at and what benefits you can expect. The only source of information in most of these cases is the company's Web site. Make sure that before you attempt to replace any proprietary component, you have visited the Web site and have obtained as much information as possible. Another factor to consider is that in most cases you will need to be certified by the manufacturer to perform the upgrade and order the parts.

Exam Essentials

Know what performance enhancements are achieved by upgrading memory.   Upgrading the amount of RAM a computer has will increase the speed of the machine by preventing the use of the hard drive to store data that is being accessed.

Know what perfomance enhancements are achieved by replacing the hard drive.   Replacing the hard drive can allow you to add to the overall storage capacity of the machine. In some cases, read/write performance can be improved by upgrading.

Know what performance enhancements are achieved by replacing the BIOS.   Replacing the BIOS can increase the number of supported devices.

Key Terms and Concepts

Flash software   This is special software provided by the motherboard manufacturer to replace or change the capabilities of the BIOS.

Overdrive chip   This special processor chip is used to upgrade the speed of the processor without the need to replace the motherboard.

Domain 2.0 Diagnosing and Troubleshooting

COMPTIA A+ EXAM OBJECTIVES COVERED IN THIS CHAPTER:

▶ **2.1 Identify common symptoms and problems associated with each module and how to troubleshoot and isolate the problems.** *(pages 81 – 100)*

- Processor/memory symptoms
- Mouse
- Floppy drive
- Parallel ports
- Hard drives
- CD-ROM
- DVD
- Sound card/audio
- Monitor/video
- Motherboards
- Modems
- BIOS
- USB
- NIC
- CMOS
- Power supply
- Slot covers
- POST audible/visual error codes
- Troubleshooting tools, e.g., multimeter
- Large LBA, LBA
- Cables
- Keyboard
- Peripherals

2.2 Identify basic troubleshooting procedures and how to elicit problem symptoms from customers. *(pages 101 – 107)*

- Troubleshooting/isolation/problem determination procedures
- Determine whether hardware or software problem
- Gather information from user

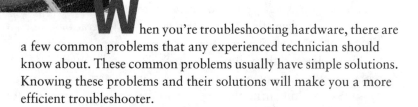

When you're troubleshooting hardware, there are a few common problems that any experienced technician should know about. These common problems usually have simple solutions. Knowing these problems and their solutions will make you a more efficient troubleshooter.

2.1 Identify common symptoms and problems associated with each module and how to troubleshoot and isolate the problems.

- Processor/memory symptoms
- Mouse
- Floppy drive
- Parallel ports
- Hard drives
- CD-ROM
- DVD
- Sound card/audio
- Monitor/video
- Motherboards
- Modems
- BIOS
- USB
- NIC
- CMOS
- Power supply
- Slot covers
- POST audible/visual error codes
- Troubleshooting tools, e.g., multimeter

- **Large LBA, LBA**
- **Cables**
- **Keyboard**
- **Peripherals**

Your job as a computer technician is to effectively troubleshoot and repair problems that arise in the day-to-day operation of a company's environment. The most cost-efficient way to fix a computer problem relates to the ability of the technician, not to the parts replaced. Whether you are employed by a manufacturing facility or by an IS consulting firm, the costs associated with maintaining a system can be quite high. Considering the cost of most components, the majority of the money spent to maintain the system goes to labor. This mean that the more efficient the technician, the lower the cost of ownership for the system.

Critical Information

Your value as a technician increases as you gain experience because of the reduced time that it takes you to accomplish common repairs. Your ability to troubleshoot by past experiences and gut feelings will make you more efficient and more valuable, which in turn will allow you to advance and earn a better income. This chapter will give you some guidelines you can use to evaluate common hardware issues that you are sure to face.

POST Routines

Every computer has a diagnostic program built into its BIOS called the *power on self-test* (*POST*). When you turn on the computer, it executes this set of diagnostics. These routines go by pretty quickly, so we'll detail them here.

NOTE   The POST described below is typical of IBM-brand PCs; other manufacturers have similar POSTs, but they may differ in certain aspects.

---

1. **Test the processor.** POST runs checks on the CPU. If the tests fail, the system stops with no error message (usually).

2. **Check the ROMs.** POST computes a checksum for the BIOS ROMs. If the checksums do not match, the system halts with no error message.

3. **Test the DMA controller.** Again, if there are problems, the system halts.

4. **Check the Interrupt controller.** If there is a problem with this component, the system will give a long beep, followed by a short beep, and then the system will stop.

5. **Test the system timing chip.** This is not the chip that tells time, but rather the chip that provides timing signals for the bus and processor. If this chip fails, the system will give a long beep, followed by a short beep, and will then halt.

6. **Test the BASIC ROMs (if they exist).** Most computers since the IBM AT have not included BASIC, so this step is usually not part of their POST routines. However, on an older computer, if the BASIC ROMs fail the POST test, the system will give a long beep, followed by a short beep, and will then halt.

7. **Check the video card.** At this point, the system runs the diagnostics for the video card. If it fails, the system issues one long beep and two short beeps and then halts. If it is successful, the video ROM BIOS is copied into RAM, and you will usually see a message about the type of video card that the computer is using.

8. **Initialize the expansion boards.** During this part of the POST routine, any expansion boards can initialize and copy their ROMs into upper memory, if necessary.

9. **Count and test RAM.** The system tests and counts all RAM that's installed in the machine by writing a bit to each bit of memory. If a 1 is written and read back successfully, the counter increments. A failure during this portion of the POST will generate a "201— Memory Error" message on the screen. (Here's a free tip for you: Any POST error numbers starting with 2 are memory-related errors.)

10. **Test the keyboard.** The system contacts the keyboard controller and sends signals to detect the presence of a keyboard. It also checks for stuck keys. If this test fails, a "301—Keyboard Failure" error is generated along with a short beep. Some systems may halt, while others may not. (Some systems also ask you to press the F1 key, which is kind of silly if the keyboard isn't working, huh?)

11. **Check the cassette interface.** This is another POST routine valid only on IBM PCs and XTs. If the cassette interface doesn't work, a "131—Cassette Interface" error is generated. The system does not halt.

12. **Test the floppy drives.** The system contacts the floppy disk adapter and asks it to activate the drive motors of any floppy disks, in order (A:, then B:). If there are problems, a "601—Floppy Disk" error is generated, and the system will try to load cassette BASIC (if it's present, on an IBM PC or XT).

13. **Check resources and boot the computer.** The POST routine queries any remaining devices (LPT ports, serial ports, etc.), makes a short beep, and then queries the disk drives looking for an operating system. If the system finds one on either a floppy drive or the hard disk, it loads it, and the computer is functional. If it can't find an operating system, most systems will issue an "Operating system not found" error (or something to that effect).

The POST routines are a great tool for troubleshooting. They usually give English descriptions of any problems that they find. Some BIOS POST routines may actually give suggestions on how to fix the problem. Tables 2.1 and 2.2 summarize the POST beep and error codes, respectively, that are most often seen on computers today.

TABLE 2.1: Common POST Beep Codes

Beep Code	Problem
No beep, system dead	Power supply bad, system not plugged in, or power not turned on
Continuous beeps	Power supply bad, not plugged into motherboard correctly, or keyboard stuck

TABLE 2.1: Common POST Beep Codes (continued)

Beep Code	Problem
Repeating short beep	Power supply problem
One short beep, nothing on screen	Video card failure
One short beep, video present, but system won't boot	Bad floppy drive, cable, or controller
Two short beeps	Configuration error (on most PS/2 systems)
One long, one short beep	System board bad
One long, two short beeps	Video card failure

TABLE 2.2: Common POST Error Codes

Error Number	Explanation
1**	Any number starting with 1 usually indicates a system board problem.
161	CMOS battery failure.
164	Memory size error. Always happens after memory has been added. Running the BIOS setup program will allow the system to recognize the memory, and the error should go away.
2**	Any number starting with 2 usually indicates a memory-related problem.
201	Memory test failed. One or more portions of RAM were found to be bad. Any numbers following this error code may indicate which RAM chip is bad. See the computer's documentation for information on interpreting those codes.
3**	Any error number starting with 3 usually indicates a problem with the keyboard. Problems include a missing or malfunctioning keyboard, as well as stuck keys.

TABLE 2.2: Common POST Error Codes *(continued)*

Error Number	Explanation
301	Keyboard error. Usually means a missing or malfunctioning keyboard or a key has been pressed too long during startup. (Are you resting your hand on the keyboard? Is something leaning against one of the keys?) Also happens if a key remains depressed during the POST keyboard routine.
4**	Monochrome video problems.
5**	Color video problems.
6**	Floppy disk system problems.
601	Floppy disk error. Either the floppy adapter or the floppy drive failed. Check to see that the floppy cable isn't attached upside down and that the power to the floppy drive(s) is hooked up correctly.
17**	Hard disk problems. The hard disk geometry might not be set correctly or the disk adapter can't communicate with the hard disk.
1780	Drive 0 (C:) failure. The C: drive or controller isn't functioning. The disk might not be configured or the adapter isn't installed correctly.
1781	Drive 1 (D:) failure. The D: drive or controller isn't functioning. The disk might not be configured or the adapter isn't installed correctly.

Motherboard Problems

The motherboard's functions are tested, for the most part, by the POST routines. The 1** errors and beep codes during startup indicate the biggest problems, so there are very few problems that don't show up in the POST. The occasional "phantom" problem does happen, however.

One problem becomes apparent when the system constantly loses time. The time will reset to 12:00 on 12/01/83, for example. At the same time, you may start seeing "1780—Hard Disk Failure" problems. When you try to reset the time, it will set correctly. But as soon as you turn off the computer and turn it back on, the time is lost.

These symptoms indicate that the system's CMOS is losing the time, date, and hard disk settings. The CMOS is usually able to retain this information when the system is shut off because a small battery powers this memory. Because it is a battery, it will eventually need replacement.

When the CMOS battery is replaced, the system settings must be reset. But they will be retained when the power is shut off.

Hard Disk System Problems

Hard disk system problems usually stem from one of three causes:

- The adapter is bad.
- The disk is bad.
- The adapter and disk are connected incorrectly.

The first and last causes are easy to identify, because in either case the symptom will be obvious: The drive won't work. You simply won't be able to get the computer to communicate with the disk drive.

However, if the problem is a bad disk drive, the symptoms aren't as obvious. As long as the BIOS POST routines can communicate with the disk drive, they are usually satisfied. But the POST routines may not uncover problems related to storing information. Even with healthy POST results, you may find that you're permitted to save information to a bad disk, but when you try to read it back you get errors. Or the computer may not boot as quickly as it used to because the disk drive can't read the boot information successfully every time.

In some cases, reformatting the drive can solve the problems described in the preceding paragraph. In other cases, reformatting brings the drive back to life only for a short while. The bottom line is that read and write problems usually indicate that the drive is malfunctioning and should be replaced soon.

WARNING   Never low-level format IDE or SCSI drives! They are low-level formatted from the factory, and you may cause problems by using low-level utilities on these types of drives.

Peripheral Problems

The most common peripheral problems are those related to modem communications. The symptoms of these problems include the following:

- The modem won't dial.
- The modem keeps hanging up in the middle of the communications session.
- The modem spits out strange characters to the terminal screen.

If the modem won't dial, first check that it has been configured correctly, including its IRQ setting. If the configuration is correct, then the problem usually has to do with initialization commands. These are the commands sent to the modem by the communications program to "initialize" it. These commands tell it such things as how many rings to wait before answering, how long to wait after the last keystroke was detected for it to disconnect, and at what speed to communicate.

Modem initialization commands are known as the *Hayes command set*, also known as the *AT command set*, since each Hayes modem command started with the letters AT (presumably calling the modem to ATtention).

Each AT command does something different. The letters AT by themselves will ask the modem if it's ready to receive commands. If it returns "OK," that means that the modem is ready to communicate.

If you receive "Error," it means that there is an internal modem problem that may need to be resolved before communication can take place.

Table 2.3 lists a few of the most common AT commands, their functions, and the problems that they can solve. These commands can be sent to the modem by opening a terminal program like Windows Terminal or HyperTerminal and typing them in. All commands should return "OK" if they were successful.

TABLE 2.3: Common AT Commands

Command	Function	Usage
AT	Tells the modem that what follows the letters AT is a command that should be interpreted.	Used to precede most commands.
ATDT *nnnnnnn*	Dials the number *nnnnnnn* as a tone-dialed number.	Used to dial the number of another modem if the phone line is set up for tone dialing.
ATDP *nnnnnnn*	Dials the number *nnnnnnn* as a pulse-dialed number.	Used to dial the number of another modem if the phone line is set up for rotary dialing.
ATA	Answers an incoming call manually.	Places the line off-hook and starts to negotiate communication with the modem on the other end.
ATH0 (or +++ and then ATH0)	Tells the modem to hang up immediately.	Places the line on-hook and stops communication. (Note: The 0 in this command is a zero, not the letter *O*.)

TABLE 2.3: Common AT Commands *(continued)*

Command	Function	Usage
AT&F	Resets the modem to factory default settings.	This setting works as the initialization string when others don't. If you have problems with modems hanging up in the middle of a session or failing to establish connections, use this string by itself to initialize the modem.
ATZ	Resets the modem to power-up defaults.	Almost as good as AT&F, but may not work if power-up defaults have been changed with S-registers.
ATS0-n	Waits n rings before answering a call.	Sets the default number of rings that the modem will detect before taking the modem off-hook and negotiating a connection. (Note: The 0 in this command is a zero, not the letter O.)
ATS6-n	Waits n seconds for a dial tone before dialing.	If the phone line is slow to give a dial tone, you may have to set this register to a number higher than 2.
,	Pauses briefly.	When placed in a string of AT commands, the comma will cause a pause to occur. Used to separate the number for an outside line (many businesses use 9 to connect to an outside line) and the real phone number (e.g., 9,555-1234).

TABLE 2.3: Common AT Commands *(continued)*

Command	Function	Usage
*70 or 1170	Turns off call waiting.	The click you hear when you have call waiting (a feature offered by the phone company) will interrupt modem communication and cause the connection to be lost. To disable call waiting for a modem call, place these commands in the dialing string like so: *70,555-1234. Call waiting will resume after the call is hung up.
CONNECT	Displays when a successful connection has been made.	You may have to wait some time before this message is displayed. If this message is not displayed, it means that the modem couldn't negotiate a connection with the modem on the other end of the line, due possibly to line noise.
BUSY	Displays when the number dialed is busy.	If displayed, some programs will wait a certain amount of time and try again to dial.
RING	Displays when the modem has detected a ringing line.	When someone is calling your modem, the modem will display this message in the communications program. You would type ATA to answer the call.

If two computers can connect, but they both receive garbage on their screens, there's a good chance that the computers don't agree on the communications settings. Settings such as data bits, parity, stop bits, and compression must all agree in order for communication to take place.

Keyboard and Mouse Problems

Keyboards are simple devices. Therefore, they either work or they don't. There are rarely any phantom problems with keyboards. Usually, keyboard problems are environmental. They get dirty and the keys start to stick. To clean a keyboard, it's best to use the keyboard cleaner sold by electronics supply stores. This cleaner foams up quickly and doesn't leave a residue behind. Spray it liberally on the keyboard and keys. Work the cleaner in between the keys with a stiff toothbrush. Blow the excess away with a strong blast of compressed air. Repeat until the keyboard functions properly. If you do have to clean a keyboard that's had a soft drink spilled on it, remove the key caps before you perform the cleaning procedure. It makes it easier to reach the sticky plungers.

TIP Remember that most of the dollars spent on systems are for labor. If you spend an hour cleaning a twelve-dollar keyboard, then you have probably just cost your company twenty dollars. Knowing how to fix certain things doesn't necessarily mean that you should fix them. Always evaluate your workload, the cost of replacement, and the estimated cost of the repair before deciding on a course of action.

With mechanical keyboards, you can de-solder a broken key switch and replace it. However, most of the time, the labor to replace one key is more expensive than a new keyboard. New keyboards can be bought for less than fifty bucks, so keep the one with the single malfunctioning key as a spare and replace it with a new one.

To clean the key caps on a keyboard, spray keyboard cleaner on a soft, lint-free cloth and rub it briskly onto the surface of each key. Be careful not to rub too hard.

Display System Problems

There are two types of video problems: no video and bad video. No video means that there is no image on the screen when the computer is powered up. Bad video means that the quality is substandard for the type of display system being used.

No Video

Any number of things can cause a blank screen. The first two are the most common: Either the power is off or the contrast or brightness is turned down.

If you've checked the power as well as the brightness and contrast settings, then it's either a bad video card or a blown monitor. An easy way to determine which one is to turn on the computer and monitor, then touch the monitor screen. The high voltage used to charge the monitor will leave a static charge on a working monitor, and it's a charge that can be felt. If there's no charge, then there's a good chance that the flyback transformer has blown and the monitor needs to be repaired. If there is a charge, then the video card or cable is suspect.

WARNING   Flyback transformers are the most common cause of monitor failure that can be affordably fixed. With falling monitor prices, the cost of other repairs may actually exceed the cost of purchasing a new monitor.

Bad Video

You may have seen a monitor that has a bad data cable. This is the monitor nobody wants; everything has a blue (or red or green) tint to it, and it gives everyone a headache. This monitor could also have a bad gun, but more often than not, the problem goes away if you just wiggle the cable (indicating a bad cable).

You may have also seen monitors that are out of adjustment. With most new monitors, this is an easy problem to fix. Old monitors had to be partially disassembled to change these settings. New monitors have push-button control panels for changing these settings.

The earth generates a very strong magnetic field. This magnetic field can cause swirls and fuzziness even in high-quality monitors. Most monitors have metal shields that can protect against magnetic fields. But eventually these shields can get "polluted" by taking on the same magnetic field as the earth, and the shield becomes useless. To solve this problem, these monitors have a built-in feature known as the "degauss" feature. This feature removes the effects of the magnetic field by creating a stronger magnetic field with opposite polarity that gradually fades to a field of zero. A special degauss button activates it. You need only press it when the picture starts to deteriorate. The image will shake momentarily during the degauss cycle, then return to normal.

TIP If you have a monitor that shows bad distortion, and changing the settings or degaussing has no effect, then look for magnetic interference caused by nearby florescent lights or large power sources. My wife-to-be, who is also an information manager, works for a manufacturing facility that's constantly fighting this problem.

Floppy Drive Problems

Most floppy drive problems result from bad media. Your first troubleshooting technique with floppy drive issues should be to try a new disk.

One of the most common problems that develop with floppy drives is misaligned read/write heads. The symptoms are fairly easy to recognize—you can read and write to a floppy on one machine but not on any others. This is normally caused by the mechanical arm in the floppy drive becoming misaligned. When the disk was formatted, it was not properly positioned on the drive, thus preventing other floppy drives from reading it.

There are numerous commercial tools available to realign floppy drive read/write heads. They use a floppy drive that has been preformatted to reposition the mechanical arm. In most cases, though, this fix is temporary—the arm will just move out of place again fairly soon. Given the inexpensive nature of the problem, the best solution is to spent a few dollars and replace the drive.

Sound Card Problems

Sound cards are traditionally one of the most problem-ridden components in a PC. They demand a lot of PC resources and are notorious for being very inflexible in their configuration. The most common sound card-related problems will involve resource conflicts (IRQ, DMA, or I/O address).

Luckily, most sound card vendors are quite aware of the problems and ship very good diagnostic utilities to help resolve them. Use your PC troubleshooting skills to determine the conflict, and then reconfigure until you find an acceptable set of resources that are not in use.

CD-ROM/DVD Issues

CD-ROM and DVD problems are normally media related. Although compact disc technology is much more reliable than floppy disks, it is still not perfect. Another factor to consider is the cleanliness of the disc. On many occasions, if a disc is unreadable, simply cleaning it with an approved cleaner and a lint-free cleaning towel will fix the problem.

Some DVD drives use a special video picture enhancement card called an *encoder*. This adds another point of failure. A failed card will cause the machine to lock up while you're watching a DVD movie or produce a poor-quality picture; however, it will not keep the disk itself from spinning. Since the cards vary by manufacturer, you should troubleshoot the device by first checking the manufacturer's Web site for information and the latest service documents.

Network Interface Card

In general, network interface cards, or NICs, are added to a PC via an expansion slot. The most common issue that prevents network connectivity is a bad or unplugged patch cable.

Cleaning crews and the rollers on the bottoms of chairs are the most common threats to a patch cable. In most cases, wall jacks are placed four to 10 feet away from the desktop. The patch cables are normally lying exposed under the user's desk, and from time to time damage is done to the cable or it is inadvertently snagged and unplugged. When you troubleshoot a network adapter, start with the most rudimentary explanations first. Make sure the patch cable is tightly plugged in, and then look at the card and see if any lights are on. If there are lights on, use the NIC's documentation to help troubleshoot. More often than not, simply shutting down the machine, unplugging the patch and power cables for a moment, and then reattaching them and rebooting the PC will fix an unresponsive NIC.

NOTE Although this is not on the test, Wake On LAN cards have more problems than standard network cards. In my opinion, this is because they are always on. In some cases, you will be unable to get the card working again unless you unplug the PC's power supply and reset the card.

BIOS Issues

Computer BIOSes don't really go bad; they just become out-of-date. This is not necessary a critical issue—they will continue to support the hardware that came with the box. It *does*, however, become an issue when the BIOS doesn't support some component that you would like to install—a larger hard drive, for instance.

Most of today's BIOSes are written to a Flash EPROM and can be updated through the use of software. Each manufacturer has its own method for accomplishing this. Check out the documentation for complete details.

WARNING If you make a mistake in the upgrade process, the computer can become unbootable. If this happens, your only option may be shipping the box to a manufacturer-approved service center! Be careful!

Power Supply Problems

Power supply problems are usually easy to troubleshoot. The system does not respond in any way when the power is turned on. When this happens, open the case, remove the power supply, and replace it with a new one.

Be aware that different cases have different types of on/off switches. The process of replacing a power supply is a lot easier if you purchase a replacement with the same mechanism. Even so, remember to document exactly how the power supply was connected to the on/off switch before removing it.

Miscellaneous Problems

Some common problems do not fit well into categories. This section lists some common hardware issues you will be faced with.

Dislodged Chips and Cards

The inside of a computer is a harsh environment. The temperature inside the case of some Pentium computers is well over 100°F! When you turn your computer on, it heats up. Turn it off, and it cools down. After several hundred cycles of this, some components can't handle the stress and start to move out of their sockets. This phenomenon is known as *chip creep* and can really be frustrating.

Chip creep can affect any socketed device, including ICs, RAM chips, and expansion cards. The solution to chip creep is simple. Open the case and reseat the devices. It's surprising how often this is the solution to phantom problems of all sorts.

Another important item worth mentioning is an unresponsive but freshly unboxed PC. With the introduction of the Type II and Type II-style of processors, the number of dead boxes increased dramatically. In fact, at that time I was leading a 2,000-unit migration for a large financial institution. As with any large migration, time and manpower were in short supply. The average dead PC ratio was about one out of every 20. When about 10 DOAs had stacked up, I stayed after work one night to assess the problem. After checking the power supply, RAM, and cables on these integrated systems, an examination of the chip provided me with the fix. These large top-heavy processors can become dislodged during shipment. Shortly after, manufacturers began using a heavier attachment point for the slot style of processor, which has helped tremendously.

Environmental Problems

Computers are like human beings. They have similar tolerances to heat and cold. In general, anything comfortable to us is comfortable to a computer. They need lots of clean, moving air to keep them functioning.

Dirt, grime, paint, smoke, and other airborne particles can become caked on the inside of the components. This is most common in automotive and manufacturing environments. The contaminants create a film that coats the components, causing them to overheat and/or conduct electricity on their surface. Simply blowing these exposed systems out with a can of condensed air from time to time can prevent damage to the components. One thing you should be sure to do while you are cleaning the components is to clean any cooling fans in the power supply or on the heat sync.

NOTE   To clean the power supply fan, blow the air from the inside of the case. When you do this, the fan will blow the contaminants out the cooling vents. If you spray from the vents toward the inside of the box, you will be blowing the dust and grime inside the case or back into the fan motor.

One way to ensure that the environment has the least possible effect on your computer is to always leave the "blanks" in the empty slots on the back of your box. These pieces of metal are designed to keep dirt, dust, and other foreign matter from the inside of the computer. They also maintain proper airflow within the case to ensure that the computer does not overheat.

Exam Essentials

Be familiar with the purpose of POST routines.   The POST routine performs entry-level hardware troubleshooting as a PC starts. Be familiar with the abilities of the POST and its use.

Know the symptoms of motherboard problems.   One motherboard problem becomes apparent when the system constantly loses time. You also may start seeing "1780—Hard Disk Failure" problems. These symptoms indicate that the system's CMOS is losing the time, date, and hard disk settings. Because a small battery powers this memory, it will eventually need replacement. When the CMOS battery is unable to provide power to the chip, the settings stored in its memory are lost when the system is turned off. Replacing the battery will fix this issue.

Know how to troubleshoot hard disk system problems.   Hard disk system problems usually stem from one of three causes:

- The adapter is bad.

- The disk is bad.

- The adapter and disk are connected incorrectly.

The most common disk error is improper configuration.

Learn to identify peripheral problems.   Peripherals are the devices that allow the user to get data into and out of computers. It stands to reason that the variety or errors can be challenging. Be familiar with some common device issues.

Be able to determine display system problems.   The most common display problems relate to power, brightness, or contrast. Simply adjusting the monitor controls should be your first step when troubleshooting.

Recognize the symptoms of floppy drive problems.   Most floppy drive problems result from bad media. Your first troubleshooting technique with floppy drive issues should be to try a new disk.

Know how to troubleshoot sound card problems. Sound cards demand a lot of PC resources and are notorious for being very inflexible in their configuration. The most common sound card–related problems will involve resource conflicts (IRQ, DMA, or I/O address).

Learn to identify BIOS issues. BIOS issues are related to the inability to support hardware. In most cases, a program or flash upgrade is available to update the BIOS so that components can be supported.

Recognize power supply problems. Power supplies are normally unique. They either work or they don't. Become familiar with the types of symptoms.

Know the symptoms of dislodged chips and cards. Dislodged components are the most common issues you will face. Become familiar with the symptoms and their fixes.

Key Terms and Concepts

POST routines The power on self-test (POST) is a diagnostic program that runs when you turn on the computer. POST routines are a great tool for troubleshooting. They usually give English descriptions of any problems that they find. Some BIOS POST routines may actually give suggestions on how to fix the problem.

Beep codes The motherboard's functions are tested by the POST routines. The errors are made known by beep codes, so there are very few problems that don't show up in the POST.

AT commands These are the commands sent to the modem by the communications program to initialize it. These commands tell it such things as how many rings to wait before answering, how long to wait after the last keystroke was detected for it to disconnect, and at what speed to communicate. Each AT command does something different. The letters AT by themselves ask the modem if it's ready to receive commands.

Flyback transformers Flyback transformers are the most common cause of monitor failure that can be affordably fixed. The flyback transformer initializes the gun and makes the connections to create the viewable images.

2.2 Identify basic troubleshooting procedures and how to elicit problem symptoms from customers.

- Troubleshooting/isolation/problem determination procedures
- Determine whether hardware or software problem
- Gather information from user

Just as all artists have their own style, all technicians have their own way to troubleshoot. Some people use their instincts; others rely on advice from other people. The most common troubleshooting tips can be condensed into a step-by-step process. You try each step, in order. If the first step doesn't narrow down the problem, you move on to the next step.

Critical Information

Let's take a look at each step in the troubleshooting process.

Step 1: Define the Problem.

If you can't define the problem, you can't begin to solve it. You can define the problem by asking questions of the user. Here are a few questions to ask the user to aid in determining what exactly the problem is:

Can you show me the problem?   This question is one of the best. It allows the user to show you exactly where and when they experience the problem.

How often does this happen?   This question establishes whether this problem is a one-time occurrence that can be solved with a reboot or whether the problem has a specific sequence of events that cause it to happen. The latter usually indicates a more serious problem that may require software installation or hardware replacement.

Has any new hardware been installed recently?   New hardware can mean incompatibility problems with existing devices. Some Plug-and-Play devices install with the same resource settings as an existing device. This can cause both devices to become disabled.

Have any other changes been made to the computer recently?   If the answer is "Yes," ask if they can remember approximately when the change was made. Then ask them approximately when the problem started. If the two dates seem related, then there's a good chance that the problem is related to the change. If it's a new hardware component, check to see that the hardware component was installed correctly.

Step 2: Check the Simple Stuff First.

This step is the one that most experienced technicians overlook. Often, computer problems are the result of some simple problem. Technicians overlook them because the problems are so simple that they assume they *couldn't* be the problem. Some examples of simple problems are shown here:

Is it plugged in?   And on both ends? Cables must be plugged in on *both ends* in order to function correctly. Cables can be easily tripped over and inadvertently pulled from their sockets.

Is it turned on?   This one seems the most obvious, but we've all fallen victim to it at one point or another. Computers and their peripherals must be turned on in order to function. Most have power switches with LEDs that glow when the power is turned on.

Is the system ready?   Computers must be ready before they can be used. "Ready" means that the system is ready to accept commands from the user. An indication that a computer is ready is when the operating system screens come up and the computer presents you with a menu or a command prompt. If that computer uses a graphical interface, the computer is ready when the mouse pointer appears. Printers are ready when the "On Line" or "Ready" light on the front panel is lit.

Do the chips and cables need to be reseated?   You can solve some of the strangest problems (random hang-ups or errors) by opening the case and pressing down on each socketed chip. This remedies the "chip creep" problem mentioned earlier in this chapter. In addition, you should reseat any cables to make sure that they are making good contact.

Step 3: Check to See If It's User Error.

This error is common but preventable. The indication that a problem is due to user error is when a user says they can't perform some very common computer task, such as "I can't print" or "I can't save my file." As soon you hear these words, you should start asking questions of the user to determine if it is simply a question of teaching the user the correct procedure. A good question to ask following their statement of the problem would be, "Were you *ever* able to perform that task?" If they answer "No" to this question, it means they are probably doing the procedure wrong. If they answer "Yes," you must move on to another set of questions.

TIP   A user can be your greatest asset or your worst opponent. If you treat each person with respect and concentrate on solving the issue, you will be better off, and you might even make a new friend.

The Social Side of Troubleshooting

When looking for clues as to the nature of a problem, no one can give you more information than the person who was there when it happened. They can tell you what led up to the problem, what software was running, and the exact nature of the problem ("It happened when I tried to print"), and they can help you re-create the problem, if possible.

Use questioning techniques that are neutral in nature. Instead of saying, "What were you doing when it broke?" be more compassionate and say, "What was going on when the computer decided not to work?" It sounds silly, but these types of changes can make your job a lot easier!

Step 4: Reboot the Computer.

It is amazing how often a simple computer reboot can solve a problem. Rebooting the computer clears the memory and starts the computer with a "clean slate." Whenever I perform phone support, I always ask the customer to reboot the computer and try again. If rebooting doesn't work, try powering down the system completely and then powering it up again. More often than not, that will solve the problem.

Step 5: Determine If the Problem Is Hardware or Software Related.

This step is an important one because it determines what part of the computer you should focus your troubleshooting skills on. Each part requires different skills and different tools.

To determine if a problem is hardware or software related, you could do a few things to narrow the problem down. For instance, does the problem manifest itself when you use a particular piece of hardware (a modem, for example)? If it does, the problem is more than likely hardware related.

This step relies on personal experience more than any of the other steps do. You will without a doubt run into several strange software problems. Each one has a particular solution. Some may even require reinstallation of the software or the entire operating system.

Step 6: If the Problem Is Hardware Related, Determine Which Component Is Failing.

Hardware problems are pretty easy to figure out. If the modem doesn't work, and you know it isn't a software problem, it's pretty safe to say that the modem is probably the piece of hardware that needs to be replaced.

With some of the newer computers, several components are integrated into the motherboard. If you troubleshoot the computer and find a hardware component to be bad, there's a good chance that the bad component is integrated into the motherboard (for example, the parallel port circuitry) and the whole motherboard must be replaced—an expensive proposition, to be sure.

Step 7: Check Service Information Sources

As you may or may not have figured out by now, I'm fond of old sayings. There's another old saying that applies here: "If all else fails, read the instructions." The service manuals are your "instructions" for troubleshooting and service information. Almost every computer and peripheral made today have a set of service documentation in the form of books, service CD-ROMs, and Web sites. The latter of the three seems to be growing in popularity as more and more service centers get connections to the Internet.

Step 8: If It Ain't Broke...

When doctors take the Hippocratic oath, they promise to not make their patients any sicker than they already were. Technicians should take a similar oath. It all boils down to, "If it ain't broke, don't fix it." When you troubleshoot, make one change at a time. If the change doesn't solve the problem, revert the computer to its previous state before making a different change.

Step 9: Ask for Help

If you don't know the answer, ask one of your fellow technicians. They may have run across the problem you are having and know the solution.

This solution does involve a little humility. You must admit that you don't know the answer. It is said that the beginning of wisdom is "I don't know." If you ask questions, you will get answers, and you will learn from the answers. Making mistakes is valuable as well, as long as you learn from them.

NOTE Throughout my career in the computer business, the reluctance to share information is the thing that most concerns me about this industry. As computer professionals, we are valued by the extent of our knowledge. Some of us intend on keeping our value high by limiting the flow of knowledge to others. My position is different than those tight-lipped people. I like to help and to teach. This factor has been my best asset as I climbed from the help desk to become an IS manager. The most amusing thing is that despite my impressive title, many certifications, and two published technical books, I still ask advice and help on a daily basis. If I don't know the answer, I ask, and it doesn't bother me a bit. If I know and I'm asked, I share and try to bring the other person to the understanding that I have of that particular subject. One of the greatest assets you can have is another opinion or another person to bounce ideas off.

Exam Essentials

Know the basic steps of troubleshooting. Troubleshooting is a process of trial and error. For the exam and your career, use this system to diagnose and repair hardware-related issues.

Check your information sources. Service manuals are your "instructions" for troubleshooting and service information. Almost every computer and peripheral made today have a set of service documentation in the form of books, service CD-ROMs, and Web sites.

Ask for help. If you don't know the answer, ask one of your fellow technicians. They may have run across the problem you are having and know the solution. This is one thing that I feel very strongly about. Don't be embarrassed to ask, and don't be too tight-lipped to help others.

Key Terms and Concepts

Social troubleshooting   In most cases, troubleshooting is 25 percent knowledge and 75 percent people skills.

Service information sources   Devices come with service manuals that can be used for troubleshooting. These manuals can come in several forms such as booklets, "readme" files on the CD-ROM or floppy disks, and the manufacturer's Web site. In most cases, the most up-to-date information is on the Web site.

Chapter

3

Domain 3.0 Preventive Maintenance

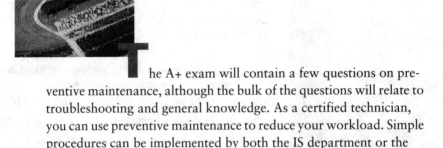

he A+ exam will contain a few questions on preventive maintenance, although the bulk of the questions will relate to troubleshooting and general knowledge. As a certified technician, you can use preventive maintenance to reduce your workload. Simple procedures can be implemented by both the IS department or the users to reduce the number of failed components.

Disposing of computer components is not only part of a technician's job, but a responsibility to the environment. Due to the ever-changing environmental laws, you should not see many—if any—exam questions relating to the proper disposal of components.

Identify the purpose of various types of preventive maintenance products and procedures and when to use and perform them.

- Liquid cleaning compounds
- Types of materials to clean contacts and connections
- Non-static vacuums (chassis, power supplies, fans)

This section outlines some preventive maintenance products and procedures. Preventive maintenance is one of the most overlooked ways to reduce the cost of ownership in any environment. Throughout this book, I have made several points on the cost savings of purchasing new equipment instead of repairing it. How can you then rationalize preventive maintenance as a cost savings? Earlier I gave an example of a keyboard repair being less cost-effective than replacement. Another factor to consider is whether the system is currently in a production environment.

In an ideal setting, all of the computers at your location would have identical software on the hard drive and all data would be saved to network locations. When a machine or component becomes unusable, a replacement would be set in its place. The technician could then work on the damaged component of the system when time allowed and not cause any interruption of its user's daily tasks. In today's work environment, lean and mean is standard procedure. For this reason, when a machine or component becomes unusable and its users are prevented from completing their tasks, dollars are lost. The lost profit relates not only to the users' salary, but also to the revenue that the users are responsible for producing.

Critical Information

In many cases, some very inexpensive maintenance can prevent downtime and lower repair costs. For example, let's say you are responsible for hardware break/fix troubleshooting and repair in a 2000-user environment. You lose an average of two keyboards per month, and your response time to the users is normally six to twelve hours with your heavy workload.

The IS manager is concerned about the amount of work that is being lost due to the inability of the users to complete their daily tasks. The IS manager asks for a proposal to reduce the impact of these failures. To reduce the keyboard failure rate, you decide to generate a memo on the benefits of using canned air to blow out the keyboards and wipes to keep the keys clean. You then outline the proper methods and distribute the needed cleaning supplies to all department heads and ask them to have the employees accomplish this task during a slow period once a month.

NOTE I have seen a company implement a plan very similar to this and reap amazing benefits. Users can perform some of the best preventive maintenance if they are educated on the proper procedures. This has other benefits besides the most apparent ones. For instance, the users feel that they are more involved with the maintenance of their computer. The ripple effect is that they take better care of their machines, which reduces service requests and allows issues to be addressed in a more timely manner.

Computer components get dirty. Dirt reduces their operating efficiency and, ultimately, their life. Cleaning them is definitely important. But cleaning them with the right cleaning compounds is equally important. Using the wrong compounds can leave residue behind that is more harmful than the dirt you are trying to remove!

Most computer cases and monitor cases can be cleaned using mild soap and water on a clean, lint-free cloth. Make sure that the power is off before putting anything wet near a computer. Dampen (not soak) a cloth with a mild soap solution and wipe the dirt and dust from the case. Then wipe the moisture from the case with a dry, lint-free cloth. Anything with a plastic or metal case can be cleaned in this manner.

In addition, if you spill anything on a keyboard, you can clean it by soaking it in distilled, demineralized water. In this type of water, the minerals and impurities have been removed and so it will not leave any traces of residue that might interfere with the proper operation of the keyboard after cleaning.

The electronic connectors of computer equipment, on the other hand, should never touch water. Instead, use a swab moistened in distilled, denatured isopropyl alcohol (also known as electronics cleaner and found in electronics stores) to clean contacts. This will take the oxidation off the copper contacts.

Finally, the best way to remove dust and dirt from the inside of the computer is to use compressed air instead of vacuuming. Compressed air can be more easily directed and doesn't produce ESD damage (like vacuuming could). Simply blow the dust from inside the computer using a stream of compressed air. However, make sure to do this outdoors so that you don't blow dust all over your work area or over yourself.

One unique challenge when cleaning printers is from spilled toner. It sticks to everything. There are two methods to deal with this. First of all, blow all the loose toner out of the printer using compressed air, being careful not to blow the toner into any of the printing mechanisms. Then, using a cool, damp cloth, wipe any remaining particles out of the printer.

Exam Essentials

Know what can be used to clean components of the computer. There are many types of cleaning solutions that can be used to perform these procedures. Be familiar with which option is best for the common situations listed above.

Know why the proper cleaning solutions should be used.   Using the wrong cleaning solution can damage components. Some of these solutions can leave a residue on the device that is more harmful than the dirt you are trying to remove.

Key Terms and Concepts

Demineralized water   Water that has had minerals and contaminants removed to prevent damage to computer components.

WARNING   Remember that no type of water should be used inside the computer's case.

Denatured isopropyl alcohol   This is the most common cleaning component found in any repair facility. You can use denatured alcohol to clean most components of a PC. It's commonly used to clean electrical connections.

Identify issues, procedures, and devices for protection within the computing environment, including people, hardware, and the surrounding workspace.

- UPS (Uninterruptible Power Supply) and suppressors
- Determining the signs of power issues
- Proper methods of storage of components for future use
- Potential hazards and proper safety procedures relating to lasers
- Special disposal procedures that comply with environmental guidelines
- ESD (Electrostatic Discharge) precautions and procedures

You will find several questions relating to power protection on the exam. It is also the most common cause of component failure. With the exception of hard drives and fans, computer components do not have moving parts. Without moving parts, the weakest link is the power source. Power fluctuations cause a wide range of problems from component failure to simple lockups. This section outlines some protection techniques that can be applied to limit the effect of power fluctuations and presents the terminology that describes the fluctuations. Make certain you spend adequate time on this section.

Critical Information

Unfortunately, it's rare for the power that comes out of the wall to be consistently 110V, 60Hz. It may be of a slightly higher or lower voltage; it may cycle faster or slower; there may occasionally be no power; or the worst, a 5000V spike may come down the power line from a lightning strike and fry the expensive electronic components of your computer and its peripherals.

There are three main classes of power problems that technicians have to deal with: problems with power quality, problems where too much power is coming out of the outlet, and problems where there is not enough power. Almost every outlet experiences at least one of these problems at some time or another.

Power Quality Problems and Solutions

The first type of power problem exists when the power coming out of the wall has a different frequency than normal (60Hz is considered normal). This type of problem manifests itself when stray electromagnetic signals get introduced into the line. This interference is called *electromagnetic interference* (*EMI*) and is usually caused by the electromagnetic waves emitted by the electric motors in appliances. In addition, televisions and other electronic devices (including the computers themselves) can produce a different type of interference, called *radio frequency interference* (*RFI*), which is really just a higher-frequency version of EMI. However, RFI is produced by integrated circuits (ICs) and other electronic devices. If your power lines run near a powerful radio broadcast antenna or factory, either of these can introduce noise into your power.

To solve these problems, companies like BEST Power Systems and APC make accessories called *line conditioners*. The function of these devices is to produce "perfect" power of 110V/60Hz. These devices will remove most of the stray EMI and RFI signals from the incoming power. They will also reduce any power overages down to 110V.

Power Overage Problems and Solutions

The most common type of power problem that causes computer damage is power overages. As the name suggests, these problems happen when too much power comes down the power lines. There are two main types of overage problems: spikes and surges. The primary difference between the two is the length of time the events last. A *spike* is a power overage condition that exists for an extremely short period of time. *Surges*, on the other hand, last for much longer, up to several seconds. Spikes are usually the result of faulty power transformer equipment at power substations. Surges can come from both power equipment and lightning strikes.

A common misconception is that a power strip can protect your computer from power overage problems. Most power strips are nothing more than multiple outlets with a circuit breaker. Real surge protectors usually cost upwards of $25.00. These devices have MOSFET (metallic oxide semiconductor field effect transistor) semiconductors that sacrifice themselves in the case of a power overage. But even these aren't perfect. They are rated in terms of clamping speed (how long it takes to go from the overvoltage to zero volts) and clamping voltage (at what voltage the MOSFET shorts out). The problem is that by the time the clamping voltage is reached, some of the overvoltage has gotten through to the power supply and damaged it. After a time, the power supply will be damaged permanently.

Realistically, having a surge protector is better than not having one, but not by much. It's better to use a line conditioner that can absorb the overvoltage than to use a circuit breaker.

NOTE   At the time that the book was written, your author was losing an average of one PC every four to six weeks at his place of employment. The latest incident caused me the most concern. I inherited white-box clones when I took my position, and the latest dead box had a two-inch square area next to the keyboard connector that was completely scorched. The motherboard itself melted in this area, and when I held a flashlight behind the board, light was visible. The amount of heat required to do this damage was pretty amazing—we were quite lucky that an electrical fire did not consume the PC and possibly the location where it sat. At first, I thought that the mortality rate was related to my predecessor's choice of PCs, but after examining the last two damaged machines and UPS devices, I had our utility provider monitor the power coming to and inside the building. The results of the monitoring showed that a faulty ground inside the building was responsible for these failures. To date, my company has lost eight PCs, three UPSs, and two modems to power issues in less than a year. In most cases, the motherboard and power supply were replaced and the machine redeployed. These repairs cost my company approximately $160 per incident, not including my time to complete the repairs. Not only that, but my employer is a retail chain store. Down equipment means fewer sales, which means lower profits. You also must consider that I was hired to provide WAN, router, server, NOS, and Web site design/implementation. I cannot perform these duties if I am constantly repairing PCs.

Undervoltage Power Problems and Solutions

Undervoltage problems generally don't cause damage to hardware. More often, they cause the computer to shut down completely (or at the very least, to reboot), thus losing any unsaved data in memory. There are three major types of undervoltage problems: sags, brownouts, and blackouts.

A *sag* is a momentary drop in voltage, lasting only a few milliseconds. Usually, you can't even tell one has occurred. Your house lights won't dim or flicker (well, actually they will, but it's too fast for you to notice). But your computer will react strangely to this sudden drop in power. Have you ever been on the "up" end of a seesaw and had someone jump off the other end? You were surprised at the sudden drop, weren't you? Your computer will experience the same kind of disorientation when the power drops rapidly to a lower voltage. A computer's normal response to this kind of "disorientation" is to reboot itself.

You've probably experienced one of the other two power undervoltage problems: brownouts and blackouts. A *brownout* occurs when voltage drops below 110 volts for a second or more. Brownouts are typically caused by a sudden increase in power consumption in your area and the lag time it takes for your power provider to respond by increasing production. You might notice when brownouts occur, because the lights in your home will dim, but not go out, then go back to full brightness a second or two later. You might also notice because your computer will reboot or the screen will flicker. (While writing this section, I counted two brownouts. Luckily, my computer hasn't rebooted, so the voltage drop probably wasn't too bad.)

Everyone has experienced a blackout. A *blackout* occurs when the power drops from 110 volts to zero volts in a very short period of time. It is a complete loss of power for anywhere from a few seconds to several minutes—or even longer. They are typically caused by a power failure somewhere in your area. Sometimes backup systems are available, but it may take anywhere from a couple of seconds to several hours to get the power back on in your area again.

There are two different hardware solutions to power undervoltage conditions: the SPS and the UPS. They each take a different approach to keeping the power at 110V. In both cases, you plug the units into the wall, then plug your computer equipment into the SPS or UPS. Let's look at the SPS first.

SPS stands for *standby power supply*. It's called that because there is a battery waiting to take over power production in case of a loss of line voltage. The SPS contains sensors that constantly monitor the line voltage and a battery with a step-up transformer. While conditions are normal, the line voltage charges the internal battery. When the line voltage drops below a preset threshold (also called the *cutover threshold*—i.e., 105V), the sensors detect that and switch the power from the wall to the internal battery. When the power comes back above the threshold, the sensors detect the restoration of power and switch the power source back to the line voltage.

The main problem with SPSs is that they take a few milliseconds to switch to the battery. During those few milliseconds, there is *no* voltage to the computer. This lack of voltage can cause reboots or crashes (rather like a brownout). An SPS is great for protecting against blackouts, but it does little for brownouts and sags. The better choice for undervoltage problems would be the *uninterruptible power supply* or *UPS*. The UPS works similarly to an SPS, but with one important difference. The computer equipment is always running off the battery. While the line voltage is normal, the battery gets charged. When power fluctuates, only the charging circuit is affected. The battery continues to provide power to the equipment uninterrupted. Because the equipment is constantly operating off the battery, the UPS also acts as a kind of line conditioner.

There is one main problem with UPSs: the quality of power they provide. Batteries provide DC power, and computer power supplies run on AC power. Inside the UPS is a power inverter that converts the DC into AC. It isn't perfect. AC power produces a 60Hz sine waveform, whereas the inverter produces a square wave. A computer's power supply will accept these square waveforms, but it doesn't like them (see Figure 3.1). However, UPS manufacturers are now using more sensitive inverters that can more closely approximate the sine wave. So, a UPS should be put on every piece of computer equipment where data loss would be a problem (in other words, almost every piece of computer equipment).

FIGURE 3.1: A comparison between line power and UPS-supplied power

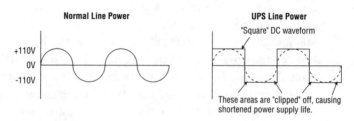

WARNING Never plug a laser printer or copier into a UPS! The large surge of power they draw when they first get turned on can burn out the inverter and battery. These devices can draw close to 15 amps when they are first turned on.

Safety

As a provider of a hands-on service, you need to be aware of some general safety tips, because if you are not careful, you could harm yourself or the equipment. First, let's talk about playing it safe. Computers, display monitors, and printers can be dangerous if not handled properly.

Perhaps the most important aspect of computers that you should be aware of is the fact that they not only *use* electricity, they *store* electrical charge after they're turned off. This makes the power supply and the monitor pretty much off-limits to anyone but a trained electrical repair person. Also, the computer's processor and various parts of the printer run at extremely high temperatures, and you can get burned if you try to handle them immediately after they've been in operation. Those are just two general safety measures that should concern you. There are plenty more. When discussing safety issues with regard to repairing and upgrading PCs, it is best to break them down into five general areas:

- The computer
- The power supply
- The printer
- The monitor
- The keyboard and mouse

The Power Supply

Do not take the issue of safety and electricity lightly. If you were to remove the power supply from its case, you would be taking a great risk. The current flowing through the power supply normally follows a complete circuit; when your body breaks that circuit, your body becomes a part of the circuit.

The two biggest dangers with power supplies are burning yourself and electrocuting yourself. These usually go hand in hand. If you touch a bare wire that is carrying current, you may get electrocuted. A large enough current passing through the wire can cause severe burns. It can also cause your heart to stop, your muscles to seize, and your brain to stop functioning. In short, it can kill you. Electricity always finds the best path to ground. And because we are basically bags of salt water, electricity will use us as a conductor if we are grounded. Because of the way electricity conducts itself, electrical burn victims usually have two kinds of wounds: the entry wound and the exit wound.

The entry wound happens at the point of contact between the conductor and the person. It's rather gruesome. The current flowing through you has enough power to boil the water in the tissues it comes in contact with, essentially cooking you from the inside out. It isn't fun. The electricity sears the tissue on its way toward whatever part of the body is closest to a ground. Then, at the point closest to a ground, the electricity bolts from the body, producing an exit wound. We hope this description will encourage you to learn proper electrical safety so you never have to experience the pain of electrical burns.

NOTE It's not often that repairing a computer is the cause of an electrical fire. You should, however, know how to extinguish one properly. There are three major classes of fire extinguishers available, one for each type of flammable substance: A for wood and paper fires, B for flammable liquids, and C for electrical fires. The most popular type of fire extinguisher today is the multipurpose, or ABC-rated, extinguisher. It contains a dry chemical powder that will smother the fire and cool it at the same time. For electrical fires (which may be related to a shorted-out wire in a power supply), make sure the fire extinguisher will work for Class C fires. If you don't have an extinguisher that is specifically rated for electrical fires (type C), you can use an ABC-rated extinguisher.

Although it is possible to work on a power supply, it is *not* recommended. Power supplies contain several capacitors that can hold *lethal* charges *long after they have been unplugged!* It is extremely dangerous to open the case of a power supply. Besides, power supplies are inexpensive, so it would probably cost less to replace them than to try to fix them, and it would be much safer.

The number of volts in a power source represents its potential to do work. But volts don't do anything by themselves. Current (amperage, or amps) is the actual force behind the work being done by electricity. Here's an analogy to help explain this concept. Say you have two boulders; one weighs 10 pounds, the other 100 pounds, and each is 100 feet off the ground. If you drop them, which one would do more work? The obvious answer is the 100-pound boulder. They both have the same potential to do work (100 feet of travel), but the 100-pound boulder has more mass, thus more force. Voltage is analogous to the distance the boulder is from the ground, and amperage is analogous to the mass of the boulder.

This is why we can produce static electricity on the order of 50,000 volts and not electrocute ourselves. Even though this electricity has a great *potential* for work, it actually does very little work because the amperage is so low. This also explains why you can weld metal with only 110 volts. Welders use only 110 (sometimes 220) volts, but they also use anywhere from 50 to 200 amps!

The Printer

Printer repair also has hazards and pitfalls. Some these hazards and pitfalls are shown here:

- When handling a toner cartridge from a laser printer or page printer, do not shake or turn the cartridge upside down. You will find yourself spending more time cleaning the printer and the surrounding area than you would have spent to fix the printer.

- Do not put any objects into the feeding system (in an attempt to clear the path) while the printer is running.

- Laser printers generate a laser that is hazardous to your eyes. Do not look directly into the source of the laser.

- If it's an ink-jet printer, do not try to blow into the ink cartridge to clear a clogged opening—that is, unless you like the taste of ink.

- Some parts of a laser printer (such as the EP cartridge) will be damaged if touched. Your skin produces oils and has a small surface layer of dead skin cells. These substances can collect on the delicate surface of the EP cartridge and cause malfunctions. Bottom line: Keep your fingers out of where they don't belong!

The Monitor

Even though we recommend not repairing monitors, the A+ exam does test your knowledge of the safety practices to use when you need to do so. If you have to open a monitor, you must first discharge the high-voltage charge on it using a high-voltage probe. This probe has a very large needle, a gauge that indicates volts, and a wire with an alligator clip. Attach the alligator clip to a ground (usually the round pin on the power cord). Slip the probe needle underneath the high-voltage cup on the monitor. You will see the gauge spike to around 15,000 volts and slowly reduce to zero. When it reaches zero, you may remove the high-voltage probe and service the high-voltage components of the monitor.

WARNING Other than the power supply, one of the most dangerous components to try to repair is the monitor, or Cathode Ray Tube (CRT). In fact, we recommend that you *not* try to repair monitors. To avoid the extremely hazardous environment contained inside the monitor—it can retain a high-voltage charge for hours after it's been turned off—take it to a certified monitor technician or television repair shop. The repair shop or certified technician will know and understand the proper procedures to discharge the monitor, which involve attaching a resistor to the flyback transformer's charging capacitor to release the high-voltage electrical charge that builds up during use. They will also be able to determine whether the monitor can be repaired or needs to be replaced. Remember, the monitor works in its own extremely protective environment (the monitor case) and may not respond well to your desire to try to open it. The CRT is vacuum-sealed. Be extremely careful when handling the CRT. If you break the glass, it will implode, which can send glass in any direction.

Environmental Concerns

It is estimated that more than 25 percent of all the lead in landfills today is a result of consumer electronics components. Because they contain hazardous substances, many states require that consumer electronics be disposed of as hazardous waste. Computers are no exception. Monitors contain several carcinogens and phosphors, as well as mercury and lead. The computer itself may contain several lubricants and chemicals as well as lead. Printers contain plastics and chemicals such as toners and inks that are also hazardous. All of these items should be disposed of properly.

Although it is relatively easy to put old machines away, thinking that you might be able to put them to good use again someday, it's really not realistic. Most computers are obsolete as soon as you buy them. And if you have not used them recently, your old computer components will more than likely never be used again.

We recycle cans, plastic, and newspaper, so why not recycle computer equipment? Well, the problem is that most computers contain small amounts of hazardous substances. Some countries are exploring the option of recycling electrical machines, but most have still not enacted appropriate measures to enforce their proper disposal. However, there are a few things that we can do as consumers and environmentalists that can promote the proper disposal of computer equipment:

- Check with the manufacturer. Some manufacturers will take back outdated equipment for parts.

- Properly dispose of solvents or cleaners used with computers, as well as their containers, at a local hazardous waste disposal facility.

- Disassemble the machine and reuse the parts that are good.

- Check out businesses that can melt the components down for the lead or gold plating.

- Contact the Environmental Protection Agency (EPA) for a list of local or regional waste disposal sites that will accept used computer equipment. The EPA's Web address is www.epa.gov.

- Check with local nonprofit or education organizations interested in using the equipment.

- Check out the Internet for possible waste disposal sites. Table 3.1 gives a few Web sites we came across that deal with disposal of used computer equipment.

- Check with the EPA to see if what you are disposing has an MSDS (Material Safety Data Sheet). These sheets contain information about the toxicity of a product and whether or not it can be disposed of in the trash. They also contain lethal dose information.

TABLE 3.1: Computer Recycling Web Sites

Site Name	Web Address
Computer Recycle Center	www.recycles.com/
Re-Compute	www.recompute.co.uk
Re-PC	www.repc.com/

In addition to hardware recycling, there are businesses that offer to recycle consumables, such as ink cartridges or printer ribbons. However, although these businesses are doing us a favor in our quest to recycle, it might not be the best way to keep up with the recycle agenda. And, recycled toner cartridges don't operate properly after refilling. However, when you are through with the old cartridges, give them to organizations that do recycle so they can have some fresh "cores." That way, you can safely dispose of your cartridge and benefit the environment at the same time.

Remember that recycling is a way to keep our environment clean and our landfills from filling up. If we can take one step to recycle or redistribute outdated computer equipment, we are one step closer to having a healthier environment. However, we should not have to sacrifice quality in the process.

In particular, you should make a special effort to recycle batteries. Batteries contain several chemicals that are harmful to our environment and won't degrade safely. Batteries should not be thrown away; they should be recycled according to your local laws. Check with your local authorities to find out how batteries should be recycled.

Electrostatic Discharge (ESD)

ESD stands for electrostatic discharge. ESD happens when two objects of dissimilar charge come in contact with one another. The two objects exchange electrons in order to standardize the electrostatic charge between them. This charge can, and often does, damage electronic components.

The likelihood that a component will be damaged increases with the increasing use of Complementary Metallic Oxide Semiconductor (CMOS) chips, because these chips contain a thin metal oxide layer that is hypersensitive to ESD. The previous generation's Transistor-Transistor Logic (TTL) chips are actually more robust than the newer CMOS chips because they don't contain this metal oxide layer. Most of today's ICs are CMOS chips, so there is more of a concern with ESD lately.

When you shuffle your feet across the floor and shock your best friend on the ear, you are discharging static electricity into the ear of your friend. The lowest static voltage transfer that you can feel is around 3,000 volts (it doesn't electrocute you because there is extremely little current). A static transfer that you can *see* is at least 10,000 volts! Just by sitting in a chair, you can generate around 100 volts of static electricity. Walking around wearing synthetic materials can generate around 1,000 volts. You can easily generate around 20,000 volts (!) simply by dragging your smooth-soled shoes across a shag carpet in the winter. (Actually, it doesn't have to be winter to run this danger. It can occur in any room with very low humidity. It's just that heated rooms in wintertime are generally of very low humidity.)

It would make sense that these thousands of volts would damage computer components. However, a component can be damaged with as little as 80 volts! That means if your body has a small charge built up in it, you could damage a component without even realizing it.

Symptoms of ESD damage may be subtle, but they can be detected. One of the authors, David Groth, relates this experience:

"When I think of ESD, I always think of the same instance. A few years ago, I was working on an Apple Macintosh. This computer seemed to have a mind of its own. I would troubleshoot it, find the defective component, and replace it. The problem was that as soon as I replaced the component, it failed. I thought maybe the power supply was frying the boards, so I replaced both at the same time, but to no avail.

"I was about to send the computer off to Apple when I realized that it was winter. Normally this would not be a factor, but winters where I live (North Dakota) are extremely dry. Dry air promotes static electricity. At first I thought that my problem couldn't be that simple, but I was at the end of my rope. So, when I received my next set of new parts, I grounded myself with an antistatic strap for the time it took to install the components, and prayed while I turned on the power. Success! The components worked as they should, and a new advocate of ESD prevention was born."

Antistatic Wrist Strap

The silver lining to the cloud described in David's story is that there are measures you can implement to help contain the effects of ESD. The first, and easiest, one to implement is the antistatic wrist strap, also referred to as an ESD strap. The ESD strap works by attaching one end to an earth ground (typically the ground pin on an extension cord) and wrapping the other end around your wrist. This strap grounds your body and keeps it at a zero charge. Figure 3.2 shows the proper way to attach an antistatic strap.

FIGURE 3.2: Proper ESD strap connection

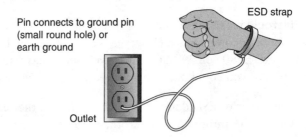

Pin connects to ground pin (small round hole) or earth ground

ESD strap

Outlet

WARNING An ESD strap is a specially designed device to bleed electrical charges away *safely*. It uses a 1-megaohm resistor to bleed the charge away slowly. A simple wire wrapped around your wrist will not work correctly and could electrocute you!
There is only one situation in which you should not wear an ESD strap. If you wear one while working on the inside of a monitor, you increase the chance of getting a lethal shock.

Antistatic Bags for Parts

Antistatic bags are important tools to have at your disposal when servicing electronic components because they protect the sensitive electronic devices from stray static charges. The bags are designed so that the static charges collect on the outside of the bags rather than on the electronic components. These bags can be obtained from several sources. The most direct way to acquire antistatic bags is to simply go to an electronics supply store and purchase them in bulk. Most supply stores will have several sizes available. Perhaps the easiest way to obtain them, however, is simply to hold onto the ones that come your way. That is, when you purchase any new component, it usually comes in an antistatic bag. Once you have installed the component, keep the bag. It may take you a while to gather a sizable collection of bags if you take this approach, but eventually you will have a fairly large assortment.

ESD Static Mats

It is possible for a device to be damaged by simply laying it on a bench top. For this reason, you should have an ESD mat in addition to an ESD strap. This mat drains excess charge away from any item coming in contact with it (see Figure 3.3). ESD mats are also sold as mouse/keyboard pads to prevent ESD charges from interfering with the operation of the computer. ESD charges can cause problems such as making a computer hang or reboot.

FIGURE 3.3: Proper use of an ESD static mat

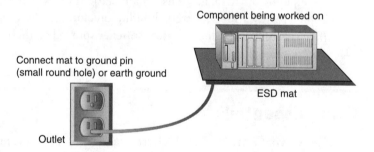

With regard to the components, vendors have methods of protecting them in transit from manufacture to installation. Vendors press the pins of ICs into antistatic foam to keep all the pins at the same potential. Also, circuit boards are shipped in antistatic bags, discussed earlier. However, keep in mind that unlike antistatic mats, antistatic bags do not "drain" the charges away, and they should never be used in place of antistatic mats.

At the very least, you can be mindful of the dangers of ESD and take steps to reduce its effects. Beyond that, you should educate yourself about those effects so you know when ESD is becoming a major problem.

NOTE If an ESD strap or mat is not available, it is possible to discharge excess static voltage by touching the metal case of the power supply. However, the power supply *must be plugged into a properly grounded outlet* for this to work as intended. Because it's plugged in, extra caution should be taken so that you don't get electrocuted. Also, continuous contact should be maintained to continuously drain excess charge away. As you can see, it would be easier to have an antistatic wrist strap.

Modifying the Relative Humidity

Another preventive measure that you can take is to maintain the relative humidity at around 50 percent. Be careful not to increase the humidity too far—to the point where moisture starts to condense on the equipment! Also, make use of antistatic spray, which is available commercially, to reduce static buildup on clothing and carpets. In a pinch, a solution of diluted fabric softener sprayed on these items will do the same thing.

Exam Essentials

Know what EMI is. EMI (electromagnetic interference) occurs when the power coming out of the wall has a different frequency than normal (60Hz is considered normal). A problem manifests itself when stray electromagnetic signals get introduced into the line. This interference is usually caused by the electromagnetic waves emitted by the electric motors in appliances.

Know what RFI is. Televisions and other electronic devices (including the computers themselves) can produce a different type of interference, called radio frequency interference (RFI), which is really just a higher-frequency version of EMI. However, ICs and other electronic devices produce RFI.

Know how overages affect a system. The most common type of power problem that causes computer damage is power overages. As the name suggests, these problems occur when too much power comes down the power lines.

Know how undervoltage affects a system. Undervoltage problems usually don't cause damage to hardware. More often, they cause the computer to shut down, thus losing any unsaved data in memory. There are three major types of undervoltage problems: sags, brownouts, and blackouts.

Know what a sag is. A sag is a momentary drop in voltage, lasting only a few milliseconds.

Know what a brownout is. A brownout occurs when voltage drops below 110 volts for a second or more. Brownouts are typically caused by an immediate increase in power consumption in your area and the lag time it takes for your power provider to respond by increasing production.

Know what a blackout is. A blackout occurs when the power drops from 110 volts to zero volts in a very short period of time. It is a complete loss of power for anywhere from a few seconds to several minutes or more. They are typically caused by a power failure somewhere in your area.

Understand standby power supply (SPS). Standby power supply is so named because there is a battery waiting to take over power production in case of a loss of line voltage. The SPS contains sensors that constantly monitor the line voltage and a battery with a step-up transformer. While conditions are normal, the line voltage charges the internal battery. When the line voltage drops below a preset threshold (also called the *cutover* threshold—i.e., 105V), the sensors detect that and switch the power from the wall to the internal battery. When the power comes back above the threshold, the sensors detect the restoration of power and switch the power source back to the line voltage.

Understand uninterruptible power supply (UPS). UPS works similarly to SPS, but with one important difference. The computer equipment is always running off the battery. While the line voltage is normal, the battery gets charged. When power fluctuates, only the charging circuit is affected.

Understand the antistatic wrist strap. The antistatic wrist strap is also referred to as an ESD strap. The ESD strap works by attaching one end to an earth ground (typically the ground pin on an extension cord) and wrapping the other end around your wrist. This strap grounds your body and keeps it at a zero charge, preventing discharges from damaging the components of a PC. It is almost a certainty that you will have questions regarding when to use this tool and where it should be connected.

Key Terms and Concepts

Electrostatic discharge (ESD) ESD happens when two objects of dissimilar charge come in contact with one another. The two objects exchange electrons in order to standardize the electrostatic charge between them. This charge can, and often does, damage electronic components.

ESD strap An ESD strap is a specially designed device to bleed electrical charges away *safely*. It uses a 1-megaohm resistor to bleed the charge away slowly. A simple wire wrapped around your wrist will not work correctly and could electrocute you! There is only one situation in which you should not wear an ESD strap. If you wear one while working on the inside of a monitor, you increase your chances of getting a lethal shock.

SPS SPS stands for standby power supply.

UPS UPS stands for uninterruptible power supply.

EMI EMI stand for electromagnetic interference.

Chapter

4

Domain 4.0 Motherboard/ Processors/Memory

COMPTIA A+ EXAM OBJECTIVES COVERED IN THIS CHAPTER:

▶ **4.1 Distinguish between the popular CPU chips in terms of their basic characteristics.** *(pages 135 – 142)*

- Popular CPU chips (Intel, AMD, Cyrix)
- Characteristics
- Physical size
- Voltage
- Speeds
- On board cache or not
- Sockets
- SEC (Single Edge Contact)

▶ **4.2 Identify the categories of RAM (Random Access Memory) terminology, their locations, and physical characteristics.** *(pages 143 – 163)*

- EDO RAM (Extended Data Output RAM)
- DRAM (Dynamic Random Access Memory)
- SRAM (Static RAM)
- RIMM (Rambus Inline Memory Module 184 Pin)
- VRAM (Video RAM)
- SDRAM (Synchronous Dynamic RAM)
- WRAM (Windows Accelerator Card RAM)
- Memory bank
- Memory chips (8-bit, 16-bit, and 32-bit)
- SIMMS (Single In-line Memory Module)
- DIMMS (Dual In-line Memory Module)
- Parity chips versus non-parity chips

4.3 Identify the most popular type of mother-boards, their components, and their architecture (bus structures and power supplies).
(pages 163 – 187)

- AT (Full and Baby)
- ATX
- Communication ports
- SIMM and DIMM
- Processor sockets
- External cache memory (Level 2)
- ISA
- PCI
- AGP
- USB (Universal Serial Bus)
- VESA local bus (VL-Bus)
- Basic compatibility guidelines
- IDE (ATA, ATAPI, ULTRA-DMA, EIDE)
- SCSI (Wide, Fast, Ultra, LVD (Low Voltage Differential))

4.4 Identify the purpose of CMOS (Complementary Metal-Oxide Semiconductor), what it contains, and how to change its basic parameters. *(pages 187 – 192)*

- Printer parallel port—Uni., bi-directional, disable/enable, ECP, EPP
- COM/serial port—memory address, interrupt request, disable
- Floppy drive—enable/disable drive or boot, speed, density
- Hard drive—size and drive type
- Memory—parity, non-parity
- Boot sequence
- Date/time
- Passwords
- Plug and Play BIOS

he processor market is one of the fastest changing component groups in the industry. Recent competition has increased the number of processors you may see in a workday. To be an effective technician, you will need to be familiar with the different types of processors and their attachment.

4.1 Distinguish between the popular CPU chips in terms of their basic characteristics.

- Popular CPU chips (Intel, AMD, Cyrix)
- Characteristics
- Physical size
- Voltage
- Speeds
- On board cache or not
- Sockets
- SEC (Single Edge Contact)

Objective 4.1 assures that you will be familiar with the basic characteristics of a vast array of processors. Although it is important to stay on top of this information to succeed as a technician, the A+ exam will probably contain a small number of questions regarding processors simply because they change so frequently.

Critical Information

Like any other component, each brand has its own unique characteristics. The next section lists the common traits of each manufacturer.

CPU Manufacturers

There are several manufacturers making CPUs for PCs today. The market leader in the manufacture of chips is Intel Corporation, with AMD gaining market share in the home PC market. Intel's competition includes Motorola, Advanced Micro Devices (AMD), Cyrix, and IBM. This list of manufacturers makes up the bulk of the IBM-compatible personal computer processor market.

Intel Processors

The Intel family of PC processors started with the 8080, which found only limited use in the computer industry. Next to be released was the 8086 with a 16-bit external data bus; however, the processor used an 8-bit bus for compatibility with older systems.

After the 808x series came the 80x86 series, otherwise known simply as Intel's x86 series. The 80286 was the first to implement the PGA, or Pin Grid Array. It ran hotter than the 8088, with speeds from 6MHz to 20MHz. Both internal and external bus structures were 16 bits wide, and it could physically address up to 16MB of RAM.

80386

Intel introduced the 80386 in 1985. The Intel x86 processor was the first to use both a 32-bit data bus and a 32-bit address bus. Other manufacturers such as AMD and Cyrix came up with a chip they called the 386SX. This chip still operated internally at 32 bits but had only a 16-bit external data path and a 16-bit address bus. In order for Intel to differentiate the capabilities, they renamed their 386 to the 386DX and introduced a 32-bit chip with a 16-bit data path and bus with the SX designation.

The 386 chips ranged from 16MHz to 33MHz. The SX was capable of utilizing 16MB of memory, while the DX would support up to 4GB. The 386 was a significant improvement over the 286, with greater speed and the introduction of multitasking support.

80486

Intel introduced the 486DX in 1989. This processor supported 32-bit internal and external data paths, a 32-bit address bus, an 8KB on-chip cache, and an integrated math coprocessor. In 1991, Intel introduced the 486SX as a cheaper version of the 486 processor. The only difference between the 486DX and the 486SX was that the internal math coprocessor was disabled on the SX. To add the math coprocessor to the chip, it was necessary to purchase a 487SX chip and insert it into the math coprocessor slot.

The 80486 operated at a maximum speed of 33MHz. To increase the speed, Intel came up with *clock doubling*, which was followed by *clock tripling*. This allowed the processor's internal clock to operate at two or three times the 33MHz external bus speed, producing up to 100MHz.

THE PENTIUM AND PENTIUM PRO

Intel introduced the Pentium processor in 1993. This processor has 3.1 million transistors using a 64-bit data path, a 32-bit address bus, and a 16KB on-chip cache, and it comes in speeds from 60MHz to 200MHz. With the release of the Pentium chips, *parallel processing* was introduced, allowing the chip to act as two separate processors. This additional power required new motherboard architecture and, as mentioned earlier, the addition of heat sinks or cooling fans to keep the heat level of the chip within design parameters.

After the initial introduction of the Pentium came the Pentium Pro, designed to meet the needs of today's server. Released in 1995, it runs at speeds around 200MHz in a 32-bit operating system environment using *dynamic execution*. Dynamic execution performs out-of-order guesses to execute program codes.

OVERDRIVE AND MMX—THE NEED FOR SPEED

Intel's 486 overdrive processor was designed to allow customers to upgrade their existing 486 PC to near-Pentium performance. Installing an overdrive chip consisted of replacing the existing CPU with the overdrive chip. The overdrive runs at approximately two and a half times the motherboard's bus speed. The drawback of the overdrive processors is that they are still 32-bit. True Pentium processors are 64-bit.

Another major change was the introduction of MMX technology. This version of the Pentium processor added three new features:

- It included 57 new instructions for better video, audio, and graphic capabilities.

- It featured Single Instruction Multiple Data (SIMD) technology, which enables one instruction to give instructions to several pieces of data rather than a single instruction per piece of data.

- Its cache was doubled to 32KB.

PENTIUM II

Intel then released the Pentium II: This chip's speeds ranged from 233MHz to over 400MHz. It was introduced in 1997 and was designed to be a multimedia chip with special on-chip multimedia instructions and high-speed cache memory. It has 32KB of Level 1 Cache, dynamic execution, and MMX technology.

The Pentium II uses a Single Edge Connector (SEC) to attach to the motherboard instead of the standard PGA package that was used with the earlier processor types.

When released, the Pentium II was designed for single-processor-only applications. Intel also released a separate processor, known as the Pentium II Xeon, to fill the need for multiprocessor applications such as servers.

CELERON

To offer a less-costly alternative and to keep their large market share, Intel released the Celeron. The Celeron was priced in some cases as much as half the retail price of the Pentium II. Since it was developed after the Pentium II, it benefited from some advancements and in certain aspects outperformed its more expensive counterpart.

PENTIUM III

The Pentium III was released in 1999 and uses the same SEC connector as its predecessor, the Pentium II. It included 70 new instructions and a processor serial number (PSN), a unique number electronically encoded into the processor. This number can be used to uniquely identify a system during Internet transactions.

NOTE As with the Pentium II, the Pentium III has a multiprocessor Xeon version as well.

SUMMARY OF INTEL PROCESSORS

Table 4.1 provides a summary of the history of the Intel processors. Table 4.2 shows the physical characteristics of Pentium (and higher) class processors.

TABLE 4.1: The Intel Family of Processors

Chip	Year Added	Data Bus Width (in bits)	Address Bus Width (in bits)	Speed (in MHz)	Transistors
8080	1974	8	8	2	6,000
8086	1978	16	20	5–10	29,000
8088	1979	8	20	4.77	29,000
80286	1982	16	24	8–12	134,000
386DX	1985	32	32	16–33	275,000
386SX	1988	32	24	16–20	275,000
486DX	1989	32	32	25–50	1.2 million
486SX	1991	32	32	16–33	1.185 million
487SX	1991	32	32	16–33	1.2 million
486DX2	1991	32	32	33–66	2.0 million
486DX4	1992	32	32	75–100	2.5 million
Pentium	1993	32	32	60–166	3.3 million
Pentium Pro	1995	64	32	150–200	5.5 million
Pentium II	1997	64	64	233–300	7.5 million

TABLE 4.1: The Intel Family of Processors *(continued)*

Chip	Year Added	Data Bus Width (in bits)	Address Bus Width (in bits)	Speed (in MHz)	Transistors
Pentium II Xeon	1998	64	64	400–600	7.5 million
Celeron	1999	64	64	400–600	7.5 million
Pentium III	1999	64	64	350–1000	9.5 million
Pentium III Xeon	1999	64	64	350–1000	9.5 million

TABLE 4.2: Physical Characteristics of Pentium-Class Processors

Processor	Speeds (MHz)	Socket	Pins	Voltage	Cache
Pentium-P5	60–66	4	273	5V	16KB
Pentium-P54C	75–200	5 or 7	320 or 321	3.3V	16KB
Pentium-P55C	166–333	7	321	3.3V	32KB
Pentium Pro	150–200	8	387	2.5V	32KB
Pentium II	233–450	SEC	N/A	3.3V	32KB
Pentium III	450–1130	SECII	N/A	3.3V	32KB

INTEL CLONES AND OTHERS

Intel clones are processors that are based on the *x*86 architecture and are produced by other vendors; the most notable is AMD. With the release of the Pentium II, AMD positioned itself to take some of the market share away from Intel, which up until this point had no viable competition. With the release of the Pentium II, computer manufacturers were looking to reduce costs, and originally the Celeron was only 15 to 20 percent less than the PII. AMD released the K6 with 3D Now technology, which in all but the most graphically intense games and video or photo-editing applications out-performed the Celeron and PII. Since then, we consumers have seen chip prices fall dramatically, which has reduced computer prices by about 20 percent.

TIP   The surest way to determine which CPU your computer is using is to open the case and view the numbers stamped on the CPU. Another way to determine a computer's CPU is to save your work, exit any open programs, and restart the computer. Watch closely as the computer returns to its normal state. You should see a notation that tells you which chip you are using. If you are using MS-DOS, you can also run Microsoft Diagnostics to view the processor type (that is, unless your computer has a Pentium processor, in which case it will report a very fast 486).

Clock Speed

The clock speed is the frequency at which a processor executes instructions. This frequency is measured in millions of cycles per second, or megahertz (MHz). This clock signal is generated by a quartz crystal, which vibrates as electricity passes through it, thereby generating a steady pulse to every component synchronized with the signal. A system cycle is generated by this pulse (called a *clock tick*), which sends a signal through the processor telling it to perform another operation. In most cases, the higher the MHz value, the faster the PC will be.

Cache Memory

Cache memory is a storage area for frequently used data and instructions. It requires a small amount of physical RAM that can keep up with the processor. It uses this RAM for storage. The processor contains an internal cache controller that integrates the cache with the CPU. The controller stores frequently accessed RAM locations to provide faster execution of data and instructions. This type of cache is known as a *Level 1 Cache*. It is also possible to have a cache external to the CPU, called a *Level 2 Cache*. This type of cache performs the same functions as a Level 1 Cache and can speed up the perceived performance. Basically, a larger cache leads to the perception of a faster CPU.

Exam Essentials

Understand the processor's job. The processor is the brain of the PC. Most actions performed by the PC require use of the processor to accomplish their task.

Understand the differences between the different classes of Pentium chips. The Intel Pentium has gone through several changes since its release. You will need to understand the differences between the various classes. One of the most notable is the physical appearance. Pentium processors are flat chips that mount directly to the motherboard. Pentium II, Pentium III, and Celeron chips are attached with a slot similar to expansion cards.

Understand what an overdrive processor is. An overdrive processor is a processor that replaces the existing processor and increases the power of the PC. When you use an overdrive processor, replacing the motherboard is not necessary.

Understand Intel clones. Other processor manufactures produce chips that sometimes meet Intel benchmarks and in most cases cost less. Their ability to replace Intel brand processors has earned them the name *clones*.

Key Terms and Concepts

Clock speed The clock speed is the frequency at which a processor executes instructions. This frequency is measured in millions of cycles per second, or megahertz (MHz).

Cache memory Cache memory is a storage area for frequently used data and instructions. It requires a small amount of physical RAM that can keep up with the processor.

4.2 Identify the categories of RAM (Random Access Memory) terminology, their locations, and physical characteristics.

- EDO RAM (Extended Data Output RAM)
- DRAM (Dynamic Random Access Memory)
- SRAM (Static RAM)
- RIMM (Rambus Inline Memory Module 184 Pin)
- VRAM (Video RAM)
- SDRAM (Synchronous Dynamic RAM)
- WRAM (Windows Accelerator Card RAM)
- Memory bank
- Memory chips (8-bit, 16-bit, and 32-bit)
- SIMMS (Single In-line Memory Module)
- DIMMS (Dual In-line Memory Module)
- Parity chips versus non-parity chips

To pass the A+ exam and be a productive computer technician, you must be familiar with memory. Not only is this subject tested on, but one of the most common upgrades performed to a PC is adding memory. Adding memory is a simple task, but before you can add memory you must have the correct type.

Critical Information

When we say the word *memory*, we are most often referring to Random Access Memory, or RAM. However, there are other types of memory. We will discuss them all in this section. Be familiar with the various types and their usage.

Physical Memory

Physically, memory is a collection of integrated circuits that store data and program information as patterns of 1s and 0s (on and off states) in the chip. Most memory chips require constant power (also called a constant *refresh*) to maintain those patterns of 1s and 0s. If power is lost, all those tiny switches revert back to the off position, effectively erasing the data from memory. Some memory types, however, do not require a refresh.

Physical Memory Types

There are many types of memory. In this section, we examine each type in detail.

SRAM

One type of memory is known as Static Random Access Memory (SRAM). It is called *static* because the information doesn't need a constant update (refresh). SRAM stores information as patterns of transistor ons and offs to represent binary digits. This type of memory is physically bulky and somewhat limited in its capacity. The original PC and XT, as well as some notebook computer systems, use SRAM chips for their memory.

Most new computers are moving away from SRAM to the newer, more efficient type of memory known as DRAM.

DRAM

Dynamic Random Access Memory (DRAM) is an improvement over SRAM. DRAM uses a different approach to storing the 1s and 0s. Instead of transistors, DRAM stores information as charges in very small capacitors. If a charge exists in a capacitor, it's interpreted as a 1. The absence of a charge is interpreted as a 0.

Because DRAM uses capacitors instead of switches, it needs to use a constant refresh signal to keep the information in memory. DRAM requires more power than SRAM for refresh signals and, therefore, is mostly found in desktop computers.

DRAM technology allows several memory units, called *cells*, to be packed to a very high density. Therefore, these chips can hold very large amounts of information. Most PCs today use DRAM of one type or another.

Let's take a brief look at some of the different types of DRAM:

- Fast Page Mode (FPM)

- Extended Data Out (EDO)

- Synchronous DRAM (SDRAM)

- Double Data Rate SDRAM (DDR SDRAM)

- Direct Rambus (RIMM)

In this section, you will learn about each type of DRAM and the differences between them.

FAST PAGE MODE

Fast Page Mode (FPM) DRAM chips, at the time of the 486/Pentium transition, were the most common type of DRAM. Although its technical designation is FPM DRAM, because it was the most common type of DRAM, everyone just started calling it "DRAM." It allowed data to be "paged" (swapped) into memory faster than earlier versions, thus providing better performance.

EXTENDED DATA OUT

In 1995, a new type of RAM became popular. EDO (Extended Data Out) RAM increases performance by 10 to 15 percent over FPM DRAM by eliminating memory wait states, which means eliminating a few steps to access memory. It's usually a bit more expensive than regular DRAM.

SYNCHRONOUS DRAM

In the final quarter of 1996, a new type of memory, Synchronous DRAM, was introduced. SDRAM was developed to match the ever-increasing processing speeds of the Pentium systems. Synchronous DRAM, as its name suggests, is synchronized to the speed of the systems it will be used in (e.g., PC66 SDRAM runs at 66MHz, PC100 runs at 100MHz, PC133 runs at 133MHz, and so on). Synchronizing the speed of the systems prevents the address bus from having to wait for the memory because of different clock speeds.

DOUBLE DATA RATE SDRAM

Essentially, Double Data Rate SDRAM (DDR SDRAM) is clock-doubled SDRAM. The memory chip can perform reads and writes on both sides of any clock cycle (the up, or start, and the down, or ending), thus doubling the effective memory executions per second. So, if you are using DDR SDRAM with a 100MHz memory bus, the memory will execute reads and writes at 200MHz and transfer the data to the processor at 100MHz. The advantage of DDR over regular SDRAM is increased throughput, thus increased overall system speed.

DIRECT RAMBUS

Direct Rambus is a relatively new and extremely fast (up to 800MHz) technology that uses, for the most part, a new methodology in memory system design. Direct Rambus is a memory bus that transfers data at 800MHz over a 16-bit memory bus. Direct Rambus memory models (often called RIMMs, or Rambus Inline Memory Module), like DDR SDRAM, can transfer data on both the rising and falling edges of a clock cycle. That feature, combined with the 16-bit bus for efficient transfer of data, results in the ultra-high memory transfer rate (800MHz) and the high bandwidth of up to 1.6GBps (more than twice that of 100MHz SDRAM).

ROM

Read-Only Memory (ROM) is used to store information permanently for easy and quick retrieval. This type of memory chip contains transistors that are manufactured permanently in the on or off position, which is the main reason why this memory is called "read only." Once these transistors have been set, they can't be changed. Because these switches are permanently in these positions, accessing the information contained in ROMs is extremely fast.

ROM is mainly used for very specialized purposes, such as storing information about how a device needs to operate. A computer's BIOS is typically stored on a type of ROM chip.

PROM

For purposes more general than those required by ROM, a type of ROM chip was developed called the Programmable ROM (PROM). The PROM is a ROM that is first manufactured with all of its circuits as logical 1s (that is, with all switches on); then, when the PROM is to be programmed, the connections that need to be set to 0 are destroyed, using a high-voltage electrical pulse. This makes the settings permanent.

EPROM

The main disadvantage of ROM is that it can't be changed once it has been manufactured. To resolve this, IC developers came up with Erasable Programmable Read-Only Memory (EPROM). EPROMs are erasable and able to be reprogrammed, making them more flexible than ROMs. They work by storing binary information as electrical charges deposited on the chip. These electrical deposits are *almost* permanent. They will stay until dislodged by a special-frequency ultraviolet light shone through a small window. Exposure to this light returns the chip to its blank state. The chip can then be completely reprogrammed. These chips are usually easily identified by their small, circular windows. Some older computers, such as the IBM PC or XT, used EPROMs for their BIOS information.

EEPROM

It is very inconvenient to remove a module every time you need to upgrade the software it contains. Removing it can be a real pain and *can* be dangerous. A way was needed to permit erasure of these chips while still maintaining their capability of keeping information intact once power is removed. Electronically Erasable PROM (EEPROM) chips were designed to solve this problem. They can be erased by sending a special sequence of electric signals to the chip while it is still in the circuit. These signals then erase all or part of the chip.

Although it might seem a good idea to use an EEPROM chip for the main memory in a computer, it would be very expensive. The primary use of this type of chip is for BIOS information; you'll see CMOS

BIOS chips in most computers. The CMOS memory keeps the computer's BIOS settings while the computer is turned off. These special EEPROM chips keep their information by means of a small battery. Although the battery's charge lasts for several years, it *will* eventually lose its ability to keep the CMOS settings. It's easy to tell when this is happening, though, because the computer begins to lose its ability to keep BIOS settings when powered off.

NOTE Because the BIOS settings can eventually be lost when the CMOS battery finally loses its charge, we encourage all technicians (and PC owners in general) to record their BIOS settings (on paper or save them to a floppy) so that you can reset them if you have to replace the CMOS battery. The BIOS settings are available from the computer's Setup program, which is accessible by a special key or key combination during startup. Some computers use the Delete key, one of the function keys, or the Escape key; others use Ctrl+Alt+Esc.

Memory Chip Package Types

The memory chips themselves come in many different types of packages. The ones most frequently encountered are discussed in the following sections.

Dual Inline Package

The first type of memory chip package is Dual Inline Package (DIP) memory, so named because the individual RAM chips use the DIP-style package for the memory module. Older computers, such as the IBM AT, arranged these small chips like rows of caskets in a small memory "graveyard." There are typically eight chips in one of these rows, although there may be nine. If data is written to memory eight bits at a time, why the ninth chip? The answer is that the ninth chip is used for *parity*, a kind of error-checking routine. Chips that have an extra chip for error checking are known as *parity chips*. Those without error checking are known as *non-parity*.

PARITY

Parity is a simple form of error checking used in computers and tele-communications. Parity works by adding an additional bit to a binary number and using it to indicate any changes in that number during transmission. There are two types of parity: even and odd.

- *Even parity* works by counting the number of 1s in a binary number and, if that number is odd, adding an additional 1 to guarantee that the total number of 1s is even. For example, the number 11101011 has an even number of 1s, so the sending computer would assign a 0 to the parity bit. The number 01101101 has five 1s, and so it would have a 1 in the parity bit position to make the total number of 1s even. If, in the second number, the computer had checked the parity position after transmission and had found a 0 instead, it would have asked the processor to resend the last bit.

- *Odd parity* works in a similar manner. But, instead of guaranteeing that the total number of 1s is even, it guarantees that the total is an odd number.

Parity works well for detecting single-bit errors (where one bit has changed its value during transmission). But if the transmission is extremely garbled, two bits might be switched at the same time. If that were the case, the value for parity would still be valid; as a consequence, the sender would not be asked to retransmit. That's why transmissions that really need to be reliable often use another method of error checking called *checksumming*.

Checksumming works as follows: When the sender is ready to transmit a unit of data, it runs a special algorithm against the binary data and computes what is known as a *checksum*. The sender then appends this checksum to the data being transmitted and sends the whole data stream to its intended recipient. The recipient decodes the entire data stream and runs a similar algorithm against the data portion. The recipient compares the value that it computed to the value contained in the received checksum. If the values are different, it rejects the data and asks the sender to retransmit it.

Most error checking done today uses checksumming, unless only a basic communication check is required. For example, parity is used in the case of modem communications, because these transfers are relatively slow to begin with. If modems used checksumming instead of parity, modem communications would be too slow to be a viable means of telecommunication. That's why it is necessary to set the parity to even or odd when setting up modem communications.

Single Inline Memory Module

The next type of RAM packaging that is commonly seen in computers is called the Single Inline Memory Module (SIMM). SIMMs were developed because DIPs took up too much "real estate" on the logic board. Someone got the idea to put several of the DIP chips on a small circuit board and then make that board easily removable. A couple of versions (there are many configurations) are shown in Figure 4.1.

FIGURE 4.1: Single Inline Memory Modules (SIMMs)

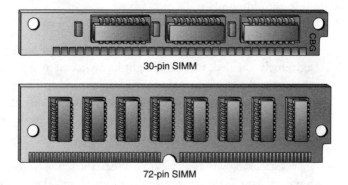

30-pin SIMM

72-pin SIMM

The first SIMMs had nine small DIP chips on them and took up less room than before, because four of them could be installed in the same space as one row of the older DIP memory chips. In order to accomplish this, the SIMMs are installed very close to each other at approximately a 45° angle. This design was also meant to prevent "chip creep"—whereby the chips that have been placed in sockets on the board start to slowly move out of their sockets from the heating and cooling of the system board.

TIP   In many cases, a machine will start behaving incorrectly after it is bumped or moved. A quick and simple fix is to reseat all chips by pressing them down securely in their sockets. Most of the time, this will solve the problem.

Most memory chips are 32-bit; so are several of the processors. You have a problem, however, when you have 32-bit memory chips and a 64-bit processor. To solve this, you must either install the SIMMs in pairs (always installing multiples of two—this is especially true for Pentium computers) or change to a DIMM installation (discussed next).

Dual Inline Memory Module

The final type of memory package is known as a DIMM (Dual Inline Memory Module). DIMMs are dual-sided memory chips that hold twice as many chips as a SIMM. (And, except for the fact that they have chips on both sides, they look just like a SIMM.) Generally, the DIMMs you'll run into will have either 72 or 168 pins. Some DIMMs are 32-bit, but more and more are 64-bit and are installed one per memory bank in Pentium-class computers.

Specialized Memory Types

There are three major specialized applications for memory besides main memory: video RAM, portable memory, and cache memory.

Video RAM

Video memory (also called video RAM or VRAM) is used to store image data for processing by the video adapter. The more video memory an adapter has, the better the quality of image that it can display. Also, more VRAM allows the adapter to display a higher resolution of image.

Portable Memory

The memory styles for portable computers are many and varied. Each portable computer manufacturer comes up with its own specification for portable memory. Installing memory in a laptop usually involves removing a specially attached panel on the bottom of the laptop and installing the memory in the slot that is under the removed panel. Then you can replace the panel.

TIP Because each laptop's memory could potentially install in completely different ways, check with the manufacturer of your laptop to determine how to upgrade the memory.

Cache Memory

In some systems, there is a small amount of very fast SRAM memory, called *cache memory*, between the processor and main memory. It is used to store the most frequently accessed information. Because it's faster than main memory and contains the most frequently used information, cache memory will increase the performance of any system.

There are two types of cache memory: on-chip (also called *internal* or *L1 Cache*) and off-chip (also called *external* or *L2 Cache*). Internal cache memory is found on Intel Pentium, Pentium Pro, and Pentium II processors, as well as on other manufacturers' chips. External cache memory is typically either a SIMM of SRAM or a separate expansion board that installs in a special processor-direct bus. In some cases, L2 Cache can be located on the chip as well.

TIP To get the most out of cache memory, if you have the option of installing an external cache card onto your motherboard, do it. It can give you as much as a 25 percent boost in speed.

Logical Memory

Logical memory is the way the physical memory is managed for the operating system. In order to use the physical memory installed in a computer, it needs to be organized in some logical manner.

There is a model that helps us understand the way that memory is laid out. This model is actually called the MS-DOS memory map. It was not created all at once but has evolved over time. The first computers to run DOS were based on the Intel 8088 processor. That processor could only access a maximum of 1MB (1024KB) of memory. So, the first memory map looked like the one illustrated in Figure 4.2. This map allows us to describe how the memory is being used. It is important to remember that this memory map is also called a *stack*, because for purposes of visualizing concepts, the memory blocks are stacked on top of one another.

FIGURE 4.2: The MS-DOS memory map

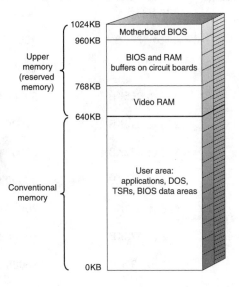

The memory map's first 1024KB is divided up into 16 blocks of 64KB each. We will describe the purpose of each of these blocks in the sections that follow.

The sixteen 64KB blocks are further divided into four "pages" of 16KB each. This division allows us to look in a more detailed way at how an application is using memory. The processor allocates memory to those applications or devices that request it. When you need to refer to these blocks, either you can refer to them by their block number (block 1, block 2, and so on), or you can refer to them as a range of hexadecimal addresses. The hexadecimal method is the most common way, since that is how the computers refer to them. These addresses are typically five-digit hex addresses, primarily because the largest five-digit hex address is FFFFF (1,048,575 decimal, corresponding to 1,048,575 bytes, or 1MB). Table 4.3 gives the blocks, their ranges in bytes, and their ranges in hexadecimal addresses.

TABLE 4.3: Memory Addresses in the MS-DOS Memory Map

Block Number	Byte Range	Hex Range
1	0 to 63KB	00000 to 0FFFF
2	64 to 127KB	10000 to 1FFFF
3	128 to 191KB	20000 to 2FFFF
4	192 to 255KB	30000 to 3FFFF
5	256 to 319KB	40000 to 4FFFF
6	320 to 383KB	50000 to 5FFFF
7	384 to 447KB	60000 to 6FFFF
8	448 to 511KB	70000 to 7FFFF
9	512 to 575KB	80000 to 8FFFF
10	576 to 639KB	90000 to 9FFFF
11	640 to 703KB	A0000 to AFFFF
12	704 to 767KB	B0000 to BFFFF
13	768 to 831KB	C0000 to CFFFF
14	832 to 895KB	D0000 to DFFFF
15	896 to 959KB	E0000 to EFFFF
16	960 to 1024KB	F0000 to FFFFF

In most utilities that scan memory to find its contents, you will see memory addresses listed as hex addresses. The table above will be valuable when you're determining where a particular program or driver is resident in memory.

Conventional Memory

The first type of memory, represented as the first 640KB in the memory map, is called *conventional memory*, as highlighted in Figure 4.3. It takes the first 10 blocks (00000 to 9FFFF). This type of memory is used for running programs, loading the operating system files, and loading drivers. With the old 8086 chip, this area was dedicated for user applications and data. Conventional memory turned out to be the Achilles' heel for a DOS-based system, as almost all DOS applications are written to be backward compatible, so they must support conventional memory.

FIGURE 4.3: The conventional memory area

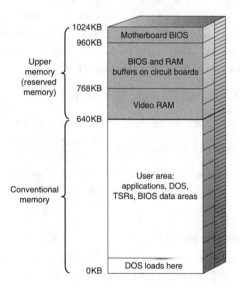

Device drivers are small pieces of software that are loaded to allow the computer to talk to hardware devices. Drivers control and understand these hardware devices. For example, if you want DOS to be able to use a sound card, a driver must be loaded for it. When you load a driver, it is allocated memory from the conventional memory area. The problem is that your applications use this area to run in. If you have too many drivers loaded, you may not have enough conventional memory to run your programs.

The first block (the first 64KB) is used for loading the DOS operating system files into memory. Also, this area contains any memory allocated to DOS disk buffers (specified by the BUFFERS= parameter in the CONFIG.SYS file). In addition, DOS uses this area to load additional memory drivers (EMM386.EXE and HIMEM.SYS). Finally, any memory that DOS needs for system operations (input/output buffers, the processing of interrupts, and so on) is also allocated from this first 64KB area.

Besides DOS itself and drivers, there are often programs that are loaded into conventional memory and then keep a portion of themselves there after they've been terminated. This behavior can be pretty handy, as programs such as e-mail software can be called up more quickly when parts of them are still located in memory. These programs are called *Terminate and Stay Resident* (*TSR*) programs. The following are a few examples of TSRs:

- Anti-virus programs, because they need to stay in memory constantly

- Disk-caching programs (for example, SMARTDRIVE.EXE)

- Network protocol stacks

All of these types of programs may want to take up more memory than is available. Therefore, the developers came up with additional types of memory.

Reserved Memory

If an 8088 can access 1MB of RAM, why can't you use all of it to run programs? The answer is that some devices in the computer also need RAM. Some RAM is reserved for use by some devices in the computer to store data so it can be accessed directly by the processor. This area of RAM, called *reserved memory* or *upper memory*, consists of the remaining six blocks—the upper 384KB—in the MS-DOS memory map. A unique characteristic of reserved memory is that various sections of this memory area are typically allocated for special purposes. Table 4.4 shows reserved memory block usage.

TABLE 4.4: Reserved Memory Block Usage

Address Range	Standard Usage	Notes
A0000 to BFFFF (128KB)	Video RAM	Varies according to type of video adapter used.
C0000 to CFFFF (64KB)	Available	Adapter ROMs sometimes mapped here; can also be used for EMS page frame.
D0000 to FFFFF (192KB)	Available	Adapter ROMs may also be mapped here.
E0000 to FFFFF (128K)	System ROMs	BIOS and BIOS "echo" may also be mapped here.

The first two blocks of reserved memory are usually used for accessing video RAM. When a computer needs to send information to the display, it writes it to this area. The adapter has its own memory mapped into this area. This area is only 128KB large, but some video cards have more than 1MB on them.

Paging allows the machine to use a portion of that 1MB and access it by swapping it into this reserved area as data needs to be written to it.

Here's an example of how this might work: Say the processor has a large graphic to draw on the screen. When this area is full, the video card swaps those full blocks for empty ones from the memory on the card. The video card takes the instructions from the full blocks and uses them to draw the picture on the screen. Table 4.5 shows the most commonly used memory addresses for video cards.

TABLE 4.5: Commonly Used Video Card Memory Addresses

Video Card	Memory Address Range
Monochrome Display Adapter (MDA)	B0000 to B1000 (4KB)
Color Graphics Adapter (CGA)	B8000 to BC000 (16KB)
Enhanced Graphics Adapter (EGA)	A0000 to BFFFF (128KB)
Video Graphics Adapter (VGA)	A0000 to BFFFF (128KB)
Super Video Graphics Adapter (SVGA)	A0000 to BFFFF (128KB)
Other VGA cards (super, accelerated, others)	A0000 to BFFFF (128KB)

In addition to the video adapter, other adapter cards may use the reserved memory area in the same way. These adapter cards are configured to use a particular range of memory in this area, typically in the area from C0000 to DFFFF. This area is used to map ROM memory addresses in upper memory. Some LAN cards have buffers that are also mapped into this area.

Finally, the area from D0000 to DFFFF is most often used for mapping the BIOS ROM information and a copy of it, called the BIOS *shadow*. This is done so that a processor can access BIOS information when it needs to. Some BIOSes have the ability to shut off the shadow, thus freeing up 64KB of upper memory.

Expanded Memory

When programs evolved and grew to the point where they were bumping up against the 640KB conventional-memory barrier, three vendors—Lotus, Intel, and Microsoft—came up with a technology to circumvent this limitation. The technology they came up with was expanded memory, or *EMS*, for *Expanded Memory System*.

EMS worked by using the same type of paging technology that video cards use. Expanded memory is divided up into 16KB chunks called *pages* that are swapped into a special memory address space in reserved memory four pages at a time. The area in reserved memory that is used to hold these pages is called the expanded *memory page frame* (or *page frame*, for short). This area normally occupies a full 64KB block in the memory map and is created when the expanded memory driver is loaded.

Computers are capable of emulating expanded memory through software, because very few programs today use expanded memory. (Most computers use the next type of memory we're going to describe, *extended memory*.) The EMS emulator is a software driver called EMM386.EXE. You load it in the CONFIG.SYS file by adding the following line:

```
DEVICE=C:\DOS\EMM386.EXE
```

This driver also allows DOS drivers and TSR programs to be loaded into the unused portions of reserved memory by adding a second line:

```
DEVICE=C:\DOS\EMM386.EXE
DOS=UMB
```

This has the benefit of freeing up conventional memory for use by your programs and is a key concept in *memory optimization*.

Extended Memory

In order to allow DOS programs to use all this memory, DOS would have to be rewritten to support the new processor. If this were done, the new version of DOS would not support old programs, since the old programs would not run above 1MB. To do this, the processor would use two different operating modes: real mode and protected mode.

In *real mode*, the 286 (and above) would operate like an 8086 (only faster) and could access only 1MB of RAM. To access memory above 1MB, the processor would have to switch to protected mode. It is called *protected mode* because each program that is running is protected from other programs that may be misbehaving and taking memory away from it. For DOS programs to use this memory, a program was written to extend DOS for those programs that can take advantage of it. This program is called a *DOS extender*.

An example of a DOS extender is the memory driver HIMEM.SYS; it allows certain programs to switch the processor to protected mode and access the memory above 1MB. It is loaded by adding the following line to the CONFIG.SYS file:

```
DEVICE=HIMEM.SYS
```

Once HIMEM.SYS is loaded, DOS can "see" the memory above 1MB. This memory is what is referred to as extended memory.

Also, when HIMEM.SYS is loaded, DOS can place the majority of itself into the first 64KB of extended memory. This first 64KB is called the *High Memory Area (HMA)*. In order to load DOS into the HMA, you modify the CONFIG.SYS file with the following two lines:

```
DEVICE=HIMEM.SYS
DOS=HIGH
```

You may have noticed that the last line is analogous to the DOS=UMB line in the last section. It is possible to have both of these lines in the CONFIG.SYS file in order to get the greatest amount of conventional memory available, although it is easier to insert them both at once, like so:

```
DEVICE=HIMEM.SYS
DEVICE=EMM386.EXE
DOS=HIGH,UMB
```

Basically, DOS can't use extended memory without the help of these extenders. However, there are several operating systems that can. These include OS/2, Unix, Windows NT, Windows 9x, Windows Me, and Windows 2000. Programs written for these non-DOS operating systems are able to take advantage of the benefits of the 286 (and above) processor, including multitasking and access to all the memory the processor can address.

NOTE Most people don't understand the MS-DOS memory map. That's okay; most people don't need to. However, it is an invaluable tool for the PC technician. Several programs report problems with memory addresses in hexadecimal. This helps us understand which programs were fighting when the error occurred. Also, in order to keep most PCs running efficiently, you must get as much conventional memory as possible. To do this, it is very important that you understand the different types of memory, their addressing, and how they work together in a PC.

With all of the different types of memory, you end up with a DOS memory map that looks like the one in Figure 4.4. With so many different types of memory, it is easy to get them confused. Most often, expanded and extended are juxtaposed. The easiest way to remember the difference is that expanded memory is paged and extended is not.

FIGURE 4.4: The Complete MS-DOS memory map

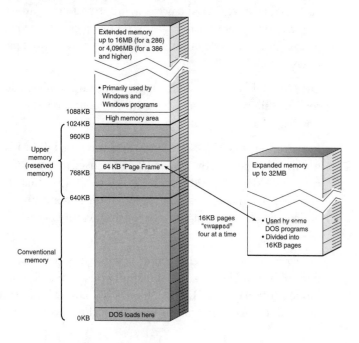

Exam Essentials

Understand what memory does.   In most cases, memory is a temporary storage location that has quicker access and read/write times than other storage media. Memory stores bits of data by setting a flag on or off. This flag represents a 1or 0 binary number.

Understand the different types and usage of memory.   Memory is used for many different types of devices in a PC. Be familiar with these types and their common usage.

Understand the memory map.   If you have a firm grip on the memory map, you can use the information to diagnose problems that cause a machine to crash or blue-screen since errors are normally displayed.

Key Terms and Concepts

Physical memory   Physically, memory is a collection of integrated circuits that store data and program information as patterns of 1s and 0s (on and off states) in the chip. Most memory chips require constant power (also called a constant refresh) to maintain those patterns of 1s and 0s.

DRAM   DRAM stores information as charges in very small capacitors. If a charge exists in a capacitor, it's interpreted as a 1. The absence of a charge is interpreted as a 0.

Synchronous DRAM (SDRAM)   Synchronous DRAM is synchronized to the speed of the systems it will be used in (e.g., PC66 SDRAM runs at 66MHz, PC100 runs at 100MHz, PC133 runs at 133MHz, and so on). Synchronizing the speed of the systems prevents the address bus from having to wait for the memory because of different clock speeds.

Direct Rambus   Direct Rambus is a memory bus that transfers data at 800MHz over a 16-bit memory bus. Direct Rambus memory models (often called RIMMs), like DDR SDRAM, can transfer data on both the rising and falling edges of a clock cycle, resulting in the ultra-high memory transfer rate (800MHz) and the high bandwidth of up to 1.6GB/second.

ROM   Read-Only Memory (ROM) is used to store information permanently for easy and quick retrieval. This type of memory chip contains transistors that are manufactured permanently in the on or off position, which is the main reason why this memory is called "read only." ROM is mainly used for very specialized purposes, such as storing information about how a device needs to operate. A computer's BIOS is typically stored on a type of ROM chip.

PROM   Programmable ROM (PROM) is ROM that is first manufactured with all of its circuits as logical 1s (that is, with all switches on); then, when the PROM is to be programmed, the connections that need to be set to 0 are destroyed, using a high-voltage electrical pulse.

Single Inline Memory Module (SIMM)   The Single Inline Memory Module (SIMM) is an easily removable circuit board that contains DIP chips.

Dual Inline Memory Module (DIMM)   DIMMs are dual-sided memory modules that hold twice as many chips as SIMMs. Generally, DIMMs have either 72 or 168 pins.

4.3 Identify the most popular type of motherboards, their components, and their architecture (bus structures and power supplies).

- AT (Full and Baby)
- ATX
- Communication ports
- SIMM and DIMM
- Processor sockets
- External cache memory (Level 2)
- ISA
- PCI
- AGP

- **USB (Universal Serial Bus)**
- **VESA local bus (VL-Bus)**
- **Basic compatibility guidelines**
- **IDE (ATA, ATAPI, ULTRA-DMA, EIDE)**
- **SCSI (Wide, Fast, Ultra, LVD (Low Voltage Differential))**

Motherboards are the backbone of a computer. The components of the motherboard provide basic services needed for the machine to operate and provide a platform for devices such as the processor, memory, disk drives, and expansion devices. This section details the popular types of motherboards and their buses.

Critical Information

Nonintegrated system boards require video, audio, or network devices to be added to the system with the expansion slots. This requirement mandates a greater assembly time for the computer and in some cases reduces the reliability of the system in transport.

Integrated system boards are so named because most of the components that would otherwise be installed as expansion cards are integrated into the motherboard circuitry. This reduces assembly time and ensures greater reliability of the system in transport but also prevents the individual replacement of a failed component.

System Board Form Factors

Let's look at three types of system board form factors: the AT, the ATX, and the NLX.

AT

The "baby" AT is the most commonly used design. Because the processor and memory are in line with the expansion slots, only one or two full-length cards can be used. Due to the location of the processor in relation to the power supply, cooling is required by addition of a heat sink or CPU fan.

AT boards are most commonly found in systems with processor speeds up to 233MHz. The easiest way to tell if a board is an AT-based form factor is to shut down the system. If the system requires you to physically press the Power button after choosing Shutdown from within a Windows 95 or higher operating system, then it is AT based.

ATX

The ATX has the processor and memory slots at right angles to the expansion cards. This puts the processor and memory in line with the fan output of the power supply, allowing the processor to run cooler. Because these components are not in line with the expansion cards, full-length expansion cards can be used. Current sales of ATX form factor boards are outpacing sales of the AT motherboards.

The ATX offers other features that are not present in the AT board, such as soft shutdowns by using the Power button. This is possible since the power is controlled by the motherboard itself.

NLX

A newer motherboard form factor that has been gaining popularity is the NLX. This form factor is used in low-profile case types. This design incorporates expansion slots that are placed on a riser board to accommodate the reduction in case size. However, this design adds another component to troubleshoot.

These motherboard form factors are usually found in what are known as "clone" machines produced by small vendors. Some manufacturers (e.g., Compaq and IBM) produce their own motherboard designs, which are known as proprietary designs. These motherboards don't conform to the standards outlined in this chapter. The components are laid out differently than the previously mentioned form factors. The large manufacturers use these designs to prevent failure during shipping and to reduce costs. Proprietary-designed motherboards can be purchased only from the vendor or an authorized repair facility and generally are much more expensive than standard form factor motherboards.

Bus—the Signal Pathways

A bus is a set of *signal pathways* that allows information and signals to travel between components inside or outside a computer. There are three types of buses inside a computer: the external bus, the address bus, and the data bus.

The *external bus* allows the CPU to talk to the other devices in the computer and vice versa. It is called that because it's external to the processor chip itself. When the CPU wants to talk to a device, it uses the *address bus* to do so. It selects the particular memory address that the device is using and uses the address bus to write to that address. When the device wants to send information back to the microprocessor, it uses the *data bus*.

Expansion Bus Features

The expansion bus allows the computer to be expanded using a modular approach. Whenever you need to add something to the computer, you plug specially made circuit boards into the expansion slots on the expansion bus. The devices on these circuit boards are then able to communicate with the CPU and are part of the computer.

THE CONNECTOR, OR SLOT

The connector slots are made up of several tiny copper "finger slots," or the row of very narrow channels that grab the fingers on the expansion circuit boards. These finger slots connect to copper pathways on the motherboard. Each set of pathways has a specific function. One set of pathways provides the voltages needed to power the expansion card (+5, +12, and ground). Another set of pathways makes up the data bus, transmitting data back to the processor. A third set makes up the address bus, allowing the device to be addressed through a set of I/O addresses. Finally, there are other lines for different functions such as interrupts, direct memory access (DMA) channels, and clock signals.

INTERRUPT LINES

Interrupts are special lines that are connected directly to the processor. Devices use an interrupt to get the attention of the CPU when they need to. A computer device uses the interrupt request (IRQ) line to get the attention of the CPU.

There are several interrupt request lines in each type of bus. Lines 0 and 1 (corresponding to IRQ 0 and IRQ 1, respectively) are used by the processor. The other lines are allocated to the various pieces of hardware installed in the computer. Not every line is used. In an average PC, there is usually at least one free IRQ line.

DMA CHANNELS

Another feature of the bus is that it allows devices to bypass the processor and write their information directly into main memory. This feature is known as *direct memory access*, or *DMA*. Each type of bus has a different number of channels that can be used for DMA.

I/O ADDRESSES

Each bus type has a set of lines that are used to allow the CPU to send instructions to the devices installed in the bus's slots. Each device is given its own unique communication line to the CPU. These lines are called *input/output (I/O) addresses* and they function a lot like unidirectional mailboxes.

CLOCK SIGNALS

Each computer has a built-in metronome-like signal called a *clock signal*. There are two types: the *CPU clock* and the *bus clock*. The former dictates how fast the CPU can run; the latter indicates how fast the bus can transmit information. The speed of the clocks is measured by how fast they "tick" and is given in millions of cycles per second, or megahertz (MHz). The bus or the CPU can perform an operation only on the occurrence of a tick signal. Think of the clock signal as a type of metronome that keeps the processor "in time."

BUS MASTERING

With DMA channels, a device can write directly to memory. But what if a device needs to read or write directly to another device (such as the hard disk)? For this purpose, bus designers came up with *bus mastering* This is a feature that allows a device to distract the CPU for a moment, "take control" of the bus, and read from or write information to the device. This feature can greatly improve the performance of the device.

Now that we have discussed the basic expansion bus concepts, we'll use these concepts to describe each of the different types of buses.

The 8-Bit Expansion Bus

The first type of expansion bus we're going discuss is the 8-bit bus. It is also sometimes known as the first PC bus. When the first PC was developed with the Intel 8088, it only had eight data lines running from the processor to the expansion connectors. Each line carried one bit of data. Thus was born the *8-bit bus*.

BUS CONFIGURATION

Configuring your devices involves assigning system resources that aren't being used by other devices. Configuration of the 8-bit bus is relatively complex, primarily because there are only one IRQ (IRQ 2) and one DMA channel (DMA 3) available. With so few system resources available, you have to decide which components will use each of the limited resources. One way to free up resources is to disable an unneeded device while using the device you need to work with.

Each card must be separately configured to operate with the computer according to the instructions that come with the card. You set the configuration on each card using jumpers and Dual Inline Package (DIP) switches so that the settings are the way you want them.

The Industry Standard Architecture Bus

This bus design uses a 16-bit pathway. It was given the same name as the computer it was designed for: the *AT bus*. It was also known as the *Industry Standard Architecture (ISA) bus*.

INFORMATION AND IDENTIFICATION

ISA expansion cards use a connector similar to the 8-bit bus but with the additional connector for the 16-bit data and address lines.

One interesting thing about the ISA bus is that it is backward compatible with the older, 8-bit bus. ISA bus slots are basically 8-bit slots with the extra signal lines required to make them 16-bit on a second connector. Expansion cards made for the PC's 8-bit bus can be inserted into ISA slots and they will function properly. There is one exception, however. Some 8-bit cards have a "skirt" extending below the bus slot. This skirt will not allow the 8-bit card to be inserted all the way into the ISA slot. This is why you will sometimes have 8-bit slots mixed in with ISA slots on the same motherboards.

BUS CONFIGURATION

Configuring expansion cards for use in ISA buses is a little less complex than configuring 8-bit buses, mainly because there are more choices available for interrupts and DMA channels. Tables 4.6 and 4.7 list the interrupts and DMA channels that are available in an ISA system.

TABLE 4.6: ISA Bus IRQ Defaults

IRQ	Default Assignment
IRQ 0	System timer
IRQ 1	Keyboard
IRQ 2	Cascade to IRQ 9
IRQ 3	COM 2 and 4
IRQ 4	COM 1 and 3
IRQ 5	LPT2 (usually available)
IRQ 6	Floppy controller
IRQ 7	LPT1
IRQ 8	Real Time Clock (RTC)
IRQ 9	Cascade to IRQ 2
IRQ 10	Available
IRQ 11	Available
IRQ 12	Bus mouse port (available if not used)
IRQ 13	Math coprocessor

TABLE 4.6: ISA Bus IRQ Defaults *(continued)*

IRQ	Default Assignment
IRQ 14	Hard disk controller board
IRQ 15	Available

TABLE 4.7: ISA Bus DMA Channel Defaults

DMA Channel	Default Assignment
DMA 0	Available
DMA 1	Available
DMA 2	Floppy controller
DMA 3	Available
DMA 4	Second DMA controller
DMA 5	Available
DMA 6	Available
DMA 7	Available

Note that COM 1 and COM 3 share the same interrupt, as do COM 2 and COM 4. The pairs are differentiated by using different I/O addresses for the different COM ports. This can work without conflict. The only problem is when you connect two devices that need to use an interrupt to the COM ports that use the same interrupt (for example, a mouse on COM 1 and a modem on COM 3). When this happens, the devices will work separately, but if you try to use both at the same time (for example, use the mouse while downloading a file with the modem), they will conflict and problems will occur.

You need to configure the card for interrupts, memory addresses, DMA channels, and I/O ports. This is done using jumpers and DIP switches.

One special case exists for interrupts when configuring them. You will notice that some interrupts are "cascaded" to each other. What this means is that in an ISA system, when the computer needs to access an interrupt higher than 9, it uses IRQ 2 to get to it. This method ensures backward compatibility with 8-bit buses.

As the ISA bus and its expansion cards evolved, manufacturers found that if they put the jumper positions into an EEPROM chip on the device, they could set them using a special software-configuration program. Because it's so easy, this method is used to configure the settings of most ISA cards today.

NOTE   There is a special case with regard to configuring ISA buses: the ISA Plug-and-Play bus. This bus consists of a standard ISA bus and a special set of BIOS extensions. The extensions examine the installed Plug-and-Play-compatible cards at startup and set them to available settings. At least that's the theory.

The Micro Channel Architecture Bus

Even though IBM developed the original 8-bit bus and had a hand in developing ISA, through the early 1980s it steadily lost its domination of the PC market. To try to regain their market share, IBM developed a higher-performance bus to rival the ISA bus. However, as with many previous industry-related failures, they chose to keep this bus type for their proprietary use. After realizing the error of their ways, IBM then tried to sell their architecture to other companies, but it was never widely adopted. This bus used a smaller, high-density connector and was known as Micro Channel Architecture (MCA).

INFORMATION AND IDENTIFICATION

MCA was a major step forward in bus design. First, it was available in either 16-bit or 32-bit versions. Second, it could have multiple bus-mastering devices installed. Third, the bus clock speed was slightly faster (10MHz instead of 8MHz). And finally, it offered the ability to change configurations with software rather than with jumpers and DIP switches.

The MCA bus connector is a high-density connector that appears similar to an ISA bus connector. However, the MCA bus connector has almost twice as many connectors in a smaller area and is segmented to provide for 16-bit, 32-bit, and video extension segments.

BUS CONFIGURATION

MCA's strengths include the ability to use software to configure it. Installing an expansion card in an MCA slot still involves the same concepts as installing an ISA card. You must configure the card to use an available IRQ, DMA channel, memory address, and I/O ports. To configure the options on these cards, you must use a reference disk and an option disk after physically installing the device into the computer.

The Extended ISA Bus

Because MCA was rather expensive and ISA slowed down their systems, manufacturers got together and came up with the Extended ISA, or EISA, bus. This bus took the best parts of the other buses and combined them into a 32-bit software-configurable bus. The 16-bit ISA cards were compatible with this new bus and the standard was open.

INFORMATION AND IDENTIFICATION

There were several new desirable features introduced with EISA. Its creators took the best of MCA's features and added to them. As we have already mentioned, EISA has a 32-bit data path. In addition, it has more I/O addresses, it allows expansion cards to be set up using software, it has no need for interrupts or DMA channels, and it allows for multiple bus-mastering devices. However, despite all these advances, it still uses the 8MHz clock speed of ISA (to ensure backward compatibility with ISA cards).

The bus slots, shown in Figure 4.5, have both 16-bit and 32-bit finger slots. The 16-bit finger slots and the 32-bit finger slots alternate every other finger slot. Also, the 16-bit finger slots are located toward the top of the connectors and the 32-bit finger slots are buried deep within the connectors. The reason for all this alternating, burying, and arranging is that when you insert a 16-bit card, it will only go in halfway and make contact with the top (16-bit) connectors. But an EISA card, shown in Figure 4.6, because of its longer fingers, will seat all the way into an EISA slot and make full contact with the deeper, 32-bit finger slots.

FIGURE 4.5: An EISA bus connector

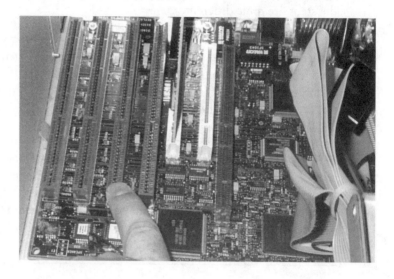

FIGURE 4.6: An EISA bus expansion card

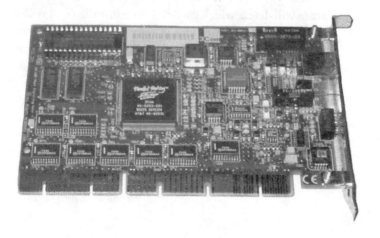

BUS CONFIGURATION

Configuring an EISA bus is similar to configuring an MCA bus, unless you install an ISA card into an EISA bus slot. If you do that, the configuration issues for ISA apply. If you are using only EISA cards, then the steps are quite different.

After installing the card and booting the PC, the computer will recognize that there is a new, unconfigured card in the bus. Then you are given the choice to run the EISA Configuration Utility or to continue and ignore the new information. If you choose the latter, the next time you boot, you will be given this choice again.

TIP To access the EISA configuration program on a Compaq server, press F10 when the flashing, white cursor appears in the upper-right corner of the screen at system startup. If the cursor doesn't appear, then the EISA Configuration program was not installed onto the boot sector(s) of the first hard disk. Boot to the Compaq EISA Configuration Utility disk the first time for assistance in this process.

If you choose to configure the bus, you must have the EISA Configuration Utility disk in a bootable drive so that the computer can boot to it. During the boot process, the EISA Configuration program will detect which card has been installed and will ask for a disk with the configuration files. These files are device specific, have the extension .cfg, and can be downloaded from the particular vendors. Also, the CFG files specific to the devices installed in the computer will be copied to the Configuration Utility disk so that you can use that disk to change the various parameters without having to have more than one disk.

VESA Local Bus

The EISA bus had several major advantages, but it had one glaring problem: It had a maximum clock speed of 8MHz. Manufacturers could speed up some components in the computer by putting them on the local bus. In addition to the memory and cache cards, one of the first components to be put on the local bus was the video circuitry, to benefit from direct communication with the processor. Some manufacturers designed a special local-bus video card slot and designed special, high-performance cards for these slots. This approach became very popular and most companies adopted it. The problem with this approach is that the local-bus video card from one vendor would not work in a local-bus slot from another vendor.

The Video Electronics Standards Association (VESA) was formed for this reason. This group made sure that cards made for one vendor's slot would work in another vendor's computer. As time passed, the slot design changed and was given a new name, the *VESA Local Bus slot*, also known as *VL-Bus*, *VLB*, or just *VESA*. This slot was a 32-bit addition to the ISA bus and was therefore backward compatible with it.

VLB has one major drawback—the configuration is still done through jumpers and DIP switches instead of through special bus-configuration programs. It's been called the "big ISA" bus because that's what it is: just a 32-bit version of ISA.

INFORMATION AND IDENTIFICATION

A VL-Bus slot is an ISA slot with the 32-bit, local bus connector added to the ISA bus connector as a third bus connector, as shown in Figure 4.7. This connector is a high-density connector that has all of its lines running directly to the processor.

FIGURE 4.7: A VL-Bus connector

The VL-Bus expansion card is also easily identifiable. The card is a bit longer than an ISA card and has one extra connector (the 32-bit, local connector). Figure 4.8 shows two typical VL-Bus expansion cards. These cards are typically used for video cards, SCSI host bus adapters, and multimedia expansion cards.

FIGURE 4.8: VL-Bus expansion cards. Top: A video card. Bottom: An IDE hard drive controller.

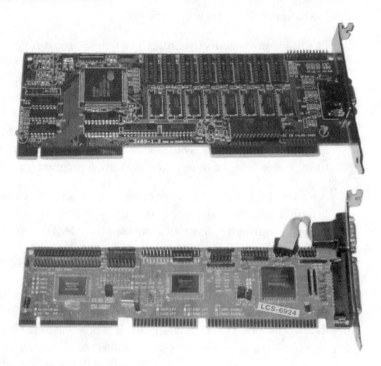

BUS CONFIGURATION

When you configure a VLB card, you perform operations that are similar to those you perform when configuring ISA cards. However, because the VL-Bus is a more modern bus, some of these cards are Plug and Play or, at the very least, software configurable.

Peripheral Component Interconnect

With the introduction of the Pentium-generation processors, all existing buses instantly became obsolete. Because the Pentiums were 64-bit processors and most buses were of the 16-bit or 32-bit variety, using existing buses would severely limit the performance of the new technology. It was primarily for this reason that the Peripheral Component Interconnect (PCI) bus was developed.

PCI has many benefits over other bus types. First, it supports both 64-bit and 32-bit data paths, so it can be used in both 486 and Pentium-based systems. In addition, it is processor independent. The bus communicates with a special bridge circuit that communicates with both the CPU and the bus. This has the benefit of making the bus an almost universal one. PCI buses can be found in PCs, Mac OS–based computers, and RISC machines. The same expansion card will work for all of them; you just need a different configuration program for each.

Another advantage of PCI over other buses is a higher clock speed. PCI (in its current revision) can run up to 33MHz. Also, the bus can support multiple bus-mastering expansion cards. These two features give PCI a maximum bus throughput of up to 265Mbps (with 64-bit cards).

The final two features of PCI that we should discuss are its backward compatibility and software setup features. The PCI bus uses a chipset that works with PCI, ISA, and EISA. It is possible to have a PC that contains all these buses on the same motherboard. Also, the PCI cards are mostly Plug and Play. The cards will automatically configure themselves for IRQ, DMA, and I/O port addresses.

NOTE   In some systems that are a combination of PCI and ISA, each PCI slot is located right next to an ISA slot. When you put a card in that PCI slot, you disable the ISA slot and vice versa. Only one card will fit in a combination slot at a time.

INFORMATION AND IDENTIFICATION

Identification of PCI bus slots is very simple. The finger slots in the bus in Figure 4.9 are packed together tightly. This connector is usually white and contains two sections. There are two versions of the PCI bus that are found in today's systems. The versions are differentiated by the voltages that they use. One uses +5.5Vdc to power the expansion cards, and the other uses +3.3Vdc. When you look at the connectors for these buses, the only difference you'll see is the different placement of the *blocker* (called a *key*) in each connector so that a +3.3Vdc card can't be plugged into a +5.5Vdc bus slot and vice versa.

FIGURE 4.9: PCI bus connectors

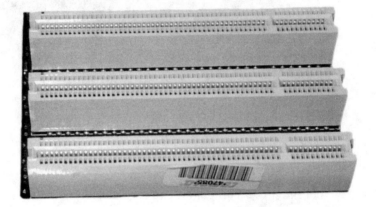

BUS CONFIGURATION

When you need to configure a PCI expansion card, shown in Figure 4.10, you simply install the card. The computer's BIOS takes care of configuring IRQ, I/O, and DMA addresses. Then you install the appropriate software so that the computer can use the device.

FIGURE 4.10: A PCI expansion card

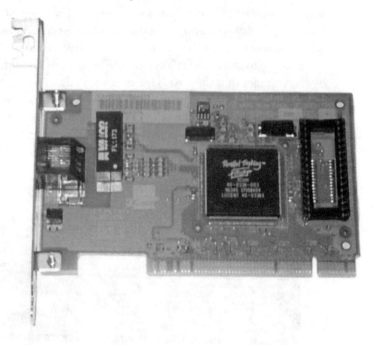

Accelerated Graphics Port

As Pentium systems got faster, PC game players wanted games that had better graphics, more realism, and more speed. However, as the computers got faster, the video technology just couldn't seem to keep up, as was the case with the VL-Bus discussed earlier. VL-Bus could run only at 33MHz, and with 100 and 200MHz processors, there was a need for a faster, processor-direct, video expansion bus. The bus that was developed to meet this need was the *Accelerated Graphics Port (AGP) bus.*

INFORMATION AND IDENTIFICATION

The AGP connector is similar in physical size and appearance to a PCI connector, as shown in Figure 4.11. But it's usually darker in color and offset from the other PCI slots to avoid confusion. The reason for the similarities is that Intel started with PCI 2.1 interface specifications to develop AGP. The bus is 32 bits wide, just like PCI. However, the similarities end there. AGP actually runs at twice the memory bus speed (as opposed to PCI, which runs at only half the memory bus speed). AGP runs at 66MHz, as opposed to PCI's 33MHz. And in its fastest mode, AGP can transfer data at 508.6Mbps! PCI is limited to 265Mbps.

FIGURE 4.11: An AGP slot on a motherboard

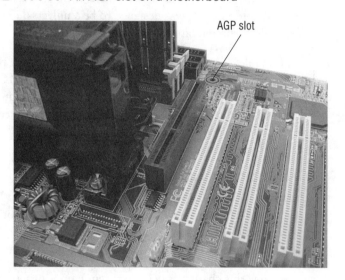

BUS CONFIGURATION

Configuration of an AGP expansion card is simplicity itself. Motherboards that support AGP have Plug-and-Play BIOSes that will automatically configure the card. To add an AGP card, simply power down the system, install the card in the AGP slot, and power the system back up. Once the system comes back up, the BIOS will configure the card automatically. Finally, you can install the drivers for your operating system. This step is unnecessary if you have a Plug-and-Play operating system.

PCMCIA

PCMCIA stands for *Personal Computer Memory Card International Association*. The bus was originally designed to provide a way of expanding the memory in a small, handheld computer. The PCMCIA was organized to provide a standard way of expanding portable computers. The PCMCIA bus has been renamed *PC card* to make it easier to pronounce. The PC card bus uses a small expansion card. Although it is primarily used in portable computers, there are PC card bus adapters for desktop PCs. It was designed to be a universal expansion bus that could accommodate any device.

The first release of the PCMCIA standard defined only the bus to be used for memory expansion. The second release (PCMCIA 2) is the most common; it is in use throughout the computer industry and has remained relatively unchanged. PCMCIA 2 was designed to be backward compatible with version 1, so memory cards can be used in the version 2 specification.

INFORMATION AND IDENTIFICATION

Currently, PCMCIA's bus width is only 16 bits, but a 32-bit version is on the way. PC cards support only one IRQ and do not support bus mastering or DMA. However, because of its flexibility, PCMCIA has quickly become a very popular bus for all types of computers.

At the time this chapter is being written, I am waiting for some wireless network gear that is manufactured by Linksys. A dentist who is a close friend of mine recently had a beautiful bar constructed in his basement for entertaining his computer friends. Dentists are detail-oriented people but lack the planning for such things as network cables. He called me over one night to see his bar and ask how he could access his MP3 files from his laptop at the bar. With no cable access paths, the only two choices were wireless networking or drilling holes in his new bar.

The new wireless gear, which is manufactured by Linksys, comes only with a PCMCIA interface. For desktop installations, Linksys also produces a PCI card that allows you to insert a PCMCIA card into a desktop. A PCMCIA card inserts into the back, which allows desktops to transmit to the base station, thereby achieving connectivity. Wireless networking and PCMCIA interfaces will become more widely used in the near future. Another friend of mine purchased from a different vendor a desktop PC that already has a PCMCIA interface in the front of the case.

There are three major types of PC cards (and slots) in use today. Each has different uses and physical characteristics; see Figure 4.12. Coincidentally, they are called Type I, Type II, and Type III:

- Type I cards are 3.3mm thick and are most commonly used for memory cards.

- Type II cards are 5mm thick and are mostly used for modems and LAN adapters. This is the most common PC card type found today, and most systems have at least two Type II slots (or one Type III slot).

- The Type III slot is 10.5mm thick. Its most common application is for the PC card hard disks. Developers have been slowly introducing these devices to the market.

FIGURE 4.12: PC card types by thickness

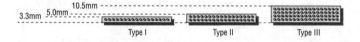

In addition to the card, there are two other components in the PC card architecture. The first one is the Socket Services software. This software is a BIOS-level interface to the PCMCIA bus slot. When loaded, it hides the details of the PC card hardware from the computer. This software can detect when a card has been inserted and what type of card it is.

The second component is the Card Services software. This software is the interface between the application and Socket Services. It tells the applications which interrupts and I/O ports the card is using. Applications that need to access the PC card don't access the hardware directly. Instead, they tell Card Services that they need access to a particular feature, and Card Services gets the appropriate feature from the PC card.

This dual-component architecture allows the PCMCIA architecture to be used in different types of computer systems (that is, not just Intel's). For example, the Apple laptop computers currently use PC cards for modems and LAN interface cards, and they are based on Motorola processors.

BUS CONFIGURATION

The process for installing a PC card is different than that for any of the other bus types, mainly because this type was designed to allow the cards to be "hot swapped"—inserted or removed while the computer is powered up. This is the only bus that allows this. However, even though you can remove a PC card while the power is on, *you shouldn't!* If you remove a PCMCIA card while the system is up, realize that some software may not like having its hardware ripped out from underneath it. That software will then have no hardware to talk to and it may crash the system. (As for other expansion cards, *never* remove them without shutting off the power to the computer first! If the power is on, you will certainly damage the card, the computer, or both.)

The process for installing a PC card is very straightforward. Just slip the card into an available slot, making sure the card type matches the slot type. Once the card is installed, you must install the software to use the card (Windows 9*x* will do this automatically).

Sometimes, there is not enough memory to load all the files for PC Card and Socket Services. In the DOS world, the software for PC Card and Socket Services loads in conventional memory (or in upper memory blocks). With many such DOS drivers being loaded, you may run out of conventional memory and not be able to run some DOS programs.

To solve this problem, PC card manufacturers have come up with a piece of software called a PC card "shim" that allows the card to be used like any other expansion card. In addition, it takes up less conventional memory. The only downside is that the shim might not be completely compatible with the system. Windows $9x$ incorporates this software as virtual device drivers, or VxDs.

Table 4.8 summarizes some of the important points concerning bus types and their specifications.

TABLE 4.8: Summary of Bus Types

Bus Type	Bus Width (Bits)	Maximum Speed (MHz)	Uses Bus Mastering?	Configuration
8-bit	8	4.77	N	Jumpers/DIP switches
ISA	16	8 (10 for Turbo)	N	Jumpers/DIP switches (Some cards are software configurable.)
MCA	16 or 32	10	Y	Software— Reference disk
EISA	32	8	Y	Software— EISA configuration disk
VL-Bus	32	33MHz	Y	Same as ISA
PCI	64	33MHz	Y	Software— Plug and Play
AGP	64	66MHz	N	Software— Plug and Play
PC card	16	33	N	Software— PC Card and Socket Services

Exam Essentials

Understand what a bus is.   PCs have several types of buses. One thing that they all have in common is that they transport data from place to place. This data pathway allows devices to utilize processor and memory resources.

Know the many different types of buses.   Know the different types of buses, their maximum speed, and their configuration.

Understand expansion buses.   You will need to be familiar with the many types of expansion buses. Spend more time on PCI, ISA, EISA, AGP, and VESA buses than other types due to their widespread usage.

Key Terms and Concepts

Bus   A bus is a set of signal pathways that allows information and signals to travel between components inside or outside of a computer. There are three types of buses inside a computer: the external bus, the address bus, and the data bus.

Expansion bus features   The expansion bus allows the computer to be expanded using a modular approach. Whenever you need to add something to the computer, you plug specially made circuit boards into the expansion slots on the expansion bus. The devices on these circuit boards are then able to communicate with the CPU and are part of the computer.

Bus mastering   Bus mastering is a feature that allows a device to distract the CPU for a moment, "take control" of the bus, and read from or write information to the device. This feature can greatly improve the performance of the device.

Extended ISA (EISA) bus   The VESA Local Bus slot, also known as VL-Bus, VLB, or just VESA, is a 32-bit addition to the ISA bus and was therefore backward compatible with it.

Peripheral Component Interconnect (PCI)   PCI supports both 64-bit and 32-bit data paths, so it can be used in both 486 and Pentium-based systems. In addition, it is processor independent. The bus communicates with a special bridge circuit that communicates with both the CPU and the bus.

Accelerated Graphics Port (AGP)   The AGP bus was developed to meet the need for increased graphics performance.

4.4 Identify the purpose of CMOS (Complementary Metal-Oxide Semiconductor), what it contains, and how to change its basic parameters.

- Printer parallel port—Uni., bi-directional, disable/enable, ECP, EPP
- COM/serial port—memory address, interrupt request, disable
- Floppy drive—enable/disable drive or boot, speed, density
- Hard drive—size and drive type
- Memory—parity, non-parity
- Boot sequence
- Date/time
- Passwords
- Plug and Play BIOS

Although you will probably have very few questions, if any, on the test that relate to menu items inside the setup utility, it is important to know the basic changes that can be made. CMOS settings can be tricky in the hands of an inexperienced user. In many cases, you will be required to use the menus in a situation when the PC is disabled. Your knowledge of CMOS settings will allow you to effectively troubleshoot and repair the PC.

Critical Information

Your PC has to keep certain settings when it's turned off and its power cord is unplugged. These settings include:

- Date

- Time

- Hard drive configuration

- Memory

CMOS Chip

Your PC keeps these settings in a special memory chip called the Complementary Metallic Oxide Semiconductor (CMOS) chip. The CMOS chip must have a constant source of power to keep its settings. To prevent the loss of data, motherboard manufacturers include a small battery, called the *CMOS battery,* to power the CMOS memory. The battery comes in different shapes and sizes, but they all perform the same function.

You can press a certain key or group of keys to access the stored settings during the POST. In most cases, you simply press the Delete key while the memory counts off to enter the CMOS setup software. This software allows you to change the configuration through a group of menus. We describe some of the most common menus and their configuration items in this section.

Standard CMOS Setup

The standard CMOS Setup menu allows you to change the time, date, hard disk, and floppy drive information. In most cases, you would not use the standard CMOS Setup menu to configure IDE hard drives since most setup software also contains a hard drive-detection utility. The most common usage for the standard Setup menu is to change the time and date.

NOTE   Not all vendors do things the same way. It is hard to find two machines that have the same configuration options and menus. Knowing what you want to accomplish before you enter the program and having a general idea of which menu should apply are the best ways to accomplish your setup requirements.

BIOS Features Setup

The BIOS Features Setup menu allows you to enable or disable the Internal Cache, External Cache, Power On Self Test (POST), Floppy Seek At Boot, and Memory Parity Check options. You can also configure in which order you would like to boot. For example, you can choose to boot from your hard drive, CD-ROM, or floppy disk in any order. If you would like your machine to boot quicker, you may disable the Floppy Seek At Boot option from the standard CMOS Setup menu and set your boot order to Hard Drive First on the BIOS Features Setup menu. After you have made these changes, the floppy will no longer be accessed after the POST, and the machine will boot from the hard drive.

Power Management

The Power Management menu controls the way the PC will act after it has been idle for certain time periods. Normally the menu offers a Power Management option, which can be set to Minimum, Maximum, or User Defined. The Minimum and Maximum settings control the HDD Off After, Doze Mode, Standby Mode, and Suspend Mode settings with predefined parameters. If you select User Defined, you must manually configure these settings to your personal preferences.

Load Setup Defaults

This option does not have any menu items. Its purpose is to configure the PC back to the default settings set by the factory. If you make changes to your settings and the machine becomes disabled, in most cases selecting this menu will return the machine to a usable state. You may then try different settings until you achieve your desired configuration.

Integrated Peripherals

The Integrated Peripherals menu allows you to set bus options or to enable or disable integrated components. These components may include PS2 Mouse, USB Ports, USB Keyboard Support, and Wake On LAN Support.

This menu is also used to assign resources to serial, COM, and printer ports. In most cases, you will use this menu to enable or disable COM 1 or 2 with one exception: Many devices other than printers can use the printer port, or parallel port. Therefore, this port can be configured in several ways, as shown in Table 4.9.

TABLE 4.9: Printer or Parallel Port Settings

Setting	Description	Use
EPP (Enhanced Parallel Port)	This configuration supports bi-directional communication and high transfer rates.	Newer inkjet and laser printers that can utilize bi-directional communication and scanners.
ECP (Enhanced Communications Port)	This configuration supports bi-directional communication and high transfer rates.	Newer inkjet and laser printers that can utilize bi-directional communication, connectivity devices, and scanners.
SPP (Standard Printer Port)	This configuration supports bi-directional communication.	Older inkjet and laser printers and slower scanners.
EPP+ECP	This is a combination of EPP and ECP capabilities.	Newer inkjet and laser printers that can utilize bi-directional communication, connectivity devices, and scanners.

When you have connected a printer, scanner, external drive, communication device, or any other type of peripheral device to the printer port and it does not function correctly, consult the documentation to see if you need to make any configuration changes. If nothing is listed, systematically change the settings: In most cases, you can fix communications problems simply by changing the port type.

Supervisor Password and User Password

Even though these are usually separate menu items, they accomplish basically the same task—setting passwords. If you select the Supervisor Password menu, you will be prompted to enter a password. After you have set a supervisor password, you must enter it in order to change any settings within the CMOS setup utility.

The User Password menu options work the same way, but after you set a password, the machine will not finish its boot process without a password being entered.

These two simple little options cause pain for users who do not understand the consequences of their actions. If they forget the password, the machine may not start or will not be able to be configured. This happens often. The truth is that the only people these passwords protect a computer from are those who know absolutely nothing about PCs. In this chapter and in Chapter 1, "Installation, Configuration, and Upgrading," we mentioned that for the CMOS settings to remain in the chip, a battery must be connected. This means that if someone has protected a machine that you need access to, or they have forgotten the password, you can simply remove the battery to erase the password.

Most motherboards have a jumper that can be used to reset the CMOS chip. In most cases, however, it will be easier to find the battery and remove it than it will be to find the correct jumper.

HDD Auto Detection

This menu allows you to detect IDE hard drives that are installed on the machine. After you have detected the drives and accepted the parameters, you exit this utility.

Save Changes and Exit, Discard Changes and Exit

These menus are self-explanatory. After you have selected either option, the machine saves or discards your changes and reboots. Once the machine reboots, you can continue to load the operating system or enter the CMOS setup utility again.

Exam Essentials

Know what the CMOS setup utility does. The CMOS setup utility allows you to configure the characteristics of certain portions of the PC.

Be familiar with the common menu items listed. Knowing these common menu items and their function can greatly aid troubleshooting.

Understand the different printer port settings. Although there is no good rule of thumb on which of these settings will fix a communication error, in most cases by systematically trying the different settings, you can resolve the issue.

Key Terms and Concepts

CMOS chip Complementary Metallic Oxide Semiconductor (CMOS) chip. This chip is used to retain system settings when the PC is turned off or unplugged.

EPP Enhanced Parallel Port. This printer or parallel port setting allows bi-directional communications and can be used with newer inkjet and laser printers.

ECP Enhanced Communication Port. This printer or parallel port setting allows bi-directional communications and can be used with newer inkjet and laser printers, scanners, and other peripheral devices.

SPP Standard Printer Port. This printer or parallel port setting allows bi-directional communications and can be used with older inkjet and laser printers.

Chapter

Domain 5.0 Printers

COMPTIA A+ EXAM OBJECTIVES COVERED IN THIS CHAPTER:

▶ **5.1 Identify basic concepts, printer operations, and printer components.** *(pages 194 – 221)*
  - Paper feeder mechanisms
  - Types of printers
  - Types of printer connections and configurations

▶ **5.2 Identify care and service techniques and common problems with primary printer types.** *(pages 221 – 240)*
  - Feed and output
  - Errors (printed or displayed)
  - Paper jam
  - Print quality
  - Safety precautions
  - Preventive maintenance

One of the most common test questions is on the process that printers go through to put toner on paper. In most cases, you will have more questions about printers—and especially laser printers—than any other topic. This is because technicians spend a great deal of time troubleshooting printers in most office environments. If you work for a consulting firm, having knowledge of your customers' printers is essential. Despite the low reliability of modern printers, they are the most commonly used peripheral.

Since printers have moving parts and rely on users to load toner and paper, you can see that this is normally the weakest link in the chain. Most consulting firms offer incentives for employees to gather certifications on specific brands of laser printers to better serve their customers. Also, if you work for a authorized repair facility, you will need to have a certification in a particular model of printer to order the parts or at the very least get reimbursed for the labor of the repairs by the manufacturer.

5.1 Identify Basic Concepts, Printer Operations, and Printer Components.

- Paper feeder mechanisms
- Types of printers
- Types of printer connections and configurations

Businesses use computers to help reduce labor and material costs. Modern offices have utilized PCs to reduce many costs; however, paper output or printed documents still abound. Since so many documents are generated on a daily basis, the A+ exam will cover printers thoroughly.

In my experience, printing problems are responsible for about one third of service calls and repairs. In most cases, these calls are quickly resolved by replacing ink and toner cartridges. In other cases, these repairs will require additional labor. Pay close attention to this section and take some additional time when covering the material on laser printers to best prepare for the exam.

Critical Information

When we conduct business, we use different types of paper documents. Contracts, letters, and, of course, money are all used to conduct business. As more and more of those documents are created on computers, printers will become increasingly important.

Printers are electro-mechanical output devices that are used to put information from the computer onto paper. They have been around since the introduction of the computer.

This section will discuss the details of each major type of printer. We will cover the following A+ exam topics:

- Impact printers
- Inkjet printers
- Laser printers (page printers)
- Interfaces and print media

WARNING   Take special note of the section on laser and page printers. The A+ exams test these subjects in detail, so we'll cover them in as much detail.

Impact Printers

There are several categories of printers, but the most basic type is the category of printers known as *impact printers*. Impact printers use some form of impact and an inked ribbon to make an imprint on the paper.

There are two major types of impact printers: daisy wheel and dot matrix. Each type has its own service and maintenance issues.

Daisy-Wheel Printers

These printers contain a wheel (called the *daisy wheel* because it looks like a daisy) with raised letters and symbols on each "petal." When the printer needs to print a character, it sends a signal to the mechanism that contains the wheel. This mechanism is called the *print head*. The print head rotates the daisy wheel until the required character is in place. An electromechanical hammer (called a *solenoid*) then strikes the back of the petal containing the character.

Daisy-wheel printers were one of the first types of impact printer developed. Their speed is rated by the number of characters per second (cps) they can print.

The daisy-wheel printer has a few advantages. First, because it is an impact printer, you can print on multipart forms (such as carbonless receipts), assuming they can be fed into the printer properly. Second, it is relatively inexpensive compared to the price of a laser printer of the same vintage. Finally, the print quality is comparable to a typewriter because it uses a very similar technology. This typewriter level of quality was given a name: *letter quality* (*LQ*).

Dot-Matrix Printers

These printers work in a manner similar to daisy-wheel printers, except that instead of a spinning, character-imprinted wheel, the print head contains a row of "pins." These pins are triggered in patterns that form letters and numbers as the print head moves across the paper.

The pins in the print head are wrapped with coils of wire to create a solenoid. Also, the pins are held in the rest position by a combination of a small magnet and a spring. To trigger a particular pin, the printer controller sends a signal to the print head, which energizes the wires around the appropriate print wire. This turns the print wire into an electromagnet, which repels the print pin, forcing it against the ink ribbon and making a dot on the paper. It's the arrangement of the dots in columns and rows that creates the letters and numbers we see on the page.

The main disadvantage to dot-matrix printers is their image quality, which can be quite poor compared to the quality produced with a daisy-wheel printer. Dot-matrix printers use patterns of dots to make letters and images, and the early dot-matrix printers used only nine pins to make those patterns.

Inkjet Printers

Inkjet printers are one of the most popular types in use today. This type of printer sprays ink on the page to print text or graphics.

Inkjet printers are very basic printers. They have very few moving parts. Every inkjet printer works in a similar fashion. First of all, every inkjet printer contains a special part called an ink cartridge (see Figure 5.1). This cartridge contains the print head and ink supply, and it must be replaced when the ink supply runs out.

FIGURE 5.1: A typical ink cartridge (size: approximately 3 inches by 1½ inches)

Inside this ink cartridge are several small chambers. At the top of each chamber is a metal plate and tube leading to the ink supply. At the bottom of each chamber is a small pinhole. These pinholes are used to spray ink on the page to form characters and images as patterns of dots (similar to the way a dot-matrix printer works, but with much higher resolution).

When a particular chamber needs to spray ink, an electric signal is sent to the heating element, energizing it. The elements heat up quickly, causing the ink to vaporize. Because of the expanding ink vapor, the ink is pushed out the pinhole and forms a bubble of ink. As the vapor expands, the bubble eventually gets large enough to break off into a droplet. The rest of the ink is pulled back into the chamber by the surface tension of the ink. When another drop needs to be sprayed, the process begins again.

Laser Printers (Page Printers)

Laser printers are referred to as *page printers* because they receive their print job instructions one page at a time. There are three major types of page printers: those that use the electrophotographic (EP) print process, those that use the Hewlett-Packard (HP) print process, and those that use the light-emitting diode (LED) print process. Each works in basically the same way, with slight differences.

Electrophotographic Laser Printer Operation

When Xerox and Canon developed the first laser printers in the late 1980s, they were designed around the electrophotographic process (a technology developed by scientists at Xerox). This technology uses a combination of static electric charges, laser light, and a black powdery substance called *toner*. Printers that use this technology are called EP process laser printers, or just *laser printers*. Every laser printer technology has its foundations in the EP printer process.

BASIC COMPONENTS

Any printer that uses the EP process contains eight standard assemblies. These assemblies are the toner cartridge, fusing assembly, laser scanner, high-voltage power supply, DC power supply, paper transport assembly (including paper pickup rollers and paper registration rollers), corona, and printer controller circuitry.

The toner cartridge   The EP toner cartridge (Figure 5.2), as its name suggests, holds the toner. Toner is a black, carbon substance mixed with polyester resins (to make it "flow" better) and iron oxide particles (to make the toner sensitive to electrical charges). These two components make the toner capable of being attracted to the photosensitive drum and capable of melting into the paper. In addition to these components, toner contains a medium called the *developer*, which "carries" the toner until it is used by the EP process. The toner cartridge also contains the EP print drum. This drum is coated with a photosensitive material that can hold a static charge when not exposed to light. Finally, the drum contains a cleaning blade that continuously scrapes the "used" toner off the photosensitive drum to keep it clean.

FIGURE 5.2: An EP toner cartridge

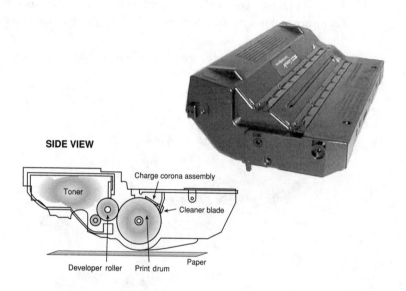

NOTE In most laser printers, "toner cartridge" means an EP toner cartridge that contains toner and a photosensitive drum in one plastic case. In some laser printers, however, the toner and photosensitive drum can be replaced separately instead of as a single unit. If you ask for a "toner cartridge" for one of these printers, all you will receive is a cylinder full of toner. Consult the printer's manual to find out which kind of toner cartridge your laser printer uses.

The laser scanning assembly The EP photosensitive drum can hold a charge if it's not exposed to light. It is dark inside an EP printer, except when the laser scanning assembly shines on particular areas of the photosensitive drum. When it does that, the drum discharges, but only in that area. As the drum rotates, the laser scanning assembly scans the laser across the photosensitive drum. Figure 5.3 shows the laser scanning assembly.

Laser light is damaging to human eyes. Therefore, the laser is kept in an enclosure and will operate only when the laser printer's cover is closed.

FIGURE 5.3: The EP laser scanning assembly (side view and simplified top view)

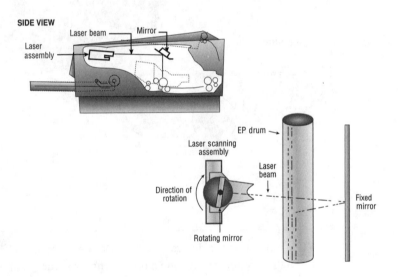

High-voltage power supply The EP process requires high-voltage electricity. The high-voltage power supply (HVPS) provides the high voltages that are used during the EP process. This component converts house AC current (120 volts, 60 Hertz) into higher voltages that the printer can use. This high voltage is used to energize both the corona wire and transfer corona wire.

DC power supply   The high voltages used in the EP process can't power the other components in the printer (the logic circuitry and motors). These components require low voltages, between +5 and +24Vdc. The DC power supply (DCPS) converts house current into three voltages: +5Vdc and −5Vdc for the logic circuitry and +24Vdc for the paper transport motors. This component also runs the fan that cools the internal components of the printer.

Paper transport assembly   The paper transport assembly is responsible for moving the paper through the printer. It consists of a motor and several rubberized rollers that each perform a different function.

The first type of roller found in most laser printers is the *feed roller* (Figure 5.4). This D-shaped roller, when activated, rotates against the paper and pushes one sheet into the printer. This roller works in conjunction with a special rubber pad to prevent more than one sheet from being fed into the printer at a time.

Another type of roller that is used in the printer is the *registration roller* (also shown in Figure 5.4). There are actually two registration rollers, which work together. These rollers synchronize the paper movement with the image-formation process in the EP cartridge. The rollers don't feed the paper past the EP cartridge until the cartridge is ready for it.

Both of these rollers are operated with a special electric motor known as an *electronic stepper motor*. This type of motor can accurately move in very small increments. It powers all of the paper transport rollers as well as the fuser rollers.

FIGURE 5.4: Paper transport rollers

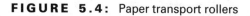
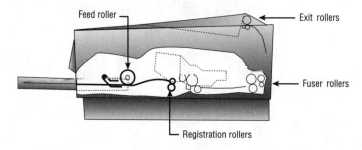

The transfer corona assembly   When the laser writes the images on the photosensitive drum, the toner then sticks to the exposed areas. The transfer corona assembly (Figure 5.5) is charged with a high-voltage electrical charge and carries the toner from the photosensitive drum onto the paper. This assembly charges the paper, which pulls the toner from the photosensitive drum.

Included in the corona assembly is a *static-charge eliminator strip*, which drains away the charge imparted to the paper by the corona. If you didn't drain away the charge, the paper would stick to the EP cartridge and jam the printer.

There are two types of corona assemblies: those that contain a *corona wire* and those that contain a *corona roller*. The corona wire is a small diameter wire that is charged by the high-voltage power supply. The wire is located in a special notch in the "floor" of the laser printer (underneath the EP print cartridge). The corona roller performs the same function as the corona wire, except that it's a roller rather than a wire. Because the corona roller is directly in contact with the paper, it supports higher speeds. For this reason, the corona wire is seldom used in laser printers any more.

FIGURE 5.5:   The transfer corona assembly

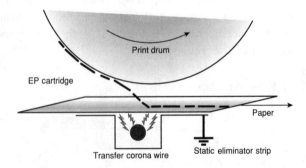

Fusing assembly   The toner in the EP toner cartridge will stick to just about anything, including paper. This is true because the toner has a negative static charge and most objects have a net positive charge. However, these toner particles can be removed by brushing any object across the page. This could be a problem if you want the images and letters to stay on the paper permanently!

To solve this problem, EP laser printers incorporate a device known as a *fuser* (Figure 5.6), which uses two rollers that apply pressure and heat to fuse the plastic toner particles to the paper. You may have noticed that pages from either a laser printer or a copier (which uses a similar device) come out warm. This is because of the fuser.

The fuser is made up of three main parts: a halogen heating lamp, a Teflon-coated aluminum fusing roller, and a rubberized pressure roller. The fuser uses the halogen lamp to heat the fusing roller to between 165 and 180 degrees C. As the paper passes between the two rollers, the pressure roller pushes the paper against the fusing roller, which melts the toner into the paper.

FIGURE 5.6: The fuser

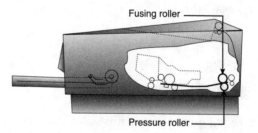

Fusing roller

Pressure roller

Printer controller circuitry   The final component in the laser printer we need to discuss is the printer controller assembly. This large circuit board converts signals from the computer into signals for the various assemblies in the laser printer, using the process known as *rasterizing*.

This circuit board is usually mounted underneath the printer. The board has connectors for each of the types of interfaces and cables to each assembly.

When a computer prints to a laser printer, it sends a signal through a cable to the printer controller assembly. The controller assembly formats the information into a page's worth of line-by-line commands for the laser scanner. The controller sends commands to each of the components telling them to "wake up" and start the EP print process.

Electrophotographic Print Process

The EP print process is the process by which an EP laser printer forms images on paper. It consists of six major steps, each for a specific goal. Although many different manufacturers call these steps different things or place them in a different order, the basic process is still the same. Here are the steps in the order you will see them on the exam:

1. Cleaning

2. Conditioning

3. Writing

4. Developing

5. Transferring

6. Fusing

Before any of these steps can begin, however, the controller must sense that the printer is ready to start printing (toner cartridge installed, fuser warmed to proper temperature, and all covers in place). Printing cannot take place until the printer is in its "ready" state, usually indicated by an illuminated Ready LED light or a display that says something like "00 READY" (on HP printers).

STEP 1: CLEANING

In the first part of the laser print process, a rubber blade inside the EP cartridge scrapes any toner left on the drum into a used-toner receptacle inside the EP cartridge, and a fluorescent lamp discharges any remaining charge on the photosensitive drum (remember that the drum, being photosensitive, loses its charge when exposed to light). This step is called the *cleaning step* (Figure 5.7).

FIGURE 5.7: The cleaning step of the EP process

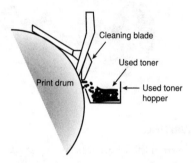

The EP cartridge is constantly cleaning the drum. It may take more than one rotation of the photosensitive drum to make an image on the paper. The cleaning step keeps the drum "fresh" for each use. If you didn't clean the drum, you would see "ghosts" of previous pages printed along with your image.

NOTE   The actual amount of toner removed in the cleaning process is quite small. The cartridge will run out of toner before the used toner receptacle fills up.

STEP 2: CONDITIONING

The next step in the EP process is the *conditioning step* (Figure 5.8). In this step, a special wire (called a *charging corona*) within the EP toner cartridge (above the photosensitive drum) gets a high voltage from the HVPS. It uses this high voltage to apply a strong, uniform negative charge (around –600Vdc) to the surface of the photosensitive drum.

FIGURE 5.8: The conditioning step of the EP process

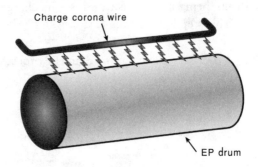

Charge corona wire

EP drum

STEP 3: WRITING

The next step in the EP process is the *writing step*. In this step, the laser is turned on and "scans" the drum from side to side, flashing on and off according to the bits of information the printer controller sends it as it communicates the individual bits of the image. The areas where the laser "touches" severely reduce the photosensitive drum's charge from –600Vdc to a slight negative charge (around –100Vdc). As the drum rotates, a pattern of exposed areas is formed, representing the images to be printed. Figure 5.9 shows this process.

FIGURE 5.9: The writing step of the EP process

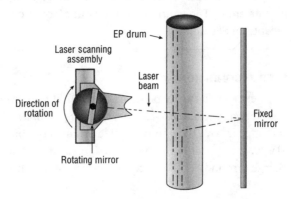

EP drum

Laser scanning
assembly

Laser
beam

Direction of
rotation

Fixed
mirror

Rotating mirror

At this point, the controller sends a signal to the pickup roller to feed a piece of paper into the printer, where it stops at the registration rollers.

STEP 4: DEVELOPING

Now that the surface of the drum holds an electrical representation of the image being printed, its discrete electrical charges need to be converted into something that can be transferred to a piece of paper. The EP process step that accomplishes this is the *developing step* (Figure 5.10). In this step, toner is transferred to the areas that were exposed in the writing step.

FIGURE 5.10: The developing step of the EP process

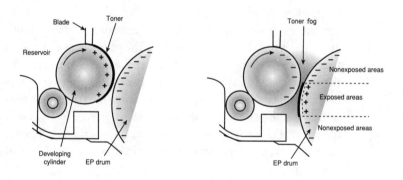

There is a metallic roller called the *developing roller* inside an EP cartridge that acquires a –600Vdc charge (called a *bias voltage*) from the HVPS. The toner sticks to this roller because there is a magnet located inside the roller and because of the electrostatic charges between the toner and the developing roller. While the developing roller rotates toward the photosensitive drum, the toner acquires the charge of the roller (–600Vdc). When the toner comes between the developing roller and the photosensitive drum, the toner is attracted to the areas that have been exposed by the laser (because these areas have a lesser charge, of –100Vdc). The toner also is repelled from the unexposed areas (because they are at the same –600Vdc charge, and like charges repel). This toner transfer creates a "fog" of toner between the EP drum and the developing roller.

The photosensitive drum now has toner stuck to it where the laser has written. The photosensitive drum continues to rotate until the developed image is ready to be transferred to paper in the next step, the transferring step.

STEP 5: TRANSFERRING

At this point in the EP process, the developed image is rotating into position. The controller notifies the registration rollers that the paper should be fed through. The registration rollers move the paper underneath the photosensitive drum, and the process of transferring the image can begin, with the *transferring step*.

The controller sends a signal to the corona wire or corona roller (depending on which one the printer has) and tells it to turn on. The corona wire/roller then acquires a strong *positive* charge (+600Vdc) and applies that charge to the paper. The paper, thus charged, pulls the toner from the photosensitive drum at the line of "contact" between the roller and the paper because the paper and toner have opposite charges. Once the registration rollers move the paper past the corona wire, the static-eliminator strip removes all charge from that "line" of the paper. Figure 5.11 details this step. If the strip didn't bleed this charge away, the paper would attract itself to the toner cartridge and cause a paper jam.

FIGURE 5.11: The transferring step of the EP process

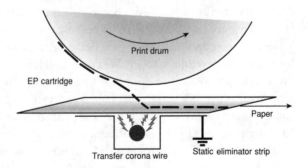

Print drum

EP cartridge

Paper

Transfer corona wire

Static eliminator strip

The toner is now held in place by weak, electrostatic charges and gravity. It will not stay there, however, unless it is made permanent, which is the reason for the next step, the fusing step.

STEP 6: FUSING

In the final step, the *fusing step*, the toner image is made permanent. The registration rollers push the paper toward the fuser rollers. Once the fuser grabs the paper, the registration rollers push for only a short time more. The fuser is now in control of moving the paper.

As the paper passes through the fuser, the fuser roller melts the polyester resin of the toner, and the rubberized pressure roller presses it permanently into the paper (Figure 5.12). The paper continues on through the fuser and eventually exits the printer.

FIGURE 5.12: The fusing step of the EP process

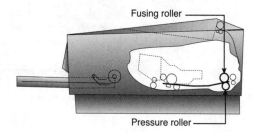

Fusing roller

Pressure roller

Once the paper completely exits the fuser, it trips a sensor that tells the printer to finish the EP process with the next step, the cleaning step. At this point, the printer can print another page and the EP process can begin again.

SUMMARY OF THE EP PRINT PROCESS

Figure 5.13 summarizes all the EP process printing steps. First, the printer uses a rubber scraper to clean the photosensitive drum. Then the printer places a uniform, negative, –600Vdc charge on the photosensitive drum by means of a charging corona. The laser "paints" an image onto the photosensitive drum, discharging the image areas to a much lower voltage (–100Vdc). The developing roller in the toner cartridge has charged (–600Vdc) toner stuck to it. As it rolls the toner toward the photosensitive drum, the toner is attracted to (and sticks to) the areas of the photosensitive drum that the laser has discharged. The image is then transferred from the drum to the paper at its line of contact by means of the corona wire (or corona roller) with a +600Vdc charge. The static-eliminator strip removes the high, positive charge from the paper, and the paper, now holding the image, moves on. The paper then enters the fuser, where the fuser roller and the pressure roller make the image permanent. The paper exits the printer, and the printer starts printing the next page or returns to its ready state.

FIGURE 5.13: The EP print process

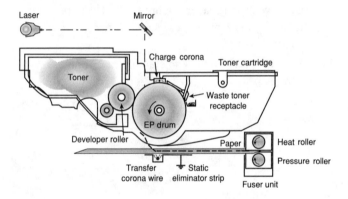

TIP To help you remember the steps of the EP print process, in order, remember them by the first letters of each step, or CCWDTF. The most often used mnemonic sentence for this combination of letters is "Charlie Can Walk, Dance, and Talk French."

Printer Interfaces and Supplies

Besides understanding the printer's operation, for the exam you will need to understand how the printer talks to a computer and all the items involved in that process. Also, you must understand how the different types of print media affect the print process. These two concepts will complete our discussion of printers.

Interface Components

A printer's *interface* is the collection of hardware and software that allows the printer to communicate with a computer. Each printer has at least one interface, but some printers have several, in order to make them more flexible in a multiplatform environment. If a printer has several interfaces, it can usually switch between them on the fly so that several computers can print at the same time.

NOTE One model of printer that can support multiple interfaces is the HP 5si. The 5si comes with the standard parallel interface. Network and serial cards can be installed into expansion bays on the back of the printer to allow multiple interface types.

There are several components to an interface, including its communication type as well as the interface software. Each aspect must be matched on both the printer and the computer. For example, an HP LaserJet 4L has only a parallel port. Therefore, you must use a parallel cable as well as the correct software for the platform being used (e.g., a Macintosh HP LaserJet 4L driver if you connect it to a Macintosh computer).

Communication Types

When we say "communication types," we're actually talking about the hardware technologies involved in getting the printed information from the computer to the printer. There are four major types: serial, parallel, Universal Serial Bus, and network.

SERIAL

When computers send data serially, they send it one bit at a time, one after another. The bits "stand in line" like people at a movie theater, waiting to get in. You must set the communication parameters (baud, parity, and start and stop bits) on both entities—in this case, the computer and its printer(s)—before communication can take place.

PARALLEL

When a printer uses parallel communication, it is receiving data eight bits at a time. Each bit travels over a separate wire (one for each bit). Parallel communication is the most popular way of communicating from computer to printer, mainly because it's faster than serial.

A parallel cable consists of a male DB-25 connector that connects to the computer and a male 36-pin Centronics connector that connects to the printer. Most of the cables are shorter than 10 feet long.

Keep printer cable lengths to less than 10 feet. Some people try to run printer cables more than 50 feet. After 10 feet, communications can become unreliable due to cross talk.

UNIVERSAL SERIAL BUS

The most popular type of printer interface as this book is being written is the Universal Serial Bus (USB). It is actually the most popular interface for just about every peripheral. The benefit for printers is that it has a higher transfer rate than either serial or parallel and it automatically recognizes new devices.

NETWORK

Most large environment printers (primarily laser and LED printers) have a special interface that allows them to be hooked directly to a network. These printers have a network interface card (NIC) and ROM-based software that allow them to communicate with networks, servers, and workstations.

The type of network interface used on the printer depends on the type of network the printer is being attached to. For example, if you're using a Token Ring network, the printer should have a Token Ring interface.

Interface Software

Computers and printers can't talk to each other by themselves. They need interface software to translate software commands into commands that the printer can understand.

There are two factors to consider with interface software: the *page description language* and the *driver software*. The page description language determines how efficient the printer will be at converting the information to be printed into signals the printer can understand. The driver software understands and controls the printer. It is very important that you use the correct interface software for the printer you are using. If you use either the wrong page description language or the wrong driver software, the printer will print garbage—or possibly nothing at all.

PAGE DESCRIPTION LANGUAGES

A page description language works just as its name says it does. It describes the whole page being printed by sending commands that describe the text as well as the margins and other settings. The controller in the printer interprets these commands and turns them into laser pulses (or pin strikes).

The most basic page description language is no page description language. The computer sends all the instructions that the printer needs in a serial stream, like so: Position 1, print nothing; Position 2, strike pins 1 and 3; Position 3, print nothing. This type of description language works great for dot-matrix printers, but it can be very inefficient for laser printers. For example, if you wanted to print a page using a standard page description language and there was only one character on the page, there would be a lot of wasted signal for the "print nothing" commands.

Also, with graphics, the commands to draw a shape on the page are relatively complex. For example, to draw a square, the computer (or printer) has to calculate the size of the square and convert that into lots of "strike pin x" (or "turn on laser") and "print nothing" commands. This is where the other types of page description languages come into the picture.

The first page description language was PostScript. Developed by Adobe, it was first used in the Apple LaserWriter printer. It made printing graphics fast and simple. Here's how PostScript works: The

PostScript printer driver "describes" the page in terms of "draw" and "position" commands. The page is divided into a very fine grid (as fine as the resolution of the printer). When you want to print a square, a communication like the following might take place:

```
POSITION 1,42%DRAW 10%POSITION 1,64%DRAW10D% . . .
```

These commands tell the printer to draw a line on the page from line 42 to line 64 (vertically). In other words, a page description language tells the printer to draw a line on the page, gives it the starting and ending points, and that's that. Rather than send the printer the location of each and every dot in the line and an instruction at each and every location to print that location's individual dot, PostScript can get the line drawn with fewer than five instructions. As you can see, PostScript uses more or less English commands. The commands are interpreted by the processor on the printer's controller and converted into the print control signals.

Another page description language is the Printer Control Language, or PCL. Currently in revision 5 (PCL 5), it was developed by Hewlett-Packard for its LaserJet series of printers as a competitor to PostScript. PCL works in much the same manner as PostScript, but it's found mainly in Hewlett-Packard printers (including its DeskJet bubble-jet printers). Other manufacturers use PCL, however. In fact, some printers support both page description languages and will automatically switch between them.

The main advantage to page description languages is that they move some of the processing from the computer to the printer. With text-only documents, they don't offer much benefit. However, with documents that have large amounts of graphics or that use numerous fonts, page description languages make the processing of those print jobs happen much faster. This makes them an ideal choice for laser printers. However, DeskJets, as well as some dot-matrix printers, also use page description languages.

DRIVER SOFTWARE

The driver software controls how the printer processes the print job. When you install a printer driver for the printer you are using, it allows the computer to print to that printer correctly (assuming you have the correct interface configured between the computer and printer).

When you need to print, you select the printer driver for your printer from a preconfigured list. The driver you select has been configured for the type, brand, and model of printer as well as the computer port to which it is connected. You can also select which paper tray the printer should use, as well as any other features the printer has (if applicable). Also, each printer driver is configured to use a particular page description language.

WARNING   If the wrong printer driver is selected, the computer will send commands in the wrong language. If that occurs, the printer will print several pages full of garbage (even if only one page of information was sent). This "garbage" isn't garbage at all, but in fact the printer page description language commands printed literally as text instead of being interpreted as control commands.

NOTE   Although HP does not recommend using any printer driver other than the one designed for the specific printer, in some cases, you can increase printing performance (speed) of HP LaserJet and DeskJet printers by using older drivers that do not support the newer high-definition printing. I have also had cases where software packages would not function with newer HP drivers. To increase speed or correct printing problems with HP LaserJet printers, try this rule of thumb: If you are using a 5 series printer (5Si), try a 4 series driver; if that does not work, reduce the driver by one series. If a LaserJet III does not work, try the "LaserJet" driver, which should be last on your list of the default drivers built into Windows. In 90 percent of the cases, this driver will fix printing problems with some applications.

Printer Supplies

Just as it is important to use the correct printer interface and printer software, you must use the correct printer supplies. These supplies include the print media (what you print on) and the consumables (what you print with). The quality of the final print job has a great deal to do with the print supplies.

Print Media

The print media are what you put through the printer to print on. There are two major types of print media: paper and transparencies. Of the two types, paper is by far the most commonly used.

PAPER

Most people don't give much thought to the kind of paper they use in their printers. It's a factor that can have tremendous effect on the quality of the hard copy printout, however, and the topic is more complex than people think. For example, if the wrong paper is used, it can cause the paper to jam frequently and possibly even damage components.

TRANSPARENCIES

Transparencies are still used for presentations made with overhead projectors, even with the explosion of programs like PowerPoint (from Microsoft) and peripherals like LCD computer displays, both of which let you show a whole roomful of people exactly what's on your computer screen. Actually, though, PowerPoint still has an option to print slides, and you can use any program you want to print anything you want to a transparent sheet of plastic or vinyl for use with an overhead projector. The problem is, these "papers" are *exceedingly* difficult for printers to work with. That's why special transparencies were developed for use with laser and bubble-jet printers.

Each type of transparency was designed for a particular brand and model of printer. Again, check the printer's documentation to find out which type of transparency works in that printer. Don't use any other type of transparency!

WARNING   *Never* run transparencies through a laser printer without first checking to see if it's the type recommended by the printer manufacturer. The heat from the fuser will melt most other transparencies and they will wrap themselves around it. It is impossible to clean a fuser after this has happened. The fuser will have to be replaced. *Use only the transparencies that are recommended by the printer manufacturer.*

Print Consumables

Besides print media, there are other things in the printer that run out and need to be replenished. These items are the print consumables. Most consumables are used to form the images on the print media. There are two main types of consumables in printers today: ink and toner. Toner is used primarily in laser printers. Most other printers use ink.

INK

Ink is a liquid that is used to "stain" the paper. There are several different colors of ink used in printers, but the majority use some shade of black or blue. Both dot-matrix printers and bubble-jet printers use ink, but with different methods.

Dot-matrix printers use a cloth or polyester ribbon soaked in ink and coiled up inside a plastic case. This assembly is called a *printer ribbon* (or *ribbon cartridge*). It's very similar to a typewriter ribbon, except that instead of being coiled into the two rolls you'd see on a typewriter, the ribbon is continuously coiled inside the plastic case. Once the ribbon has run out of ink, it must be discarded and replaced with a new one. Ribbon cartridges are developed closely with their respective printers. It is for this reason that ribbons should be purchased from the same manufacturer as the printer. The wrong ribbon could jam in the printer as well as cause quality problems.

Bubble-jet cartridges actually have a liquid ink reservoir. The ink in these cartridges is sealed inside. Once the ink runs out, the cartridge must be removed and discarded. A new, full one is installed in its place. Because the ink cartridge contains ink as well as the printing mechanism, it's like getting a new printer every time you replace the ink cartridge.

In some bubble-jet printers, the ink cartridge and the print head are in separate assemblies. In this way, the ink can be replaced when it runs out and the print head can be used several times. This works fine if the printer is designed to work this way. However, some people think they can do this on their integrated cartridge/print head system, using special ink cartridge refill kits. These kits consist of a syringe filled with ink and a long needle. The needle is used to puncture the top of an empty ink cartridge. The syringe is then used to refill the reservoir. Don't use these kits! See the warning about using them for more information.

WARNING *Do not use ink cartridge refill kits!* These kits (the ones you see advertised with a syringe and a needle) have several problems. First, the kits don't use the same kind of ink that was originally in the ink cartridges. The new ink may be thinner, causing the ink to run out or not print properly. Also, the print head is supposed to be *replaced* around this same time. Just refilling it doesn't replace the print head. This will cause print quality problems. Finally, the hole the syringe leaves cannot be plugged and may allow ink to leak out. The bottom line: *Buy new ink cartridges from the printer manufacturer.* Yes, they are a bit more expensive, but you will actually save money because you won't have any of the problems described above.

TONER

The final type of consumable is toner. Each model of laser printer uses a specific toner cartridge. The different types of toner cartridges were covered in the discussions of the different types of printers. All we would add here is to check the printer's manual to see which toner cartridge it needs.

WARNING   Just as with ink cartridges, always buy the exact model toner cartridge recommended by the manufacturer. The toner cartridges have been designed specifically for a particular model. Also, *never* refill toner cartridges, for most of the same reasons we don't recommend refilling ink cartridges. The printout quality will be poor, and the fact that you're just refilling the toner means you're *not* replacing the photosensitive drum (which is usually inside the cartridge), and it might be that the drum *needs* to be replaced. Simply replacing the refilled toner cartridges with proper, name-brand toner cartridges has solved most laser printer quality problems we have run across. We keep recommending the right ones, but clients keep coming back with the refilled ones. The result is that we take our clients' money to solve their print quality problems when all it involves is a toner cartridge, our (usually repeat) advice to buy the proper cartridge next time, and the obligatory minimum charge for a half hour of labor, even though the job of replacing the cartridge takes all of five minutes!

Exam Essentials

Know the common types of printers.   Know and understand the types of printers such as impact printers, bubble-jet printers, and laser printers (page printers), as well as their interfaces and print media.

Understand the process of printing for each type of printer.   Each type of printer puts images or text on paper. Understand the process that each type of printer uses to accomplish this task.

Know the specific components of each type of printer.   Each type of printer uses similar components to print. Know the different components that make up each type of printer and their job.

Know and understand the print process of a laser printer.   You will almost certainly be asked questions on certain processes of a laser printer. Know and understand the different steps that make up the print process of a laser printer.

Key Terms and Concepts

Toner cartridge   The EP toner cartridge holds the toner. Toner is a black, carbon substance mixed with polyester resins and iron oxide. In most cases, the toner cartridge contains a medium called the *developer*, the print drum, and a cleaning blade.

DC power supply (DCPS)   The DC power supply (DCPS) converts house current into three voltages: +5Vdc and −5Vdc for the logic circuitry and +24Vdc for the paper transport motors. This component also runs the fan that cools the internal components of the printer.

Paper transport assembly   The paper transport assembly is responsible for moving the paper through the printer. It consists of a motor and several rubberized rollers that each perform a different function.

Transfer corona assembly   When the laser writes the images on the photosensitive drum, the toner then sticks to the exposed areas. The corona is charged with a high-voltage electrical charge and carries the toner from the photosensitive drum onto the paper. This assembly charges the paper, which pulls the toner from the photosensitive drum.

Printer controller circuitry   This large circuit board converts signals from the computer into signals for the various assemblies in the laser printer.

Interface components   A printer's interface is the collection of hardware and software that allows the printer to communicate with a computer. Each printer has at least one interface, but some printers have several.

Communication types   There are four major types: serial, parallel, Universal Serial Bus (USB), and network.

Interface software   Interface software translates commands into commands that the printer can understand.

Page description languages   A page description language describes the whole page being printed by sending commands that describe the text as well as the margins and other settings.

Print media   The print media are what you put through the printer to print on. There are two major types of print media: paper and transparencies.

5.2 Identify care and service techniques and common problems with primary printer types.

- Feed and output
- Errors (printed or displayed)
- Paper jam
- Print quality
- Safety precautions
- Preventive maintenance

Not only is printer troubleshooting on the test, but you have to accomplish these tasks on a daily basis. The worst thing about repairing printers is the lack of redundancy. Most large companies share printers to reduce costs. In the quest to reduce costs, there are seldom backup printers to provide fail-over when a printer becomes disabled. Workflow can be drastically affected by downtime. Your ability to get a down printer working will make you more valuable to your employer.

Critical Information

As I mentioned earlier in this chapter, a large portion of all service calls relates to printing problems. This section will give some general guidelines and common printing solutions to resolve printing problems.

Printer Troubleshooting

This section covers the most common types of printer problems you will run into. We break the information into three areas, for the three different types of printers in use today.

Dot-Matrix Printer Problems

Dot-matrix printers are relatively simple devices. Therefore there are only a few problems that usually arise. We cover the most common problems and their solutions here.

LOW PRINT QUALITY

Problems with print quality are easy to identify. When the printed page comes out of the printer, the characters may be too light or have dots missing from them. Table 5.1 details some of the most common print quality problems, their causes, and their solutions.

TABLE 5.1: Common Dot-Matrix Print Quality Problems

Characteristics	Cause	Solution
Consistently faded or light characters	Worn-out print ribbon	Replace ribbon with a new, vendor-recommended ribbon.
Print lines that go from dark to light as the print head moves across the page	Print ribbon advance gear slipping	Replace ribbon advance gear or mechanism.
A small, blank line running through a line of print (consistently)	Print head pin stuck inside the print head	Replace the print head.
A small, blank line running through a line of print (intermittently)	A broken, loose, or shorting print head cable or a sticking print head	Secure or replace the print head cable. Replace the print head or clean it.

TABLE 5.1: Common Dot-Matrix Print Quality Problems *(continued)*

Characteristics	Cause	Solution
A small, dark line running through a line of print	Print head pin stuck in the "out" position	Replace the print head. (Pushing the pin in may damage the print head.)
Printer makes printing noise, but no print appears on page	Worn, missing, or improperly installed ribbon cartridge or the print head gap set too large	Replace ribbon cartridge correctly or adjust the print head gap.
Printer prints "garbage"	Cable partially unhooked, wrong driver selected, or bad printer control board (PCB)	Hook up cable correctly, select correct driver, or replace PCB (respectively).

PRINTOUT JAMS INSIDE THE PRINTER

Printer jams are very frustrating because they always seem to happen more than halfway through your 50-page print job, requiring you to take time to remove the jam before the rest of your pages can print. A paper jam happens when something prevents the paper from advancing through the printer evenly. Print jobs jam for two major reasons: an obstructed paper path and stripped drive gears.

Obstructed paper paths are often difficult to find. Usually it means disassembling the printer to find the bit of crumpled-up paper or other foreign substance that's blocking the paper path. A very common obstruction is a piece of the "perf"—the perforated sides of tractor-feed paper—that has torn off and gotten crumpled up and then lodged into the paper path. It may be necessary to remove the platen roller and feed mechanism to get at the obstruction.

TIP Use extra caution when printing peel-off labels in dot-matrix printers. If a label or even a whole sheet of labels becomes misaligned or jammed, *do not* roll the roller backward to realign the sheet. The small plastic paper guide that most dot-matrix printers use to control the forward movement of the paper through the printer will peel the label right off its backing if you reverse the direction of the paper. And once the label is free, it can easily get stuck under the platen, causing paper jams. A label stuck under the platen is almost impossible to remove without disassembling the paper feed assembly. If a label is misaligned, try realigning the whole sheet of labels *slowly* using the *feed roller,* with the power off, moving it in very small increments.

STEPPER MOTOR PROBLEMS

A *stepper motor* is a motor that can move in very small increments. Printers use stepper motors to move the print head back and forth as well as to advance the paper (these are called the *carriage motor* and *main motor*, respectively). These motors get damaged when they are forced in any direction while the power is on. This includes moving the print head over to install a printer ribbon as well as moving the paper feed roller to align paper. These motors are very sensitive to stray voltages. And, if you are rotating one of these motors by hand, you are essentially turning it into a small generator, damaging it!

A damaged stepper motor is easy to detect. Damage to the stepper motor will cause it to lose precision and move farther with each "step." Lines of print will be unevenly spaced if the main motor is damaged (which is more likely). Characters will be "scrunched" together if the print head motor goes bad. In fact, if the motor is bad enough, it won't move at all in any direction. It may even make high-pitched squealing noises. If any of these symptoms show themselves, it's time to replace one of these motors.

Stepper motors are usually expensive to replace. They are about half the cost of a new printer! Damage to them is very easy to avoid, using common sense.

NOTE   If I had a wish for the service department I worked in, I would wish that all the dot-matrix printers ever bought would be made by Okidata. Okidata dot-matrix printers are a technician's dream machine. With nothing but a flat-bladed screwdriver and your hands, you can completely disassemble an Okidata dot-matrix printer in less than 10 minutes. Replacing parts on them is just as easy. All parts "snap" into place, including the covers. They also have an excellent reputation. If a customer asks you for a recommendation when buying a dot-matrix printer, you can't go wrong recommending an Okidata.

Inkjet Printers

Inkjet, or bubble-jet, printers are the most commonly sold printers for home use. For this reason, you need to understand the most common problems with bubble-jet printers so your company can service them effectively. Let's take a look at some of the most common problems with bubble-jet printers and their solutions.

PRINT QUALITY

The majority of bubble-jet printer problems are quality problems. Ninety-nine percent of these can be traced to a faulty ink cartridge. With most bubble-jet printers, the ink cartridge contains the print head and the ink. The major problem with this assembly can be described by "If you don't use it, you lose it." The ink will dry out in the small nozzles, blocking them if they are not used at least once a week.

An example of a quality problem is when you have thin, blank lines present in every line of text on the page. This is caused by a plugged hole in at least one of the small, pinhole ink nozzles in the print cartridge. Replacing the ink cartridge solves this problem easily.

WARNING Some people will try to save a buck by refilling their ink cartridge when they need to replace it. If you are one of them, *stop it!* Don't refill your ink cartridges! Almost all ink cartridges are designed *not* to be refilled. They are designed to be used once and thrown away! By refilling them, you make a hole in them, and ink can leak out and the printer will need to be cleaned. Also, the ink will probably be of the wrong type, and print quality can suffer. Finally, a refilled cartridge may void the printer's warranty.

If an ink cartridge becomes damaged or develops a hole, it can put too much ink on the page and the letters will smear. Again, the solution is to replace the ink cartridge. (You should be aware, however, that a very small amount of smearing is normal if the pages are laid on top of each other immediately after printing.)

One final print quality problem that does not directly involve the ink cartridge is when the print goes from dark to light quickly, then prints nothing. As we already mentioned, ink cartridges dry out if not used. That's why the manufacturers included a small suction pump inside the printer that "primes" the ink cartridge before each print cycle. If this "priming pump" is broken or malfunctioning, this problem will manifest itself and the pump will need to be replaced.

TIP If the problem of the ink going from dark to light quickly and then disappearing ever happens to you, and you really need to print a couple of pages, try this trick I learned from a fellow technician: Take the ink cartridge out of the printer. Squirt some window cleaner on a paper towel and gently tap the print head against the wet paper towel. The force of the tap plus the solvents in the window cleaner should dislodge any dried ink, and the ink will flow freely again.

PAPER JAMS

Bubble-jet printers usually have very simple paper paths. Therefore, paper jams due to obstructions are less likely. They are still possible, however, so an obstruction shouldn't be overlooked as a possible cause of jamming.

Paper jams in bubble-jet printers are usually due to one of two things:

- A worn pickup roller

- The wrong type of paper

The pickup roller usually has one or two D-shaped rollers mounted on a rotating shaft. When the shaft rotates, one edge of the "D" rubs against the paper, pushing it into the printer. When the roller gets worn, it gets smooth and doesn't exert enough friction against the paper to push it into the printer.

If the paper used in the printer is too smooth, it causes the same problem. Pickup rollers use friction, and smooth paper doesn't offer much friction. If the paper is too rough, on the other hand, it acts like sandpaper on the rollers, wearing them smooth. Here's a rule of thumb for paper smoothness: Paper slightly smoother than a new dollar bill will work fine.

Laser and Page Printers

I've got good news and bad news. The bad news is that laser printer problems are the most complex, because the printer is the most complex. The good news is that most problems are easily identifiable and have specific fixes. Most of the problems can be diagnosed with knowledge of the inner workings of the printer and a little common sense. Let's discuss the most common laser and page printer problems and their solutions.

PAPER JAMS

Laser printers today run at copier speeds. Because of this, their most common problem is paper jams. Paper can get jammed in a printer for several reasons. First of all, feed jams happen when the paper feed rollers get worn (similar to feed jams in bubble-jet printers). The solution to this problem is easy: Replace the worn rollers.

TIP If your paper feed jams are caused by worn pickup rollers, there is something you can do to get your printer working while you're waiting for the replacement pickup rollers. Scuff the feed roller(s) with a Scotch-Brite® pot-scrubber pad (or something similar) to roughen up the feed rollers. This trick works only once. After that, the rollers aren't thick enough to touch the paper.

Another cause of feed jams is related to the drive of the pickup roller. The drive gear (or clutch) may be broken or have teeth missing. Again, the solution is to replace it. To determine if the problem is a broken gear or worn rollers, print a test page, but leave the paper tray out. Look into the paper feed opening with a flashlight and see if the paper pickup roller(s) are turning evenly and don't skip. If they turn evenly, the problem is more than likely worn rollers.

Worn exit rollers can also cause paper jams. These rollers guide the paper out of the printer into the paper-receiving tray. If they are worn or damaged, the paper may "catch" on its way out of the printer. These types of jams are characterized by a paper jam that occurs just as the paper is getting to the exit rollers. If the paper jams, open the rear door and see where the paper is. If the paper is very close to the exit roller, the exit rollers are probably the problem.

The solution is to replace all the exit rollers. You must replace all of them at the same time since even one worn exit roller can cause the paper to jam. Besides, they're inexpensive. Don't be cheap and skimp on these parts if you need to have them replaced.

Paper jams can actually be the fault of the paper. If your printer consistently tries to feed multiple pages into the printer, the paper isn't dry enough. If you live in an area with high humidity, this could be a problem. I've heard some solutions that are pretty far out but that work (like keeping the paper in a Tupperware-type of airtight container or microwaving it to remove moisture). The best all-around solution, however, is humidity control and to keep the paper wrapped until it's needed. Keep the humidity around 50 percent or lower (but above 25 percent if you can, in order to avoid problems with electrostatic discharge).

Finally, there is a metal, grounded strip called the *static eliminator strip* inside the printer that drains the corona charge away from the paper after it has been used to transfer toner from the EP cartridge. If that strip is missing, broken, or damaged, the charge will remain on the paper and may cause it to stick to the EP cartridge, causing a jam. If the paper jams after reaching the corona assembly, this may be the cause.

BLANK PAGES

Blank pages are a somewhat common occurrence in laser and page printers. Somehow, the toner isn't being put on the paper. There are three major causes of blank pages:

- The toner cartridge

- The corona assembly

- The high-voltage power supply (HVPS)

TONER CARTRIDGE

The toner cartridge is the source for most quality problems, because it contains most of the image-formation pieces for laser and page printers. Let's start with the obvious. A blank page will come out of the printer if there is no toner in the toner cartridge. It's very easy to check: Just open the printer, remove the toner cartridge, and shake it. You will be able to hear if there's toner inside the cartridge. If it's empty, replace it with a known, good, manufacturer-recommended toner cartridge.

Another problem that crops up rather often is the problem of using refilled or reconditioned toner cartridges. During their recycling process, these cartridges may get filled with the wrong kind of toner (for example, one with an incorrect charge). This may cause toner to be repelled from the EP drum instead of attracted to it. Thus, there's no toner on the page because there was no toner on the EP drum to begin with. The solution is to replace the toner cartridge with the type recommended by the manufacturer.

A third problem related to toner cartridges happens when someone installs a new toner cartridge and forgets to remove the sealing tape that is present to keep the toner in the cartridge during shipping. The solution to this problem is as easy as it is obvious: Just remove the toner cartridge from the printer, remove the sealing tape, and reinstall the cartridge.

CORONA ASSEMBLY

The second cause of the blank pages is a damaged or missing corona wire. If there is a lost or damaged wire, the developed image won't transfer from the EP drum to the paper. Thus, no image appears on the printout. To determine if this is causing your problem, do the first half of the self-test (described later in this section). If there is an image on the drum but not on the paper, you will know that the corona assembly isn't doing its job.

To check if the corona assembly is causing the problem, open the cover and examine the wire (or roller, if your printer uses one). The corona wire is hard to see, so you may need a flashlight. You will know if it's broken or missing just by looking (it will either be in pieces or just not there). If it's not broken or missing, the problem may be related to the HVPS.

The corona wire (or roller) is a relatively inexpensive part and can be easily replaced with the removal of two screws and some patience.

HIGH-VOLTAGE POWER SUPPLY

The HVPS supplies high-voltage, low-current power to both the charging and transfer corona assemblies in laser and page printers. If it's broken, neither will work properly. If the self-test shows an image on the drum but none on the paper, and the corona assembly is present and not damaged, then the HVPS is at fault.

All Black Pages

This happens when the charging unit (the charging corona wire or charging corona roller) in the toner cartridge malfunctions and fails to place a charge on the EP drum. Because the drum is grounded, it has no charge. Anything with a charge (like toner) will stick to it. As the drum rotates, all the toner will be transferred to the page and a black page is formed.

This problem wastes quite a bit of toner, but it can be fixed easily. The solution (again) is to replace the toner cartridge with a known, good, manufacturer-recommended one. If that doesn't solve the problem, then the HVPS is at fault (it's not providing the high voltage that the charging corona needs to function).

Repetitive Small Marks or Defects

Repetitive marks occur frequently in heavily used (as well as older) laser printers. The problem may be caused by toner spilled inside the printer. It can also be caused by a crack or chip in the EP drum (this mainly happens with recycled cartridges). These cracks can accumulate toner. In both cases, some of the toner will get stuck onto one of the rollers. Once this happens, every time the roller rotates and touches a piece of paper, it will leave toner smudges spaced a roller circumference apart.

The solution is simple: Clean or replace the offending roller. To help you figure out which roller is causing the problem, the service manuals contain a chart like the one in Figure 5.14. To use the chart, place the printed page next to the chart. Align the first occurrence of the "smudge" with the top arrow. The next smudge will line up with one of the other arrows. The arrow it lines up with tells which roller is causing the problem.

FIGURE 5.14: Laser printer roller circumference chart

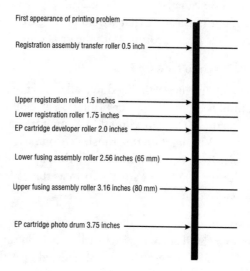

NOTE Remember that the chart in Figure 5.14 is only an example. Your printer may have different size rollers (and thus need a different chart). Check your printer's service documentation for a chart like this. It is valuable in determining which roller is causing a smudge.

Vertical Black Lines on Page

A groove or scratch in the EP drum can cause the problem of vertical black lines running down all or part of the page. Since a scratch is "lower" than the surface, it doesn't receive as much (if any) of a charge as the other areas. The result is that toner will stick to it as though it were discharged. Since the groove may go around the circumference of the drum, the line may go all the way down the page.

Another possible cause of vertical black lines is a dirty charge corona wire. A dirty charge corona wire will prevent a sufficient charge from being placed on the EP drum. Since the EP drum will be almost zero, toner will stick to the areas that correspond to the dirty areas on the charge corona wire.

The solution to the first problem is, as always, to replace the toner cartridge (or EP drum if your printer uses a separate EP drum and toner). You can also solve the second problem with a new toner cartridge, but in this case that would be an extreme solution. It's easier to clean the charge corona with the brush supplied with the cartridge.

Vertical White Line on Page

Vertical white lines running down all or part of the page are relatively common problems on older printers, especially ones that see little maintenance. They are caused by some foreign matter (more than likely toner) caught on the transfer corona wire. The dirty spots keep the toner from being transmitted to the paper (at those locations, that is), with the result that streaks form as the paper progresses past the transfer corona wire.

The solution is to clean the corona wires. LaserJet Series II printers contain a small corona wire brush to help in this procedure. It's usually a small, green-handled brush located near the transfer corona wire. To use it, remove the toner cartridge and run the brush in the charge corona groove on top of the toner cartridge. Replace the cartridge and use the brush to brush away any foreign deposits on the transfer corona. Be sure to put it back in its holder when you're finished.

Image Smudging

If you can pick up a sheet from a laser printer, run your thumb across it, and have the image come off on your thumb, then you have a fuser problem. The fuser isn't heating the toner and fusing it into the paper. This could be caused by a number of things—but all of them would be taken care of with a fuser replacement. For example, if the halogen light inside the heating roller has burned out, that would cause the problem. The solution is to replace the fuser. The fuser can be replaced with a rebuilt unit, if you prefer. Rebuilt fusers are almost as good as new fusers, and some even come with guarantees. Plus, they cost less.

TIP   The whole fuser may not need to be replaced. Fuser components can be ordered from parts suppliers and can be rebuilt by you. For example, if the fuser has a bad lamp, you can order a lamp and replace it in the fuser.

Another problem similar to this is when there are small areas of smudging that repeat themselves down the page. Dents or "cold spots" in the fuser heat roller cause this problem. The only solution is to replace either the fuser assembly or the heat roller.

Ghosting

Ghosting is what you have when you can see light images of previously printed pages on the current page. This is caused by one of two things: bad erasure lamps or a broken cleaning blade. If the erasure lamps are bad, the previous electrostatic discharges aren't completely wiped away. When the EP drum rotates towards the developing roller, some toner will stick to the slightly discharged areas. A broken cleaning blade, on the other hand, causes old toner to build up on the EP drum and consequently present itself in the next printed image.

Replacing the toner cartridge solves the second problem. Solving the first problem involves replacing the erasure lamps in the printer. Since the toner cartridge is the least expensive cure, you should try that first. Usually, replacing the toner cartridge will solve the problem. If it doesn't, you will then have to replace the erasure lamps.

Printer Prints Pages of Garbage

This has happened to everyone at least once. You print a one-page letter and 10 pages of what looks to be garbage come out of the printer. This problem comes from one of two different sources: the print driver software or the formatter board.

PRINTER DRIVER

The correct printer driver needs to be installed for the printer you have. For example, if you have a HP LaserJet III, then that is the driver you need to install. Once the driver has been installed, it must be configured for the correct page description language: PCL or PostScript. Most HP LaserJet printers use PCL (but can be configured for PostScript). Determine what page description your printer has been configured for and set the print driver to the same setting. If this is not done, you will get garbage out of the printer.

TIP   Most printers that have LCD displays will indicate that they are in PostScript mode with a "PS" or "PostScript" somewhere in the display.

If the problem is the wrong driver setting, the "garbage" that the printer prints will look like English. That is, the words will be readable, but they won't make any sense.

FORMATTER BOARD

The other cause of several pages of garbage being printed is a bad formatter board. This circuit board takes the information that the printer receives from the computer and turns it into commands for the various components in the printer. Usually problems with the formatter board produce wavy lines of print or random patterns of dots on the page.

It's relatively easy to replace the formatter board in a laser printer. Usually this board is installed underneath the printer and can be removed by loosening two screws and pulling the board out. Typically, replacing the formatter board also replaces the printer interface; another possible source of "garbage" printouts.

HP LaserJet Testing

Now that we've defined some of the possible sources of problems with laser printers, let's discuss a few of the testing procedures that you use with laser printers. We'll discuss HP LaserJet laser printers since they are the most popular types of laser printer, but the topics covered here can be applied to other types of laser printers as well.

When you troubleshoot laser printers, there are three tests you can perform on the printer to narrow down which assembly is causing the problem. (These tests are internal diagnostics for the printers and are included with most laser printers.)

Self-Tests

The three significant printer self-tests—tests that the printer runs on its own (albeit when directed by the user)—are the engine self-test, the print engine half self-test, and the secret self-test.

Engine self-test   The engine self-test checks the print engine of the LaserJet, bypassing the formatter board. This test will cause the printer to print a single page with vertical lines running its length. If an engine self-test can be performed, you will know that the laser print engine can print successfully. To perform an engine self-test, you must press the printer's self-test button, which is hidden behind a small cover on the side of the printer. The location of the button varies from printer to printer, so you may have to refer to the printer manual. Using a pencil or probe, press the button and the print engine will start printing the test page.

Half self-test   A print engine half self-test is performed the same as the self-test, but you interrupt it halfway through the print cycle by opening the cover. This is useful in determining which part of the print process is causing the printer to malfunction. If you stop the print process and part of a developed image is still on the EP drum and part has been transferred to the paper, you know that the pickup rollers, registration rollers, laser scanner, charging roller, EP drum, and transfer roller are all working correctly. You can stop the half self-test at various points in the print process to determine the source of a malfunction.

Secret self-test   To activate this test, you must first put the printer into service mode. To accomplish this, turn the printer on while simultaneously holding down the On Line, Continue, and Enter buttons (that's the first secret part, because nobody knows it unless somebody tells them). When the screen comes up blank, release the keys and press, in order, Continue, then Enter. The printer will perform an internal self-test and then display "00 READY." At this point, you are ready to initiate the rest of the secret self-test by taking the printer offline and pressing the Test button on the front panel and holding it until you see the "04 Self-Test" message. When you see this message, release the Test button. This will cause the printer to print one self-test page. (If you want a continuous printout, then instead of releasing the Test button at the "04 Self-Test" message, keep holding the Test button down until the message "05 Self-Test" is displayed. The printer will print continuous self-test pages until you power off the printer or hit On Line, or until the printer runs out of paper.)

Error Codes

In addition to the self-tests, you have another tool for troubleshooting HP laser printers. Error codes are a way for the LaserJet to tell the user (and a service technician) what's wrong. Table 5.2 details some of the most common codes displayed on an HP LaserJet.

TABLE 5.2: HP LaserJet Error Messages

Message	Description
00 Ready	The printer is in standby mode and ready to print.
02 Warming Up	The fuser is being warmed up before the 00 Ready state.
05 Self-Test	A full self-test has been initiated from the front panel.
11 Paper Out	The paper tray sensor is reporting that there is no paper in the paper tray. The printer will not print as long as this error exists.
13 Paper Jam	A piece of paper is caught in the paper path. To fix, open the cover and clear the jam (including all pieces of the jam). Close the cover to resume printing. The printer will not print as long as this error exists.
14 No EP Cart	There is no EP cartridge (toner cartridge) installed in the printer. The printer will not print as long as this error exists.
15 Engine Test	An engine self-test is in progress.
16 Toner Low	The toner cartridge is almost out of toner. Replacement will be necessary soon.
50 Service	A fuser error has occurred, most commonly caused by fuser lamp failure. Power off the printer and replace the fuser to solve the problem. The printer will not print as long as this error exists.
51 Error	Laser scanning assembly problem. Test and replace, if necessary. The printer will not print as long as this error exists.
52 Error	The scanner motor in the laser scanning assembly is malfunctioning. Test and replace as per service manual. The printer will not print as long as this error exists.

TABLE 5.2: HP LaserJet Error Messages *(continued)*

Message	Description
55 Error	Communication problem between the formatter and the DC controller. Test and replace as per service manual. The printer will not print as long as this error exists.

Troubleshooting Tips for HP LaserJet Printers

There is a set of troubleshooting steps that are usually used by printer technicians to help them solve HP LaserJet printing problems. Let's detail each of them to bring our discussion of laser printer troubleshooting to a close.

1. **Is the exhaust fan operational?** This is the first component to receive power when the printer is turned on. If you can feel air coming out of the exhaust fan, this confirms that AC voltage is present and power is turned on, that +5Vdc and +24Vdc are being generated by the AC power supply (ACPS), and that the DC controller is functional. If there is no power to the printer (no lights, fan not operating), the ACPS is at fault. Replacement involves removing all printer covers and removing four screws. You can purchase new ACPS modules, but it is usually cheaper to replace it with a rebuilt unit.

2. **Do the control panel LEDs work?** This means that the formatter board can communicate with control panel. If the LEDs do not light, it could mean that the formatter board is bad, the control panel is bad, or the wires connecting the two are broken or shorting out.

3. **Does the main motor rotate at power up?** Turn the power off. Remove the covers from the side of the printer. Turn the printer back on and carefully watch and listen for main motor rotation. If you see and hear the main motor rotating, this indicates that the toner cartridge is installed, all photosensors are functional, all motors are functional, and the printer can move paper (assuming there are no obstructions).

4. **Does the fuser heat lamp light up after the main motor finishes its rotation?** You will need to have the covers removed to notice. The heat lamp should light after the main motor rotation and stay lit until the control panel says "00 Ready."

5. **Can the printer perform an engine test print?** A sheet of vertical lines indicates that the print engine works. This test print bypasses the formatter board and will indicate if the print problem resides in the engine or not. If the test print is successful, the engine can be ruled out as a source of the problem. If the test print fails, you will have to further troubleshoot the printer to determine which engine component is causing the problem.

6. **Can the printer perform a control panel self-test?** This is the final test to ensure printer operation. If you can press the "Test Page" control panel button and receive a test printout, this means the entire printer is working properly. The only possibilities for problems would be outside the printer (i.e., interfaces, cables, and software problems).

Exam Essentials

Know the common printing problems listed.   Understand the most common problems that occur in an environment.

Know the possible fixes for the common problem types.   Each type of printer has its own common issues. Be familiar with the most likely repair options for each common problem.

Key Terms and Concepts

High-voltage power supply   The HVPS supplies high-voltage, low-current power to both the charging and transfer corona assemblies in laser and page printers.

Image smudging   Image smudging occurs when the toner is not properly fused to the paper. The text or graphics that were printed can be smudged by wiping a finger across it.

Ghosting   Ghosting is what you have when you can see light images of previously printed pages on the current page.

Printer driver   The printer driver is a software component that allows the application to interface with the hardware of a printer.

Formatter board   This circuit board takes the information that the printer receives from the computer and turns it into commands for the various components in the printer.

Chapter

6

Domain 6.0 Basic Networking

COMPTIA A+ EXAM OBJECTIVES COVERED IN THIS CHAPTER:

▶ 6.1 Identify basic networking concepts, including how a network works and the ramifications of repairs on the network. *(pages 242 – 287)*
- Installing and configuring network cards
- Network access
- Full-duplex, half-duplex
- Cabling—twisted pair, coaxial, fiber optic, RS-232
- Ways to network a PC
- Physical network topographies
- Increasing bandwidth
- Loss of data
- Network slowdown
- Infrared
- Hardware protocols

he A+ exam will test your basic networking skills—those skills needed to effectively troubleshoot and repair desktop PCs in a corporate environment. To pass the test and be effective in your troubleshooting, you will need to understand the basic concepts and terminology in this chapter. A good deal of this information—especially the concepts listed in the Open Systems Interconnect networking model—is for information purposes only. For the exam, spend more time on learning the different types of cables and connectors. If you find the more in-depth information interesting, consider pursuing your CompTIA Network+ Certificate.

6.1 Identify basic networking concepts, including how a network works and the ramifications of repairs on the network.

- Installing and configuring network cards
- Network access
- Full-duplex, half-duplex
- Cabling—twisted pair, coaxial, fiber optic, RS-232
- Ways to network a PC
- Physical network topographies
- Increasing bandwidth
- Loss of data
- Network slowdown
- Infrared
- Hardware protocols

This chapter focuses on the basic concepts surrounding how a network works, including the way it sends information and what it uses to send information. This information is covered only to a minor degree by the A+ certification exam. However, if you have interest in becoming a service technician, this information will prove to be very useful, as you will in all likelihood be asked to troubleshoot both hardware and software problems on existing networks. Included in this chapter is information on the following topics:

- What is a network?

- Network types

- Media types

- Connectivity devices

NOTE If you find that the material in this chapter interests you, you might consider studying for, and eventually taking, CompTIA's Network+ exam. It is a generic networking certification (similar to A+, except that it is for network-related topics). You can study for it using Sybex's Network+ Study Guide materials available at www.sybex.com.

Critical Information

Since I entered the workforce in 1988, things have changed dramatically. My first job was working as a sales/service representative for a local IBM retailer. Back then, personal computers were not used for area businesses. My largest customer was one of the largest multinational pharmaceutical companies. At that time, IBM Personal Wheel Writers littered the desktops, and dumb terminals were on every fifth desk. When I began working in the Information Systems industry, my travels took me back to the same desktops nearly 10 years later. I had to chuckle to myself every time I bumped into one of the dinosaurs that had IBM convinced that the PC would never become a prolific item in a business environment.

Now that same pharmaceutical company has a PC on every desktop connected to Microsoft, Novell, DEC, and IBM mainframe networks.

The in-baskets that used to be stacked several inches high with yellow inter-company mail folders are gone, replaced with Lotus Notes, Microsoft Chat, and other communication software. Now instead of large pools of secretaries typing, you see only a few. Executives wearing headsets can be seen "talking instead of typing" into voice-recognition software.

Once when I was called onsite to modify some shipping software and place it on an application server, I realized just how far that business had come in such a short period. At the age of 32, I suddenly felt old.

Networking

Stand-alone personal computers, first introduced in the late 1970s, gave users the ability to create documents, spreadsheets, and other types of data and save them for future use. For the small business user or home computer enthusiast, this was great. For larger companies, however, it was not enough. The larger the company, the greater the need to share information between offices—and sometimes over great distances. The stand-alone computer was inadequate for the following reasons:

- Their small hard drives were inefficient.

- To print, each computer required a printer attached locally.

- Sharing documents was cumbersome. People grew tired of having to save to a disk, then taking that disk to the recipient.

- There was no e-mail. Instead, there was interoffice mail, which was not reliable and frequently was not delivered in a timely manner.

What Is a Network?

To address these problems, networks were born. A *network* links two or more computers together to communicate and share resources. Their success was a revelation to the computer industry as well as businesses. Now, departments could be linked internally to offer better performance and increase efficiency.

You have heard the term "networking" in the business context, where people come together and exchange names for future contact and to get access to more resources. The same scenario is true with a computer network. A computer network allows computers to link to each other's resources. For example, in a network every computer would not need a printer connected locally to print. Instead, one computer would have a printer connected to it and allow the other computers to access this resource. Because they allow users to share resources, networks offer an increase in performance as well as a decrease in the outlay for new hardware and software.

LANs vs. WANs

Local Area Networks (LANs) were introduced to connect computers in a single office. Wide Area Networks (WANs) expand the LANs to include networks outside of the local environment and also to distribute resources across distances. Today, LANs can be seen in most businesses, from small to large. WANs are widely accepted, as businesses are more mobile and spanning greater distances. It is important to have an understanding of LANs and WANs as a service professional, because when you're repairing computers, you are likely to come in contact with problems that are associated with the computer being connected to a network.

Local Area Networks

The 1970s brought us the mini-mainframe computer, which was a smaller version of the mainframe. Like the mainframe computers, mini-mainframe computers utilize centralized processing. Centralized processing is the concept that all work done to the data, such as calculations and queries, is performed by the mainframe or minicomputer. The dumb terminals that sit on each user's desktop are merely devices used to view and enter commands. They should be thought of as TV sets to watch what is taking place on the centralized processor rather than as computers.

With the introduction of network operating systems such as Novell NetWare, LANtastic, and Microsoft LAN Manager, microcomputer networking was born. Microcomputer networking uses distributed processing rather than centralized processing. Distributed processing is much more scalable than centralized processing since adding additional clients or workstations does not affect the application's performance as much. The difference is that a special PC, referred to as a *server*, provides a place to house data that is processed by the local PC, known as a *client*, where the user is working. Server PCs are nothing more than high-performance PCs with increased processor, memory, and disk space resources.

With the introduction of microcomputer networking, the cable that connected each device (computer or network device, also referred to as a *node*) began to change. First came the variants of coaxial cable, then came the introduction of twisted pair and fiber optic cable (we'll explain the types of cable in more detail later in this chapter). Figure 6.1 shows an example of a simple LAN.

FIGURE 6.1: A simple LAN

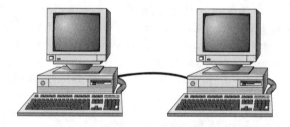

One important exception in the server's role is application serving and Windows-based thin clients. Application servers normally house large databases and do some or all of the processing, such as calculations or queries on the data housed in the database. Examples of application servers are company databases and/or business-management software housed in Microsoft SQL or Oracle databases.

With the introduction of Citrix products, such as Win Frame and Meta Frame, and Microsoft Terminal server, centralized processing has come back into style like baggy bell-bottom jeans. Thin client environments utilize beefed-up servers and clients that in most cases have no disk storage. The server does all processing and data storage, while the Windows-based thin clients merely process the images to be viewed on the monitor at each station.

Wide Area Networks

By the late 1980s, networks were expanding to cover ranges considered geographical in size. Wide Area Networks, first implemented with mainframes at massive government expense, started attracting PC users as networks went to this whole new level. Businesses with offices across the country communicated as if they were only desks apart. Soon the whole world would see a change in its way of doing business, across not just a few miles but across countries. Whereas LANs are limited to single buildings, WANs are able to span buildings, states, countries, and even continental boundaries. Figure 6.2 gives an example of a simple WAN.

FIGURE 6.2: A simple WAN

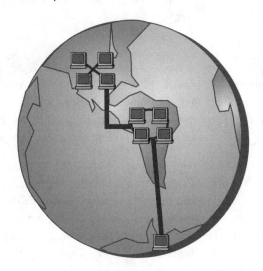

Networks of today and tomorrow are no longer limited by the inability of LANs to cover distance and handle mobility. WANs play an important role in the future development of corporate networks worldwide. Although the primary focus of this chapter is LANs, we will feature a section on WAN connectivity. This section will briefly explain the current technologies and what you should expect to see in the future. If you are interested in more information on LANs or WANs, or if you plan on becoming a networking technician, check your local library resources or the Internet.

Primary Network Components

Putting together a network is not as simple as it was with the first PC network. You can no longer consider two computers cabled together a fully functional network. Today, networks consist of three primary components:

- Servers
- Clients or workstations
- Resources

No network would be complete without these three components working together.

Servers

Servers come in many shapes and sizes. The server is a core component of the network, providing a link to the resources necessary to perform any task. The link it provides could be to a resource existing on the server itself or a resource on a client computer. The server is the "indentured servant," filling the client computer's request for resources.

Servers offer networks the capability of centralizing the control of resources and can thus reduce administrative difficulties. They can be used to distribute processes for balancing the load on the computers, thereby increasing speed and performance. They can also departmentalize files for improved reliability. That way, if one server goes down, not all of the files are lost.

Servers perform several tasks. For example, servers that provide files to the users on the network are called *file servers*. Likewise, servers that host printing services for users are called *print servers*. (There are other tasks as well, such as remote access services, administration, mail, etc.) Servers can be multi-purpose or single-purpose. If they are multi-purpose, they can be, for example, both a file server and a print server at the same time. If the server is a single-purpose server, it is a file server only or a print server only.

With the expansion of microcomputer networks, two big competitors, Microsoft and Novell, emerged. They had very different views on what a server should and should not do. With Microsoft Windows NT, the server console could be used as a workstation, but this practice should not be encouraged because of the importance of the server.

Novell believed that the server should not be a fully functional workstation and did not provide any type of graphical interface to allow the addition of standard applications on the server's console. Both companies have changed their views slightly. Novell NetWare 5.*x* and above now has a more graphical interface, and Microsoft has changed Windows 2000's default system security to allow users to log on locally. Their original views lead to a somewhat fuzzy classification of server types, as *dedicated* and *nondedicated.*

NONDEDICATED SERVERS

These are assigned to provide one or more network services *and* local access. A nondedicated server is expected to be slightly more flexible in its day-to-day use than a dedicated server. Nondedicated servers can be used not only to serve client requests and perform administrative actions, but often to serve as a front end for the administrator to work with other applications or services. The nondedicated server is not really what some would consider a true server, because it can act as a workstation as well as a server.

DEDICATED SERVERS

These are assigned to provide specific applications or services for the network and nothing else. Because a dedicated server specializes in only a few tasks, it requires fewer resources from the computer that is hosting it than a nondedicated server might require. This savings in overhead may translate to a certain efficiency and can thus be considered as having a beneficial impact on network performance.

Many networks use both dedicated and nondedicated servers in order to incorporate the best of both worlds, offering improved network performance with the dedicated servers and flexibility with the non-dedicated servers.

Workstations or Client Computers

Workstations are the computers on which the users on a network do their work, such as word processing, database design, graphic design, e-mail, and other office or personal tasks. Workstations are basically nothing more than an everyday computer, except for the fact that they are connected to a network that offers additional resources. Workstations can range from a diskless thin client to a desktop system. As clients, they are allowed to communicate with the servers in the network in order to use the network's resources.

It takes several items to turn a workstation into a client. You must install a network interface card (NIC), a special expansion card that allows the PC to talk on a network. You must connect it to a cabling system that connects to another computer (or several other computers). And you must install some special software, called *client software*, which allows the computer to talk to the servers. Once you've accomplished all this, the computer will be "on the network."

To the client, the server may be nothing more than just another drive letter. However, because it is in a network environment, the client is able to use the server as a doorway to more storage or more applications or to communicate with other computers or other networks. To a user, being on a network changes a few things:

- They can store more information, because they can now store data on other computers on the network.

- They can now share and receive information from other users, perhaps even collaborating on the same document.

- They can use programs that would be too large for their computer to use by itself.

Network Resources

We now have the server to share the resources and the workstation to use them, but what about the resources themselves? A *resource* (as far as the network is concerned) is any item that can be used on a network. Resources can include a broad range of items, but the most important ones include the following:

- Printers and other peripherals

- Files

- Applications

- Disk storage

When an office can purchase paper, ribbons, toner, or other consumables for only one, two, or maybe three printers for the entire office, the costs are dramatically lower than the costs for supplying these items to printers at every workstation. Networks also give more storage space to files. Client computers are not always able to handle the overhead involved in storing large files (for example, database files) because they are already heavily involved in the day-to-day work activities of the users. Because servers in a network can be dedicated to only certain functions, a server could be allocated to store all the larger files that are worked with every day, freeing up disk space on client computers. Similarly, applications (programs) no longer need to be on every computer in the office. If the server is capable of handling the overhead an application requires, the application could reside on the server and be used by workstations through a network connection.

Network Operating Systems

PCs use a disk operating system that controls the file system and how the applications communicate with the hard disk. Networks use a network operating system (NOS) to control the communication with resources and the flow of data across the network. The NOS runs on the server. Many companies offer software to start a network. Some of the more popular network operating systems at this time include

Unix, Novell NetWare, and Microsoft Windows 2000 Server. Although several other network operating systems exist, these three are the most popular.

NOTE Microsoft Windows NT 3.51 and 4.0 are still very abundant in today's businesses; however, Microsoft stopped supporting the software as of 01-01-2001. Another mentionable NOS is Linux. Although it has a long way to go before the interface is as comfortable to use as other products, it has become the NOS of choice for Internet Service Providers (ISPs). A recent report showed that nearly 80 percent of local and regional ISPs use Linux. Within the past two years, its growth has been amazing. Yet in the business world, where support and program compatibility are major decision factors, it has not had any noticeable effect on Microsoft's market domination.

Back in the early days of mainframes, it took a full staff of people working around the clock to keep the machines going. With today's NOSes, servers are able to monitor memory, CPU time, disk space, and peripherals, without a baby-sitter. Each of these operating systems allows processes to respond in a certain way with the processor.

With the new functionality of LANs and WANs, you can be sitting in your office in Milwaukee and carry on a real-time electronic "chat" with a coworker in France, or maybe print an invoice at the home office in California, or manage someone else's computer from your own while they are on vacation. Gone are the days of passing disks, phone messages left but not received, or having to wait a month to receive a letter from someone in Hong Kong. NOSes provide this functionality on a network.

Network Resource Access

Now that we have discussed the makeup of a typical network, let's discuss the way resources are accessed on a network. There are generally two resource access models: peer-to-peer and server-based. It is important to choose the appropriate model. How do you decide what type of resource model is needed? You must first think about the following questions.

- What is the size of the organization?
- How much security does the company require?
- What software or hardware does the resource require?
- How much administration does it need?
- How much will it cost?
- Will this resource meet the needs of the organization today and in the future?
- Will additional training be needed?

Networks today cannot just be put together at the drop of a hat. A lot of planning is required before implementation of a network to ensure that whatever design is chosen will be effective and efficient—and not just for today but for the future as well. In each network, it is important to develop a plan to answer the previous questions. The answers will help decide the type of resource model to be used.

Peer-to-Peer Networks

A *peer-to-peer network* is a network where the computers act as both workstations and servers. An example of a peer-to-peer resource model is shown in Figure 6.3.

FIGURE 6.3: The peer-to-peer resource model

Peer-to-peer networks are great for small, simple, and inexpensive networks. In fact, this model can be set up almost immediately, with little extra hardware required. Windows 9x, Windows ME, Windows 2000, and Windows NT are popular operating system environments that support a peer-to-peer resource model.

There is no centralized administration or control in the peer-to-peer resource model. However, this very lack of centralized control can make it difficult to administer the network; for the same reason, it's not very secure. Moreover, because each computer is acting as both a workstation and server, it may not be easy to locate the resources. The person who is in charge of the file may have moved it without anyone's knowledge. Also, the users who work under this arrangement need more training, because they are not only users but also administrators.

Server-Based Resource Model

The *server-based model* is better than the peer-to-peer model for large networks (more than 10 users) that need a more secure environment and centralized control. Server-based networks use a dedicated, centralized server. All administrative functions and resource sharing are performed from this point. This makes it easier to share resources, perform backups, and support an almost unlimited number of users. It also offers better security. However, it does need more hardware than that used by the typical workstation/server computer in a peer-to-peer resource model. Additionally, it requires specialized software (the NOS) to manage the server's role in the environment. With the addition of a server and the NOS, server-based networks can easily cost more than peer-to-peer resource models. However, for large networks, it's the only choice. An example of a server-based resource model is shown in Figure 6.4.

FIGURE 6.4: The server-based resource model

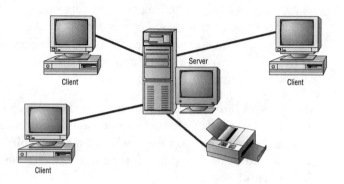

Server-based resource models are the desired models for companies that are continually growing or that need to initially support a large environment. Server-based networks offer the flexibility to add more resources and clients almost indefinitely into the future. Hardware costs may be more, but, with the centralized administration, managing resources becomes less time-consuming. Also, only a few administrators need to be trained, and users are responsible for only their own work environment.

TIP If you are looking for an inexpensive, simple network with very little setup required, and there is really no need for the company to grow in the future, then the peer-to-peer network is the way to go. If you are looking for a network to support many users (more than 10), strong security, and centralized administration, consider the server-based network your only choice.

A network is not something you can just "throw together." You don't want to find out a few months down the road that the type of network you chose does not meet the needs of the company. This could be a time-consuming and costly mistake.

Network Topologies

A *topology* is a way of "laying out" the network. Topologies can be either physical or logical. *Physical topologies* describe how the cables are run. *Logical topologies* describe how the network messages travel. Deciding which type of topology to use is the next step when designing your network.

You must choose the appropriate topology in which to arrange your network. Each type differs by its cost, ease of installation, fault tolerance (how the topology handles problems like cable breaks), and ease of reconfiguration (like adding a new workstation to the existing network).

There are five primary topologies (some of which can be both logical and physical topologies):

- Bus (can be both logical and physical)
- Star (physical only)
- Ring (can be both logical and physical)
- Mesh (can be both logical and physical)
- Hybrid (usually physical)

Each topology has its advantages and disadvantages. At the end of this section, check out the table that summarizes the advantages and disadvantages of each topology.

Bus

A *bus* is the simplest physical topology. It consists of a single cable that runs to every workstation, as shown in Figure 6.5. This topology uses the least amount of cabling but also covers the shortest distance. Each computer shares the same data and address path. With a logical bus topology, messages pass through the trunk, and each workstation checks to see if the message is addressed to itself. If the address of the message matches the workstation's address, the network adapter copies the message to the card's on-board memory.

FIGURE 6.5: The bus topology

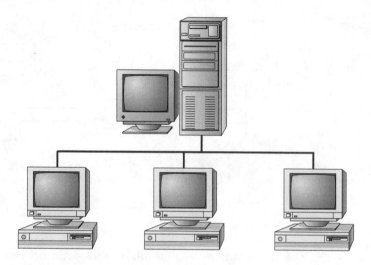

Cable systems that use the bus topology are easy to install. You run a cable from the first computer to the last computer. All the remaining computers attach to the cable somewhere in between. Because of the simplicity of installation, and because of the low cost of the cable, bus topology cabling systems (such as Ethernet) are the cheapest to install.

Although the bus topology uses the least amount of cabling, it is difficult to add a workstation. If you want to add another workstation, you have to completely reroute the cable and possibly run two additional lengths of it. Also, if any one of the cables breaks, the entire network is disrupted. Therefore, it is very expensive to maintain.

Star

A *physical star topology* branches each network device off a central device called a *hub*, making it very easy to add a new workstation. Also, if any workstation goes down, it does not affect the entire network. (But, as you might expect, if the central device goes down, the entire network goes down.) Some types of Ethernet and ARCNet use a physical star topology. Figure 6.6 gives an example of the organization of the star network.

FIGURE 6.6: The star topology

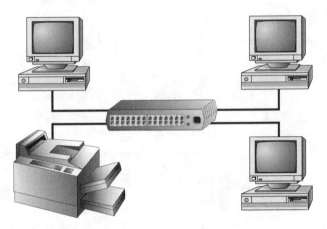

Star topologies are easy to install. A cable is run from each work-station to the hub. The hub is placed in a central location in the office (for example, a utility closet). Star topologies are more expensive to install than bus networks because there are several more cables that need to be installed, in addition to the cost of the hubs that are needed.

Ring

A *physical ring topology* is a unique topology. Each computer connects to two other computers, joining them in a circle, creating a unidirectional path where messages move from workstation to workstation. Each entity participating in the ring reads a message, then regenerates it and hands it to its neighbor on a different network cable. See Figure 6.7 for an example of a ring topology.

FIGURE 6.7: The ring topology

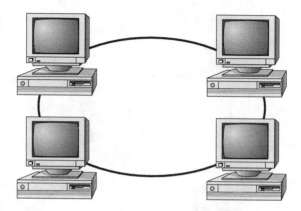

The ring makes it difficult to add new computers. Unlike a star topology network, the ring topology network will go down if one entity is removed from the ring. Few physical ring topology systems still exist, mainly because the hardware involved was fairly expensive and the fault tolerance was very low. However, one type of logical ring still exists: IBM's Token Ring technology. We'll discuss this technology later in the "Network Architectures" section.

Mesh

The *mesh topology* is the simplest logical topology, in terms of data flow, but it is the most complex in terms of physical design. In this physical topology, each device is connected to every other device, as shown in Figure 6.8. This topology is rarely found in LANs, mainly because of the complexity of the cabling. If there are x computers, there will be $(x \times (x-1)) \div 2$ cables in the network. For example, if you have five computers in a mesh network, it will use $5 \times (5 - 1) \div 2$, which equals 10 cables. This complexity is compounded when you add another workstation. For example, your five-computer, 10-cable network will jump to 15 cables just by adding one more computer. Imagine how the person doing the cabling would feel if you told them you had to cable 50 computers in a mesh network—they'd have to come up with $50 \times (50 - 1) \div 2 = 1225$ cables!

FIGURE 6.8: The mesh topology

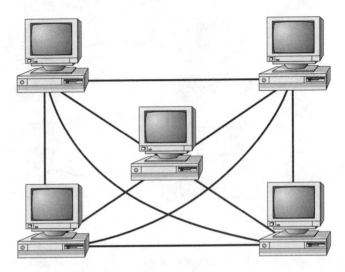

Because of its design, the physical mesh topology is very expensive to install and maintain. Cables must be run from each device to every other device. The advantage you gain from it is high fault tolerance. With a logical mesh topology, however, there will always be a way of getting the data from source to destination. It may not be able to take the direct route, but it can take an alternate, indirect route. It is for this reason that the mesh topology is still found in WANs to connect multiple sites across WAN links. It uses devices called *routers* to search multiple routes through the mesh and determine the best path. However, the mesh topology does become inefficient with five or more entities.

Hybrid

The *hybrid topology* is simply a mix of the other topologies. It would be impossible to illustrate it, because there are many combinations. In fact, most networks today are not only hybrid, but heterogeneous (by *heterogeneous* I mean they include a mix of components of different types and brands). The hybrid network may be more expensive, on the one hand, than some types of network topologies, but, on the other hand, it takes the best features of all the other topologies and exploits them. Believe it or not, this is almost the most popular topology (second only to the star topology).

Summary of Topologies

Table 6.1 summarizes the advantages and disadvantages of each type of network topology. This table is a good study aid for the A+ exam. (In other words, memorize it!)

TABLE 6.1: Topologies—Advantages and Disadvantages

Topology	Advantages	Disadvantages
Bus	Cheap. Easy to install.	Difficult to reconfigure. Break in bus disables entire network.
Star	Cheap. Easy to install. Easy to reconfigure. Fault tolerant.	More expensive than bus.
Ring	Efficient. Easy to install.	Reconfiguration difficult. Very expensive.
Mesh	Simplest. Most fault tolerant.	Reconfiguration extremely difficult. Extremely expensive. Very complex.
Hybrid	Combines best features of each topology used.	Complex (less so than mesh, however).

Network Communications

You have chosen the type of network and arrangement (topology). Now the computers need to understand how to communicate. Network communications use protocols. A *protocol* is a set of rules that govern communications. Protocols detail what "language" the computers are speaking when they talk over a network. If two computers are going to communicate, they both must be using the same protocol.

There are different methods used to describe the different protocols. We will discuss two of the most common: the OSI model and the IEEE 802 standards.

OSI Model

The International Organization for Standardization introduced the *Open Systems Interconnection (OSI)* model to provide a common way of describing network protocols. They put together a seven-layer model providing a relationship between the stages of communication, with each layer adding to the layer above or below it.

NOTE This OSI model is just that—a model. It was introduced as a standard that software and hardware vendors could use to create cross-platform connectivity.

The theory behind the OSI model is that as transmission takes place, the higher layers pass data through the lower layers. As the data passes through a layer, the layer will tack its information (also called a *header*) onto the beginning of the information being transmitted until it reaches the bottom layer. At this point, the bottom layer sends the information out on the wire.

At the receiving end, the bottom layer receives the information, reads its information from its header, removes its header from the information, and then passes the remainder to the next highest layer. This procedure continues until the topmost layer receives the data that the sending computer sent.

The OSI model layers from top to bottom are listed here. We'll describe each of these layers from bottom to top, however. After the descriptions, we'll summarize the entire model.

- Application layer
- Presentation layer
- Session layer

- Transport layer
- Network layer
- Data Link layer
- Physical layer

TIP There are several mnemonics that will help you remember the layers (as well as their order). For example, a popular one that indicates the layers from top to bottom is "All People Seem To Need Data Processing." One that indicates the layers from bottom to top is "People Design Networks To Send Packets Accurately." (There's also "Please Do Not Trust Sales People Always.")

PHYSICAL LAYER

At the bottom of the OSI model is the Physical layer. This layer describes how the data gets transmitted over a physical medium. It defines how long each piece of data is and the translation of each into the electrical pulses that are sent over the wires. It decides whether data travels unidirectionally or bidirectionally across the hardware. It also relates electrical, optical, mechanical, and functional interfaces to the cable.

DATA LINK LAYER

The next layer is the Data Link layer. This layer arranges data into chunks called *frames*. Included in these chunks is control information indicating the beginning and end of the data stream. This layer is very important because it makes transmission easier and more manageable and allows for error checking within the data frames.

NETWORK LAYER

Addressing messages and translating logical addresses and names into physical addresses occurs at the Network layer. The Network layer is something like the traffic cop. It is able to judge the best network path for the data based on network conditions, priority, and other variables. This layer manages traffic through packet switching, routing, and controlling congestion of data.

TRANSPORT LAYER

The Transport layer signals "all clear" by making sure the data frames are error-free. It also controls the data flow and troubleshoots any problems with transmitting or receiving data frames. This layer's most important job is to provide error checking and reliable, end-to-end communications. It can also take several smaller messages and combine them into a single, larger message.

SESSION LAYER

The Session layer allows applications on different computers to establish, use, and end a session. A session is one virtual "conversation." For example, all the procedures needed to transfer a single file make up one session. Once the session is over, a new process is begun. It enables network procedures such as identifying passwords, logons, and network monitoring. It can also handle recovery from a network failure.

PRESENTATION LAYER

The look, or format, of the data, network security, and file transfers is determined by the Presentation layer. It performs protocol conversion and manages data compression. Data translation and encryption are handled at this layer. Also, the character set information is determined there. (The character set determines which numbers represent which alphanumeric characters.)

APPLICATION LAYER

Finally, the Application layer allows access to network services. This is the layer at which file services and print services operate. It also is the layer that workstations interact with, and it controls data flow and, if there are errors, recovery.

SUMMARY OF THE OSI MODEL

Figure 6.9 shows the complete OSI model. Note the relation of each layer to one another and the function of each layer. Also note that when data is sent from one computer to another, the transmission starts above the Application layer and passes down to the Physical layer. Each layer, as it receives information from the layer above, adds its own information and passes the amended packet to the next layer down. At the bottom, the Physical layer places the packet on the wire. The receiver does the exact opposite procedure. The Physical layer takes the packet off the wire, removes the Physical layer header, and transfers the information to the layer above. Each layer reads the information given to it by the transmitting counterpart layer, removes its header, and passes the remainder up the stack until the data being transmitted is received by the Application layer.

FIGURE 6.9: OSI model and characteristics

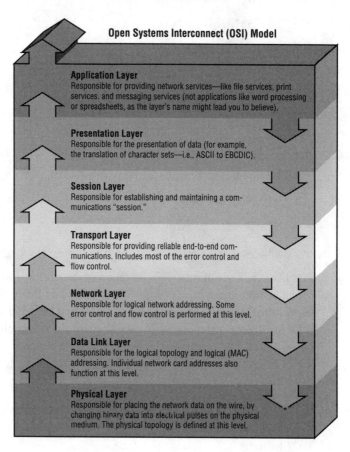

Open Systems Interconnect (OSI) Model

Application Layer
Responsible for providing network services—like file services, print services, and messaging services (not applications like word processing or spreadsheets, as the layer's name might lead you to believe).

Presentation Layer
Responsible for the presentation of data (for example, the translation of character sets—i.e., ASCII to EBCDIC).

Session Layer
Responsible for establishing and maintaining a communications "session."

Transport Layer
Responsible for providing reliable end-to-end communications. Includes most of the error control and flow control.

Network Layer
Responsible for logical network addressing. Some error control and flow control is performed at this level.

Data Link Layer
Responsible for the logical topology and logical (MAC) addressing. Individual network card addresses also function at this level.

Physical Layer
Responsible for placing the network data on the wire, by changing binary data into electrical pulses on the physical medium. The physical topology is defined at this level.

IEEE 802 Project Models

The Institute for Electrical and Electronics Engineers (IEEE) formed a subcommittee to create the 802 standards for networks. These standards specify certain types of networks, although not every network protocol is covered by the IEEE 802 committee specifications. This model breaks down into the following 12 categories:

- 802.1 Internetworking
- 802.2 Logic Link Control
- 802.3 CSMA/CD LAN
- 802.4 Token Bus LAN
- 802.5 Token Ring LAN
- 802.6 Metropolitan Area Network
- 802.7 Broadband Technical Advisory Group
- 802.8 Fiber Optic Technical Advisory Group
- 802.9 Integrated Voice/Data Networks
- 802.10 Network Security
- 802.11 Wireless Networks
- 802.12 Demand Priority Access LAN

The IEEE 802 standards were designed primarily for enhancements to the bottom three layers of the OSI model. The IEEE 802 model breaks the Data Link layer into two sublayers: a Logical Link Control (LLC) sublayer and a Media Access Control (MAC) sublayer. In the Logical Link Control sublayer, data link communications are managed. The Media Access Control sublayer watches out for data collisions and assigns physical addresses.

We will focus on the two predominant 802 models that existing network architectures have been based on: 802.3 CSMA/CD and 802.5 Token Ring.

IEEE 802.3 CSMA/CD

The 802.3 CSMA/CD model defines a bus topology network that uses a 50-ohm coaxial baseband cable and carries transmissions at 10Mbps. This standard groups data bits into frames and uses the Carrier Sense Multiple Access with Collision Detection (CSMA/CD) cable access method to put data on the cable.

CSMA/CD specifies that every computer can transmit at any time. As sometimes happens, when two machines transmit at the same time, a "collision" takes place and no data can be transmitted for either machine. The machines then back off for a random period of time and try to transmit again. This process repeats until transmission takes place successfully. The CSMA/CD technology is also called *contention*.

The only major downside to 802.3 is that with large networks (more than 100 computers on the same cable), the number of collisions increases to the point where there are more collisions than transmissions taking place.

An example of a protocol based on the IEEE 802.3 CSMA/CD standard is Ethernet.

NOTE   CSMA/CD and Ethernet are discussed in more detail later in this chapter.

IEEE 802.5 TOKEN RING

The IEEE 802.5 standard specifies a physical star, logical ring topology that uses a token-passing technology to put the data on the cable. IBM developed this technology for their mainframe and minicomputer networks. IBM's name for it was Token Ring. The name stuck, and any network using this type of technology is called a *Token Ring* network.

In token passing, a special chunk of data called a *token* circulates through the ring from computer to computer. Any computer that has data to transmit must wait for the token. A transmitting computer that has data to transmit waits for a "free" token and takes it off the ring. Once it has the token, this computer modifies it in such a way that tells the computers who has the token. The transmitting computer then places the token (along with the data it needs to transmit) on the ring and it travels around the ring until it gets to the destination computer. The destination computer takes the token and data off the wire, modifies the token (indicating that it has received the data), and places the token back on the wire. When the original sender receives the token back and sees that the destination computer has received the data, the sender modifies the token to set it "free." It then sends the token back on the ring and waits until it has more data to transmit.

The main advantage to the token-passing access method over contention (the 802.3 model) is that it eliminates collisions. Only workstations that have the token can transmit. It would seem that this technology has a lot of overhead and would be slow. But remember that this whole procedure takes place in a few milliseconds. This technology scales very well. It is not uncommon for Token Ring networks based on the IEEE 802.5 standard to reach hundreds of workstations on a single ring.

Network Architectures

Network architectures define the structure of the network, including hardware, software, and layout. We differentiate each architecture by the hardware and software required to maintain optimum performance levels. The major architectures in use today are Ethernet, Token Ring, ARCNet, and AppleTalk.

Ethernet

The original definition of the 802.3 model included a bus topology using a baseband coaxial cable. From this model came the first Ethernet architecture. Ethernet was originally co-developed by Digital, Intel, and Xerox and was known as *DIX Ethernet*.

Ethernet has several specifications, each one specifying the speed, communication method, and cable. The original Ethernet was given a designation of 10Base5. The "10" in Ethernet 10Base5 stands for the 10Mbps transmission rate. "Base" stands for the baseband communications used. Finally, the "5" stands for the maximum distance of 500 meters to carry transmissions. This method of identification soon caught on, and as vendors changed the specifications of the Ethernet architecture, they followed the same pattern in the way they identified them.

After the 10Base5 came 10Base2 and 10BaseT. These quickly became standards in Ethernet technology. Many other standards (including 100BaseF, 10BaseF, and 100BaseT) have developed since then. But those three are the most popular.

Ethernet 10Base2 uses thin coaxial cables and bus topology and transmits at 10Mbps, with a maximum distance of 200 meters. If that is the case, what does the Ethernet 10BaseT use? Actually, Ethernet 10BaseT uses twisted-pair cabling, transmitting at 10Mbps, with a maximum distance of 100 meters, and physical star topology with a logical bus topology.

Token Ring

Token Ring networks are exactly like the IEEE 802.5 specification because the specification is based on IBM's Token Ring technology. Token Ring uses a physical star, logical ring topology. All workstations are cabled to a central device, called a *multistation access unit* (*MAU*). The ring is created within the MAU by connecting every port together with special circuitry in the MAU. Token Ring can use shielded or unshielded cable and can transmit data at either 4Mbps or 16Mbps.

ARCNet

A special type of network architecture that deserves mention is the *Attached Resource Computer Network* (*ARCNet*). Developed in 1977, it was not based on any existing IEEE 802 model. However, ARCNet is important to mention because of its ties to IBM mainframe networks and also because of its popularity, which comes from its flexibility and price. It is flexible because its cabling uses large trunks and physical star configurations, so if a cable comes loose or is disconnected, the network will not fail. In addition, since it uses inexpensive coaxial cable, networks could be installed fairly cheaply.

Even though ARCNet enjoyed an initial success, it died out as other network architectures became more popular. The main reason for this was its slow transfer rate of only 2.5Mbps. Thomas-Conrad (a major developer of ARCNet products) did develop a version of ARCNet that runs at 100Mbps, but most people have abandoned ARCNet for other architectures. ARCNet is also not based on any standard, which makes it difficult to find compatible hardware from multiple vendors. Because of its speed and compatibility limitations, ARCNet is quickly being replaced in networks.

AppleTalk

Another architecture not based on any existing IEEE 802 models is AppleTalk. AppleTalk is a proprietary network architecture for Macintosh computers. It uses a bus and typically uses either shielded or unshielded cable. There are a few things to note about AppleTalk.

First, AppleTalk uses a Carrier Sense Multiple Access with Collision Avoidance (CSMA/CA) technology to put data on the cable. Unlike Ethernet, which uses a CSMA/CD method, this technology uses "smart" interface cards to detect traffic *before* it tries to send data. A CSMA/CA card will listen to the wire. If there is no traffic, it will send a small amount of data. If no collisions occur, it will follow that amount of data with the data it wants to transmit. In either case, if a collision does happen, it will back off for a random amount of time and try to transmit again.

A common analogy is used to describe the difference between CSMA/CD and CSMA/CA. Sending data is like walking across the street. With CSMA/CD you just cross the street. If you get run over, you go back and try again. With CSMA/CA you look both ways and send your little brother across the street. If he makes it, you can follow him. If either of you gets run over, you both go back and try again.

Another interesting point about AppleTalk is that it's fairly simple. Most Macintosh computers already include AppleTalk, so it is relatively inexpensive. It will assign itself an address. In its first revision (Phase I), it allowed a maximum of 32 devices on a network. With its second revision (Phase II), it supports faster speeds and multiple networks with EtherTalk and TokenTalk. EtherTalk allows AppleTalk network protocols to run on Ethernet coaxial cable (used for Mac II and above. TokenTalk allows the AppleTalk protocol to run on a Token Ring network.

Network Media

We have taken a look at the types of networks, network architectures, and the way a network communicates. To bring networks together, we use several types of media. A *medium* is the material on which data is transferred one point to another. There are two parts to the medium: the network interface card and the cabling. The type of network card you use depends on the type of cable you are using, so let's discuss cabling first.

Cabling

When the data is passing through the OSI model and reaches the Physical layer, it must find its way onto the medium that is used to physically transfer data from computer to computer. This medium is cable. It is the network interface card's role to prepare the data for transmission, but it is the cable's role to properly move the data to its intended destination. It is not as simple as just plugging it into the computer. The cabling you choose must support both the network architecture and topology. There are four main types of cabling methods: twisted-pair cable, coaxial cable, fiber optic cable, and wireless. We'll summarize all four cabling methods following the brief descriptions below.

Twisted-Pair

Twisted-pair is one of the most popular methods of cabling because of its flexibility and low costs. It consists of several pairs of wire twisted around each other within an insulated jacket, as shown in Figure 6.10. Twisted-pair is most often found in 10BaseT Ethernet networks, although other systems can use it.

FIGURE 6.10: Twisted-pair cable

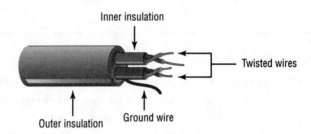

We usually break twisted-pair cabling into two types: unshielded twisted-pair (UTP) and shielded twisted-pair (STP). UTP is simply twisted-pair cabling that is unshielded. STP is the same as UTP except that STP has a braided foil shield around the twisted wires (to decrease electrical interference).

UTP comes in six grades to offer different levels of protection against electrical interference.

- Category 1 is for voice-only transmissions and is used in most phone systems today. It contains two twisted pairs.

- Category 2 is able to transmit data at speeds up to 4Mbps. It contains four twisted pairs of wires.

- Category 3 is able to transmit data at speeds up to 10Mbps. It contains four twisted pairs of wires with three twists per foot.

- Category 4 is able to transmit data at speeds up to 16Mbps. It contains four twisted pairs of wires.

- Category 5 is able to transmit data at speeds up to 100Mbps. It contains four twisted pairs of copper wire to give the most protection.

- Category 5e is able to transmit data at speeds up to 1Gbps. It also contains four twisted pairs of copper wire, but they are physically separated and contain more twists per foot than Category 5 to provide maximum interference protection.

Each of these six levels has a maximum transmission distance of 100 meters.

Coaxial

The next choice of cable for most LANs is coaxial cable. The cable consists of a copper wire surrounded by insulation and a metal foil shield, as shown in Figure 6.11. It is very similar to the cable used to connect cable television.

FIGURE 6.11: Coaxial cable

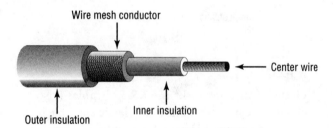

Coaxial cable comes in many thicknesses and types. The most common use for this type of cable is for Ethernet 10Base2 cabling. It is known as *Thinnet* or *Cheapernet*.

Fiber Optic

Fiber optic cabling has been called one of the best advances in cabling. It consists of a thin, flexible glass fiber surrounded by a rubberized outer coating (see Figure 6.12). It provides transmission speeds from 100Mbps up to 1Gbps and a maximum distance of several miles.

Because it uses pulses of light instead of electric voltages to transmit data, it is completely immune from electric interference and from wiretapping.

Fiber optic cable has not become a standard in networks, however, because of its high cost of installation. Networks that need extremely fast transmission rates, transmissions over long distances, or have had problems with electrical interference in the past often use fiber optic cabling.

FIGURE 6.12: Fiber optic cable

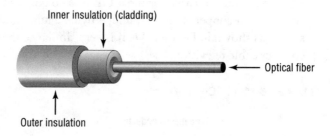

Inner insulation (cladding)

Optical fiber

Outer insulation

RS-232

Occasionally, networks use *RS-232* cables (also known as *serial cables*) to carry data. The most classic example is in older mainframe and minicomputer terminal connections. Connections from the individual terminals go to a device known as a *multiplexer* that combines the serial connections into one connection and connects all the terminals to the host computer. This cabling system is seen less and less as a viable LAN cabling method, however, because LAN connections (like twisted-pair Ethernet) are faster, more reliable, and easier to maintain.

Wireless Networks

One of the most fascinating cabling technologies today—and, actually, it's one that doesn't really *use* cable—is wireless. Wireless networks offer the ability to extend a LAN without the use of traditional cabling methods. Wireless transmissions are made through the air by infrared light, laser light, narrow-band radio, microwave, or spread-spectrum radio.

Wireless LANs are becoming increasingly popular as businesses are becoming more mobile and less centralized. You can see them most often in environments where standard cabling methods are not possible or wanted.

Wireless networks also make workstation relocation fast, easy, and cheap. Restructuring is a part of today's business. Corporations are bought and sold frequently. When a buyout occurs, the purchaser normally tries to centralize business services such as accounting, payroll, and human resources. Employees of the purchased company are relocated, and cubicles are disassembled and moved. From the IS standpoint, existing networks are incorporated or migrated to allow communication between the two entities.

With wireless networks, cable relocation is obsolete. Vast amounts of money are not expended on upgrading or relocating jacks and wall outlets. Another thing to consider is point of failure. Critics of wireless networks state that wireless is less reliable because of interference. These people have not supported a 2,000-user network on a Monday morning after cleaning crews have butchered, unplugged, or bumped a static-charged vacuum cleaner into a patch cable. Wireless networks utilize encryption to prevent eavesdropping; however, anytime you use unbound media, your data is somewhat vulnerable.

NOTE Wireless is still in a state of development. At the time that this book was being written, 11Mbps was the maximum speed available from various manufacturers. While writing this chapter, I had the opportunity to install a wireless network. The components were manufactured by Linksys and included a base station and wireless NICs. I was extremely impressed with the performance and the range. The system was installed for a friend of mine (whom I referenced in a previous chapter), and it has outperformed my expectations. The ease of use and cost savings that we enjoyed (considering where the workstations were located) have me excited about what will happen over the next few years. I firmly believe that wireless networking will become a major architecture as performance continues to increase and prices drop.

Summary of Cabling Types

Each type of cabling has its own benefits and drawbacks. Table 6.2 details the most common types of cabling in use today. As you look at this table, pay particular attention to the cost, length, and maximum transmission rates of each cabling type.

TABLE 6.2: Cable Types

Characteristics	Twisted-Pair	Coaxial	Fiber Optic	Wireless
Cost	Least expensive	More than twisted-pair	Expensive	Most expensive
Maximum length	100 meters (328 feet)	185 meters (607 feet) to 500 meters (1640 feet)	>10 miles	2 miles
Transmission rates	10Mbps to 100Mbps	10Mbps	100Mbps or more	10Mbps
Flexibility	Most flexible	Fair	Fair	Limited

TABLE 6.2: Cable Types *(continued)*

Characteristics	Twisted-Pair	Coaxial	Fiber Optic	Wireless
Ease of installation	Very easy	Easy	Difficult	Somewhat difficult
Interference	Susceptible	Better than UTP, more susceptible than STP	Not susceptible	Susceptible
Special features	Often pre-installed; similar to wiring used in telephone systems	Easiest installation	Supports voice, data, and video at highest transmission speeds	Very flexible
Preferred uses	Networks	Medium-size networks with high security needs	Networks of any size requiring high speed and data security	WANs and radio/TV communications
Connector	RJ-45	BNC-T and AUI	Special	Dish or transceiver
Physical topology	Star	Bus	Star (typically)	Bus or star
Other info	Five categories of quality	RG-58 and RG-59 family; also called Thinnet and Thicknet, respectively	Requires special training to configure	Most must comply with FCC regulations

The Network Interface Card

The network interface card (NIC) provides the physical interface between computer and cabling. It prepares data, sends data, and controls the flow of data. It can also receive and translate data into bytes for the CPU to understand. It communicates at the Physical layer of the OSI model and comes in many shapes and sizes.

The various NICs are distinguished by the PC bus type and the network for which they are used. This section describes the role of the NIC and how to choose the appropriate one. The following factors should be taken into consideration when choosing a NIC:

- Preparing data
- Sending and controlling data
- Configuration
- Drivers
- Compatibility
- Performance

Preparing Data

In the computer, data moves along buses in parallel, as on a four-lane interstate highway. But on a network cable, data travels in a single stream, as on a one-lane highway. This difference can cause problems transmitting and receiving data, because the paths traveled are not the same. It is the NIC's job to translate the data from the computer into signals that can flow easily along the cable. It does this by translating digital signals into electrical signals (and in the case of fiber optic NICs, to optical signals).

Sending and Controlling Data

For two computers to send and receive data, the cards must agree on several things. These include the following:

- The maximum size of the data frames
- The amount of data sent before giving confirmation

- The time needed between transmissions

- The amount of time needed to wait before sending confirmation

- The amount of data a card can hold

- The speed at which data transmits

If the cards can agree, then the sending of the data is successful. If the cards cannot agree, the sending of data does not occur.

In order to successfully send data on the network, you need to make sure that the network cards are of the same type (i.e., all Ethernet, all Token Ring, all ARCNet, etc.) and that they are connected to the same piece of cable. If you use cards of different types (for example, one Ethernet and one Token Ring), neither of them will be able to communicate with the other (unless you use some kind of gateway device, such as a router).

In addition, network cards can send data in either full-duplex or half-duplex modes. *Half-duplex communications* means that between the sender and receiver, only one of them can transmit at any one time. In *full-duplex communications*, a computer can send and receive data simultaneously. The main advantage of full-duplex over half-duplex communications is performance. Network cards (specifically Fast Ethernet network cards) can operate twice as fast (200Mbps) in full-duplex mode as they do normally in half-duplex mode (100Mbps).

Configuration

The NIC's configuration includes such things as a manufacturer's hardware address, IRQ address, base I/O port address, and base memory address. Some may also use DMA channels to offer better performance.

Each card must have a unique hardware address. If two cards have the same hardware addresses, neither one of them will be able to communicate. For this reason, the IEEE committee has established a standard for hardware addresses and assigns blocks of these addresses to NIC manufacturers, who then hard-wire the addresses into the cards.

Configuring a NIC is similar to configuring any other type of expansion card. The NIC usually needs a unique IRQ channel and I/O address, and possibly a DMA channel. Token Ring cards often have two memory addresses that must be allocated in reserved memory for them to work properly.

Drivers

For the computer to use the network interface card, it is very important to install the proper device drivers. These drivers communicate directly with the network redirector and adapter. They operate in the Media Access Control sublayer of the Data Link layer of the OSI model.

PC Bus Type

When choosing a NIC, use one that fits the bus type of your PC. If you have more than one type of bus in your PC (for example, a combination ISA/PCI), use a NIC that fits into the fastest type (the PCI, in this case). This is especially important in servers, as the NIC can very quickly become a bottleneck if this guideline isn't followed.

Performance

The most important goal of the network adapter card should be to optimize network performance and minimize the amount of time needed to transfer data packets across the network. There are several ways of doing this, including assigning a DMA channel, using a shared memory adapter, and deciding to allow bus mastering.

If the network card can use DMA channels, then data can move directly from the card's buffer to the computer's memory, bypassing the CPU. A shared memory adapter is a NIC that has its own RAM. This feature allows transfers to and from the computer to happen much more quickly, increasing the performance of the NIC. Shared system memory allows the NIC to use a section of the computer's RAM to process data. Bus mastering lets the card take temporary control of the computer's bus to bypass the CPU and move directly to RAM. This is more expensive, but it can improve performance by 20 to 70 percent. However, EISA and MCA cards are the only ones that support bus mastering.

Each of these features can enhance the performance of a network interface card. Most cards today have at least one, if not several, of these features.

Media Access Methods

You have put the network together in a topology. You have told the network how to communicate and send the data, and you have told it how to send the data to another computer. You also have the communications medium in place. The next problem you need to solve is how to put the data on the cable. What you need now are the *cable access methods*, which define a set of rules for how computers put data on and retrieve it from a network cable. The four methods of data access are shown here:

- Carrier Sense Multiple Access with Collision Detection (CSMA/CD)

- Carrier Sense Multiple Access with Collision Avoidance (CSMA/CA)

- Token passing

- Polling

Carrier Sense Multiple Access with Collision Detection

As we've already discussed, NICs that use CSMA/CD listen to, or "sense," the cable to check for traffic. They compete for a chance to transmit. Usually, if access to the network is slow, it means that there are too many computers trying to transmit, causing traffic jams.

Carrier Sense Multiple Access with Collision Avoidance

Instead of monitoring traffic and moving in when there is a break, CSMA/CA allows the computers to send a signal that they are ready to transmit data. If the ready signal transmits without a problem, the computer then transmits its data. If the ready signal is not transmitted successfully, the computer waits and tries again. This method is slower and less popular than CSMA/CD.

Token Passing

As previously discussed, token passing is a way of giving every NIC equal access to the cable. A special packet of data is passed from computer to computer. Any computer that wants to transmit has to wait until it has the token. It can then transmit its data.

Polling

An old method of media access that is still in use is *polling*. There aren't very many topologies that support polling anymore, mainly because it has special hardware requirements. This method requires a central, intelligent device (meaning that the device contains either hardware or software "intelligence" to enable it to make decisions) that asks each workstation, in turn, if it has any data to transmit. If the workstation answers "yes," the controller allows the workstation to transmit its data.

The polling process doesn't scale very well. That is, you can't take this method and simply apply it to any number of workstations. In addition, the high cost of the intelligent controllers and cards has made the polling method all but obsolete.

Connectivity Devices

Cabling links computer to computer. Most cabling allows networks to be hundreds of feet long. But what if your network needs to be bigger than that? What if you need to connect your LANs to other LANs to make a WAN? What if the architecture you've picked for your network is limiting the growth of your network along with the growth of your company? The answer to these questions is found in a special class of networking devices known as *connectivity devices*. These devices allow communications to break the boundaries of local networks and let your computers talk to other computers in the next building, the next city, or the next country.

There are several categories of connectivity devices, but we are going to discuss the six most important and most often used:

- Repeaters

- Hubs

- Bridges

- Routers

- Brouters

- Gateways

These connectivity devices have made it possible to lengthen the distance of the network to almost unlimited distances.

Repeaters

Repeaters are very simple devices. They allow a cabling system to extend beyond its maximum allowed length by amplifying the network voltages so they travel farther. Repeaters are nothing more than amplifiers and, as such, are very inexpensive.

Repeaters operate at the Physical layer of the OSI model. Because of this, repeaters can only be used to regenerate signals between similar network segments. I can, for example, extend an Ethernet 10Base2 network to 400 meters with a repeater. But I can't connect an Ethernet and Token Ring network together with one.

The main disadvantage of repeaters is that they just amplify signals. These signals include not only the network signals, but any noise on the wire as well. Eventually, if you use enough repeaters, you could possibly drown out the signal with the amplified noise. For this reason, repeaters are used only as a temporary fix.

Hubs

Hubs are devices used to link several computers together. They are most often used in 10BaseT Ethernet networks. They are also very simple devices. In fact, they are just multiport repeaters. They repeat any signal that comes in on one port and copy it to the other ports (a process that is also called *broadcasting*).

There are two types of hubs: active and passive. *Passive hubs* simply connect all ports together electrically and are usually not powered. *Active hubs* use electronics to amplify and clean up the signal before it is broadcast to the other ports. In the category of active hubs, there is also a class called *intelligent hubs*, which are hubs that can be remotely managed on the network.

Bridges

Bridges operate in the Data Link layer of the OSI model. They join similar topologies and are used to divide network segments. Bridges keep traffic on one side from crossing to the other. For this reason, they are often used to increase performance on a high-traffic segment.

For example, with 200 people on one Ethernet segment, the performance would be mediocre, because of the design of Ethernet and the number of workstations that are fighting to transmit. If you divide the segment into two segments of 100 workstations each, the traffic would be much lower on either side and performance would increase.

Bridges are not able to distinguish one protocol from another, because higher levels of the OSI model are not available to them. If a bridge is aware of the destination address, it is able to forward packets; otherwise a bridge will forward the packets to all segments. They are more intelligent than repeaters but are unable to move data across multiple networks simultaneously. Unlike repeaters, bridges *can* filter out noise.

The main disadvantage of bridges is that they can't connect dissimilar network types or perform intelligent path selection. For that function, you would need a router.

Routers

Routers are highly intelligent devices that connect multiple network types and determine the best path for sending data. They can route packets across multiple networks and use routing tables to store network addresses to determine the best destination. Routers operate at the Network layer of the OSI model.

The advantage of using a router over a bridge is that routers can determine the best path that data can take to get to its destination. Like bridges, they can segment large networks and filter out noise.

However, they are slower than bridges because they are more intelligent devices; as such, they analyze every packet, causing packet-forwarding delays. Because of this intelligence, they are also more expensive.

Routers are normally used to connect one LAN to another. Typically, when a WAN is set up, at least two routers will be used.

Switches

Like hubs, *switches* are devices used to link several computers together. They differ from hubs in a few important ways. Switches repeat signals, like hubs do, to the ports with one exception. Rather than send network traffic to all ports, switches have enough intelligence to send the traffic directly to the port the packet was intended for. This reduces the work done by the OSI layers below the Network layer. The lower layers do not process the data to determine if it was intended for that machine.

All switches are active and some are manageable. Manageable hubs allow remote management and in higher-end devices can also act similarly to a router. This feature can be used to logically divide the network into segments and reduce network traffic.

Brouters

Brouters are truly an ingenious idea because they combine the best of both worlds—bridges and routers. They are used to connect dissimilar network segments and also to route only one specific protocol. The other protocols are bridged instead of being dropped. Brouters are used when only one protocol needs to be routed or where a router is not cost-effective (as in a branch office).

Gateways

Gateways connect dissimilar network environments and architectures. Some gateways can use all levels of the OSI model, but they are frequently found in the Application layer. It is there that gateways convert data and repackage it to meet the requirements of the destination address. This makes gateways slower and more costly than other connectivity devices. An example of a gateway is the NT Gateway Service for NetWare, which, when running on a Windows NT Server, can connect a Microsoft Windows NT network with a Novell NetWare network.

Exam Essentials

Understand Local Area Networks (LAN).   Local Area Networks (LANs) connect computers in a single office.

Understand peer-to-peer networks.   A peer-to-peer network is a network where the computers act as both workstations and servers.

Understand the role of nondedicated servers.   Nondedicated servers can be used not only to serve client requests and perform administrative actions, but often to serve as a front end for the administrator to work with other applications or services.

Key Terms and Concepts

Star   A physical star topology branches each network device off a central hub, making it very easy to add a new workstation. If any workstation goes down, it does not affect the entire network.

Ring   Each computer connects to two other computers, joining them in a circle, creating a unidirectional path where messages move from workstation to workstation. Each entity participating in the ring reads a message, then regenerates it, and hands it to its neighbor on a different network cable.

Server-based resource model   Server-based networks use a dedicated, centralized server. All administrative functions and resource sharing are performed from this point.

Network interface card   The network interface card (NIC) provides the physical interface between the computer and cabling. It prepares data, sends data, and controls the flow of data. It can also receive and translate data into bytes for the CPU to understand.

Twisted-pair   Twisted-pair is one of the most popular methods of cabling because of its flexibility and low costs. It consists of several pairs of wire twisted around each other within an insulated jacket.

Hubs   Hubs are devices used to link several computers together. They repeat any signal that comes in on one port and copy it to the other ports (a process that is also called broadcasting).

Routers   Routers are highly intelligent devices that connect multiple network types and determine the best path for sending data. They can route packets across multiple networks and use routing tables to store network addresses to determine the best destination.

Switches   Like hubs, switches are devices used to link several computers together. They differ from hubs in a few important ways. Switches repeat signals, as hubs do, to the ports with one exception. Rather than send network traffic to all ports, switches have enough intelligence to send the traffic directly to the port the packet was intended for. This reduces the work done by the OSI layers below the Network layer.

A+: Operating System Technologies Exam

PART

II

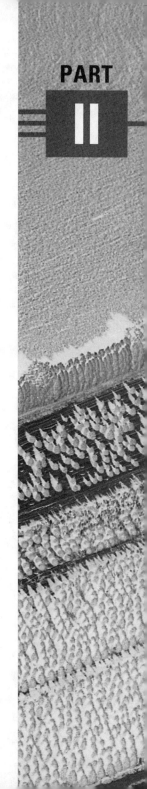

Chapter 7

Domain 1.0 Operating System Fundamentals

As a child, you had to learn to walk before you learned to run. The same is true of mastering computer maintenance. Domain 1.0 of the A+ Operating System exam objectives basically covers the "learning to walk" aspects of using computer operating systems. More specifically, it deals with the basic concepts behind Microsoft's Windows operating systems. Previous versions of this test had focused on MS-DOS and Windows 3.x systems, but those are rarely used today, and the test now deals exclusively with the current Windows versions: Windows 95, Windows 98, Windows NT, and Windows 2000. Windows Me was just released when the objectives came out and is not covered. Also, although the A+ exam is vendor-neutral, the test basically equates "operating system knowledge" with "Microsoft operating system knowledge." Check your Linux, Macintosh, and OS/2 information with your coat when you arrive at the testing center. You won't need it for this exam.

Domain 1.0 consists of two major conceptual groups. The first of these is 1.1, and it deals with information on using a Windows machine. Components of the graphical user interface (GUI), how to use applications and utilities, and where to find important system files are all part of this objective. For most test-takers, the information in part 1.1 is second nature, so those who regularly use Windows 95/98/NT/2000 will probably find most of this is simply a review.

Part 1.2, on the other hand, deals with how to go in and configure, or reconfigure, the operating system (OS). This is where you would begin to look at issues that are outside the scope of daily usage. Utilities and concepts from 1.2 are used to monitor, manage, and even permanently modify the operating system or even used to reconfigure the computer's hardware.

The information in this domain is essential to the knowledge base of any computer technician. Some of the material covered in this chapter is remedial for many of you, while for others much of it may be new. Wherever your knowledge level is now, though, both for the test and for your later usage, this is stuff you simply have to know.

1.1 Identify the operating system's functions, structure, and major system files to navigate the operating system and how to get to needed technical information.

- **Major Operating System functions**
- **Major Operating System components**
- **Contrasts between Windows 9x and Windows 2000**
- **Major system files: what they are, where they are located, how they are used, and what they contain**

There are a lot of subobjectives covered by objective 1.1, but even so, the objective really deals with just three basic questions:

- What does an operating system do?

- Which files are needed for a particular OS to work?

- How can you navigate and work with the OS?

Again, we are looking at only two classes of operating systems here. Windows 95/98 is Microsoft's home user and low-end corporate desktop OS, while Windows NT/2000 is a more powerful OS with enhanced security and stability for "power users."

For purposes of the exam—and the real world—the first question is largely irrelevant, although it is certainly of academic interest. There is an extension of this question, though: "What can one OS do that another can't?" This information is useful when you are deciding which OS a client needs, and it is also a great source of test questions like the following: "A user needs to run an old DOS modem-dialing program. Which OS should they use, Windows 98 or Windows NT?" Answer: "Windows 98. DOS applications are not generally supported in Windows NT or 2000."

The second question is an extremely important one. A knowledge of the boot and system files for an OS is critical for troubleshooting and configuring the OS. This is information that is not necessarily common knowledge, as well. If you don't know what AUTOEXEC.BAT and NTBOOTDD.SYS are now, you should before you take the test!

You need to review your knowledge of the Windows interface, from the Start button up. You will be given the chance to review the primary components of the GUI and how they work. Also, we discuss how to use installed programs or command-line utilities.

Critical Information

Now let's run through the specific information mentioned in content area 1.1 of CompTIA's objectives. We'll examine each of these content areas separately, with an eye toward the essential information needed to understand and do well on that section.

Major Operating System Functions

As you read about various software products, try to think about the ways in which they differ from one another and the reasons they were designed in that fashion. The A+ exam focuses only on OS options available from Microsoft, and it will be those systems that are given the most time in this chapter. Although Macintosh, for instance, has a strong following in certain niche markets, Intel/Windows machines dominate the corporate market almost completely. You may come across any of the following OSes over the course of your time as a technician, as all are still in use:

- DOS
- Windows 3.1 or 3.11 for Workgroups

- OS/2

- Windows 95 or 98

- Windows NT Workstation

- Windows 2000 Professional

- Linux

- Macintosh

The operating system provides a consistent environment for other software to execute commands. The OS gives users an interface with the computer so they can send commands to (input) and receive feedback or results back (output). To do this, the OS must communicate with the computer hardware to perform the following tasks:

- Disk and file management

- Device access

- Memory management

- Input/output

Once the operating system has organized these basic resources, users can give the computer instructions through input devices (such as a keyboard or a mouse). Some of these commands are built into the operating system, while others are issued through the use of applications. The OS becomes the center through which the system hardware, other software, and the user communicate, and all the rest of the components of the system work together through the OS, which coordinates their communication.

Disk and File Management

The Create Folders option within this heading of the test objectives seems to be incredibly badly placed, as it really a bit too specific and is more a part of content area 1.2, which also talks about "creating, viewing and managing files, directories and disks."

Even so, the process of managing how information is stored and retrieved from the system is crucial to understanding how an operating system works. There are two major elements to this process. The first is the creation of partitions and drives. In Windows 95/98, this is done through a tool called FDISK. In Windows NT, it is done through Disk Administrator, and in Windows 2000, disks are managed through the Computer Management tool's Storage area.

Once a drive has been created, the OS needs to be able to prepare the drive for use through a process called *formatting* and to then write information to the drive and retrieve it.

As with the Creating Folders objective, the specifics of disk and file management will be covered in content area 1.2.

Device Access

Another responsibility of the operating system is to manage the way that software on the system interacts with the computer's hardware. More advanced OSes have the capability to avoid conflicts between devices and to prevent applications from interfering with each other. We'll have more to say on this in content area 2.4.

Memory Management

Computers are designed so that in order for information to be used by the processor, it must be in the machine's memory (RAM). How the operating system manages the transfer of information from storage on the hard drive to a place in RAM is referred to as *memory management*. This topic is covered later in this chapter.

Input/Output

Generally called *I/O*, this is the process by which the machine accepts instructions (from the mouse, keyboard, etc.) and provides output (to a monitor, file, or printer). Printing and other output functionality will be covered later, and for input there are only a very few crucial things you will need to know. Primary among these are the ways that the mouse is used to allow you to access information. There are numerous mouse options available to Windows:

Primary mouse click   A single click used to select an object or place a cursor.

Double-click   Two primary mouse clicks in quick succession. Used to open a program through an icon or for other specific application functions.

Secondary mouse click   Most mice have two buttons. Clicking once on the secondary button (usually the one on the right side, although that can be modified) is interpreted differently from a left mouse click. Generally in Windows, this displays a context-sensitive menu from which you are given the ability to perform tasks or view object properties.

Click and drag   Allows you to pick something up and move it.

WARNING   If you are not familiar enough with Windows that these are already second nature to you, you have a lot of work ahead of you before you take the OS test!

Major Operating System Components

When you look at the monitor of a machine running Windows 98 and then look at the monitor of a machine running Windows 2000, it is difficult to tell the two apart. If you look closely, you will notice that the names of some icons have changed, but for the most part the two are identical and look very much like the screen in Figure 7.1.

FIGURE 7.1: The Windows interface

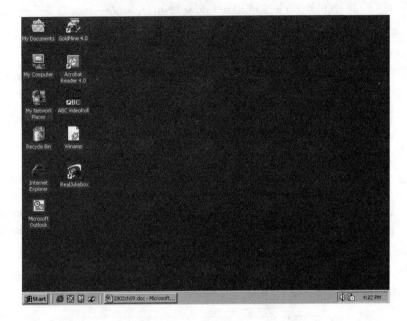

The following are the key elements of the Windows GUI. If you have a copy of Windows 9x or Windows NT4/2000 available, you may want to explore the various menus and options by examining each of the elements as they are discussed. If you are able to follow along, you may also notice that there are numerous additional icons and options that are not mentioned. They should not be on the test, but you may want to browse through them on your own just in case.

Much of this information will be review for those of you who have experience using Windows operating systems, but you may want to simply refresh your mind as to the specific names and attributes of these components.

The Desktop

The Desktop is the virtual desk upon which all of your other programs and utilities run. By default it contains the Start menu, the Taskbar, and a number of icons. The Desktop can also contain additional elements, such as Web page content, through the use of the

Active Desktop option. Because it is the base on which everything else sits, how the Desktop is configured can have a major effect on how the GUI looks and how convenient it is for users.

You can change the Desktop's background patterns, screen saver, color scheme, and size by right-clicking any area of the Desktop that doesn't contain an icon. The menu that appears allows you to do several things, such as creating new Desktop items, changing how your icons are arranged, or selecting a special command called Properties. You can also access the Display Properties settings by choosing Display Control Panel under Start ➢ Settings ➢ Control Panel.

TIP   Windows is designed to allow each user to access information in the way that they are most comfortable with, and as such there are generally at least two ways to do everything. When getting ready for the test, try to make sure that you know *all* the ways to perform a task, not just the way that you are used to.

The Taskbar

The Taskbar is another standard component of the Windows interface. It contains two major items: the Start menu and the System Tray. The Start menu is on the left side of the Taskbar and is easily identifiable by the fact that it is a button that has the word "Start" on it. The System Tray is located on the right side of the Taskbar and contains only a clock by default, but other Windows utilities (for example, screen savers or virus-protection utilities) may put their icons here to indicate that they are running and to provide the user with a quick way to access their features.

Besides containing the Start button and the System Tray, the Taskbar provides an area to display information about the applications you have open. Whenever you open a new window or program, it gets a button on the Taskbar with an icon that represents that window or program. To bring a window or program to the front (or to maximize it if it was minimized), click its button on the Taskbar. As the middle area of the Taskbar fills up with buttons, the buttons become smaller in order to display all of them.

You can increase the size of the Taskbar by moving the mouse pointer to the top of the Taskbar and pausing until the pointer turns into a double-headed arrow. Once this happens, you can click the mouse and move it up to make the Taskbar bigger. Or, you can move it down to make the Taskbar smaller. You can also move the Taskbar to the top or sides of the screen by clicking the Taskbar and dragging it to the new location, or you can use the Auto Hide feature in the Taskbar Properties window—which is accessed by right-clicking the Taskbar and clicking Properties. Auto Hide causes the Taskbar to vanish when you do not need it, giving you more screen area.

The Start Menu

When Microsoft officially introduced Windows 95 to the world, it bought the rights to use the Rolling Stones' song "Start Me Up" in its advertisements and at the introduction party. They chose that particular song because the Start menu was the central point of focus in the new Windows interface, and it has retained this position in all subsequent versions.

To display the Start menu, click the Start button in the Taskbar. From the Start menu, you can select any of the various options the menu presents. An arrow pointing to the right means that there is a submenu. To select a submenu, move the mouse pointer over the submenu title and pause. The submenu will then appear; you don't even have to click. (You have to click to choose an option *on* the submenu, though.)

Another handy feature of the Start menu is that it usually displays the name of the operating system type along its side when you activate it. This provides an excellent way to quickly see whether you are on Windows 95, 98, NT, or 2000. You can also check which operating system you are using by right-clicking the My Computer icon on the Desktop and selecting Properties. The operating type and version will be displayed on the first tab. The exam objectives specify that you need to be able to determine the version of an OS, so this is something you should look into for the test. We'll show yet another way of checking on a version later.

PROGRAMS SUBMENU

The Programs submenu holds the program groups and program icons that you can use. You can add programs to this submenu in many ways. The three most popular ways are as follows:

- Using the application's installation program
- Using the Taskbar Properties screen
- Using the Windows Explorer program

DOCUMENTS SUBMENU

The Documents submenu has one and only one function: to keep track of the last 15 data files you opened. Whenever you open a file, a shortcut to it is automatically made in this menu. Just click the document in the Documents menu to reopen it in its associated application.

SETTINGS SUBMENU

The Settings submenu provides easy access to the configuration of Windows. There are numerous submenus to the Settings submenu, including Control Panel, Printers, and Taskbar & Start Menu. Additional menus are available depending on which version of Windows you are using. These submenus give you access to the Control Panel, printer driver, and Taskbar configuration areas, respectively.

SEARCH (FIND) SUBMENU

The name of this menu changes between Windows 98 and Windows 2000, but its purpose doesn't. The Windows 98 Find submenu is used to locate information on your computer or on a network. The Search submenu of Windows 2000 has the same functionality.

HELP COMMAND

Windows includes a *very* good help system. Not only is it arranged by topic, but it is also fully indexed and searchable. Because of its usefulness and power, it was placed on the Start menu for easy access. When you select this command, it will bring up Windows Help. From this screen, you can double-click a manual to show a list of subtopics and then click a subtopic to view the text of that topic. You can also view indexed help files or do a specific search through the help documents' text.

RUN COMMAND

The Run command can be used to start programs if they don't have a shortcut on the Desktop or in the Programs submenu. To execute a particular program, just type its name and path in the Open field. If you don't know the exact path, you can browse to find the file by clicking the Browse button. Once you have typed in the executable name and path, click OK to run the program.

NOTE   Paths and files will be covered later.

SHUT DOWN COMMAND

Windows $9x$ and 2000 are very complex operating systems. At any one time, they have several files open in memory. If you accidentally hit the power switch and turn the computer off while these files are open, there is a good chance these files will be corrupted. For this reason, Microsoft has added the Shut Down command under the Start menu. When you select this option, Windows presents you with at least three choices:

Shut Down The Computer   This option will write any unsaved data to disk, close any open applications, and get the computer ready to be powered off. When you see a black screen with the message "It's now safe to turn off your computer" in orange text, it is, in fact, safe to power off the computer. You can also hit Ctrl+Alt+Del to reboot the computer at this point.

Restart The Computer   This option works the same as the first option but instead of shutting down completely will automatically reboot the computer with a warm reboot.

Restart The Computer In MS-DOS Mode (Windows $9x$ only)
This option is special. It does the same tasks as the previous options, except upon reboot, Windows $9x$ will execute the command prompt

only and will not start the graphical portion of Windows 9x. You can then run DOS programs as though the machine were a DOS machine. When you have finished running these programs, type **exit** to reboot the machine back into the "full" Windows 9x with the GUI.

Log Off   If you have user profiles enabled, a Log Off option is also available either from this menu or as a separate menu command. Profiles are automatic on NT and 2000 and optional on 95/98.

Stand By   On laptops or other machines with APM (advanced power management) the Stand By option may also be available. This allows the machine to go into a "sleep mode" where it shuts down most functions to save energy. Utilizing Stand By can significantly extend battery time on laptops.

Icons

Icons are shortcuts that allow a user to open a program or a utility without knowing where that program is or how it needs to be configured. Icons consist of four elements:

- Icon label
- Icon graphic
- Program location
- Working directory location

The label and graphic simply tell the user the name of the program and give a visual hint as to what that program does. Solitaire, for instance, is labeled Solitaire, and its icon graphic is a deck of cards. By right-clicking an icon once, you make that icon the active icon, and a drop-down menu appears. One of the selections is Properties. Clicking Properties brings up the attributes of an icon and is the only way to see exactly which program an icon is configured to start. The working directory location tells Windows where to save documents created through this icon. This is the default and can be overridden.

There are a number of icons that are automatically placed directly on the Desktop. Some of the important common icons include those listed here. Note that some of these icons have been given new names in Window 2000, but they continue to perform the same job. In such cases, both names are listed.

My Computer If you double-click the My Computer icon, it will display all the disk drives installed in your computer as well as the Control Panel and Printers folders. If you double-click a disk drive, you will see the contents of that disk drive. In addition to allowing you access to your computer's files, the My Computer icon allows you a view of your machine's configuration and hardware, also called the System Properties.

Recycle Bin All files, directories, and programs in Windows are represented by icons and are generally referred to as *objects*. When you want to remove an object from Windows, you do so by deleting it. Deleting doesn't just remove the object; it also removes the ability of the system to access the information or application that the object represents. Because of this, Windows includes a special directory where all deleted files are placed: the Recycle Bin. This Recycle Bin allows users the opportunity to recover files that they deleted accidentally.

You can retrieve a file that you have deleted by opening the Recycle Bin, then dragging the file from the Recycle Bin back to the disk it came from. To permanently erase the file, you need to empty the Recycle Bin, thereby permanently deleting any items in it and freeing up the hard drive space they took up.

Network Neighborhood/My Network Places Used to access the network, this icon appears only if you have a network connection of some sort available. More on this when we get to domain 4.0.

What's in a Window?

Applications and utilities are used and managed through the use of windows, the rectangular application environments for which the Windows family of operating systems is named.

A *program window* is a rectangular area created on the screen when an application is opened within Windows. This window can have a number of different forms, but most windows include at least a few basic elements. Figure 7.2 shows the Control box, Title bar, Minimize button, Restore button, and resizable border in a text editor called Notepad (`Notepad.exe`) that has all of the basic window elements and little else!

FIGURE 7.2: The basic elements of a window

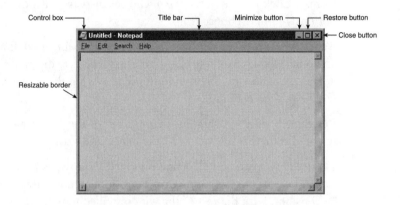

Control box   Located in the upper-left corner of the window, the Control box is used to control the state of the application. It can be used to maximize, minimize, and close the application. Clicking it once brings up a selection menu. Double-clicking it closes the window and shuts down the application.

Minimize and Restore buttons   Used to change the state of the window on the Desktop. They will be explained further later in this chapter.

Close button   Used to easily end a program and return any resources it was using to the system. It essentially does the same thing as double-clicking the Control box, but with one less click. The Close button is identified by an X and is in the upper-right corner of the window.

Title bar   The area between the Control box and the Minimize button. It simply states the name of the program and in some cases gives information as to the particular document being accessed by that program. The color of the Title bar indicates whether or not a particular window is the active window.

Menu bar   Used to present useful commands in an easily accessible format. Clicking one of the menu choices displays a list of related options you may choose from.

Active window   The window that is currently being used. It has two attributes: First, any keystrokes that are entered are directed there by default. Second, any other windows that overlap the active window will be pushed behind it.

Resizable border   A thin line that surrounds the window in its restored state that allows it to be widened and shortened.

These elements are not all found on every window, as programmers can choose to eliminate or modify them. Still, in most cases, these will be constant, with the rest of the window filled in with menus, toolbars, a workspace, or other application-specific elements. For instance, Microsoft Word adds an additional Control box and Minimize and Maximize buttons for each document. It also has a menu bar, a number of optional toolbars, scroll bars at the right and bottom of the window, and a status bar at the very bottom. Application windows can become very cluttered.

Notepad is a very simple Windows program. It has only a single menu bar and the basic elements seen previously in Figure 7.2. Figure 7.3 shows a Microsoft Word window. Both Word and Notepad are used to create and edit documents, but Word is far more configurable and powerful and therefore has many more optional components available within its window.

FIGURE 7.3: A window with more components

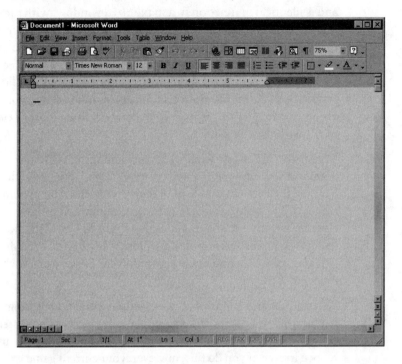

There is more to the Windows interface than the physical parts of a window itself, however. Windows also are movable, stackable, and resizable, and they can be hidden behind other windows (often unintentionally!).

When an application window has been launched, it will exist in one of three states:

Maximized A maximized window is one that takes up all available space on the screen. When it is in front of the other programs, it is the only thing visible except the Taskbar— even the Desktop is hidden. The middle button in the upper-right corner displays two rectangles rather than one, and the sides of the window no longer have borders because the window is flush with the edges of the screen.

Restored   A restored window is one that can be used interactively and is identical in function to a maximized window, with the simple difference that it does not necessarily take up the entire screen. Restored windows can be very small, or they can take up almost as much space as maximized windows. How large the restored window becomes is the user's choice. Restored windows display a restore box (the middle button in the upper-right corner) containing a single rectangle; this is used to maximize the window. Restored windows have a border.

Minimized   The last window state is minimized. Minimized program windows are represented by nothing but an icon on the Taskbar, and they are not usable until they have been either maximized or restored. The only difference between a minimized program and a closed program is that a minimized program is out of the way but is still taking up resources and is therefore ready to use if you need it. It will also leave the content of the window in the same place when you return to it as when you minimized it.

When a program is open and you need to open another program (or maybe need to stop playing a game because your boss has entered the room), you have two choices. First, you can close the program and reopen it later. If you do this, however, your current game will be lost and you will have to start over. Minimizing the game window, on the other hand, will remove the open window from the screen and leave the program open but display nothing more than an icon in the lower-left corner of the Taskbar.

While it is unlikely that you will have a lot of questions on what a window is, many of the questions on the test require you to know the names and functionality of the components in order to understand and answer the rest of the question.

Contrasts between Windows 9x and Windows 2000

Windows 9x and Windows 2000 Professional are similar in many ways, but they also have important differences. Windows 2000 is a more powerful desktop operating system option, and it is designed as the preferred OS for corporate users or home power users. The reason for the extra expense of Windows 2000 Pro is that it provides the following enhancements to the Windows platform:

- Support for more hardware

- Advanced security and stability

- Greater application stability

NOTE   In the Exam guide, note that sometimes Windows 2000 is referred to as Windows 2K, Windows 2000, Windows 2000 Pro, or Windows 2000 Professional. There are actually a number of additional versions of Windows 2000 (Server, Advanced Server, and Datacenter Server), but the A+ exam tests your knowledge of desktop operating systems only, and as such deals only with Professional. When you read "Windows 2000," remember that it is Windows 2000 Professional that is being referenced here. The Server+ and Network+ tests examine the other versions.

Hardware Requirements

One of the major considerations for which OS you will want to put on a machine is the sort of hardware the computer has. Older machines run better with older, less resource-intensive operating systems, while newer machines generally want a more current OS to take advantage of their power. Table 7.1 lists the hardware levels for Windows 95 and 98, and Table 7.2 lists the required and recommended levels for Windows 2000 Professional.

TABLE 7.1: Windows 9x Hardware Requirements

Hardware	95 Requirement	98 Requirement
Processor	386DX or higher processor (486 recommended).	386DX or higher processor (Pentium recommended).
Memory	4MB (8MB recommended).	8MB (16–32MB recommended).
Free hard disk space	50–55MB for typical install (40MB if upgrading from a previous version of Windows). Could go as high as 85MB for a custom install with all options.	120MB for typical install. Could go as high as 250MB for a custom install with all options.
Floppy disk	One 3½-inch disk drive (if doing installation from floppy disks).	One 3½-inch disk drive (if doing installation from floppy disks).
CD-ROM	Required if installing from CD (preferred method).	Required if installing from CD (preferred method).
Video	VGA or better.	VGA or better.
Mouse	Required.	Required.
Keyboard	Required.	Required.

Because of the fact that it is a "power workstation," the hardware requirements for Windows 2000 are higher than those for Windows 9x, and it also is less forgiving of older, less-efficient software.

TABLE 7.2: Windows 2000 Hardware Prerequisites

Hardware	Windows 2000 Pro Required	Windows 2000 Pro Recommended
Processor	Pentium 133	Pentium II or higher
Memory	64MB	128MB or higher
Free hard disk space	2GB	2GB plus what is needed for your applications and storage
Floppy disk	Required only if installing from the boot disks	Yes
CD-ROM	Required only if installing from CD	Yes
Video	VGA	SVGA
Mouse	Yes	Yes
Keyboard	Yes	Yes

NOTE The "recommended" levels are simply a guideline from Microsoft. Remember that the hardware levels in the Required column of Table 7.2 are the ones you need for the test. Even so, the required levels would be very low for an actual functioning system.

Besides the basic resources listed, you should also note that Windows 98 supports more hardware out of the box than Windows 95, and Windows 2000 has built-in support for many new technologies, such as smart cards and DVD drives, which Windows 9x either does not support or requires additional software to run. Once you have found a machine that you feel will run Professional acceptably, your next step is to determine whether all of the hardware in it is compatible with Windows 2000. There are a number of ways to do this, but probably the most dependable is to go to www.microsoft.com/windows2000 and download a copy of the most recent Hardware Compatibility List (HCL). This list will tell you which hardware has been tested with Windows 2000 and should run properly. If your hardware is not on the HCL, contact your vendor for compatibility information and updated Windows 2000 drivers. Many Windows NT drivers will work with 2000, but Windows 95 or 98 drivers will *not* work! Most hardware on the HCL also has drivers that ship with Windows 2000, so supported hardware should be installed and configured automatically during setup. If your hardware is extremely new or if your vendor did not submit the hardware to Microsoft for testing, then you may find that you need to supply your own drivers. Also, if the hardware is very old, it may also either be unsupported or require you to provide your own drivers.

Application Compatibility

There are three types of applications you will need to consider when looking at Windows compatibility: DOS applications, Windows 16-bit applications, and Windows 32-bit applications.

DOS apps   True DOS applications are apps that are written for use with Microsoft's Disk Operating System (DOS). DOS is pretty much dead, but even so there are a number of older DOS programs still floating around. Windows 95 and 98 are built to be backward compatible with support for DOS applications, while Windows NT and 2000 are not. NT and 2000 do support some DOS applications, but in order to provide greater system security, the OS in NT/2000 requires that all applications go through the OS to use hardware. Most older DOS applications try to directly access resources such as serial ports, printer ports, or disk drives, and if they do so, NT/2000 simply ends the program rather than let that happen.

Windows 16-bit apps   Both Windows 9*x* and Windows NT/2000 will run pretty much all Windows 16-bit applications. The question here is efficiency, as 16-bit apps are designed for use with the Windows 3.*x* cooperatively multitasked architecture. The 16-bit apps run in a special environment under both 9*x* and 2000. This environment simulates a DOS/Windows environment but limits the processor and memory access of the application. Also, 16-bit applications can interfere with each other and are generally less stable.

Windows 32-bit apps   Written specifically for the newer architecture of modern Microsoft operating systems, these are the most efficient and the most compatible of the applications listed. The 32-bit apps are able to take advantage of enhancements such as multithreading (the ability to send multiple commands to the processor at a single time) and preemptive multitasking (which allows the operating system to control when the application can access the processor).

NOTE   Applications will be covered more in the material for domain 2.4.

Security and Stability

Due to the fact that they are a "compromise" OS that supports both newer 32-bit Windows applications and older DOS applications, Windows 95 and 98 are susceptible to a number of security and stability problems. By being far pickier about which applications they allow to run, and by controlling those applications more tightly, Windows NT and 2000 are able to prevent many of the problems that cause Windows 95 and 98 to lock up. Also, they use an advanced file system called NTFS (NT File System), which allows for files to be secured or even encrypted. This is done through the enforcement of usernames and passwords for all users. These are stored in a local user database called the Security Accounts Management (SAM) database. Windows 9*x* does not have a SAM or equivalent database.

Major System Files: What They Are, Where They Are Located, How They Are Used, and What They Contain

The information in this content area is pretty straightforward, but the objectives as listed by CompTIA are not. For instance, IO.SYS and BOOT.INI are listed under the heading "System, Configuration, and

User Interface files," and then each is listed again later. For simplicity, we'll deal with these files together here under a slightly more coherent framework. Since the startup files for Windows 9x and 2000 are almost completely different, we'll discuss the important files for Windows 9x first, along with 9x's configuration tools. Then we will consider Windows 2000's files and tools.

System, Configuration, and User Interface Files

We'll cover the specific name and function of each of these more fully in the next few sections:

System files   These are files that are used to start up or support the operating system. They provide OS functionality.

Configuration files   These are used to modify the behavior of either the OS or a particular application. Windows uses initialization (.ini) files for this purpose, as well as Registry information.

User interface files   These are used to support the GUI. Windows will not run without system files, but it can run in a non-graphical mode without these files.

Memory Management

In both Windows 9x and Windows NT/2000, memory management is accomplished in much the same way. Physical memory—the RAM that you put into a computer—is where all processing needs to be done. In addition, Windows uses an area set aside on the hard drive as extra storage space and then "swaps" information between the hard drive and RAM. More on that in a minute.

First, though, there are a number of other memory-related distinctions that you may want to keep in mind, simply because they are mentioned in the objective guide:

Conventional memory   In DOS, this is the first 640KB of memory. In DOS/Windows 3.x, this memory area is used to load drivers and system code.

High memory   This is the remaining memory in the first 1MB. Usually this is where DOS or the active application is loaded and running.

Extended memory   Because DOS was not designed to deal with large amounts of memory, extended memory was developed to allow the system to see memory over 1MB. Extended memory is managed by HIMEM.SYS.

Expanded memory   In DOS/Windows 3.*x*, additional memory could be gained by using expanded memory to create a paged memory area on the hard drive. This was an early form of the virtual memory structure we will look at under Windows 9*x* and 2000. Expanded memory is managed by EMM386.SYS.

NOTE   Although you will want to know these terms for the test, the simple fact is that there are very few programs left that use these settings, and they are available on 9x/2000 only for backwards compatibility. To set extended/expanded memory, create a DOS shortcut on Windows 9x or 2000 and view its properties. Windows 16-bit or 32-bit programs do not have these options, because they don't use this ancient and inefficient memory scheme.

Virtual memory   The swap file is used to provide virtual memory to Windows 9*x* and 2000 systems. The swap file is hard drive space where idle pieces of programs are placed, while other active parts of programs are kept in or swapped into main memory. The programs running within Windows believe that their information is still in RAM, but Windows has simply moved it into "near-line" storage on the hard drive. When the application needs the information again, it is swapped back into RAM so that the processor can use it. The larger the swap file, the fewer times it has to do intensive drive searches. These searches, called *page faults*, are occasions when needed information is not already somewhere in memory (virtual or RAM).

The default behavior for virtual memory is that Windows simply handles it for you. This is a good thing, and unless you have a particular need to modify the size of the page file, you are best served by letting the computer handle it. If a particular application does require extensive virtual memory, you can modify it easily, though, through the System icon. If you do modify the automatic settings, do not set the swap file to an extremely low size. Another general rule is that the swap file should be at least as big as the amount of RAM in the machine. If you make the swap file too small, the system can become unbootable or at least unstable.

Windows 9*x* has a maximum memory size of 4GB, which is the most memory that can be allocated in the 95/98 memory map. Of this 4GB, 2GB are available to the OS, while the other 2GB are available to applications. The odd thing here is that each application is led to believe that it has the entire 2GB space to itself, so that it does not know of the existence of other programs and can place information at any memory location it would like. This information is then organized into the actual memory map by the Windows virtual memory manager (VMM), which keeps applications from conflicting with each other.

Windows 9*x* Major System Files

There are a number of files stored in the root of C:, as well as in the WINDOWS directory, that can be used to modify your system's configuration and affect how your computer starts. Some of the files listed in the following subsections are critical to the functioning of a Windows 9*x* computer, whereas others are simply holdovers from earlier operating systems. Due to the fact that the Registry actually handles most of the startup tasks in Windows 9*x*, many system files are there mostly for compatibility with older programs. You may never use them, but since many of these obsolete files are listed in CompTIA's test objectives, you need to know about them! Files with an * by them are required to boot Windows.

MSDOS.SYS* Function is primarily to handle disk I/O, hence the name disk operating system (DOS). Just like IO.SYS, MSDOS.SYS is loaded into memory at bootup and remains in memory at all times.

IO.SYS* Allows the rest of the operating system and its programs to interact directly with the system hardware and the system BIOS. IO.SYS includes hardware drivers for common hardware devices. It has built-in drivers for such things as printer ports, serial or communication ports, floppy drives, hard drives, auxiliary ports, console I/O (input and output), and so on.

WIN.INI Sets particular values corresponding to the Windows environment. It's used extensively by 16-bit Windows 3.*x* applications; it's almost entirely replaced by the Registry for Windows 9*x* 32-bit apps.

WIN.COM* Initiates the Windows 9*x* protected load phase.

SYSTEM.INI Used in DOS and Windows 3.1 to store information specific to running the operating system. This and other .ini files were used to configure 16-bit DOS and Windows apps.

COMMAND.COM Called the *DOS shell* or the *command interpreter*, it provides the command-line interface that the DOS user sees. This is usually, but not always, the C:\> prompt.

CONFIG.SYS Loads device drivers and uses the information from the AUTOEXEC.BAT file to configure the system environment. Memory-management tools and DOS peripheral drivers can be added here.

AUTOEXEC.BAT Used to run particular programs during startup. Also declares variables (such as search paths).

TIP A batch file, named with a .bat extension, is simply a set of commands that Windows can execute or run. These commands may run utilities, or they may point toward full-blown applications. AUTOEXEC.BAT is a batch file that is automatically executed when the system starts up.

STARTUP FILES CONFIGURATION TOOLS

There are a number of ways to modify the configuration of a Windows 9x machine. You can, of course, modify many text files by simply using a text editor such as NOTEPAD.EXE, but both Windows 95 and Windows 98 allow you to use a tool called SYSEDIT.EXE to modify certain files, and Windows 98 has added MSCONFIG.EXE as well.

SYSEDIT.EXE Allow you to examine, compare, and if needed, modify the PROTOCOL.INI, SYSTEM.INI, WIN.INI, CONFIG.SYS, and AUTOEXEC.BAT files. All that the SYSEDIT program really does is open multiple text editors, each of which has one of the key text files preloaded into it.

MSCONFIG.EXE Provided as a new addition to Windows 98, the System Configuration Utility has a number of tabs, each of which has specific options. The thing that makes the System Configuration Utility different is that it lets you use your mouse to browse and modify settings that previously were accessible only through manual text configuration. You can also enable or disable Windows 98-specific elements. The MSCONFIG utility therefore merges Windows 98 configuration information with a way for non-DOS-savvy users to work with DOS-era configuration files. Table 7.3 lists the tabs on the System Configuration Utility window.

TABLE 7.3: System Configuration Utility Tabs

Tab	Function
General	Used to set startup options, as well as to determine which files to load during startup. This tab also allows you to back up your critical system files or to restore a previous backup.
Config.sys	Used to graphically view and edit the CONFIG.SYS file.
Autoexec.bat	Used to graphically view and edit the AUTOEXEC.BAT file.
System.ini	Allows you to modify the SYSTEM.INI file using a Registry-type interface.

TABLE 7.3: System Configuration Utility Tabs *(continued)*

Tab	Function
Win.ini	Allows you to modify the WIN.INI file using a Registry-type interface.
Startup	Can be used to enable or disable particular startup options, such as which programs automatically run and whether the Registry is scanned at startup.

THE WINDOWS 9X REGISTRY

The Windows 9x Registry is a database that is made up of two files: USER.DAT and SYSTEM.DAT. Between them, these two files store configuration information about nearly everything that happens within Windows 9x.

USER.DAT Contains environmental settings for each user who logs in to Windows 9x. By default, Windows 9x uses a single profile for all users, and in that case only a single USER.DAT is maintained in the Windows directory. If users each have their own profile, though, a separate USER.DAT file is created and maintained for each user. This file is then stored in the user's profile directory.

SYSTEM.DAT Contains information about the hardware configuration of the computer that Windows is running on. The SYSTEM.DAT file is stored in the Windows directory and is shared by all users of the computer.

USER.DAT and SYSTEM.DAT cannot be edited with a text editor because they aren't text files (like AUTOEXEC.BAT, CONFIG.SYS, or the .ini files). To edit the Windows 95 Registry, you need to use a tool specifically designed for that purpose: the aptly named Registry Editor (REGEDIT.EXE).

To start the editor, choose Start ≻ Run and type **REGEDIT**. On the left side of this screen you will see the areas of the Registry. Each area (called a *key*) contains different types of settings. Table 7.4 explains these six keys and their functions.

TABLE 7.4: Registry Keys and Their Functions

Key	Description
HKEY_CLASSES_ROOT	Contains file extension associations. This tells Windows when a file with a particular extension should be opened in a particular application. Much of the data in this key is duplicated in the HKEY_LOCAL_MACHINE key (described below).
HKEY_CURRENT_USER	Contains user profile information for the person currently logged in to Windows. It contains the preferences for color settings and Desktop configuration. It is a subset of the HKEY_USERS key (described below).
HKEY_LOCAL_MACHINE	Contains settings and information for the hardware that is installed in the computer. When troubleshooting hardware issues, you might make changes to this section.
HKEY_USERS	Contains the default user profile and the profile for the current user (HKEY_CURRENT_USER, described above).
HKEY_CURRENT_CONFIG	Contains the current hardware configuration. This key is a subset of HKEY_LOCAL_MACHINE (described above).
HKEY_DYN_DATA	Contains the dynamic settings for any Plug-and-Play devices in your computer. This setting is kept in RAM and doesn't require a reboot when changes are made.

SYSTEM POLICY EDITOR

Besides using the Registry Editor, one other way to modify the Registry is through the use of System Policies. A third file—CONFIG.POL—can be used to specify particular security settings for a particular user or group of users. This file is used to "lock down" the Windows 9*x* interface so a user can't change it (useful if you have a user who is constantly changing their settings and messing up their computer). The CONFIG.POL file is created and edited with a utility called the Policy Editor (POLEDIT.EXE), which is available as an optional add-in on the Windows 95 and 98 installation CD-ROMs.

Windows 2000 Major System Files

Almost all of the files needed to boot Windows 3.1 or 9*x* are unnecessary for Windows 2000. Windows 2K requires, in fact, only a very few files, each of which performs specific tasks:

NTLDR   This file "bootstraps" the system. In other words, it is the file that starts the loading of an operating system on the computer.

BOOT.INI   Holds information about which operating systems are installed on the computer.

BOOTSECT.DOS   In a dual-boot configuration, this file keeps a copy of the DOS or Windows 9*x* boot sector so that the Windows 9*x* environment can be restored and loaded as needed.

NTDETECT.COM   Parses the system for hardware information each time Windows 2000 is loaded. This information is then used to create dynamic hardware information in the Windows 2000 Registry.

NTBOOTDD.SYS   On a system with a SCSI boot device, this file is used to recognize and load the SCSI interface. On EIDE systems, this file is not needed and is not even installed.

System files   Besides the previously listed files listed, all of which are located in the root of the C: partition on the computer, Windows 2000 also needs a number of files from its system directories, including the hardware abstraction layer (HAL.DLL) and the Windows 2000 command file (WIN.COM).

Numerous other DLL (dynamic link library) files are also required, but usually the lack or corruption of one of these will simply produce a non-critical error, while the absence of WIN.COM or HAL.DLL will cause the system to be nonfunctional.

THE REGISTRY EDITOR(S)

The Registry in Windows NT and Windows 2000 has the same purpose as the Windows 9x Registry. Unlike Windows 9x, though, NT/2000 requires that each user have their own profile and maintains that profile automatically for them. There are no longer any USER.DAT or SYSTEM.DAT files, as the Windows 2000 user info is stored in NTUSER.DAT, and the system information is split among a number of files stored in the WINNT\SYSTEM32\CONFIG directory. The key Windows NT/2000 Registry files follow closely the subfolders under the HKEY_LOCAL_MACHINE hive and are as follows:

SAM Used to store the machine's Security Accounts Management database, which is where the Registry stores information about user accounts and passwords.

SECURITY This key stores information about file and folder security on the machine.

SOFTWARE Holds configuration data for programs and utilities installed on the machine. Also has numerous areas corresponding to the OS itself.

SYSTEM This key holds information that affects the operating system's operation, especially during startup.

NOTE There is one key conspicuously absent. This is the Hardware key, which is dynamically constructed by NT/2000 each time it boots. This information is stored exclusively in memory and so is not written to a file.

Command Prompt Procedures (Command Syntax)

The Microsoft Disk Operating System, or MS-DOS, was never extremely friendly. It had its roots in CP/M, which, in turn, had its roots in Unix. Both of these older operating systems were command-line-based, and so was MS-DOS. In other words, they all used long strings of commands typed in at the computer keyboard to perform operations. Although Windows has now left the full command-line interface behind, there are still DOS-like elements in Windows 9*x* and NT/2000. Primary among these are the programs and utilities available through the command prompt.

We will look at a number of graphical utilities in the next few chapters and, believe it or not, the command prompt is one of them. Although you can't tell from looking at it, the crazy thing about the Windows command prompt is that it is actually a 32-bit Windows program that is intentionally *designed* to have the look and feel of a DOS command line!

Because it is, despite its appearance, a Windows program, the command prompt provides all of the stability and configurability that you would expect from Windows.

In general, Windows 98 uses more text-based commands than Windows 2000, and a number of standard commands are stored in the Windows 98 command directory. This can be found in whichever directory (usually Windows) that Windows 98 is installed into. See Table 7.5 for a list of Windows text commands, some of which are available only in Windows 98, while others are available in Windows 2000, such as the IPCONFIG utility that allows you to check on the TCP/IP settings of a 2000 machine.

TABLE 7.5: Windows Command-Line Utilities

Command	Purpose
ATTRIB	Allows the user to set or remove file attributes.
CD	Changes your current folder to another folder.
CHECKDSK	Examines the hard drives of the machine.
COPY	Copies a file into another directory.
DEFRAG	Defragments (reorganizes) the files on your machine's hard drives, which can result in better performance.
DEL	Deletes a file from the folder.

TABLE 7.5: Windows Command-Line Utilities *(continued)*

Command	Purpose
DELTREE	Deletes files and subdirectories. A more powerful extension of the DEL command.
DIR	Displays the contents of the current folder.
DISKCOPY	Duplicates floppy disks.
DOSKEY	Lists recently issued commands with a prompt session.
EDIT	A simple ASCII text editor.
FDISK	Creates, deletes, and manages hard disk partitions.
FORMAT	Prepares a drive for use.
MD	Creates a new folder.
MEM	Provides information on how much memory is available to the system.
MOVE	Moves files from one folder to another.
MSCDEX	Accesses CD-ROMs.
REN	Renames a file.
SCANDISK	Similar to CHECKDSK.
SCANREG	Scans the Registry by starting a Windows application that checks for errors and allows you to back up the Registry files.
SETVER	Sets the version and reports version numbers of DOS utilities.
SYS	Prepares a drive to be used to start a computer.
VER	Checks the current version of the operating system.
XCOPY	Duplicates files and subdirectories. An extension of the COPY command.

To issue a command from the command prompt, you need to know the structure that the command uses, generally referred to as its *syntax*. The following graphic shows how to learn about a command and then run that command. The command in the exercise is ATTRIB, which is used to allow a user to set one of four attributes on a file: Read Only, Archive Needed, System, or Hidden. As shown in the graphic, if you don't know the options for a DOS command, you can usually find them out using the online help for that command. Simply type the command followed by a forward slash (/) and a question mark (?). This will display all the options for that command and how to use them properly, as shown in Figure 7.4.

FIGURE 7.4: Options available for ATTRIB.EXE

Exam Essentials

Know how to navigate the Windows GUI. Knowledge of the Windows interface is pretty much a prerequisite for any of the rest of the OS exam information. Know what the elements of the Windows 9x and Windows NT/2000 systems are, how they work, and where to find them.

Know how to check the OS version. Either the System Properties window or the VER command will give you this information.

Know the major differences between Windows 9x and Windows 2000. Stability, security, and application compatibility are all important here. You may also get questions that give you a machine's hardware specifications and ask you which OS would be best for it.

Know how the Windows virtual memory system works. You should be able to describe how information is handled by the virtual memory manager and how to change the default virtual memory settings.

Understand the distinctions between DOS memory types. Know what conventional, high, extended, and expanded memory are. Also know how to set these memory levels in both Windows 9x and NT/2000.

Know the function of the major system files for Windows 9x. If you have questions on the exam about these, they should be relatively straightforward, such as "Which file is used to load DOS device drivers?" (CONFIG.SYS). Know the files and their most common uses.

Know the function of the major system files for Windows NT/2000. NT and 2000 have identical boot files, so the same information works for both systems. The NTBOOTDD.SYS file is an extremely common test item.

Know the function of common system configuration tools and how to use them. Getting in some practice working with the system tools mentioned for both 9x and 2000 is highly recommended.

Know about the Windows Registry—both what it contains and how to modify it. Understanding the component parts of the Registry is critical to understanding Windows. You need to know where the Registry files are located in the file system and what each one stores, and you will need to be able to use REGEDIT and REGEDT32 to browse and modify the system configuration.

Know how to open up a command prompt and enter text commands. One of the things you should probably do is go through each of the commands listed in the objectives and read through their help screens. Find out which switches are available for each, and what they do.

Key Terms and Concepts

Window   A rectangular area of the screen in which a particular application or utility runs.

Icon   A graphic that sits on the Desktop, in the Start menu, or in a directory. These graphics can be opened to start the applications that they are linked to.

Desktop   The "back" of the Windows operating system. All components and windows are placed on the Desktop.

HCL   The Hardware Compatibility List can be used to determine whether the components in your machine are supported by a particular Windows operating system.

Version   A version is a particular revision of a piece of software, normally described by a number that tells you how new the product is in relation to other versions of the product.

Shell   A shell is a program that runs "on top of" the operating system and allows the user to issue commands through a set of menus or some other graphical interface. Shells make an operating system easier to use by changing the user interface. The Windows shell is called the Explorer.

Graphical user interface (GUI)   The user interface is the method by which a person communicates with a computer. GUIs use a mouse, touch pad, or another mechanism (in addition to the keyboard) to interact with the computer to issue commands.

Cooperative multitasking   A multitasking method that depends on the application itself to be responsible for using and then freeing access to the processor. This is the way that Windows 3.1 managed multiple applications. If any application locked up while using the processor, the application was unable to properly free the processor to do other tasks, and the entire system locked, usually forcing a reboot.

Preemptive multitasking A multitasking method in which the operating system allots each application a certain amount of processor time and then forcibly takes back control and gives another application or task access to the processor. This means that if an application crashes, the operating system takes control of the processor away from the locked application and passes it on to the next application, which should be unaffected. Although unstable programs still lock, only the locked application will stall, not the entire system.

Extended memory Memory over 1MB in DOS/Windows 3.1 machines.

Expanded memory Memory created by using a portion of a DOS/Windows 3.1 machine's hard drive. Replaced by virtual memory in Windows 9x.

Virtual memory A portion of the hard drive providing extra memory for the system.

SAM The Security Accounts Management database allows Windows NT and 2000 to manage users and passwords. It then allows these OSes to provide other security-related features such as file security and encryption.

Switch In command-prompt utilities, switches are options appended to the command that modify its functionality.

System Policy System Policies allow an administrator to control what users see and what they can do.

Profile A profile keeps track of a user's preferences and settings, so that if multiple users work on a single machine, each of them can have their own Desktop and settings.

▶ 1.2 Identify basic concepts and procedures for creating, viewing and managing files, directories and disks. This includes procedures for changing file attributes and the ramifications of those changes (for example, security issues).

- File attributes - Read Only, Hidden, System, and Archive attributes
- File naming conventions (Most common extensions)
- Windows 2000 COMPRESS, ENCRYPT
- IDE/SCSI
- Internal/External
- Backup/Restore
- Partitioning/Formatting/File System
- Windows-based utilities

This objective concentrates on the syntax used with commands, file types, file-naming conventions, and the use of the ATTRIB command and the results associated with setting a file's attributes.

Critical Information

Objectives within the 1.2 content area are focused around the way that Windows 9*x* and NT/2000 interact with the hard disk on a computer. Content to be reviewed includes how disks are created and prepared for use and how Windows then allows you to save and retrieve information using these disks. The objectives are in a relatively odd order on the CompTIA list. To put them into logical study order, please mentally reorder them for this section as shown below:

Drive Types

IDE/SCSI

Internal/External

Device Manager

Creating and Managing Partitions

Partitioning

FDISK

Computer Management

Formatting

FAT

FAT16

FAT32

NTFS4

NTFS5

HPFS

FORMAT

Cvt1

CONVERT

Working with the File System

File Naming Conventions (Most Common Extensions)

System Information

File Attributes (Read Only, Hidden, System, and Archive)

ATTRIB

Windows 2000 Compress, Encrypt

Maintaining the File System

Scandisk

EXTRACT

DEFRAG

SCANREG

ASD

WSCRIPT

Backup/Restore

MSCONFIG

REGEDIT/REGEDT32

If you reorder these and check them off, you will notice that not everything is included in the above list. Never fear, true believer, I haven't forgotten them. Some of them are duplicates from area 1.1, while others just don't make sense. Here are the things that didn't belong anywhere else.

System Manager   This is the weirdest part of the entire exam blueprint. Put quite simply, the "System Manager" does not exist in any version of Windows that I know of. Moreover, all of us at Sybex looked for this utility, and no one could unearth anything. My suspicion here is that the intended utility is the "System Information" tool, but this tool is relatively out of place in this segment. Although we won't be talking about it here, you may want to explore the Windows 98 and Windows 2000 versions of the System Information tool, just in case. This is probably the tool CompTIA intended to refer to.

Computer Manager   Another typo, as near as I can tell, as there is no "Computer Manager" tool in Windows either. "Computer Management" is the tool that replaces FDISK in Windows 2000, and we will look at it.

EDIT.COM   This tool was important in DOS, as it was the primary text editor for that OS. EDIT is still available in Windows 9*x*, NT, and 2000, but generally users now use NOTEPAD for text-editing tasks instead.

Drive Types

This objective is a bit odd, in that it mentions information such as the following:

- IDE/SCSI

- Internal/External

What this has to do with anything, I am not exactly sure. These items are generally more of an issue at the hardware level, but nonetheless we will review them just a bit in case the test throws you a curve.

There are two storage device architectures that can be used with Intel-architecture computers. The most common consumer drives are IDE (Integrated Drive Electronics) or EIDE (Enhanced IDE) drives. IDE drives are attached to the motherboard by a ribbon cable, which is connected to the IDE interface. Most modern machines have two of these interfaces, although some have only one. Each interface can support two drives, one of which will be configured as the master, while the other will be set up as the slave. These settings can be explicitly configured, or a Cable Select option can be used to let the drives determine this order themselves. Because of their architecture, there can be only four IDE devices on a single computer (two interfaces times two devices on each). This limitation can be an issue in modern machines, as these devices can include Zip drives, CD-ROM drives, Writeable/Re-writeable CD-ROM drives, and DVD drives. Even so, the IDE architecture is cheaper and easier to configure than SCSI, so most consumer machines use these drives.

SCSI drives come in many types, but they also connect to an interface on the motherboard using a ribbon cable. The difference is that instead of a master/slave configuration, SCSI uses a more flexible device ID to enumerate its devices. This allows for far more devices on a controller—either eight or 16 normally. The SCSI interface (also called a *controller*) takes one of these, but that still leaves seven (or 15) other IDs per controller. Because of this, SCSI-based systems can allow you to have more devices, although they are sometimes more difficult to configure, as each ID must be set individually on the drive. The SCSI architecture is faster and more flexible than the IDE, but as with nearly everything in life, better is more expensive, and SCSI drives generally are used only in server machines or high-performance workstations.

Now, you may ask yourself, "What the heck does this have to do with the OS?" The simple answer, of course, is "Pretty much nothing at all." The only way that the SCSI/IDE difference affects the OS is that while an IDE controller is generally built to a standard and does not need any special drivers, SCSI controllers often do need to have drivers supplied before they will work. This will generally be pretty obvious, as you won't even be able to see the drives to set up the OS without having the proper drivers. Once the drivers are loaded, they can be looked at and updated using the Device Manager. The drives themselves (IDE or SCSI) do not need any drivers and simply do what the controller tells them.

NOTE   Most older SCSI controllers are recognized by Windows systems without much problem. Newer controllers may not be recognized, especially by older systems such as Windows 95 or Windows NT. In that case, you will have to have the drivers or go out to a Web site and find them.

Even more vexing is the presence of a content objective called "Internal/External," which is completely irrelevant to the OS exam. External drives are the same as internal in the way they are configured, partitioned, formatted, and accessed. The only difference is that they are, as you might have guessed, mounted in cases outside the computer rather than mounted inside it. Your author humbly apologizes for not even being able to comprehend how a relevant OS question can be formulated from this difference.

TIP While this is not certain, it is possible that what the test formulators were actually referring to are "removable" drives. These are devices that allow you to take out the media and replace it. Examples of this are Zip drives, Read/Write CD drives, and Bernouli drives. There are issues with removable devices that you may want to look into, but because they are not technically in the objectives, we won't cover them here.

Creating and Managing Partitions

Once the drives are in the machine and the controller is set up, you will need to prepare the hard drives for use before an operating system can be installed on the machine. This generally consists of two steps, both of which fall under objective 1.2.

Partitioning

Windows 9x and Windows NT/2000 manage disks in different ways. Windows NT/2000 includes a partitioning option during setup and also has a tool called Disk Management (NT) or Computer Management (2000) that can be used to manage partitions on an existing system.

Windows 9x, though, requires that partitions be created before the OS is installed, and this is done through a DOS or Windows startup disk.

NOTE The procedure for creating the startup disk is covered in domain 2.3.

Partitioning refers to establishing large allocations of hard drive space. A *partition* is a continuous section of sectors that are next to each other. In DOS and Windows, a partition is referred to by a drive letter, such as C: or D:. Partitioning a drive into two or more parts gives it the appearance of being two or more physical hard drives.

When a drive is partitioned in DOS, the first partition you create will be a *primary partition*, which needs to be marked *active*. The active partition is the location of the bootup files for DOS or Windows. It is possible for no partitions to be marked active on a particular drive. In this case, the machine will not be able to boot to the drive. If this is the case, you must use FDISK to set an active partition before you will be able to properly install Windows 9*x*. One and only one partition can be marked active at a time.

If there is additional space, a second partition called an *extended partition* can be created. An extended partition contains one or more *logical partitions*. One or more logical partitions must be defined within the extended partition, and they can then have drive letters attached to them so users can access them. Due to limitations with the way that DOS and Windows 9*x* access partition structures, only one primary and one extended partition can be created per disk using the Windows 95 disk utility, FDISK.

Using FDISK

With FDISK, you can create partitions, delete partitions, mark a partition as active, or display available partitioning information. FDISK can be run off the Windows 9*x* startup disk, as discussed above, or can be run from a command prompt within Windows 9*x*. Either way, FDISK has a number of major functions:

Creating partitions and logical drives   Partitions are created from unused space on the drive. Until the space has been partitioned, it is unusable by most systems.

Deleting partitions and logical drives   If a partition is no longer needed, and space needs to be made on the drive for the creation of other partitions, deleting a partition removes all information about the partition and also deletes any information that had been stored on the partition. Think before you do this!

Setting a partition as active   In order to boot the system, the computer must know where to look for the "bootstrap" files that start the system load phase. Setting a partition as active identifies it as the place to look for these files.

Viewing the partitions on a disk FDISK also allows you to simply browse through the partition information on a disk. If the machine has more than one disk, you can choose which one to look at.

Disk Administrator/Computer Management

Windows NT and 2000 use different tools to manage partitions. Windows NT has an icon for Disk Administrator in its Administrative Tools folder, while Windows 2000 has a Storage area in its Computer Management utility.

The two utilities are actually very similar, as both allow you to modify partition information in a graphical manner. These tools have far more options than FDISK, though. First off, instead of just two partitions, Windows NT/2000 can recognize four per disk. You can still have just one extended partition (with up to three primaries) or you can simply make four primary partitions.

NOTE Just because you *can* have four partitions per drive doesn't mean you *have* to. In many cases, a single large partition is best.

Among the important differences between FDISK and these advanced disk tools is the ability of Disk Administrator and Computer Management to do the following:

- Format partitions
- Change drive letters
- Check other drive properties

Format Options

The next step in the management of a hard drive is formatting, initiated by the FORMAT command. During a format, the surface of the hard drive platter is briefly scanned to find any possible bad spots, and the areas surrounding a bad spot are marked as bad sectors. After this, magnetic tracks are laid down in concentric circles. These tracks are where information is eventually encoded.

Past this, there are a number of options as far as how the system will store information. Each of these methods of storing information is known as a *file system*, and you will need to know about several of these for the test:

FAT   Short for File Allocation Table. The FAT keeps track of where information is stored and how to retrieve it.

FAT16   Used with DOS and Windows 3.*x*, as well as early versions of Windows 95, FAT16 (generally just called FAT) has a number of advantages. First, it is extremely fast on small (under 500MB) drives. Second, it is a file system that nearly all operating systems can agree on, making it excellent for dual-boot system. However, FAT also has limitations that started causing problems as Windows got bigger and faster. First off, FAT has a limit of 4GB per partition. Once you have hard drives that are 10–30GB, this becomes a serious issue. Also, sectors on hard drives are arranged in what is called a *cluster* or *allocation unit*. In general, as a FAT16-formatted drive or drive partition increases in size, the number of sectors per cluster increases. A drive between 16MB and 128MB will have four sectors per cluster, while a drive of up to 256MB will have eight sectors per cluster, and drives of up to 512MB will have 16 sectors per cluster.

TIP   Another limit of FAT is so wonderfully obscure that test preparers rarely can resist it. The root of any FAT drive (C:\, D:\) has a hard-coded limit of 512 entries. This includes directories, files, etc. Also, long filenames may take up more than one entry. If a user reaches this limit, they will be unable to save any other files in the root. This limit does not apply to subdirectories or to FAT32 or NTFS drives.

FAT32   Introduced with Windows 95 OSR2, FAT32 is similar to FAT but has a number of advantages. First, FAT32 supports larger drives and smaller allocation units. As a comparison of how the new system saves you space, a 2GB drive with FAT16 has clusters of 32KB; with FAT32, the clusters sizes are 4KB. Because of this, if you save a 15KB file, FAT will need to allocate an entire 32KB cluster. FAT32 would use four 4KB clusters, for a total of 16KB. FAT32 wastes an unused 1KB, while FAT wastes 15 times as much!

The disadvantage of FAT32 is that it is not compatible with older DOS, Windows 3.*x*, and Windows 95 operating systems. This means that when you boot a Windows 95 Rev B. or Windows 98 FAT32-formatted partition with a DOS boot floppy, you can't read the partition.

One tool included with Windows 98 is the FAT32 Drive Converter tool (CVT1.EXE), which allows you to upgrade FAT disks to FAT32 without having to reformat them. This preserves all of the information on the drive but allows you to take advantage of FAT32's enhancements.

NTFS4 Windows NT's file system. NTFS4 includes enhanced attributes for compressing files or for setting file security. Updating a FAT drive to NTFS is relatively easy and can be done through a command called CONVERT. This conversion does not destroy any information but simply updates the file system.

NTFS5 Windows 2000 updated the NTFS system, so as to include enhancements such as file encryption. NTFS5 also includes support for larger drive sizes.

HPFS This is the OS/2 file system, which is supported only under Windows NT. Windows 9*x* cannot create or access HPFS, and neither can Windows 2000. Even NT can only read these partitions, not create them.

Formatting a Drive

If you are installing Windows 9*x*, you will need to use a boot disk to first partition and then format the drive. The FORMAT command is located on the boot disk and is simple to use. If you want to format the first partition on the system, type **FORMAT C:** and it will start the process. You will be reminded that this procedure will destroy any information currently on the drive and will be asked to verify your decision to format. Once the format is complete, you can start the install process.

Windows NT and 2000 allow you to format as part of the install, so no advance preparation with FDISK or FORMAT is necessary when installing those OSes.

Once Windows (9*x*, NT, or 2000) is up and running, you can format or reformat drives by using FORMAT from a command prompt or graphically through the Windows interface, which also allows formatting through the Explorer or the My Computer icon.

Working with the File System

After you have your partitions created and formatted, you can put information onto them. Generally, the first information to be put onto the drive is placed there by the OS installation program. Once this is done and the system is up and running, you can then perform additional modifications as needed. This section of the chapter deals with how users can access and work with the Windows file system management tools.

The Windows file system is arranged like a filing cabinet. In a filing cabinet, paper is placed into folders, which are inside dividers, which are in a drawer of the filing cabinet. In the file system, individual files are placed in subdirectories, which are inside directories, which are stored on different disks. Windows also protects against duplicate filenames, since no two files on the system can have exactly the same name and path. A *path* indicates the location of the file on the disk; it is composed of the logical drive letter the file is on, and if the file is located in a directory or subdirectory, the names of those directories. For instance, a file named AUTOEXEC.BAT is located in the root of the C: drive—meaning it is not within a directory—so the path to the file is simply C:\AUTOEXEC.BAT. Another important file, FDISK.EXE, is located in the COMMAND directory under Windows under the root of C:, so the path to FDISK is therefore C:\WINDOWS\COMMAND\FDISK.EXE (Windows 9*x* only). The *root* of any drive is simply the place where the hierarchy of that drive begins. On a C: drive, for instance, C:\ is the root directory of the drive.

File Naming Conventions (Most Common Extensions)

First, let's look at some of the basics. Windows filenames are used to identify particular application, configuration, or data files. Each file must have a unique name within the directory it is created in and must obey certain rules. The following characters are not usable in filenames in Windows: \ / : * ? " | < >.

Besides the filename itself, each file can also have an optional filename extension, which is one or more characters long and allows the file to be identified by Windows as being of a certain type. Text files are given .txt extensions, batch files are given .bat extensions, and executable files are given .exe extensions. Each is then handled differently when it is accessed. The behavior of a file with a particular extension is determined by a process called *association*.

When a file extension is associated with a particular filename, the association defines what application will open the file and what the default actions for the file are. To check on a file association, use Windows Explorer. Click Tools ➢ Folder Options, and go to the File Types tab. From there you can view and modify the extensions for that computer. Among the most common filename extensions are those shown in Table 7.6.

TABLE 7.6: Filename Extensions

Extension	File type
.bat	Batch files
.sys	System files
.exe	Executable files
.txt	Text files
.dll	Dynamic Link Library code files
.doc	MS Word document files
.xls	MS Excel spreadsheet files
.ini	DOS/Windows 3.x application initialization files
.bmp	Bitmap graphic files
.inf	Setup information files

All Windows filenames share the elements we have looked at so far. There are, however, two very different naming schemes in Windows:

Short filenames These filenames come out of the DOS legacy. Files that are created using the short "8.3" naming convention are allowed a name of only one to eight characters, with an optional extension of one to three characters. While this works fine, it does not allow for names that make a great deal of sense. These names are seldom used anymore, but both DOS and Windows 3.1 used this naming convention, so the DOS prompt and any Windows 16-bit applications still are likely to use 8.3 naming. Short names do not allow blank spaces.

Long filenames Beginning with Windows 95, Microsoft expanded the namespace by allowing names of up to 256 (215 in Windows 2000) characters. All newer MS operating systems support long filenames, which do allow blank spaces in the name.

File Attributes (Read Only, Hidden, System, and Archive)

Besides their names, files also have a series of attributes that can be attached to them to further identify or categorize them. In DOS, Windows 3.*x*, and 9*x*, there are four such attributes, while Windows NT and 2000 add additional attributes through NTFS. These attributes are listed below, along with their function. The ATTRIB command can be used to set and remove the four base "RASH" attributes (the first four below), while Windows Explorer can be used to set any of the attributes that are available by viewing a file's properties.

Read Only This attribute prevents the file from being modified or deleted.

Archive This tells the system whether the file has been modified since it was last backed up and allows the backup program to know which files to process in an incremental or differential backup.

System Identifies the file as one needed by the system. You will be warned if you attempt to delete a file labeled as System.

Hidden Often, system files are hidden to prevent them from showing up in normal searches of the hard drive. To see a list of hidden files in a directory, type **DIR /ah**.

Compress Used to specify that the file is to be compressed when not in use. This saves space on the drive but slows access to the file (NT and 2000).

Index Allows the Index Service to add the file to its indexes. This increases the speed of any searches you do on the system (2000 only).

Encrypt Used to secure a file through an encryption algorithm. This makes it extremely difficult for anyone other than the user to access the file by encoding it using a public/private key technology (2000 only).

Folders and Files

Now that we have the basics of file naming and attributes, you will also need to know how to view, create, and manage files and folders for the test. *File management* is the process by which a computer stores data and retrieves it from storage. The process of managing files is similar across all current Windows platforms (Windows 95/98/NT/2000). Most folder and file management is done through a tool called Windows Explorer.

WARNING Watch out for all the "Explorers" when reading test questions. There are three different Explorers in Windows: Internet Explorer, Windows Explorer, and EXPLORER.EXE, which is the Windows shell program. Make sure you know which one the question is asking you about.

Capabilities of Windows Explorer

Although it is technically possible to simply use the command-line utilities provided within the command prompt to manage your files, this generally is not the most efficient way to accomplish most tasks. The ability to use drag-and-drop techniques and other graphical tools to manage the file system makes the process far simpler. Windows Explorer is a utility that allows the user to accomplish a number of important file-related tasks from a single graphical interface.

Some of the tasks you can accomplish using Windows Explorer include:

- Viewing files and directories
- Opening programs or data files
- Creating directories and files
- Copying objects (files or directories) to other locations
- Moving objects (files or directories) to other locations
- Deleting or renaming objects (files or directories)
- Searching for a particular file or type of file
- Changing file attributes
- Formatting new disks (such as floppy disks)

Navigating and Using Windows Explorer

Using Windows Explorer is actually pretty simple. Just a few basic instructions are all you will need to start working with it. First off, the Explorer interface itself has a number of parts, each of which serves a specific purpose. The top area of the Explorer is dominated by a set of menus and toolbars that allow easy access to common commands. The main section of the window is divided into two panes. The left pane displays the drives and folders available to the user, while the right pane displays the contents of the currently selected folder. Along the bottom of the window, the status bar displays information about the used and free space on the current directory. Some common actions in Explorer include the following:

Expanding a folder   You can double-click a folder to expand the folder (i.e., show its subfolders in the left panel) and display the contents of the folder in the right pane. Simply clicking the plus sign (+) to the left of a folder will expand the folder without changing it.

Collapsing a folder   Clicking a minus sign (–) next to a folder will unexpand it.

Selecting a file   If you click a file in the right pane, Windows will highlight the file by marking it with a darker color.

Selecting multiple files   The Ctrl and Shift keys allow you to select multiple files at once. Holding down Ctrl while clicking individual files selects each new file while leaving the currently selected file or files selected as well. Holding down Shift while selecting two files selects both of them and all files in between.

Opening a file   Double-clicking a file in the right pane opens the program if it is an application; if it is a file, it opens it using whichever file extension is configured for it.

Changing the view type   There are four different primary view types: Large Icons, Small Icons, List, and Details. You can move between these views by clicking the View menu and selecting the view you prefer.

Finding specific files   You access this option under View ➤ Find in Windows 98 or by using the Search button in Windows 2000. Either way, you can search for files based on their name, file size, file type, and other attributes.

TIP   When searching, wildcards can also be used. Wildcards are characters that act as placeholders for a character or set of characters, allowing, for instance, a search for all files with text (.txt) extensions. To perform such a search, you'd type an asterisk (*) as a stand-in for the filename: *.txt. Asterisks are used to take the place of any number of characters in a search, while question marks (?) are used to take the place of a single number or letter; for example, **AUTOEX??.BAT** would return the file AUTOEXEC.BAT as part of its results.

Creating new objects   To create a new file, folder, or other object, navigate to the location where you want to create the object, and then right-click in the right pane. In the menu that appears, select New and then choose the object you want to create.

Deleting objects   Select the object and press the Delete key on the keyboard, or right-click the object and select Delete from the menu that appears. This will send the file or folder to the Recycle Bin. In order to permanently delete the object, you must then empty the Recycle Bin. Alternatively, you can hold down Shift while deleting an object, and it will be permanently deleted immediately.

Besides simplifying most file-management commands as shown above, the Explorer also allows you to easily complete a number of disk-management tasks. Floppy disks can be formatted and labeled, and the Windows system files can be copied to a floppy so that a disk may be used to boot a machine. Before you take the test, you will want to be extremely familiar with the Windows file system and how the above tasks are accomplished.

NOTE   *Labeling* is an optional process of giving a name to a disk. You can label both hard drives and floppies.

Maintaining the File System

For the most part, the Windows operating system is self-regulating, and there is little that needs to be done to keep it running. Even so, some tools have been provided to allow you to check on the health and performance of your system and to take action if there are problems. For the test, you will want to know how each of these tools works.

Most of these utilities, if installed, can be found in the Start menu: Start ➢ Programs ➢ Accessories ➢ System Tools. The programs in this folder can be very useful to a technician. Other utilities (such as ASD.EXE) are not commonly used and do not have an icon. You can find them in the Windows (or WINNT) directory or the System32 sub-directory. Some common Windows utilities, along with their purpose, are listed in Table 7.8.

TABLE 7.7: Windows System Tools

System Tool	Function
Automatic Skip Driver	Checks for ASD failures on the system.
Backup	Makes archival copies of important files.
Character Map	Determines which type of letters, numbers, and nonalphanumeric characters the machine will use.
Clipboard Viewer	Allows you to see what has been copied onto the system clipboard.
Drive Space 3	Allows you to compress the files on a drive to get more information onto it (although compressing files makes them slower to access).
Compression Agent	Used with DriveSpace 3. Allows you to set up parameters for automatically determining which files to compress.
Disk Cleanup	Goes through the system and deletes unneeded files to free up drive space.
Disk Defragmenter	Arranges data on the computer's disk drives so that it will be more easily available. Also can be run from the command line as DEFRAG.EXE.
Extract	New to Windows 2000, the Extract command allows you to browse through a cabinet file (.cab) and retrieve selected files out of it.
Maintenance Wizard	Sets up a system maintenance plan.
Net Watcher	Checks the performance of the network.
Resource Meter	Gives a quick, graphical display of how heavily basic system resources are being used.

TABLE 7.7: Windows System Tools *(continued)*

System Tool	Function
Scan Disk	Checks a disk drive for errors or problems. Also can be run from the command line as SCANDISK.EXE.
Scanreg	Checks the Windows Registry for errors or problems.
Scheduled Tasks	Enables the running of recurring tasks automatically.
System Configuration Utility	Graphical tool for modifying and backing up system files and choosing startup options.
System Information	Finds information on the hardware and software installed on a PC.
System Monitor	A more complex version of Resource Meter. Monitors specific resources and watches how they are used in real time.
Windows Scripting Host	Often known as WSH, or by its filename, WSCRIPT.EXE, this tool allows users to create and run scripts from their Windows 2000 machines far more easily and flexibly than previously possible.

Windows 2000 also has a folder called Administrative Tools where additional system configuration utilities are kept. Many of the tools in Table 7.7 are available in both Windows 98 and Windows 2000 but have different names or are in different locations. For instance, Windows 98's System Monitor is expanded into a more powerful tool in Windows 2000 called Performance, which you can access by clicking Start ➤ Control Panel ➤ Administrative Tools. Many common system tools are also available in Windows 2000 through the Computer Management tool, as shown in Figure 7.5.

FIGURE 7.5: Windows 2000 Computer Management Utility

Maintaining the Registry

Configuration information for Windows is stored in a special configuration database known as the *Registry*. This centralized database contains environmental settings for various Windows programs. It also contains what is known as *registration* information, which details which types of file extensions are associated with which applications. So, when you double-click a file in Windows Explorer, the associated application runs and opens the file you double-clicked.

The Registry was introduced with Windows 95. Most operating systems up until Windows 95 were based on text files, which can be edited with almost any text editor. However, the Registry database is contained in special binary file, which can be edited only with the special Registry Editor provided with Windows. The Registry Editor program is called REGEDIT.EXE, and its icon is not typically created during Windows installation—you must create the icon manually. You can also run the program manually by selecting Start ➤ Run, typing **REGEDIT**, and clicking OK. Windows NT and 2000 have two applications that can be used to edit the Registry, REGEDIT and REGEDT32 (notice there is no *I* in REGEDT32). Both work similarly, but each has slightly different options for navigation and browsing. Windows extensively uses the Registry to store all kinds of information. Indeed, it holds most, if not all, of the configuration information for Windows 98 and 2000. It is a potentially dangerous task to modify the Registry in Windows. The reason why the Control Panel and other configuration tools are provided for you is so that you will have graphical tools for modifying system settings. Directly modifying the Registry can have unforeseen—and unpleasant—results. Users should modify the Registry only when told to do so by an extremely trustworthy source.

For the test, you will want to be familiar with the Registry Editor interface and with how configuration information is stored and modified.

Backup and Restore

Outside of keeping a system running, the most important thing you will need to know how to do is to get a system back up and running after a critical failure. Critical failures come in a number of flavors, all of which leave a bad taste. The ones we will be looking at here are two of the most common you may have to face—both in the real world and on the exam:

- Recovering from a hard drive failure
- Recovering from a Registry failure

Recovering from a Hard Drive Failure

First off, I want to note that any part in a computer can go bad. Motherboards can short out, power supplies can burn out, and network cards can die. None of these, though, is nearly as difficult to deal with as a hard drive gone bad. The reason for this is that a power supply or motherboard does not contain unique information, and all you need to do is replace the hardware and restart the system. Hard drives are different, as you not only need to replace the hardware, but the information on it as well. To do this, you need to have the information on the drive backed up to another location. This can either be another disk, a writeable CD, or a tape. Because they are relatively inexpensive and have large capacities, tape drives are the most common form of backup.

A *backup* is a duplicate copy of all the files and software on your hard disk. This copy is usually stored in a safe place (like a safe) in case of a system failure. When a system failure occurs, the backup can be copied back onto the system, restoring the system to the state it was in at the time of the last backup. This process of restoring the system is known as a *restore*.

Most backups are done the same way: Select what you want to back up, then select where you want to back up to, then finally begin the backup. The files and directories you want to back up (and, subsequently, the drive they are stored on) are called the *backup source*. The device that you are backing up to is called the *backup target*. Once you have selected these items, some backup software will let you save these selections in a file known as a *backup set* so that you can reselect them later for restore by simply retrieving the backup set file from the backup media.

BACKUP TYPES

There are four major types of backup that most backup software can use when backing up files: Full, Differential, Incremental, and Custom. Each type differs in the amount that it backs up, the time it takes to perform the backup, and the time it takes to restore the system to its pre-backup condition.

Full A Full backup, as its name suggests, backs up everything on the entire disk at once. It simply copies everything from the disk being backed up to the backup device. The backup takes a long time to perform (relative to the other types of backup), but the advantage is that the backup (and, subsequently, the restore) will use only one backup set. Full backups are most often performed on systems that require that there be very little downtime.

Differential A Differential backup backs up the files on a disk that have changed since the last Full backup, regardless of whether a Differential or Incremental backup has been done since the last Full backup. The Full backup is done usually once a week (e.g., on Friday) and copies all the files from the disk to the backup device. The Differential backup is done every day, so the size of a Differential backup increases every day following the Full backup. The advantage to a Differential backup style is that during the week, the backups don't take as long, but when you restore from a Differential backup, you will need two tapes: the Full backup from the previous week and the current Differential backup. You will need to restore the Full backup first, then restore the Differential backup to restore the changes made since the last Full backup.

Incremental The Incremental backup works similarly to the Differential backup but uses fewer tapes in a large backup situation. An Incremental backup does a Full backup once a week, then the backup software backs up all the files that have changed since the previous backup (not necessarily the last Full backup). Each day, the backup software backs up a different amount of data, depending on the amount of data that was created that day.

The upside to the Incremental backup is that only the files that have changed that day will be backed up. If only three files changed today, then only three files will be backed up. Incremental backups tend to be very quick. The downside to Incremental backups is that to restore, you need the last Full backup tape and all the Incremental backup tapes from the day of the failure back to the day of the last Full backup.

Custom The last type of backup that is performed is the Custom backup. A Custom backup is any combination of the above three types.

BACKING UP FILES

Because of the importance of backing up your data, there are many different Backup programs to choose from. Microsoft has ensured that you will have one to use by including one with each of its major operating systems. The Backup program should be found in the following locations:

- Windows 9x—System Tools

- Windows NT—Administrative Tools

- Windows 2000—System Tools

If the program icon is not present, the Backup utility may not be installed. To install it, simply go to Add/Remove programs. For the test, you will want to know how to open Backup on each OS and also how to create and schedule backups.

Backup is a rather simple yet powerful program and is basically the same across all Windows OSes. The Backup window contains two panes that work very similarly to the Windows Explorer program. If you double-click an item in the right pane, it will open and allow you to see what's inside. You can also use the right pane and click the + signs next to items to "tree them out" and show the directory structure. These two panes allow you to select items to be backed up. First, you select what you want to back up, then you indicate where you want to back up those files and directories, and then you initiate the backup. If you have a tape drive installed, it will show up in the list on the left. You can then select it as the target device and click Start Backup to begin the backup. If you don't have a tape drive (or don't want to use it), you can select one of the drives as the target device by clicking its name.

Once you have a backup set, it is important to remember that you will need to schedule backups to occur regularly (generally weekly or nightly). In Windows 2000, this can be done through the Backup utility itself, while in Windows 9x and NT, a scheduler program must be used. NT uses the Scheduler service, while Windows 9x uses the Scheduled Tasks utility.

Note that besides simply backing up the files on the drive, many Backup programs also allow you to back up the Registry and other system information separately. You may also need to have special backup "agents" to allow you to properly back up databases and other files, as open files are generally skipped by the backup process.

One other, less-complete backup process you will want to look at is the Windows 98 System Configuration Utility's (MSCONFIG) option for backing up system files. This allows the user to back up files such as the AUTOEXEC.BAT before making changes to them and to restore the original versions later if they need to go back to the original files. This is a limited, but very useful, backup type.

RESTORING FILES

In order to ensure that your backups are good and that you know what to do in case of a disaster-recovery situation, you should perform a test restore every once in a while. Whatever Backup program you used will need to be used to perform the restore as well. In most cases, this means that you will have to install a test machine with a new copy of the OS you backed up and install the tape drive and drivers for the tape drive on that machine. There is no "RESTORE.EXE" program; in order to restore files, you simply run the Backup utility again and choose the Restore tab.

Backup will then allow you to choose where you want to restore from and which files you wish to bring back. In doing this, you will be overwriting any files on the machine that have the same name and path as those being restored. Once you have made your selections, you start the restore, and the appropriate files will be found on the tape or disk you have specified and will be returned to the hard drive. When Backup finishes restoring all the files you have selected, it will present you with a summary of the restore, detailing how much data was restored and how long it took.

Normally, I would recommend forgetting the MS Backup options and using a third-party option like Backup Exec or ArcServe. For the purposes of the A+ test, though, the ones you need to know are the Microsoft Backup products.

Recovering from a Registry Failure

Other than a complete drive crash, probably the next most destructive problem you may encounter is the corruption of your system Registry. Both Windows 9x and Windows NT/2000 have relatively stable Registries, but even so they are still just databases, and corruption is always a risk with any database.

Windows 9*x* automatically makes backup copies of the two Registry files USER.DAT and SYSTEM.DAT. Each time that Windows 9*x* restarts, your Registry is examined, and if problems are found, the backup copy of the Registry is located and is used to start Windows. The application used to do this is SCANREG.EXE. You can run this application separately from Windows if you want to verify the Registry at any time. SCANREG is great, as long as the automatic Registry backup is good. Just in case, though, it is always a good idea to back up the Registry files regularly. If both the current and backup copies of the Registry are corrupt, a backup copy of the Registry files can simply be saved over the corrupt files and the system restarted.

In Windows NT and 2000, the situation is more complex. There are more files that make up the Registry, and they are not backed up automatically. The Registry in NT/2000 can be backed up using the Backup program or through the creation of an Emergency Repair Disk. Note that when creating an ERD, you have to add the /s switch to back up the security information from the Registry. When the ERD is updated, the /REPAIR directory on the hard drive can also be updated with the same current configuration information that is written to the floppy disk.

Another option in all versions of Windows is to use REGEDIT or REGEDT32 to save the Registry out to a file, which can then be re-added later. This file can include all Registry information or only particular parts of the Registry's hierarchy.

For the test, you will want to know the locations of the key Registry files in all Windows versions, as well as how the repair process works for each.

Exam Essentials

Know the different types of drives and how they affect the system configuration process. Focus on the difference between SCSI and IDE hardware, and be sure to look at all of the tools that allow you to access information about your drives, notably Device Manager.

Be able to plot the course a drive takes from being blank to running Windows.   An understanding of the key tools used to partition and format drives is critical, with FDISK and FORMAT being the main tools for Windows 9*x*, and Setup and Disk Administrator/Computer Management the main tools for Windows NT/2000.

Understand the key differences between FAT16, FAT32, and NTFS. The most important elements here are partition size, allocation unit size, available attributes, and compatibility.

Understand how short and long filenames work and what the limits and advantages of each are.   Short names are nasty things but are backward-compatible. Long names are more descriptive but can cause problems with older systems.

Understand the types and function of file attributes.   Know the four basic FAT attributes (RASH) and also the extended attributes available under NTFS.

Know the tools available for maintaining the health of a file system. You will need to know how and why you would use tools such as DEFRAG and SCANDISK.

Know how to back up files in all current versions of Windows and how to restore those backups as needed.   Focus on what a Differential backup does as opposed to an Incremental backup. Work with the various backups so that you know what their options are.

Understand how the Registry works and how it is maintained. Know how REGEDIT and REGEDT32 work. Understand how the Registry replaces .ini files. Know how the Registry repair process works and how to perform Registry backups.

Understand how to create and modify files in Windows Explorer and how to navigate through the file system.   This is pretty basic stuff, but according to the objectives, this is stuff you may be tested on. Brush up on your knowledge of Windows file management, including the toolbars and menus, just in case.

Key Terms and Concepts

Attribute   An option set on a file that identifies it as part of a particular class of files or changes it in some way.

Extension   A set of characters appended to a filename that define how the file should be handled by the operating system.

IDE and SCSI   The two common PC hard disk architectures.

Backup   The process of saving a copy of a file to another location for redundancy.

Restore   The process of replacing a file that has been lost or corrupted with a copy that had been backed up.

Partition   A region of space on a hard drive set aside for use by a tool such as FDISK.

Logical drive   An area of space within a partition mapped for use by the operating system and identified by a drive letter, for instance C: or D:.

File system   The structure by which information is stored to and retrieved from a disk.

Format   The process by which a file system is written onto a partition.

Convert   Converting a drive differs from formatting it in that although you update the file system on the drive, you do not destroy the information currently on that drive.

Registry   The configuration database of Windows 9x, NT, and 2000. It contains information about both the computer and the users on the system.

Chapter

8

Domain 2.0 Installation, Configuration and Upgrading

COMPTIA A+ EXAM OBJECTIVES COVERED IN THIS CHAPTER:

▶ **2.1 Identify the procedures for installing Windows 9*x* and Windows 2000 for bringing the software to a basic operational level.** *(pages 359 – 384)*

- Start Up
- Partition
- Format drive
- Loading drivers
- Run appropriate set up utility

▶ **2.2 Identify steps to perform an operating system upgrade.** *(pages 385 – 399)*

- Upgrading Windows 95 to Windows 98
- Upgrading Windows NT Workstation 4.0 to Windows 2000
- Replacing Windows 9x with Windows 2000
- Dual-boot Windows 9x/Windows NT 4.0/2000

▶ **2.3 Identify the basic system boot sequences and boot methods, including the steps to create an emergency boot disk with utilities installed for Windows 9*x*, Windows NT, and Windows 2000.** *(pages 399 – 416)*

- Startup disk
- Safe Mode
- MS-DOS mode
- NTLDR (NT Loader), BOOT.INI
- Files required to boot
- Creating emergency repair disk (ERD)

2.4 Identify procedures for loading/adding and configuring application device drivers and the necessary software for certain devices.
(pages 416 – 438)

- Windows 9x Plug and Play and Windows 2000

- Identify the procedures for installing and launching typical Windows and non-Windows applications. (Note: There is no content related to Windows 3.1.)

- Procedures for set up and configuring Windows printing subsystem.

Domain 2.0 contains four separate subdomains, each of which actually covers very different material. This is, in other words, a very large domain, even though it doesn't take up much space on the objectives pages. There's a lot of information here, and this information is great to know, not only for the test, but also for working in the industry. The information here deals with issues of installation and architecture, as well as setting up operating systems, applications, and devices.

2.1 Identify the procedures for installing Windows 9*x* and Windows 2000 for bringing the software to a basic operational level.

- Start Up
- Partition
- Format drive
- Loading drivers
- Run appropriate set up utility

This is a very tightly focused objective that deals with information needed to install Windows 9*x* or Windows 2000 on a system that does not currently have an operating system installed. The test information covered here includes drive preparation (already covered in the previous domain, but there are a number of places where the objectives overlap) as well as a look at the setup process from blank disks to final reboot.

Critical Information

This section breaks down each of the content areas of this domain and looks at the most important aspects to focus on.

Start Up

Each Windows system that you will need to know for the test has a different way of starting its install. There are three possible ways for the install to start.

Booting from CD

The Windows NT and 2000 CDs are bootable, so installing them is pretty simple. Put the disk in, turn on the machine, and wait for Setup to start. The only catch is that if you have an older machine, its BIOS may not allow it to boot from a CD. In that case, you will need to resort to another method for the install. Windows 95 and 98 CDs are not bootable.

When booting to an NT installation CD, Setup will automatically start. With Windows 2000, an option will appear during startup asking if you want to enter Setup or continue a normal boot.

Booting from Disk to Access a Local CD

All four current versions of Windows allow you to create bootable disks or disk sets. Windows 98, NT, and 2000 use these disks to load the basic operating system and CD drivers that will allow access to most IDE and SCSI drives.

In Windows 98, the startup disk automatically presents you with an option to load CD-ROM support on startup. Some Windows 95 startup disks also have this option, but if not, you can modify the AUTOEXEC.BAT and CONFIG.SYS files to load a CD-ROM driver. The exact modifications you will need to make depend on the type and manufacturer of your CD-ROM drive, but a sample of some lines you may need to add to the CONFIG.SYS and AUTOEXEC.BAT follow. In this case, the drivers are for a Panasonic CD-ROM. The drivers you need to load in the DEVICE and MSCDEX.EXE options will depend on the drive you are using:

```
CONFIG.SYS:
        Files=25
        Buffers=9,256
        DEVICE=C:\PANCD.SYS /B:25 /N:PANCD001

AUTOEXEC.BAT
        PATH=C:\;C:\DOS
        MSCDEX.EXE /D:PANCD001 /L:D /M:100
```

Notice that these aren't big changes, but they are crucial to make the CD-ROM functional under DOS; once Windows 95 or 98 is loaded, these files won't be needed because Windows has its own drivers for accessing the CD drive, and they will be loaded during the install. These lines can be added to and later removed from AUTOEXEC.BAT and CONFIG.SYS using any text editor.

Once you have gained access to the CD, you will need to then start the setup process by finding the Setup executable. In Windows 9x, this will be in the Win95 or Win98 directory and will be named SETUP.EXE. If you are using a boot disk to install Windows NT or 2000, this file will be in the I386 directory and will be called WINNT.EXE.

NOTE Windows NT and 2000 boot disks generally automatically start Setup, so there is little work to do on them other than ensure that you have the proper CD drivers and (if needed) SCSI drivers.

Booting from Disk to Access a Network Install Share

If you are installing a number of machines with any operating system, you may find it best to place the installation files on a network file server and then install the workstations over the network. To do this, you will need a DOS or Windows 9x boot disk, with the proper network interface card (NIC) and client software. This often means that you will need to have a different boot disk for every type of network card on your network. Knowing how to access network resources by setting up client software is an important skill and will be covered in domain 4.0.

When doing an install from the network, it is a good idea to copy the install files to the local hard drive and then start the install from there.

Partition (Win 9*x*)

Once you have decided upon your install method, you will also need to decide how you wish to partition the computer on which you plan to do the install. Remember that Windows 95 and 98 require that you partition and format before starting Setup, while NT and 2000 allow you to do so during the setup process.

FAT32 and NTFS both can support partition sizes that allow you to simply use a single partition for the entire drive. Normally, this is the easiest—and therefore the best—solution to your partitioning needs. Only in cases where you are using Windows 95 pre-OSR2 or are booting multiple operating systems should you need more than one partition on a drive. Because FAT supports only partitions of 4GB, and DOS supports only 2GB FAT partitions, you often do not have the option of using the entire drive under FAT. This is one of the reasons why FAT is not commonly used anymore.

If you do have multiple partitions or multiple drives, from an operating system standpoint, there are two types of partitions: system and boot. The system partition (generally C:) stores the files that will initially start the computer, while the boot partition holds the actual operating system files. For instance, in a standard dual-boot scenario, the C: drive would be the system partition and also the boot partition for Windows 98, installed in C:\Windows. Windows 2000 would then be installed in D:\Winnt, and its boot partition would be D:.

Format Drive (Win 9*x*)

We covered the basics of drive formatting in the Chapter 7, "Operating System Fundamentals," and the key here is to just remember that Windows 9*x* requires the drive to be formatted before starting the install, while Windows NT and 2000 can do it during the install. The

FORMAT command is relatively simple to use and is generally done through a command line. In Windows 9*x*, the options for FORMAT include those shown in Table 8.1. For space reasons, this book won't cover most text commands as completely as FORMAT is covered below, but every time you see a command in the text or the objectives, you should go to *both* a 9*x* machine and a 2000 machine and type *COMMANDNAME /?* at the prompt. For instance, the information below was obtained by typing **FORMAT /?** at a command prompt on each OS. The reason for this is that "What function does format c: /s perform?" is a very possible test question. The same goes for switches on other command-line programs.

TABLE 8.1: Windows 9*x* FORMAT Options

Option	Function
/V	Specifies a volume label.
/Q	Performs a quick format.
/F	Specifies the size of the floppy disk to format.
/B	Allocates space for system files.
/S	Copies system files.
/T	Specifies the number of tracks per side.
/N	Specifies the number of sectors per track.
/1	Formats a single side of floppy.
/4	Formats a 5.25-inch 360K floppy disk in a high-density drive.
/8	Formats eight sectors per track.
/C	Tests clusters currently marked as bad.

In Windows 2000, the FORMAT options are enhanced, as shown in Table 8.2. Because 2000 rolls the format into the install, you won't need to use this command during a 2000 setup, but you may use it later to format additional partitions on the drive or insert new drives into the machine.

TABLE 8.2: Windows 2000 FORMAT Options

Option	Function
volume	Specifies the drive letter mount point, or volume name.
/FS:filesystem	Specifies the type of the file system (FAT, FAT32, or NTFS).
/V:label	Specifies the volume label.
/Q	Performs a quick format.
/C	Compresses files created on the new volume by default.
/X	Forces the volume to dismount first if necessary. All opened handles to the volume would no longer be valid.
/A:size	Overrides the default allocation unit size. Default settings are strongly recommended for general use. NTFS supports 512, 1024, 2048, 4096, 8192, 16K, 32K, 64K. FAT supports 512, 1024, 2048, 4096, 8192, 16K, 32K, 64K, (128K, 256K for sector size > 512 bytes). FAT32 supports 512, 1024, 2048, 4096, 8192, 16K, 32K, 64K, (128K, 256K for sector size > 512 bytes).
/F:size	Specifies the size of the floppy disk to format (160, 180, 320, 360, 640, 720, 1.2, 1.23, 1.44, 2.88, or 20.8).
/T:tracks	Specifies the number of tracks per disk side.
/N:sectors	Specifies the number of sectors per track.

TABLE 8.2: Windows 2000 FORMAT Options *(continued)*

Option	Function
/1	Formats a single side of a floppy disk.
/4	Formats a 5.25-inch 360K floppy disk in a high-density drive.
/8	Formats eight sectors per track.

Loading Drivers

The test objectives for the A+ exam have a feel to them that is, to put it gently, archaic. This heading is yet another example of that, as it deals with the need to load drivers before starting Setup. While this is something that needs to be done, we generally don't have to worry a lot about loading MOUSE.COM and such anymore. Nearly all of the drivers you will need for a standard install of Windows will be included on the boot disk. In Windows 9*x*, NT, and 2000, a standard driver database is included with the software, and this database is used to identify and install your critical hardware (drive controllers, mouse, video, etc.) during Setup. If a particular piece of hardware can't be located, a "default" low-end driver is used to bring the system up. At the conclusion of Setup in Windows 9*x* and 2000, Plug and Play then asks you to identify and provide appropriate drivers for any hardware for which a driver could not be found.

The only time when this may not be enough is if you are trying to install on more advanced hardware or oddball hardware. An unidentified SCSI controller, for instance, will cause Setup to fail, and in such a case, you will need to find the proper driver. From a test standpoint, remember that an unsupported SCSI controller or CD-ROM is really the only thing that can stop a CD-based install from starting, while on a network install, either an unsupported SCSI controller or an unsupported NIC can stop you.

Windows 9x and NT need to access the installation files after a reboot to finish the Setup process. Therefore, if you use a DOS disk to access the installation directory and start Setup, but then you do not have an adapter that is supported by 9x or NT, Setup will be unable to finish (which is why I recommended earlier that you copy files to the local drive before starting Setup). Windows 2000 solves this problem by creating a local install directory.

Run Appropriate Setup Utility

Once you have the CDs, boot disks, and/or network shares ready, it's time to start the actual install. The test requires that you know the install process for two systems: Windows 9x and Windows 2000. The problem here, of course, is that Windows 9x is a group of products, not a single one. Windows 95, 95 OSR2, and 98 all are slightly different in their installation methods, but they do follow a set of basic steps, and these are the things you should concentrate on for the test. Here, then, are those steps, for each of the operating system classes we are discussing.

Windows 9x

The first thing you will want to know is the type of hardware required for a Windows 9x install. Please see Table 8.3 for the Windows 9x hardware requirements.

TABLE 8.3: Windows Hardware Prerequisites

Hardware	95 Requirement	98 Requirement
Processor	386DX or higher processor (486 recommended).	386DX or higher processor (Pentium recommended).
Memory	4MB (8MB recommended).	8MB (16–32MB recommended).

TABLE 8.3: Windows Hardware Prerequisites *(continued)*

Hardware	95 Requirement	98 Requirement
Free hard disk space	50–55MB for a typical install (40MB if upgrading from a previous version of Windows). Could go as high as 85MB for a custom install with all options.	120MB for a typical install. Could go as high as 250MB for a custom install with all options.
Floppy disk	One 3½-inch disk drive (if doing installation from floppy disks).	One 3½-inch disk drive (if doing installation from floppy disks).
CD-ROM	Required if installing from CD (preferred method).	Required if installing from CD (preferred method).
Video	VGA or better.	VGA or better.
Mouse	Required.	Required.
Keyboard	Required.	Required.

Once you know you have hardware that is acceptable and have the drive prepared, you are ready to start the Windows install process. To do this, boot to the startup disk and either put the CD-ROM into the drive or connect to the appropriate network share.

The program that performs the *9x* installation is called SETUP.EXE, and it's located either in the root directory of Disk 1 of the set of installation floppies (really only an option for Windows 95) or in the WIN95/WIN98 directory of the installation CD-ROM. There are a few options that you can use with the Setup program. To use them, you type them after the SETUP command at the command line, separated by a single space. Table 8.4 details these Setup startup switches for Windows 95. Windows 98 has some different options but is similar.

TABLE 8.4: Windows 95 SETUP Command-Line Options

Option	Function
/d	Tells Setup to ignore your existing copy of Windows. It applies only during an upgrade.
<*filename*>	Used without the < and >, specifies the preconfigured SETUP file that Setup should use (e.g., SETUP MYFILE.INI causes Setup to run with the settings contained in MYFILE.INI).
/id	Tells Setup to skip the disk space check.
/im	Tells Setup to skip the available memory check.
/in	Runs Setup without setting up network components.
/ip	Tells Setup to skip the check for any Plug-and-Play devices.
/iq	Tells Setup to skip the test for cross-linked files.
/is	Tells Setup to skip the routine system check.
/it	Tells Setup to skip the check for Terminate and Stay Resident programs (TSRs) that are known to cause problems with Windows 95 Setup.
/l	Enables a Logitech mouse during Setup.
/n	Causes Setup to run without a mouse.
/T:C:\tmp	Specifies which directory (C:\tmp in this case) Setup will copy its temporary files to. If this directory doesn't exist, Setup will create it.

Setup examines your hard disk and makes sure there is enough room to install Windows 9x, then copies a few temporary files to your hard disk. These temporary files are the components of the Installation Wizard that will guide you through the installation of Windows 9x. A basic Windows system then starts the full Setup process, and a Windows-like screen appears and welcomes you to the installation.

The Setup Wizard will ask you a number of questions. For Windows 95, these come in three main categories:

- Gathering information
- Copying files to your computer
- Finishing the installation

Windows 98 Setup actually does pretty much the same thing, but installation tasks are divided into the following areas:

- Preparing to run Windows 98 Setup
- Collecting information about your computer
- Copying Windows 98 files to your computer
- Restarting your computer
- Setting up hardware and finalizing settings

There are only so many things about the install process that seem logical to test about. I doubt, for instance, that you will get any questions about "Do you have to accept the license agreement?" (Yes!) The answer is just too obvious and is not a "configurable" part of Setup. Still, there are a number of parts of the Setup process that could be test fodder.

INSTALLATION DIRECTORY

For most installations, you will want to install Windows 9x to the default C:\WINDOWS directory. This can be changed to another place, though, if you want to.

PRODUCT IDENTIFICATION NUMBERS

Licensing issues are important to becoming a professional tech, and it is very possible that CompTIA will throw in a question to test your understanding of licensing. The product identification number helps to ensure that you aren't illegally installing Windows 9x and also is used to authorize technical support if you ever need it.

SETTING UP HARDWARE

Windows 95 and 98 actually differ significantly on hardware detection. First, as 98 is three years newer, it has native support for much more hardware than 95. Second, 98 handles the hardware phase much more transparently. Windows 95 stops to ask you if you have a CD-ROM or a sound card in the machine, while 98 just checks for them automatically. The hardware-detection process may take several minutes. During this time, you will hear the hard drive searching for files (or at least you'll see the hard drive light flash madly). When Setup finds a piece of hardware, it makes a note of what it is, so that it can copy over the driver for it later. If Setup finds something that it doesn't have a driver for, it later asks you whether you want to provide one or to not install the device at all.

After the hardware detection is finished, Setup will automatically move on to the next step. Another great test question deals with the way that this works. During hardware detection, there is always a possibility that the machine will lock up while trying to contact a particular device. Because of this, Setup does the following: First, it makes a note to itself in a file called DETLOG.TXT that says "I am going to try to detect a modem using this driver." It then tries the driver and records the result of the test. If the driver locks the system when it is tried, no record of the test can then be written. This is fine. Simply restart, and Windows will check the file and realize not to try that driver again. Setup will then continue from that point but won't make the same mistake again! Therefore, the best way to recover from a Setup problem, oddly, is to just reboot and start again—without deleting the partially finished install.

Another file, SETUPLOG.TXT, records the entire install, from the components you are installing to every piece of hardware and all things that are attempted during Setup. This can be an excellent tool for troubleshooting an installation gone bad!

CHOOSING WHICH WINDOWS COMPONENTS TO INSTALL

You will have a choice of four different Setup options. These are listed below in Table 8.5. You may want to look through which options are included with each type of install, as there may be questions that ask you which type of install you would perform given a particular circumstance or that ask you which install you would need to do to install a particular component.

TABLE 8.5: Windows 95 Setup Types

Setup Option	Description
Typical	Allows Setup to choose the most popular features during the rest of the setup process.
Portable	Sets up the most common applications and utilities for portable computers. This option installs PCMCIA support and Advanced Power Management (APM).
Compact	Installs the minimum components Windows 95 needs to function.
Custom	Allows you to choose which components to install. If you select this option, Setup will present you with a list of utilities and programs to install. This option allows you to make the most choices about how Windows 95 gets installed. This is the method most commonly used by technicians to install Windows 95.

If you use Custom, you will be presented with a window that allows you to select the components you want to install. If a check box is cleared, the component will not be installed. If it has a white background and is checked, the component will be fully installed, and if the box is gray with a check mark in it, some but not all the components of that category are going to be installed. If you highlight the category containing the gray check box and click the Details button, a screen will appear that will allow you to select or deselect additional components. Know which applications are available to Windows 95 and 98 and what their functions are.

NETWORK CONFIGURATION

The next step in the installation of Windows 95 shows up only if a network card is detected in the machine. You can customize which networking components are installed and how they are configured.

The computer identification screen allows you to give the machine a unique network name. On Microsoft networks, each computer has to have a name and should belong to a workgroup or domain. There is information here that you will need to know for the test, but it will be easiest to review that with the rest of the networking info, in domain 4.0.

CREATING A STARTUP DISK

During the Windows 9x installation, a startup disk can be created. Unlike the emergency repair disk (ERD) for NT/2000, the Windows 9x startup disk is the same for all PCs, so most technicians make their own Windows 9x startup disk, copy all their diagnostic utilities to it, and never use this option again.

There should be at least one Windows 9x startup disk at each location where Windows 9x PCs are in use.

SETTING UP HARDWARE AND SOFTWARE AFTER INSTALLATION

After the initial reboot that follows the installation of Windows 9x files, 9x will restart and will finish the install by setting up hardware and taking a long look for any non-Plug-and-Play devices. If there are any devices for which Windows 9x can't determine the settings (or find drivers), it will pop up a screen asking you to specify them.

If you have a legacy (non-PnP) device, and the detection process does not find it, you probably have some sort of resource conflict. In that case, you may have to modify the settings in the machine or reserve an IRQ for the device. We cover this topic in domain 3.0.

NOTE   Briefly, a *driver* is a small program or piece of program code that runs in the background and translates the information going to and from an application and a piece of hardware. For example, a program such as WordPerfect doesn't keep track of all the different types of printers that are available; instead, it uses a Windows printer driver for a particular printer. (Windows 9*x*, NT, and 2000 each use their own specific printer drivers.) WordPerfect is loaded into memory along with a printer driver that is specific to the user's printer. If a different type of printer is attached to that system, then a different printer driver will be required.

Those are most of the sticking points with a Windows 9*x* install. Once the install is over, or if you have a problem during the installation, there are two files you may want to take a look at: BOOTLOG.TXT and DETLOG.TXT. DETLOG.TXT is created during the install and is a record of all the hardware found in the machine, along with any problems encountered. BOOTLOG.TXT, on the other hand, is created during the system boot phase and records any problems during startup.

Windows NT/2000

The installation of Windows 2000 is actually extremely simple. Put the disk in, turn on the computer, and start hitting Next on the Wizard. Okay, not *quite* that simple, but pretty close. Because of that, there are not a lot of questions to ask about 2000 Setup. The areas from which you are likely to see test information drawn follow.

TIP   Although the objectives mention the installation of only Windows 2000, and that is all that this section will cover, Windows NT Setup is very similar, differing only in how it presents information. You shouldn't get any NT install questions, but if you do, your best bet is to answer them as if they were 2000 questions. Also, if you have the chance, it would be a good idea to do a quick NT Workstation install just to see the menus.

INSTALLATION PREREQUISITES

Because of the fact that it is a "power workstation," the hardware requirements of Windows 2000 are higher than those of Windows 9*x*, and it also is less forgiving of older, less-efficient software. Even so, the hardware requirements to install Windows 2000 Professional are actually rather low—a Pentium 133 and 32MB of RAM, as shown in Table 8.6. Almost any machine that is still being used in a corporate environment will meet these basic requirements from Microsoft. More than any other OS we have looked at, though, more is better for Windows 2000, and the system will be happier if you ensure that it has a PII-class machine with 64–128MB of RAM.

NOTE The "recommended" levels are simply a guideline from Microsoft. Remember the hardware levels in the Required column of Table 8.6 are the ones you need for the test!

TABLE 8.6: Windows 2000 Hardware Prerequisites

Hardware	Required	Recommended
Processor	Pentium 133	Pentium II or higher
Memory	32MB	128MB or higher
Free hard disk space	2GB	2GB plus what is needed for your applications and storage
Floppy disk	Required only if installing from the boot disks	Yes
CD-ROM	Required only if installing from CD	Yes
Video	VGA	SVGA
Mouse	Yes	Yes
Keyboard	Yes	Yes

Once you have found hardware that you feel is going to run Windows 2000 Professional acceptably, your next step is to determine whether this hardware is compatible with the OS. There are a number of ways to do this, but probably the most dependable is to go to www.microsoft.com/windows2000 to download a copy of the most recent Hardware Compatibility List (HCL). This list tells you which hardware has been tested with Windows 2000 and should run properly. If your hardware is not on the HCL, contact your vendor for compatibility information and updated Windows 2000 drivers. Many Windows NT drivers will work with 2000, while Windows 95 or 98 drivers will *not* work!

THE WINDOWS 2000 BOOT DISKS

Unlike Windows *9x* Setup, which must run from a functioning operating system (an earlier version of DOS or Windows or a boot disk), Windows 2000 will generally be a breeze to install on a machine. To start the install process, simply place the Windows 2000 Professional CD into the CD-ROM drive and restart the computer. After the POST routine for the computer has completed, a message will appear that says, "Press any key to boot from CD...." Hit a key, any key, and the Windows 2000 Setup program will start.

That scenario is a "perfect world" situation, and sometimes reality intrudes. If the message mentioned above does not appear, it generally means that your PC is not configured to boot from CD-ROM or does not have that capability. In such a case, you will need to do one of two things:

- Go into the BIOS to set the machine to boot to its CD drive. Consult your computer's user guide for more information on examining and making changes to the BIOS.

- Create and use Windows 2000 boot disks to start Setup.

Although most modern machines support booting from CD-ROM, you may occasionally need to use a boot disk to start Setup. This disk can either be a Windows boot disk with CD-ROM support or the startup disk set that can be made from the Windows 2000 CD. To create the 2000 boot disks, you will need access to the Windows 2000 CD and a computer with a CD-ROM drive. There is a directory on the CD called BOOTDISK. In this directory is an executable file called MAKEBOOT.EXE, which is used to make Windows 2000 startup disks from any version of DOS or Windows.

STARTING A WINDOWS 2000 INSTALLATION

All the startup options listed above eventually lead you to the same point: executing the Setup routine for Windows 2000 Professional. Professional has two different executables used to start Setup, depending on the OS you are using to start the install. These executables are WINNT.EXE (used from DOS or Windows 9x) and WINNT32.EXE (used during an upgrade from Windows NT or an earlier version of 2000). These commands have various options associated with them, as shown in Tables 8.7 and 8.8.

TABLE 8.7: Common WINNT.EXE Options

Option	Function
/s:sourcepath	Allows you to specify the location of the Windows 2000 source files.
/t:tempdrive	Allows you to specify the drive that Setup uses to store temporary installation files.
/u:answer file	Used in an unattended installation to provide responses to questions the user would normally be prompted for.
/udf:id [,UDB_file]	If you are installing numerous machines, each must have a unique computer name. This setting lets you specify a file with unique values for these settings.
/e:command	Allows you to add a command (such as a batch script) to execute at the end of Setup.
/a	Tells Setup to enable accessibility options.

TABLE 8.8:   Common WINNT32.EXE Options

Option	Function
/s:*sourcepath*	Allows you to specify the location of the Windows 2000 source files.
/tempdrive:*drive_letter*	Allows you to specify the drive that Setup uses to store temporary installation files.
/unattend	Used to run install without user intervention.
/unattend[*num*]:[*answer_file*]	Allows you to specify custom settings for machines during an unattended installation.
/cmd:*command_line*	Executes a command (such as a batch file at the end of Setup).
/debug[*level*]:[*filename*]	Used to troubleshoot problems during an upgrade.
/udf:*id*[,*UDB_file*]	Allows certain values that need to be unique to be set separately for each machine installed.
/checkupgradeonly	Performs all the steps of an upgrade, but only as a test. The results are saved to an upgrade.txt file that can be examined for potential problems.
/makelocalsource	Specifies that the I386 installation directory from the CD should be copied to the hard drive, allowing for easier updates later.

PARTITIONING THE DRIVE

During Setup, you will be shown a list of the partitions currently configured on the machine. If one of these is acceptable, simply select that partition, then hit Enter. If you wish to create a new partition, you can do so using the Setup program itself, which replaces FDISK as a way to set up the system's hard drive(s).

To delete an existing partition, highlight the partition and press the *D* key. You will be asked to confirm your choice and will be reminded that all information on the partition will be lost. If the disk is new or if the old information is no longer needed, this is fine.

WARNING If you are not sure what is on the drive, find out before you repartition it!

To create a new partition, highlight some free space, and press C. You will be asked how big you want the partition to be. Remember that Windows 2000 Workstation wants you to have about 2GB as a minimum, but the partition can be as large as the entire drive.

FORMATTING

Once you have created or decided on a partition to use, you will be asked to format that partition. In doing so, you will need to choose between NTFS, FAT, or FAT32. In most cases, you will find that it will be better to go with the newer and more advanced NTFS, but certain dual-boot scenarios require FAT or FAT32. Your formatting options normally include three basic possibilities:

Leave the current file system. This option simply leaves the partition as it is. If you already have data on the partition you are installing onto, this option will leave that data intact.

Format with a new file system. Formatting with FAT, FAT32, or NTFS cleans the disk and gives you a nice blank partition to start the install on. On most new installs, this option will be your choice.

Convert to NTFS. To gain the advantages of NTFS (explained in domain 1.1) without destroying the information currently on the drive, you can simply convert the partition during Setup. This does require an additional reboot but is generally a better option than leaving a partition as FAT or FAT32.

WARNING If Setup detects any problems during the partition check, it will attempt to fix the problem and will immediately ask you to reboot. At that point, the install must start over. If it finds problems, this can often be an indicator that there are problems with the hard drive, and you may want to run a full Scandisk before returning to the install.

HARDWARE DETECTION

During Setup, 2000 will attempt to identify and configure the hardware in the computer, which may take a few minutes. One of the more unsettling parts of Setup occurs during this time, as the screen flickers—and often goes completely black—while monitor-detection occurs. Windows 2000 comes packaged with an impressive array of drivers and is able to identify and load most modern hardware. Still, not all devices have compatible drivers on the Windows 2000 CD-ROM, so if your hardware is not detected during startup, you can install additional device drivers after Setup completes, as discussed in objective 2.4.

After hardware detection is completed, the ever-polite Windows 2000 Setup Wizard welcomes you once again. To move through the wizard, simply click the Next and Back buttons along the bottom of the window. The screens of the Setup process are as follows:

Regional Settings The first screen rarely needs to be modified if you are configuring the machine for use in the U.S., but users in other countries can change keyboard and language settings here.

Personalize Your Software This screen is used to enter the name (required) and organization (optional) of the person to whom the software is registered. Both fields are just text boxes. Enter any values that apply.

Computer Name and Administrator Password The computer name is the name by which a machine will be known if it participates on a network. This name generally contains 15 characters or fewer. The administrator password is used to protect access to the powerful administrator account. Unlike Windows 9x, where usernames and password security are optional, all users must log on with a username and password to use a Windows 2000 Professional Desktop.

Modem Dialing Information If a modem has been detected, you will be asked for country, area code, and dialing preference information. If you do not have a modem, this screen will be skipped.

Date and Time Settings The Date and Time Settings dialog box has time zone and daylight saving time information. Any data on this screen can easily be changed later.

Networking Settings/Installing Components After configuring the date and time settings, you must wait for a minute or two as Windows 2000 installs any networking components that it has found and prepares to walk you through the configuration of the network. While you are waiting, you will see which components are being installed in the Status area.

Performing Final Tasks Once you have made it through the component install, the Setup process is in the home stretch. The Performing Final Tasks page reports on Setup's progress while it does the following:

Installs Start menu items This is where shortcuts are created to the applications and options installed during Setup.

Registers components The Registry is updated with Setup information.

Saves settings Configuration information is saved to disk, and other defaults and user selections are applied (such as area code and time zone).

Removes any temporary files used   The temporary files saved to the hard drive at the start of Setup and used to install Windows are removed to free up drive space.

Eventually, the wizard will complete, and you will be asked to reboot by clicking the Finish button. When the system restarts, Windows 2000 Professional Setup will be complete, and the standard 2000 boot process will initiate.

It is difficult to imagine you being tested on any of these minute details of the Setup process, but it is possible, as the objectives clearly talk about installation. A better guess is that it is the work leading up to the installation (finding SCSI and CD-ROM drivers, creating a network boot disk, creating a 98 startup disk or 2000 boot disks, etc.) that will be the focus of most installation questions.

LOGGING ON TO WINDOWS 2000

Users are presented with a number of options when they start Windows 2000. The user logon system comes up immediately at the end of the Windows 2000 startup process, and the system requires, at the very least, a username and password, but it allows for other choices. This is due to the fact that its security structure requires that every user on a Windows 2000 Professional system identify themselves for purposes of setting their security context and their configuration.

The options available on the logon screen include the following:

Username   The username is the name that defines a particular individual on the computer. Each user has their own Desktop and personal settings and can be given access to or restricted from particular files or tasks. This field displays the letters as you type them and is not case-sensitive.

Password   A password is a personal identifier that is used to verify the identity of the user. Without a verified username and password set, a user cannot log onto a Windows 2000 Professional station. The Password field displays only asterisks (*) as you type, and the field is case-sensitive.

From This field allows the user to set the security context that they will be using to authenticate. Windows 2000 Professional stations have their own user database, but they can also authenticate using a shared database, such as the Windows 2000 Server Active Directory. You cannot type new information into the From field, but if you have multiple authentication options configured, you will be able to select from among them using the down arrow.

Log On Using Dial-Up Networking This option allows a user to establish a dial-up connection to a remote network and then authenticate against a database over that connection. This option is rarely used, but it may be needed in high-security environments.

In order to log on, you will need to enter valid credentials. You may have created an administrator account and password during Setup, or you may need to get this information from a network administrator.

Once you have entered your credentials, Windows 2000 will configure your desktop and will load any personal settings and any User Policy settings associated with your account. At that point, you will be able to begin using Windows 2000.

If this is your first time logging on to the system as a particular user, it may take a minute or two for your initial system environment to be set up. A number of wizards will run and an introduction screen will be displayed.

Necessary Procedures

Among the procedures you should know well for the exam are those listed below.

Preparing a New Drive to Install Windows 98

1. Insert the Windows 98 Startup Disk in the A: drive.

2. Start the computer, and choose to boot without CD support. This saves time.

3. Type **FDISK** at the prompt. When the menu appears, type *Y* to use large disk support. This also causes 98 to format any partitions you create with FAT32.

4. If the disk has no partitions, select the Create option. Choose to use all space for this partition (unless you will be dual-booting). If you use all the space for C:, the partition is automatically set as active. If not, remember to set C: as active.

5. Reboot after the partition is created.

6. After the reboot, choose to boot the system with CD support, and type **FORMAT C:** at the prompt. Click *Y* to verify that you want to format the partition.

7. After the format of C: is finished, place the Windows 98 CD in the CD-ROM drive, and type **D:\WIN98\SETUP.EXE**. This starts the Setup process.

Creating the Windows 2000 Boot Disks

1. Place the Windows 2000 CD into a DOS or Windows machine.

2. Browse to the BOOTDISK directory on the CD-ROM.

3. Run the MAKEBOOT program, and provide each of the four floppy disks needed as they are requested.

Exam Essentials

Know how to boot to an installation CD or a network share point. Understand how to access a CD-ROM from DOS or how to modify the BIOS to allow a bootable CD to start the system. Also, know the basics of how an installation can be done across a network and when a network install is appropriate.

Know how SCSI and IDE hardware differ. Look into how systems that use SCSI controllers boot, and note how you can load drivers to boot SCSI hardware that is not supported by default.

Understand how partitioning and formatting work. With Windows 9*x*, this involves understanding how to create and format partitions before starting the install. With Windows NT and 2000, it involves understanding how to create and format partitions during the install.

Understand the hardware requirements of each Windows OS. Windows 95, 98, and 2000 hardware requirements are all test fodder. Also, remember which type of tasks each OS was "designed" for so that you can answer "which OS should you use" type of questions.

Work through the Setup of Windows 95, 98, and 2000. While Setup is automated enough that there are not a lot of things to quiz on, focus on what is happening during Setup, which files are created, and how Setup performs tasks such as hardware detection in each OS.

Key Terms and Concepts

Boot disk   A disk used to troubleshoot or install an operating system.

Partition   A separate physical space on a hard drive.

Format   The process by which a partition is prepared to have information written to it.

Driver   Software used to access a particular piece of hardware.

Windows component   A part of the operating system that can be individually installed or uninstalled.

DETLOG.TXT   File used to record hardware found during a Windows 9*x* install.

HCL   Hardware Compatibility List, which lists all hardware that has been verified to work with a particular operating system.

2.2 Identify steps to perform an operating system upgrade.

- **Upgrading Windows 95 to Windows 98**
- **Upgrading Windows NT Workstation 4.0 to Windows 2000**
- **Replacing Windows 9x with Windows 2000**
- **Dual-boot Windows 9x/Windows NT 4.0/2000**

This subdomain looks at the various upgrade paths available within the Windows family of operating systems and examines how Setup is different when you are either upgrading or creating a dual-boot scenario.

Critical Information

An operating system upgrade is a process by which the OS on a machine is updated to a newer or more powerful version. Upgrades can be preferable to a complete reinstall of the machine because they preserve the user's settings as well as any applications that are currently installed on the older OS. Upgrades can also be a disaster, as older programs or device drivers may not be compatible with the new OS and will need to be replaced anyway. Before deciding to do an upgrade, carefully research how the OS change will affect your hardware and software. Once you have decided that you do want to upgrade, the process in Windows is actually relatively straightforward. Here are the main things to review for the test.

Upgrading Windows 95 to Windows 98

Note that you cannot "upgrade" Windows 98 to Windows 95. The upgrade process generally checks the current version of your operating system and verifies that it can be upgraded. If you wish to install an OS that is not eligible for an upgrade, you will need to perform a new install, often overwriting the existing installation or rendering it unusable. Machines running Windows 3.*x* can be upgraded to Windows 95 or 98, and Windows 95 machines can be upgraded to Windows 98.

In truth, Windows 95 to 98 is a relatively basic upgrade. Besides the fact that most of the changes were relatively modest, most of them were generally also available to interested Windows 95 users through free Internet updates. As you will see, for most configuration and troubleshooting tasks, Windows 95 and 98 are identical.

The following are the enhancements of Windows 98:

- Better Internet support through the integration of Internet Explorer

- Year 2000 fixes

- Support for newer hardware, such as USB, AGP, and DVD

- FAT32

- DOS 7 (16-bit) replaced by DOS 32 (32-bit)

- Enhancements for MMX processors; better use of RAM and disk resources

The Upgrade Process

In order to start the upgrade, you simply start the SETUP.EXE program. If you are upgrading using a CD-ROM with a working installation of Windows 95, things couldn't be much simpler. Insert the disk into the CD drive, and a window appears asking if you wish to upgrade.

NOTE When a compact disc is inserted into a drive, it often automatically starts a program, such as an install routine. This is done through the Autorun option. Not all discs have this option, but both the Windows 98 and Windows 2000 installation CDs do. You can also just use the Explorer to access the CD if you prefer to browse to the SETUP.EXE program in the WIN98 directory on the CD.

Simply click Yes at the Autorun screen, and the SETUP.EXE program will load. You will be able to see the progress of the setup process along the left side of the window as the Setup program shows you which part of the install you're in.

The first part of the setup routine is pretty basic. All that happens during the initial preparation is that the drives are given a quick examination and the files needed to run the setup are loaded. There are a couple of things that Windows checks for at this time, such as whether you have enough free drive space for the install and whether you have any programs running that may interfere with the upgrade.

TIP   During a system upgrade, you will generally want to shut down all nonessential programs, including those that are sitting in your System Tray. This will help avoid conflicts and make it more likely that the install will go smoothly. It is especially important that any virus-detection programs are closed, as they will otherwise cause problems.

Once the Setup program is convinced that you are ready to install, it will begin to gather the details needed for this install. A wizard appears and goes through the following screens:

License Agreement   This is where you give Bill your firstborn. Few people bother to read these, and fewer still understand them. The most important thing that you need to remember is that if you don't accept the license agreement, you can't complete the install. It's that simple.

Product Key   These just keep getting longer and more annoying. Microsoft keys have gone from 10 characters long in Windows 95 to 25 in Windows 98.

Install Directory Here you enter the directory in which the Windows 98 files will be stored. By default, this is the same directory that the current version of Windows is in—generally C:\WINDOWS. You can change this directory, but if you do, the upgrade reminds you that existing programs and drivers from Windows 95 will not be migrated, and you will need to install all programs and drivers over again (as in a new install).

At this point, Setup does some system checks and again checks for drive space. It also looks at the install directory you have specified. If you are upgrading over an existing Windows install, you're given the option to save your existing system files so that you can revert back if you have problems with Windows 98. If you decide to save these files, they will be saved at this point.

NOTE To save the files needed to revert back to Windows 95, you must have about 50MB of extra disk space. In most cases, you will not need these files and will choose not to save them. If you have any doubt about the compatibility of the hardware or software on the machine, though, this is a reassuring option.

Next you are presented with choices as to which Windows components you wish to install. There are the same as during a normal install. This screen and the naming and networking screens try to take their cues from the currently installed OS, so you can usually just leave the components and other information as it is.

Once these fields have been filled in, Setup confirms the keyboard layout and regional settings, as well as country or regional information. You are then given the opportunity to make a Windows 98 startup disk. Since this is an upgrade, you may not have a Windows 98 startup disk, and this is an excellent time to create one. After you have given the machine the information it wants, it copies files and then restarts, as with a normal install.

HARDWARE DETECTION AND DRIVER UPGRADES

During the reboot, Windows collects information about the hardware installed in the machine, exactly as it did during an installation under Windows 95. Plug-and-Play devices are listed and activated if possible. Setup will load and test drivers to detect other hardware.

Once your hardware has been detected, you will be given the chance to specify driver locations for any devices that are not supported out of the box by Windows 98. The upgrade process will generally find and update the device drivers that were in use under Windows 95. This is good, in that it makes for an easy install, but you should check vendor Web sites to see if they have updated Windows 98 drivers. If so, you will need to upgrade to the new driver. Also, older DOS drivers are 16-bit "real-mode" software. These are slower and less stable than drivers written for Windows 9*x*. Because these drivers are not always uninstalled properly by Setup, you may also have real-mode drivers loading in the CONFIG.SYS file that are then conflicting with 32-bit drivers loaded from Registry entries.

TIP Remember that the AUTOEXEC.BAT and CONFIG.SYS files are no longer required in Windows 9*x*. They still exist only for reasons of backward compatibility. When upgrading, you should generally try renaming (*not* deleting!) these files, and then rebooting. If everything still works, they are no longer needed. If problems occur, go into the files and find out which commands or device drivers are still needed.

FINISHING THE UPGRADE

Once Windows has detected and installed drivers for all of the hardware it can find, it will reboot a second time in order to initialize the new configuration and present your Desktop.

After the reboot, you're almost there. You can be pretty sure that you are nearing the finish line when you see in the Windows 98

Setup window that the basic settings for each of the following are being configured:

- Control Panel
- Programs on the Start menu
- Windows Help
- MS-DOS program settings
- Tuning up application start
- System configuration

For the test, just remember that these are user-based settings that are usually configured for each profile as it is created. Windows 98 sets up the Desktop and other user-specific system elements according to the system defaults, after which point you are presented with a Windows 98 Desktop. If the machine has already been in use, individual user profiles are simply updated with whatever information is new, while their existing profile choices are preserved.

Upgrading Windows NT Workstation 4.0 to Windows 2000

If the machine that you want to install Windows 2000 Professional on already has Windows 9*x* or Windows NT up and running, you may want to upgrade to the advanced security and performance of Windows 2000 without losing your installed programs or system configuration. Windows 2000 allows for this by providing a very sophisticated upgrade mechanism that can check your hardware and software and then update an existing Windows 9*x* install while preserving the look, feel, and functionality of your current environment.

DOS and Windows 3.*x*

Windows 2000 cannot upgrade Windows 3.1 or DOS systems to 2000 Professional. Most machines running 3.1 or DOS probably will be running older hardware, but if you do want to upgrade such a system, you will need to perform a new full install rather than an upgrade. All programs or drivers that were installed on DOS or Windows 3.*x* will then need to be reinstalled under 2000. Also, remember that Windows 2000 cannot use real-mode drivers and does not like DOS programs, so getting Windows 2000 versions of all needed software prior to the reinstall is highly recommended.

Starting Setup

Compared to the work involved in setting up a new Windows 2000 Professional install, running the 2000 upgrade is almost completely effortless. The basic hardware requirements are the same for an upgrade as they are for a new install, and again you will have the option of either doing a CD-based install or a network-based install.

Generally, the simplest option is to place the Windows 2000 Professional disk into the CD-ROM drive of the Windows 9x or Windows NT Workstation machine to be upgraded. A window should automatically appear asking if you want to upgrade to Windows 2000.

If you click Yes to accept the offered upgrade, the Windows 2000 Setup Wizard will begin. This wizard will perform a number of pre-upgrade tasks and will then start the upgrade itself. The first choice of the wizard is also probably the most important. You must decide whether to perform an upgrade of your existing system or to simply install a fresh copy of Windows 2000 onto the drive. Both of these have their advantages.

Upgrade to Windows 2000 (recommended)   The upgrade allows you to keep your existing programs, but it also retains any existing problems. Because of this, any system configuration glitches or files that are no longer used will continue to plague you in the new install, just like they did in Windows NT.

Install a new copy of Windows 2000 (clean install)   A clean install has two major advantages. First, it allows you to start fresh without the baggage of your Windows NT Setup. Second, it allows you to dual-boot back to your original Windows NT OS. The disadvantage, of course, is that you will have to re-install all of your programs in this scenario.

Windows 2000 and Windows NT can't exist on the same partition in a dual-boot scenario, since certain drive locations (such as the location of Internet Explorer) are hard-wired to the same directory for both. To install a new copy of Windows 2000 and also dual-boot to an existing Windows NT install, you need to have a second partition on your disk or a second disk. Windows NT should be installed on the C: partition first, and then Windows 2000 can be installed afterwards on the D: partition. If you choose to upgrade, you will continue through the wizard. If you choose to install a new copy of the OS, you will be immediately funneled into the Windows 2000 installation process described in domain 2.1.

Assuming you have continued the upgrade, you're required to complete the next two screens, License Agreement and Product Key, just as you would during the install itself. There is a different Windows 2000 product key for the upgrade than for the install, but as with the regular install, this key is an obscene 25 characters in length and can usually be found on the case of the CD.

The Upgrade Wizard

With the bookkeeping out of the way, you can now get down to the business of the upgrade itself. The big difference between an upgrade and a new install is the Upgrade Wizard, which is used to examine your existing configuration to see whether there are any problems that will make upgrading difficult. The Upgrade Wizard also provides a link to Microsoft's Windows Compatibility Web site for product updates and compatibility information.

During the upgrade, Setup will try to contact Microsoft's site for information and updates, including the upgrade packs it's looking for on the next page of the wizard. If you do not have a connection to the Web as you are upgrading, you will be asked to connect, but you can choose to continue to work offline. If you do work offline, any updates must be applied manually later. If you have an Internet connection, we recommend going out to the Web site and looking for updates.

PROVIDING UPGRADE PACKS

If you do work offline, one of the things you may need to provide is application upgrade packs. Most 32-bit applications will continue to function without any problems. If you have any 16-bit DOS or Windows 3.x applications, though, they may not work. Also, any new or odd hardware may not be upgraded properly, as we will see in the next section. If you have been out to the Microsoft upgrade site or a vendor site and have obtained updated files for 2000, you may add them now by choosing the Yes, I Have Upgrade Packs option. If not, simply select the No, I Don't Have Any Upgrade Packs option. In such a case, you can still apply upgrades later if applications do not function after the upgrade.

UPGRADING TO THE WINDOWS 2000 NTFS

Another upgrade option you will be given is to upgrade your drive's file system to Windows 2000's advanced NTFS. The upgrade to NTFS enables increased file security, disk quotas, and disk compression. NTFS also makes better use of large drives by using a more advanced method of saving and retrieving data. While upgrading to NTFS has a number of advantages, only Windows NT and Windows 2000 understand the file system. Moreover, Windows 2000 uses NTFS 5, and so partitions formatted in this manner cannot be used by Windows NT. If you want to reinstall Windows NT on a drive formatted with NTFS 5, you will have to completely reformat. To upgrade to NTFS 5 and sever all ties to Windows NT, select the Yes, Upgrade My Drive option. To retain your links to the past and allow for dual-boot scenarios, select the No, Do Not Upgrade My Drive option.

PREPARING AN UPGRADE REPORT

Once you have made your choices, Setup will finally go through and examine your system for compatibility issues. This involves checking all hardware and software that is currently installed and creating a detailed upgrade report. Once the upgrade report is finished, you will be allowed to do two things: provide updated files for any incompatible hardware and view a report of what the compatibility check has found.

PROVIDE UPDATED PLUG-AND-PLAY FILES

In upgrading any system, there is a chance that incompatible hardware may be found. In upgrading certain systems, such as older machines or laptops, the chances are even greater. IBM's ThinkPad series has hardware support for DVD playback available through an

MPEG-2 Decoder Card. This is an optional piece of hardware that is specifically built by IBM for IBM, and as such it is not common enough to be recognized by the setup process. In order for this device to work, you must obtain updated files from IBM.

If you don't have updated files at present for any unsupported hardware, you can still continue with the install but will have to update the files before the hardware will function under Windows 2000. If the functioning of the hardware is essential to the operation of the system (network card, video card, etc.) you may want to stop the install and get the new drivers before continuing. For nonessential hardware such as a DVD decoder, you can continue and simply fix the problem later, but it is a good idea to at least verify that the hardware is compatible with Windows 2000, just so you won't be surprised later.

WARNING As noted earlier, you cannot use the same Windows 9x drivers that are currently installed, but if you are upgrading Windows NT Workstation to 2000 Professional, existing drivers will generally still work.

UPGRADE REPORT

Once you have added any Plug-and-Play drivers, the Setup Wizard will provide you with a detailed report of what it thinks may cause you "issues" as you upgrade. The following topics are included:

Hardware Any devices that cannot be confirmed as compatible with Windows 2000 will be listed here.

Software Programs that do not work with Windows 2000 are listed here. The ThinkPad upgrade, for instance, found that not only was the DVD decoder not supported, but the installed DVD player also will not work. In these cases, you are directed to uninstall the program before the upgrade, because it will not function and may not uninstall properly after the upgrade.

Program Notes   Besides incompatibilities, some programs simply need to be reconfigured to work with Windows 2000. The Program Notes area details some of these known issues, such as how Microsoft Outlook 2000 works with Windows 2000 but must be reinstalled after the upgrade.

General Information   This section details information best described as "other." Some of the upgrade issues that came up during a recent upgrade included notes concerning hardware profiles, backup files, and the Recycle Bin.

If you wish to save the upgrade report information for later use, you have two options: print it or save it to a file. If you feel that the machine has major compatibility issues, you should probably save or print the report and visit `www.microsoft.com/windows2000/compatible` and `www.hardware-update.com` for information or updates.

Once you have checked out the upgrade report, you have to choose whether to proceed with the upgrade immediately or to exit from the upgrade in order to regroup and obtain needed updates. If you are ready to proceed, click Next to continue with the install. If you would rather wait, click Cancel, and the upgrade will end without affecting your existing Windows 9*x* or NT install.

Proceeding with the Upgrade

If you have made it this far, the tough part is now over. As the wizard states, "This process is completely automatic, and you will not have to answer any additional questions." All you need to do is click the Next button and head off to get some coffee—or preferably some lunch. About one hour and three restarts later, you should find that the process has completed, and a Windows 2000 logon screen should be waiting for you when you return.

After the first reboot, the existing Windows install will be deleted, and Windows 2000 files will be copied to the drive. After the second, a graphical setup will start, and your settings from Windows 9*x* or NT will be automatically reapplied.

Replacing Windows 9x with Windows 2000

This particular objective area really doesn't need a great deal of discussion. The term "replacing" Windows 9x is odd, but it seems to include both upgrading and installing over the existing OS. We have covered the general aspects of installing a fresh copy of Windows 2000 Pro and have also covered upgrading from Windows NT. The thing to remember here is that if you plan to install over a Windows 9x install, the best idea is to simply delete the existing information on the partition and start over from scratch. Depending on how the disk is partitioned, you may want to even delete and re-create. If you do not do this, your installation will have far too many leftover files on the drive, since Windows 2000 uses a completely different set of system files than Windows 9x.

If you choose to upgrade from your existing Windows 9x system, Microsoft does provide that the same Upgrade Wizard that we discussed earlier can be used to upgrade Windows 9x as well as Windows NT. In such a case, the only real thing to consider is whether the software—applications and drivers—currently installed under Windows 9x will properly upgrade. Generally, this involves checking the documentation for the products, either on the Web or in manuals.

When you run the Upgrade Wizard, there may be files left on the hard drive that are no longer needed. Go through and clean up unneeded files and directories to reclaim space, but be careful not to delete things you still need!

Dual-Boot Windows 9x/Windows NT 4.0/2000

One additional option you have when installing Windows 2000 Professional is to keep your existing system and install the upgrade OS into a different location. This actually is an excellent option if you need to do development work or are just interested in having multiple operating systems on a single system—say while studying for an exam.

The various boot scenarios that are available include the following:

- Windows 9x and Windows NT
- Windows 9x and Windows 2000

- Windows NT and Windows 2000

- Windows 9x, Windows NT, and Windows 2000

In each of these cases, the best option is to use a different partition, or even a different drive, for each OS to be installed. In most cases, the best option will be to install the earliest OS first and then layer on the newer ones. The resulting configuration gives you a Windows 9x install on the C: drive and a Windows NT/2000 install on the D: (or D: and E:) drive.

The reason that you cannot put, for instance, Windows 98 and Windows 2000 on the same drive is that they share common locations, such as the default location for the Internet Explorer and program files. Applications must be installed separately for each OS on the machine (this means two installs of MS Office, two installs of any games, etc.), and if they try to save to the same place, conflicts often occur. By keeping all 98 system files and apps on one drive and all 2000 files on another, you prevent version conflicts and other problems.

Boot Managers

Both Windows NT and 2000 Pro install a boot manager and will automatically recognize and add an option for a previously installed operating system. This allows you to select from among whichever OSes are available during the boot process. You may also use third-party boot managers, but these will not be on the test.

Remember that Windows 95 and 98 do not have boot managers, so installing 98 over an NT Workstation install will not produce a dual-boot system. Windows 98 will simply overwrite the boot sector, and NT will no longer be available. To dual-boot, always install NT or 2000 *after 9x.*

File Systems

Other than the one-OS-per-partition recommendation, the key problem to watch out for in a dual-boot environment is incompatible file systems. Remember that each of the MS operating systems support different file systems:

- **Windows 95 rev A:** FAT

- **Windows 95 rev B and 98:** FAT and FAT32
- **Windows NT:** FAT and NTFS (and HPFS for what it's worth)
- **Windows 2000:** FAT, FAT32, and NTFS

The first drive (C:) should be formatted with a file system common to all of the operating systems on the machine. Generally this is FAT32 today. Other partitions can be formatted however the OS on that partition prefers.

Exam Essentials

Know which upgrade paths are possible. Windows 95 upgrades Windows 3.*x*, Windows 98 upgrades 3.*x* and 95, NT upgrades 3.*x* and 9*x*, and 2000 Professional upgrades 9*x* and NT Workstation. Besides this simple information, also understand the issues involved with each type of upgrade.

Know the difference between an upgrade and a fresh install. Upgrades are installations that examine the existing environment and preserve it as closely as possible in the updated OS. Fresh installs simply cover up an older install but do not learn from it. Upgrade installs generally preserve existing software, user settings, and other configuration details.

Know how the Windows 2000 Upgrade Wizard works. The Upgrade Wizard is new with 2000; NT doesn't have it. It checks the system and then interacts with the user and the Internet to verify and update the system as accurately as possible.

Key Terms and Concepts

Upgrade   An installation that preserves existing settings.

Autorun   A feature that allows a CD-ROM to immediately start a program when inserted into a CD-ROM drive.

Install directory   The location of the operating system's files on the hard drive.

Wizard A utility that helps a user perform a particular task.

Dual-boot The ability to run more than one operating system on a single machine by choosing which operating system you wish to use at startup.

2.3 Identify the basic system boot sequences and boot methods, including the steps to create an emergency boot disk with utilities installed for Windows 9*x*, Windows NT, and Windows 2000.

- **Startup disk**
- **Safe Mode**
- **MS-DOS mode**
- **NTLDR (NT Loader), BOOT.INI**
- **Files required to boot**
- **Creating emergency repair disk (ERD)**

With subdomain 2.3, the focus turns from installation to architecture, and this content area involves examining the key files needed to boot Windows 9*x*, NT, and 2000. We have a full plate in a few words, though, as the objective also discusses emergency repair scenarios and Safe Mode. This subdomain is one of the few areas on the test objectives where NT is specifically mentioned.

The 2.3 subdomain includes three interrelated but different topics you will need to be ready for:

- What are the major files needed to boot Windows 9*x* and Windows NT/2000, and what are their functions?

- How does the boot process work on these operating systems?

- What options are available to troubleshoot and repair problems with the boot process?

Critical Information

Tests love questions with specific answers, and the information in this section is lends itself easily to such questions. Also, this is not the sort of information that you get simply by working with the systems, as often these files and boot processes operate in complete anonymity (at least until they have problems).

In order to bring an operating system up to an operational level, two types of files are required: boot files and system files. Boot files have the job of starting up the computer and preparing the system for the operating system. System files then load the OS itself, including its graphic interface and other system components. Boot files are stored in the root of the active partition (generally C:) while system files are found in the place where the OS was installed, such as C:\Windows or C:\Winnt.

Windows 9x Boot Process Essentials

Because Windows 9x is a very different operating system than Windows 3.x (which it replaced), most of its configuration is done using different tools than were used in Windows 3.x. Even so, Windows 9x shares a few configuration similarities with its ancestors (Windows 3.x and DOS) for compatibility's sake. The AUTOEXEC.BAT and CONFIG.SYS files are used to a limited extent by some older programs, but they're not actually needed and are still available only for older hardware and software compatibility. In addition, INI files are still used for some Windows programs (generally, older 16-bit apps) to hold configuration settings.

The Registry of Windows 9x (and NT/2000) has taken the place of most INI files. In addition to software extension information, it also contains software configuration information and hardware configuration information. Generally speaking, most of the Windows 9x settings that were previously stored in INI files are now stored in the Registry.

TIP   Due to the fact that the Registry actually handles most of the startup tasks in Windows 9*x*, many system files are there mostly for compatibility with older programs. Because of that, you may never use them. Regardless, many of these obsolete files are listed in CompTIA's test objectives, so you still need to know about them!

Examining the Windows 9*x* Boot Process

First, let's look at the process you use when you boot the system. When Windows 9*x* first starts up, it goes through a number of steps before presenting you with a Desktop. The basic elements of a Windows 9*x* startup are as follows:

System self-checks and enumerates hardware resources.   Each machine has a different startup routine, called the POST (power on self-test), which is executed by the commands written to the motherboard of the computer. Newer Plug-and-Play boards not only check memory and processors, they also poll the systems for other devices and peripherals.

MBR loads and finds the boot sector.   Once the system has finished with its housekeeping, the master boot record (MBR) is located on the first hard drive and loaded into memory. The MBR finds the bootable partition and searches it for the boot sector of that partition. Information in the boot sector allows the system to locate the root directory of C: and to find and load into memory the IO.SYS file located there.

IO.SYS loads into memory and starts the processor in real mode.   The IO.SYS file performs a number of tasks, each of which is done in real mode. Real mode is simply a method of accessing the processor in 16-bit mode. Drivers loaded through the CONFIG.SYS file therefore can continue to function in real mode even after the next step, unless they are replaced by 32-bit Windows drivers. The IO.SYS file performs the following tasks:

- Provides basic file system access to allow the rest of the boot files to be found.

- Accesses the MSDOS.SYS file to obtain boot configuration parameters.

- Loads LOGO.SYS (Windows bitmap display) and DRVSPACE.BIN (compressed drive access) if they are present and needed.

- Loads the Registry file SYSTEM.DAT into memory but does not access it.

- Selects a hardware profile (or allows the user to do so).

- Processes the commands in the CONFIG.SYS and AUTOEXEC.BAT files if they are present.

WIN.COM loads and transfers the processor to protected mode.
Once the AUTOEXEC.BAT file is parsed and processed, the WIN.COM file is automatically executed. This file then loads various drivers as instructed by the Registry. It also examines the SYSTEM.INI and WIN.INI files to obtain additional configuration information. Once the Registry files have been loaded, the processor is transferred into 32-bit protected mode.

Virtual device drivers, the Windows kernel, and the GDI load.
Once the system is in 32-bit mode, various 32-bit virtual device drivers load to manage hardware resources, often replacing 16-bit real-mode drivers. The Windows kernel, which controls access to the processor from Windows 9x, is loaded into memory, and once the graphic display interface (GDI) loads to manage screen I/O, the system is ready to accept customers.

The Explorer shell loads and the user is presented with a Desktop.
The last part of the boot process is the loading of the "shell" program: EXPLORER.EXE. The Explorer is the program that manages the graphical interface—the toolbar, the Desktop, and the Start menu. Once this loads, network connections are restored and programs in the

STARTUP folder are run, all of which are determined by the USER.DAT Registry settings for that user.

Windows 9x Startup Files

We discussed a number of files in the section "Examining the Windows 9x Boot Process." Now we will take a minute to explain each one further (we've placed an asterisk next to the names of the files that are required in order to boot Windows 9x):

MSDOS.SYS* Function is primarily to handle disk I/O, hence the name *disk operating system (DOS)*. Just like IO.SYS, MSDOS.SYS is loaded into memory at bootup and remains in memory at all times.

EMM386.EXE Provides the operating system with a mechanism to see additional memory. The memory space that EMM386.EXE controls has come to be known as *upper memory*, and the spaces occupied by programs in that region are known as *upper memory blocks (UMBs)*.

HIMEM.SYS Used to access upper memory.

IO.SYS* Allows the rest of the operating system and its programs to interact directly with the system hardware and the system BIOS. IO.SYS includes hardware drivers for common hardware devices. It has built-in drivers for such things as printer ports, serial or communication ports, floppy drives, hard drives, auxiliary ports, console I/O, and so on.

WIN.INI Sets particular values corresponding to the Windows environment. It's used extensively by 16-bit Windows 3.x applications; it's almost entirely replaced by the Registry for Windows 9x 32-bit apps.

WIN.COM* Initiates the Windows 9x protected-load phase.

SYSTEM.INI Used in DOS and Windows 3.1 to store information specific to running the operating system. This and other INI files were used to configure 16-bit DOS and Windows apps.

COMMAND.COM Called the *DOS shell* or the *command interpreter*. It provides the command-line interface that the DOS user sees. This is usually, but not always, the C:\> prompt.

CONFIG.SYS   Loads device drivers and uses the information from the AUTOEXEC.BAT file to configure the system environment. Memory-management tools and DOS peripheral drivers can be added here.

AUTOEXEC.BAT   Used to run particular programs during startup. Also declares variables (such as search paths).

TIP   A batch file, named with a .bat extension, is simply a set of commands that Windows can execute or run. These commands may run utilities, or they may point toward full-blown applications. AUTOEXEC.BAT is a batch file that is automatically executed when the system starts up.

Startup Files Configuration Tools

There are a number of ways to modify the INI files on a Windows $9x$ machine. First, you can open up a copy of Notepad, or the text editor of your choice, and go to town. This is still probably the most common method of modifying INI configuration files. If you prefer to have things a bit easier, though, there are a couple of tools provided with Windows $9x$ for dealing with these files. Both Windows 95 and Windows 98 allow you to use a tool called SYSEDIT.EXE to modify certain files, and Windows 98 has added MSCONFIG.EXE as well.

SYSEDIT

SYSEDIT allows you to access a number of key configuration files all at once. From there, you can examine, compare, and, if needed, modify any of these files. All that the SYSEDIT program really does is open multiple text editors, each of which has one of the key text files in it. SYSEDIT can be used to view and edit the PROTOCOL.INI, SYSTEM.INI, WIN.INI, CONFIG.SYS, and AUTOEXEC.BAT files.

MSCONFIG

The thing that makes the System Configuration Utility (MSCONFIG.EXE) different is that it lets you use your mouse to browse and modify settings that previously were accessible only through manual text configuration. You can also enable or disable Windows 98-specific elements. The MSCONFIG utility therefore merges Windows 98 configuration information with a way for non-DOS-savvy users to work with DOS-era configuration files. See Table 8.9 for an explanation of the tabs on the System Configuration Utility.

TABLE 8.9: System Configuration Utility Tabs

Tab	Function
General	Used to set startup options, as well as to determine which files to load during startup.
Config.sys	Used to graphically view and edit the CONFIG.SYS file.
Autoexec.bat	Used to graphically view and edit the AUTOEXEC.BAT file.
System.ini	Allows you to modify the SYSTEM.INI file using a Registry-type interface.
Win.ini	Allows you to modify the WIN.INI file using a Registry-type interface.
Startup	Can be used to enable or disable particular startup options.

Windows 2000 Boot Process Essentials

Windows 2000 uses completely different startup procedures and different startup files. In this section, we will discuss how Windows 2000 boots and which files are needed to keep it healthy and happy.

Key Boot Files

Almost all of the files needed to boot Windows 3.1 or *9x* are unnecessary for Windows 2000. Windows 2000 requires, in fact, only a very few boot files, each of which performs specific tasks:

NTLDR   This file "bootstraps" the system. In other words, it is the file that starts the loading of an operating system on the computer.

BOOT.INI   Holds information about which operating systems are installed on the computer.

BOOTSECT.DOS   In a dual-boot configuration, this file keeps a copy of the DOS or Windows 9*x* boot sector so that the Windows 9*x* environment can be restored and loaded as needed.

NTDETECT.COM   Parses the system for hardware information each time Windows 2000 is loaded. This information is then used to create dynamic hardware information in the Windows 2000 Registry.

NTBOOTDD.SYS   On a system with a SCSI boot device, this file is used to recognize and load the SCSI interface. On EIDE systems, this file is not needed and is not even installed.

System files   Besides the previously listed files, all of which are located in the root of the C: partition on the computer, Windows 2000 also needs a number of files from its system directories (\WINNT and WINNT\System32 generally) including the Hardware Abstraction layer (HAL.DLL) and the Windows 2000 command file (WIN.COM). Numerous other DLL (dynamic link library) files are also required, but usually the lack or corruption of one of these will simply produce a noncritical error, while the absence of WIN.COM or HAL.DLL will cause the system to be nonfunctional.

The Boot Process

When Windows 2000 starts, the computer's BIOS performs a number of system checks, and then it looks for an operating system to load. What it finds is Windows 2000's NTLDR (NT loader) file, which is then read into memory. The NTLDR file (which does not have a file extension, by the way—it is just NTLDR) prepares the system for the boot process and invokes a rudimentary file system access that allows it to read the BOOT.INI file in the root of C:. This file is then used to construct a menu from which a user may select an operating system. If Windows 2000 is the only OS installed on the machine, the choice is moot, but if the system dual-boots, you may choose your OS at this point and boot directly into Windows 9*x*, Windows 2000, Linux, or whatever. The system waits a predetermined amount of time for a user choice and then simply loads the default OS. Both the default option and the time can be configured in Windows 2000's System properties. Modifications to the menu itself can be made through the BOOT.INI file, which is a text file configurable with any editor.

Once you have chosen to start Windows 2000 Professional, NTLDR will invoke NTDETECT.COM to check the system's hardware and will load NTBOOTDD.SYS if the system uses a SCSI boot device. Once this process is complete, NTLDR will then pass control of the system to WIN.COM, and the graphical phase of startup will begin.

During this time, you will be presented with a series of screens that show the system's progress during startup; the interface will be initiated and network connections and computer policies (if present) will be loaded. Once this has completed, Windows 2000 will present you with a logon screen as discussed earlier, and you can now start to use the system.

NOTE   If you choose to boot back to a previous OS, NTLDR will immediately pass control to BOOTSECT.DOS, and the other files mentioned will not be used.

Startup Options

In most cases, you will want to simply start the computer running Windows 9*x* or 2000, and within a few moments (or minutes) the logon screen or Desktop will appear. Occasionally, either by choice or disaster, this does not work. For the exam, you will definitely want to know about how to get a system back up and running if it is in a problem state. This part of domain 2.3 is odd in that it closely overlaps with domain 3.0, which deals with troubleshooting. We will look at how to create startup disks and use Safe Mode here, and we will deal with the scenarios under which you will have to use these tools later.

Safe Mode in Windows 9*x*

If the computer seems to start up fine but Windows 9*x* doesn't function properly, try rebooting in Safe Mode. This mode of operation loads Windows 98 with a minimal set of drivers and can help you determine if the problem is hardware or software related. To see the boot menu, turn the computer on and press the F8 key when you see the words *Starting Windows 98*. Doing so will present you with a list of bootup choices, including booting the computer in Safe Mode. The choices include:

Normal This is the default selection and loads both the graphical interface and all drivers.

Logged (\BOOTLOG.TXT) If you are having problems starting, this option can help by saving all information about the boot process to a file. This file can then be examined later for information that may help identify the problem.

Safe Mode Starts Windows using only basic files and drivers (mouse, except serial mice; monitor; keyboard; mass storage; base video; default system services; and no network connections). Once in Safe Mode, you can restore files that are missing or fix a configuration error.

Step-By-Step Confirmation If you want to watch the entire boot process, or selectively exclude lines from AUTOEXEC.BAT or CONFIG.SYS from the boot process, this option presents you with each option before Startup executes it and asks you whether to perform that action or not.

Command Prompt Only Starts Windows 98 without the graphic interface, presenting you instead with a DOS-like command prompt shell. This can be helpful if you are having serious problems with the Windows interface files

Safe Mode Command Prompt Only This is Windows at its most basic. Only essential drivers are loaded and no GUI.

When Windows 98 is booted up in Safe Mode, you can then check on drivers, conflicts, and so on and make changes to the configuration as needed. To exit Safe Mode, restart the computer. If you have fixed the problem, upon reboot, the computer should be operating normally.

Safe Mode in Windows 2000

Rather than simply booting into Windows 2000 using standard startup options, you may also make additional selections by pressing the F8 key. In most cases, you will be able to just boot into Windows 2000 without worrying about the advanced options. Occasionally, though, problems may arise. If you have a problem that makes it difficult to get 2000 up and running, the advanced options offer a number of useful tools.

Safe Mode   Starts Windows 2000 using only basic files and drivers (mouse, except serial mice; monitor; keyboard; mass storage; base video; default system services; and no network connections). Once in Safe Mode, you can restore files that are missing or fix a configuration error.

Safe Mode With Networking   Same as Safe Mode, but tries to load networking components as well.

Safe Mode With Command Prompt   Similar to Safe Mode but doesn't load the Windows GUI. Presents the user with a Windows 2000 command prompt interface.

Enable Boot Logging   Logs all boot information to a file called NTBTLOG.TXT. This file can be found in the \WINNT directory. You can then check the log for assistance in diagnosing system startup problems.

Enable VGA Mode   Starts Windows 2000 using the basic VGA driver but loads the rest of the system as normal. If you happen to install an incorrect video driver or a video driver corrupts, this allows you to get into the system to fix the problem.

Last Known Good Configuration   This option is useful if you have changed a configuration setting in the Registry, which then causes the system to have serious problems. LKGC will not save you from a corrupt file or a deleted file error.

Debugging Mode   A sort of advanced boot logging, Debugging Mode requires that another machine be hooked up to the computer through a serial port. The debug information is then passed to that machine during the boot process. This option is rarely used by technicians because it usually only solves problems involving poorly written applications. This is a great tool for developers, but for technicians simply reinstalling and avoiding the offending application is far faster!

Creating and Using a Startup Disk (Windows 9*x*)

What happens when your Windows computer has a problem so severe the computer won't boot? Oftentimes, if the Registry is corrupt, the Windows interface won't come up—not even in Safe Mode. All versions of Windows 9*x* come with a utility that allows you to create a disk that can be used to fix Windows. This disk is called the Windows startup disk. It contains enough of the Windows startup files to boot the computer from floppy disk, allowing you to perform various diagnostic and repair tasks. The disk contains files and utilities such as FDISK, ATTRIB, CHKDSK, DEBUG, EDIT, FORMAT, RESTART, SCANDISK, and SYS. These files are used to correct basic disk problems as well as file boot problems. However, the Windows 9*x* emergency disk *cannot* be used to restore a corrupt Registry (apart from copying the USER.DAT and SYSTEM.DAT files from their backup locations).

USING THE WINDOWS 9*X* STARTUP DISK

If you have a problem with your Windows installation and you suspect the disk has a problem, you can boot to the startup disk and try to repair the hard disk. Simply insert the floppy you made into your floppy drive and boot to it. This startup disk will create a small, virtual disk drive (usually labeled D: or something similar) with all the repair utilities installed on it. You can then use these utilities to repair the disk or files. In addition, since you are booted up to a command line, you can copy new files over old, corrupt ones, if necessary.

TIP There are differences between the Windows 95 and Windows 98 repair disks. Before taking the exam, create one of each and compare them. For instance, the Windows 98 disk has built-in CD support, but partly because of this it has little room for additional utilities you might wish to add.

Windows NT Emergency Repair Disk

When compared to Windows 9*x*, Windows NT is a much more advanced operating system that relies more heavily on the Registry than any of its predecessors did. The Windows NT Emergency Repair

Disk (ERD) is a special disk you can create in Windows NT that can be used to repair the Registry as well as startup files. One important difference between the NT ERD and the Windows *9x* startup disk is that the NT ERD contains only information—it is *not* a bootable disk. You must use this disk from a menu within the Setup utility, which means booting using a startup disk set or the NT installation CD itself.

The Windows NT ERD typically contains the following files:

- System Registry hive (SYSTEM.)

- Software Registry hive (SOFTWARE.)

- Default user profile (default.)

- New user profile (ntuser.da_) Windows NT version 4.0 only

- Setup.log

- Autoexec.nt

- Config.nt

The above files can be used to restore a Windows NT system to proper operation. One important note is that a crucial part of the Registry is not backed up on the ERD by default. This is the security information, which includes the users, groups, passwords, and security structure of the local Windows NT Workstation. In order to back this information up, you must add the /S switch (RDISK /S), which will add the following critical security files:

- The Security Accounts Management database (SAM.)

- The Security Registry hive (SECURITY.)

USING THE WINDOWS NT ERD

To use the ERD, you must first boot the NT computer using either an NT Setup Boot Disk set or the Windows NT CD-ROM. Once you get to the screen that asks you to "Press Enter to install Windows NT or press R to repair a damaged installation," go ahead and press *R*.

Insert the ERD into your floppy drive when prompted by the Setup program. Once you have started the emergency repair, you will have four options:

- Inspect Registry Files

- Inspect Startup Environment

- Verify Windows NT System Files

- Inspect Boot Sector

The option(s) you choose will depend on what you suspect is wrong with your computer, and we will look at this in domain 3.0.

The Windows 2000 ERD

In Windows 2000, if your system won't start and either Safe Mode or the Recovery Console hasn't helped, you may also need to use an emergency repair disk. The Create Emergency Repair Disk option is part of the Windows 2000 Backup program. This program includes a wizard to help you create a disk to repair your system. Then, as with Windows NT, you can start the machine with either the startup disks or the Setup CD-ROM and use the ERD to restore the system files.

USING A WINDOWS 2000 ERD

If you want to use or test your newly created ERD, simply boot to either the Windows 2000 startup floppy disks or the Windows 2000 CD-ROM. When prompted, choose the Repair option by pressing *R*. You can also choose to either run a manual repair (by selecting *M*) or a fast repair (by selecting *F*). During this process, the selected portions of the system are then restored from the disk to the setup of Windows 2000. The system will restart automatically when the repair is successfully completed.

NOTE Note that the ERD creation process also allows you to update the \WINNT\REPAIR directory on the hard drive. This keeps the same information as the ERD and may be more convenient.

Necessary Procedures

Creating a Windows 9x Startup Disk

1. Select Start ➢ Settings ➢ Control Panel.

2. Select Add/Remove Programs.

3. Select the Startup Disk tab.

4. Insert a blank floppy disk in your A: drive and click the Create Disk icon. Windows 9x will start the process of creating the disk.

5. You will be asked to verify that the disk in the A: drive should be overwritten, and then Windows 9x will format the disk and make it bootable. It will also copy numerous utilities to the disk so that you can use them to fix Windows 9x.

6. When Windows 9x finishes copying files to the disk, remove the disk from the drive, label it "Windows 9x Startup Disk," and put it in a safe place so that you can get to it easily if there is ever a problem.

Creating a Windows NT ERD

To create a Windows NT Emergency Repair Disk, you must use the RDISK utility. This utility is installed with the default installation of Windows NT and by default is installed to the C: drive in the WINNT\SYSTEM32 directory.

1. Click Start ➢ Run and type **RDISK /S.**

2. The graphic below will display. At this screen, click the Create Repair Disk button.

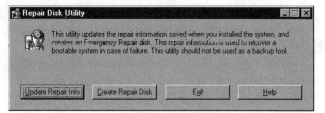

3. RDISK will prompt you to insert a disk. Insert a blank disk (or one that is okay to format) and click OK.

4. RDISK will format the disk and copy the configuration files to it.

5. When Windows NT has finished creating the disk and copying files to it, it will present a screen telling you that this disk contains security-sensitive data and to store it only in a safe location.

6. Click OK to finish creating the disk, remove the disk from the drive, label it "Windows NT ERD for <WORKSTATION NAME>," and put it in a safe place so that you can get to it easily if there is ever a problem.

7. Remember that the ERD is unique to each NT machine. Repeat this process at other NT Workstations as necessary.

Creating a Windows 2000 ERD

To create an Emergency Repair Disk in Windows 2000, use the following steps:

1. Select Start ➢ Programs ➢ Accessories ➢ System Tools ➢ Backup.

2. From the Welcome tab, click Emergency Repair Disk.

3. Backup prompts you to insert a disk. Insert a blank, formatted 1.44MB floppy disk into your floppy disk drive.

4. Select the check box on this screen that will put a copy of the Registry in the C:\WINNT\REPAIR directory (assuming Windows 2000 was installed to C:\WINNT).

WARNING When you finish installing Windows 2000 successfully, information about the setup is stored in the *systemroot*\Repair folder on the system partition. *Do not delete this folder.* It contains the information the ERD requires to restore your system to its original state.

---

5. Click OK to start copying ERD files. Backup will display a progress bar as the files copy.

6. When finished, Backup will display a message that the disk was created successfully. Remove the disk, label it as your Windows 2000 ERD, and include the name of the computer it was created for. Put it in a safe place so it will be available when your computer has a problem.

Exam Essentials

Know the files necessary to boot Windows 9x and how the boot process works.   Don't get obsessive about the details, such as "How does WIN.COM transfer the processor into protected mode?" It doesn't matter. Just know *that it does it*!

Know the files necessary to boot Windows 2000 and how the boot process works.   Remember that Windows NT and Windows 2000 boot files are identical, so any questions about "What does the BOOT.INI file do in Windows NT?" will have the same answer as "What does the BOOT.INI file do in Windows 2000?"

Know how to edit Windows 9x startup files.   Text editors, MSCONFIG, and SYSEDIT are all things you should know. The only Windows 2000 boot file that can be edited is the BOOT.INI, which can be modified with a text editor such as NOTEPAD.EXE.

Understand Safe Mode.   Both Windows 9x and 2000 have Safe Mode. *Windows NT does not have this option!* Know when it is appropriate to enter Safe Mode, how to do this, and what options are available.

Know how to create a Startup Disk (9x) or an ERD (NT/2000).   Know where to go within Windows to create these utility disks and how to use them.

Key Terms and Concepts

Boot files   Files used to start the computer and prepare it for use by the operating system.

System files Files used to load the operating system itself, including its graphic interface and other system components.

Real mode Sixteen-bit hardware access.

Batch file A file used to run a series of commands.

Safe Mode A method of running Windows using a minimal set of system drivers.

2.4 Identify procedures for loading/adding and configuring applications, device drivers, and the necessary software for certain devices.

- Windows 9x Plug and Play and Windows 2000
- Identify the procedures for installing and launching typical Windows and non-Windows applications. (Note: There is no content related to Windows 3.1.)
- Procedures for set up and configuring Windows printing subsystem.

This last subdomain is a rather oddly written one, as the objective as of 11/02/00 talks about an "application device driver." I believe that the domain should read "Identify procedures for loading/ adding and configuring applications, device drivers, and the necessary software for certain devices," meaning that this is just a typo, and have corrected it in the above heading.

Critical Information

Again, there's considerable information in this section as this subdomain deals with the way that Windows operating systems deal with hardware and software configuration. This is, practically speaking, information used by techs on a daily basis.

Managing Hardware

There are three ways to install hardware. Knowing all of these is critical for understanding how Windows works with hardware:

Automatically during the OS install   If a piece of hardware is in the computer when you install the OS and is supported by operating system's default driver database, it will simply be installed and configured automatically during setup.

Automatically through detection by Plug and Play   If hardware is installed after the installation of the OS, Plug and Play can detect and automatically install the device when you restart the machine. In such a case, you can provide your own drivers, or you can often use standard drivers provided for you. Plug and Play is an industry standard that allows peripheral devices to interact with the operating system. The device can report on what it is and what resources it needs, and the OS and device can negotiate particular settings, such as IRQs.

Manually through the Add/Remove Hardware icon in Control Panel   If your hardware is not detected by Plug and Play, it may be a legacy device. These are components that are not designed to work with Plug and Play and that need to be configured manually. In order to do this, you will generally need to have information on the IRQ and DMA settings of the device. You will also have to provide drivers or choose the proper driver from the default list.

Plug and Play

Among the most important of the other enhancements debuted by Microsoft with Windows 95 was support for the Plug-and-Play standard (PnP). This meant that if a device was designed to be Plug and Play, a technician could install the device into the computer, start the machine, and have the device automatically recognized and configured by Windows 95. This was a major advance, but unfortunately for Plug and Play to work properly, three things had to be true:

- The OS had to be PnP compatible.

- The computer motherboard had to support PnP.

- All devices in the machine had to be PnP compatible.

Unfortunately, at the time Windows 95 came out, many manufacturers were creating their hardware for use in DOS/Windows machines, and DOS did not support PnP, so most pre-1995 computer components were not PnP compliant. Because of this, these components—generally referred to as *legacy devices*—often interfered with the Plug-and-Play environment. Legacy devices are sound cards, modems, etc. that do not support the Plug-and-Play standard. Such devices are not able to dynamically interact with newer systems. They therefore require manual configuration or must be replaced by newer devices, which don't usually need manual configuration. Due to problems managing legacy hardware under Windows 95, many people soured on PnP technology. Worse, they blamed Windows 95 for their problems, not the old hardware. "It worked fine in DOS" was the standard logic! Now, half a decade later, nearly all PC components are PnP compliant, and configuring computer systems is far easier than it was under DOS.

Windows 9x and 2000 work very similarly in dealing with hardware issues. Windows 2000 supports a broader range of hardware (mostly because it is newer), but 9x and 2000 both rely on Plug and Play and use all three of the above methods to install hardware. Windows NT, on the other hand, does not have Plug-and-Play support—except for some rudimentary detection capability through the PNPISA utility. As such, NT is a different animal. Since it is not mentioned in the objectives, Windows NT hardware management will be ignored here, but you should note that it is different.

There are a number of tools and options for letting you install, update, and configure your system. We will first look at how you can examine the hardware that is installed on your machine, and then we'll examine how to install a new device.

Device Manager

Device Manager is found on the Hardware tab of the System icon in Control Panel. It gives a graphical view of all the hardware installed in your computer that Windows 9x or 2000 has detected. Device

Manager is not available in Windows NT. Device Manager is used to display all the hardware that Windows "knows about" and to configure the hardware settings of those devices. If you click the plus sign (+) next to a category of devices, it will "tree out" that category and allow you to see the devices in the category. If you then select a device and click Properties, you can view the information about that device. Figure 8.1 shows the result of selecting a network card and clicking Properties. Notice that there are three tabs under Device Manager: General, Driver, and Resources. Most devices have these tabs (although some devices may have only one or two). The General tab shows information about the device and its status. It also allows you disable the device in the current hardware profile.

FIGURE 8.1: Displaying the properties of a device in Device Manager

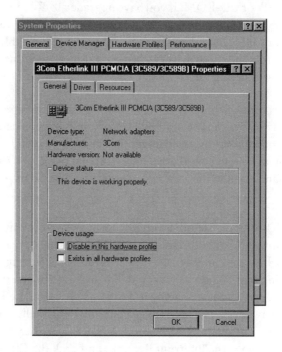

NOTE For more information about hardware profiles, refer to either the Windows Help files or the Windows 95, 98, or 2000 Resource Kits by Microsoft. Don't worry about it too much on test day, though, as hardware profiles aren't covered on the exam.

UPDATING A DEVICE'S PROPERTIES OR DRIVER

The Driver tab allows you to see the driver name for the device as well as the driver version, if available. You can see whether any drivers have been loaded for a device or if drivers specified for a device are not compatible. If you need to load a driver (or update a driver), click the Update Driver button. Windows will present you with a list of drivers to select from or allow you to install your own from floppy disk or CD-ROM. If you have upgraded to Windows 98 or 2000, you may find that the system continues to use old drivers from the previous OS. A number of updated drivers are available on vendor Web sites, and these drivers often are far more efficient, and stable, than the older drivers.

TIP To add drivers available on the Web, you usually must download the compressed driver files and then expand them onto a floppy disk or into a hard drive folder. At that point, you can run the update and point to the location where you extracted the files.

The right-most tab is usually Resources. From this tab, you can view and configure the system resources that the device is using. Most often, the check box next to Use Automatic Settings is checked, meaning that Windows Plug and Play has determined the settings for the device and is managing it. However, if the device is not a Plug-and-Play device and needs to be configured manually, simply uncheck the Use Automatic Settings check box. You can then select the setting (for example, the Interrupt Request) and click the Change Setting button to pick the correct setting from a list. When you configure settings manually, Windows lets you know if the setting you have chosen conflicts with another device.

Installing a New Device

Adding new hardware devices is very simple under Windows. When you start Windows after installing a new hardware device, it will normally detect the new device using Plug and Play and automatically install the software for it. If not, you need to run the Add New Hardware Wizard.

INSTALLING A DEVICE USING PLUG AND PLAY

To start adding the new device, double-click the My Computer icon. Then double-click Control Panel. To start the wizard, double-click the Add New Hardware icon in the Control Panel window.

Once you have started the Add New Hardware Wizard, you will see a screen similar to the one in Figure 8.2. To start the configuration of the new hardware, click Next.

FIGURE 8.2: The Add New Hardware Wizard

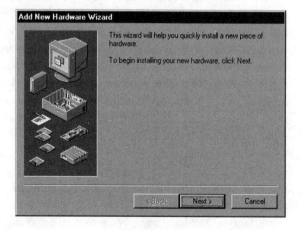

The next screen that is presented allows you to decide whether the wizard will search for the hardware. If you choose Yes, then in the next step, Windows will search for the hardware and install the drivers for it automatically. It is the easiest method (especially if the hardware is Plug-and-Play-compliant) and is the least complex. If you choose No, the wizard will present a screen from which you will have to select the type, brand, and settings for the new hardware. If you choose to let Windows detect the device, the next screen will tell you that Windows is ready to search for the new hardware. To begin the detection, Windows will make an intensive scan of the hardware (you should notice that the hard disk light will be on almost constantly and you will hear the hard disk thrashing away during the detection).

Eventually, Windows will tell you that it found some hardware that it can install. You can see which hardware it found by clicking the Details button. To finish the setup of the new hardware, click the Finish button. Windows will copy the drivers from the installation disks or CD for the device. Once it has done that, it may ask you for configuration information, if necessary. To finish the hardware setup, it will ask you to reboot Windows so that the changes can take effect and Windows can recognize (and use) the new hardware.

INSTALLING A DEVICE MANUALLY

Occasionally, you will find that when you install a new piece of hardware, it is not automatically detected. In this case, one of two things has happened: Either the device is not Plug-and-Play-capable, or there is some sort of problem that is keeping the device from being recognized. This could range from an interrupt conflict to a malfunction of the hardware itself. If there is an actual problem, you can find that information in domain 3.0. If the device simply is not Plug and Play, though, all you need to do is go to Control Panel and run the Add New Hardware (or Add/Remove Hardware) program. This will allow you to attempt to force-detect the hardware, and if that does not work, you can manually install the driver and specify the needed resource settings for the device. If you have all the information, this is easy. If you don't, it can be extremely frustrating. Before trying to install undetected hardware, be certain to go to the Web site of the vendor that made the device. Verify that the hardware is supported under the OS you are trying to install it on, and obtain any new drivers that are available. Also check to see what the default IRQ/DMA settings are. Let's hope no one changed them! Some companies even have configuration programs that allow you to check for the settings on the device and test its functionality.

Managing Software

Once all the hardware is running, it's time to install some programs on the PC. When you start looking at installing applications on a Windows machine, the first thing to note is that the installation is generally pretty similar regardless of whether the program is installed on Windows 9*x* or Windows 2000. Even so, there are a number of differences in applications, and you should take these into account. One of the first things you will want to look for when getting ready to install a new application is what types of operating system the product supports. Not all programs install on all operating systems, and the following sections detail the key questions you will want to ask.

Is It a DOS or a Windows Application?

In order to make it easier for third-party vendors to write applications for Windows, Microsoft provides APIs (application programming interfaces) for Windows 3.*x*, 9*x*, NT, and 2000. These APIs allow programmers to write applications more easily because Windows itself provides much of the functionality. For instance, when a programmer wants to write a routine that prints out a result, they can simply call printing APIs instead of writing out the entire print process. This does two things: First, it makes programming more simple, and second, it standardizes the way that certain tasks are performed. Almost all print or file-save screens in Windows, for example, look about the same because all of them use a standardized API set.

If a program is written for Windows, it should run on either 9*x* or 2000. We will see in the next section that it may not run optimally, but generally, it will work. If the application was written for DOS, though, it could be a different story. Windows 9*x* provides an environment that allows you to use older DOS applications, but Windows 2000 does not. Most non-Windows applications will fail if you attempt to run them on Windows 2000! We will deal with how Windows 9*x* runs DOS applications later in the chapter.

Is It a 32-Bit or 16-Bit Windows Application?

Applications that are written for older versions of Windows are referred to as *16-bit applications* or *Windows 3.x applications*. Newer applications written specifically for Windows 9*x* or Windows 2000 are designed for use on more modern hardware and take advantage of the fact that 9*x* and 2000 are 32-bit operating systems. Although both 16-bit and 32-bit Windows applications will generally run on either of the 32-bit Windows platforms, 32-bit applications are faster and more stable and should be used whenever possible.

Does the Application Use Any Nonstandard Windows APIs?

As I just mentioned, most 16-bit and 32-bit Windows applications will run on either Windows 98 or Windows 2000. Unfortunately, though, this is a guideline, not a rule. Because of the fact that there are Windows APIs that are supported by Windows 9*x* but not by Windows 2000, and vice versa, you will occasionally find that a 32-bit Windows application will work only on the 9*x* or the 2000 platform.

TIP Because the operating systems are very similar architecturally, applications written for Windows 95 will work with Windows 98, and those written for Windows NT will work with Windows 2000. Those written for the newer systems, however, are not always backward compatible.

Installing Applications

Once you have determined that an application is able to run on your Windows machine (or you think it will!), you need to transfer the files and settings for that application onto the computer. In Windows, this is generally done through the use of a Setup program, although, as you will see with Windows 2000, Microsoft has debuted a new way of installing and managing applications that could mean the end of Setup as we know it. Because of this, installation information is divided into two sections: The first describes a standard application setup, and the second describes a setup using the Windows Installer (MSI) files. We will not divide this up in a Windows 9*x*/Windows 2000 fashion because they are identical in the way they handle each setup. You may or may not get MSI questions on the test. The Windows Installer is not mentioned in the objectives, but it could easily be added.

TIP   Because it is the application that controls the setup procedures, both Windows 9*x* and Windows 2000 machines will be able to use the new setup method of Office 2000.

Applications are really nothing more than software code installed onto the hard drive of your machine. Because of this, it shouldn't be a big surprise to know you have to obtain a copy of the software installation files before running the setup. The most common installation methods today are as follows:

CD-ROM   Most programs are sold on CD-ROM. To install them, you simply put the disk into the disk drive, and an install routine should start up. If it doesn't, you may have to browse to the setup file.

Network   In organizations where network installations are available, they are generally preferred to CD-ROM installs because there is no need to carry around the disk (or in my case, to *find* the disk I need). Network installs are also generally faster than CD-ROM installs.

Internet   Installing software that is downloaded directly over the Internet is becoming increasingly popular because of its convenience and flexibility.

WARNING   Installing applications acquired off the Internet can also be dangerous to the health of your machine. Most viruses and other malicious problems are passed on through opening and using executable files, and SETUP.EXE is one such file. Download and use content directly from vendor sites or respected mirror sites only.

RUNNING A STANDARD SETUP ROUTINE

Once you have the installation CD or have downloaded the files you need, find the installation file—it will usually be SETUP.EXE or INSTALL.EXE.

NOTE Nonstandard setup filenames are relatively common among software distributed over the Internet. As updates become available and the version number changes, so will the filename, because the version numbers are incremented.

Setup generally runs a wizard, and you are given options as to how the install will proceed. Once the Setup routine has completed, you will find that a number of changes have been made to your system. First, there are changes to the GUI consisting of a new group of icons in the Start menu.

In addition to these changes, the setup file also makes changes under the hood. A number of files are installed onto the hard drive to support the application. These files consist of DLLs (which are code libraries) and other informational and executable files, but there are no configuration files such as INI text files. Rather, configuration elements are set by adding a number of entries to the Registry, which can be found (among other places) in HKEY_LOCAL MACHINE\SOFTWARE\.

INSTALLING MICROSOFT OFFICE 2000 USING THE NEW WINDOWS INSTALLER

There are some significant limitations to Setup programs, and Microsoft recently began using a new method of setting up applications called the Windows Installer. The installer has the following advantages over traditional installation methods:

- The ability to logically group application elements for installation

- The ability to install components only when they are needed, through the Install On First Use option

- The ability to automatically detect and restore deleted or corrupt files

- Easier customization through the use of MST files, which are used to save customized installation options for reuse

One of the most common programs to now use the Installer is Microsoft Office 2000. Office 2000 has a number of versions—and each is a collection of collection of programs, called an *application suite*. Office Standard includes Word (word processing), Excel (spreadsheet), Outlook (personal information manager), and Power-Point (presentation). Office Professional adds Access, which is a database, and Office Premium adds the FrontPage Web editor and a number of other tools.

Microsoft Office has a SETUP.EXE file that it uses to start its installation routine. To start the install, simply insert the Office 2000 disk into your disk drive. Setup will begin automatically and will install Windows Installer onto your machine. If you already have a current version of the MS Installer software, the install continues. If not, an update will occur, and you may need to reboot and restart the install.

After this, you will be asked for a CD key, and you will need to agree to the license agreement. Once you have typed in the ridiculously long 25-digit key and have signed away your organs to Microsoft, you will be presented with a choice of a standard or a custom install.

Custom is nice because you can see exactly which applications and options you are installing. If you choose Custom, you will be asked not only to decide which options you want, but also how you want them to be installed. Components can be selected to run from CD, can be removed from the install, or can be installed only if they are used. This can't be done in an older standard setup! These installation options are available because of the flexibility of the Windows Installer program, which actually stays on your hard drive and can start a small install any time you need it, such as when someone wants to use an option that is installed on first use. Not all programs support these options yet, but many more will in the coming years.

Because new information is written to the Registry during the install process and may not be properly read until the system is reinitialized, you may need to reboot after the install. Some programs do not need to reboot. Others do, however, and generally it is best to restart immediately if prompted to do so.

Uninstalling an Application

Occasionally, you will install an application on a PC and then decide that you no longer need it. In order to free up hard drive space, you may then want to remove that application from the PC. This is done through a process called *uninstalling*. The Uninstall feature, which completely removes a program from the computer, also goes into the Registry and other system areas and removes references to the application. To access the Uninstall feature for an application in Windows, you generally have one of two options (or sometimes both):

- Use the Uninstall icon from the application's program group.

- Use Add/Remove Programs and choose to remove all or uninstall, depending on what terminology the program uses.

WARNING It is crucial to the health of your system that you do not simply go into Windows Explorer and delete the files for an application. Removing the files without performing an uninstall will cause Registry problems and other difficulties and may even make the system unstable.

Installing and Launching Non-Windows Applications

There are two ways to install DOS programs onto a Windows 9x machine. Many older DOS programs can simply be copied; newer, more complex DOS programs will have to be installed with a setup routine specific to that application. In either case, Windows 9x has the ability to let you configure the DOS environment to allow DOS applications to run as well as, well, a DOS application is going to run.

WARNING   The process for installing and using DOS applications is the same in Windows 2000 as it is in Windows 9x. That said, there is one critical difference: DOS applications generally run pretty well under Windows 9x and generally won't run at all under Windows 2000. If you are thinking of installing a 16-bit DOS application on Windows 2000 Professional, you need to test it carefully to make certain it will function properly.

Windows 3.x 16-bit applications' setup routines look similar to those of the Windows 32-bit applications we looked at earlier except that they use INI and other configuration files and are generally completely ignorant of the Registry.

Installing an Application by Copying

Many years ago, DOS applications were simple executable COM or EXE files that could be run from a floppy. Copying these files to the hard drive was a common practice (if the computer had a hard drive) because programs run faster from a hard drive than they do from a floppy drive. As programs became larger, with many pieces and added-in drivers, it became more than just practical to copy the files to the hard drive; it became necessary. DOS programs generally do not have INI files and do not interact with the Registry. Therefore, installing or uninstalling them is as simple as copying or deleting them.

The problem comes in when these programs start trying to execute commands on the system. In order for the application to work, an environment must generally be set up to allocate resources and workspace to the app. This is done through editing the AUTOEXEC.BAT or CONFIG.SYS file or through custom DOS configuration files.

Installing an Application with a Setup Routine

More complex DOS programs may need to be installed, rather than just copied, to work properly. Many DOS programs *can* be copied onto the hard drive but still come with an installation program that aids in the copy process by locating or creating a subdirectory for the files to be copied to. The install program also prompts you to insert each floppy disk as it is needed.

More complex programs require a more intricate installation procedure, usually meaning that you'll have to make decisions throughout the setup process. DOS programs generally use device drivers that are specific to that program; you may have to select a display driver for fitting more text or typed data on a screen.

NOTE   If you have questions about installing a DOS-based program, refer to the user guide that comes with the DOS software.

Launching an Application

Launching an application in DOS usually means typing in its name or the name of its main executable file at a DOS command prompt. You can also create an icon shortcut to the executable. Generally, programs are put into their own subdirectories, so a path must exist pointing to that subdirectory, or you must already be in that subdirectory.

Uninstalling an Application

As noted earlier, with most DOS programs, the uninstall process is easy: You simply erase all the files associated with the program.

Of course, sometimes an installation will have made modifications to the CONFIG.SYS and AUTOEXEC.BAT files. Depending on the nature of these configuration modifications, there may be no side effects from the removal of a program, or there may be some error messages about files not being found.

Rarely are these configuration changes harmful if left in, although many times the changes will leave extra and unneeded drivers loaded or memory configurations that are not optimized for the applications left on the hard drive. If you find these entries in the CONFIG.SYS or the AUTOEXEC.BAT files, and they refer to a program that has been removed, remarking out or deleting the offending statements will usually fix the problems.

DOS Optimization

Compatibility with older programs is important because people have a significant investment in the money spent on their programs and in their time learning how to use them. Microsoft built a number of features into Windows 9x that allow previous users of DOS and Windows 3.x to capitalize on their investment and that allow technicians access to DOS-based troubleshooting.

According to Microsoft (see, for example, the Microsoft Windows 95 Resource Kit), memory management for conventional memory while running the Windows 9x operating system is the same as for MS-DOS 6.x. This applies to the management of conventional memory only because all other memory management in Windows 9x is essentially automatic. If 16-bit DOS and 16-bit Windows 3.x programs are not even going to be used, then these techniques are unnecessary.

If you do need to use DOS/Windows 3.1 real-mode programs, you have three options:

- The user can initiate a DOS shell from inside of Windows 9x. This Virtual DOS Machine (VDM) is actually a 32-bit Windows application that emulates a DOS environment.

- The user can exit from Windows 9x into DOS mode. To do this, simply choose Start ➤ Shut down ➤ Restart in MS-DOS Mode. Any programs you are currently running will be shut down, and a DOS session will be opened. The advantage of this is that some DOS applications require actual control of the computer and will not work through a VDM.

- In some cases, the user can boot the computer straight into DOS. This requires having a copy of MS-DOS installed on the machine and using a dual-boot scenario, with Windows 9x installed and DOS coexisting as a totally different, stand-alone system.

In any of these cases, special configuration tasks can potentially make DOS/3.1 programs function more efficiently. To maximize available memory for real-mode programs, load the extended memory manager, HIMEM.SYS, and the expanded memory manager, EMM386, in the

CONFIG.SYS file. If possible, remove the real-mode drivers from the AUTOEXEC.BAT file and utilize the protected-mode drivers that are built into Windows 9x. You should not load SMARTDRIVE because the VCACHE disk caching that comes with Windows 9x is superior and does not detract from conventional memory.

MEMMAKER, which came with DOS 6.2x, is found on the Windows 9x CD in the directory OTHER\OLDDOS. MEMMAKER may be used to optimize the CONFIG.SYS and AUTOEXEC.BAT files for conventional memory.

NOTE If you want to dual-boot to DOS, you must use the FAT file system and keep your C: partition below 2GB; FAT32 and partition sizes over 2GB are not supported by DOS. Don't worry about this too much, though, because finding a machine that is still running DOS 6.x or lower is extremely rare. Because Windows 95 (DOS 7) and 98 (DOS32) support DOS applications well enough in most cases and have far more functionality, "real" 6.x and earlier DOS has largely gone the way of the Atari 2600 and laserdiscs.

Setting Up and Configuring Windows Printing Subsystem

One of the most common aspects of a technician's job is configuring Windows printing properly. The A+ exam will test your ability to do so. There are two ways to configure Windows printing: with a local printer or a network printer. You will need to know about both options. As with other device management, when it comes to configuring a printer, the steps for both Windows 9x and 2000 are essentially the same.

Microsoft was thoughtful enough to provide a wizard to help us install printers. The Add Printer Wizard (APW) will guide you through the basic steps of installing a printer by asking you questions about how you would like the printer configured.

To start the Add Printer Wizard, you must first open the PRINTERS folder (Start ➤ Settings ➤ Printers). Once you get to the PRINTERS folder, you can double-click the Add Printer icon. Doing so will display a screen that tells you the wizard is going to help you install your printer.

Local Printing Installation

The first question the wizard will ask you is where this printer is located. If it is connected to the network, click the button next to Network Printer. What the wizard is looking for here is whether you want to create a printer and print queue on this machine (local) or use an existing printer that is already set up on another machine elsewhere on the network. In setting up a local printer, you will have to supply the following:

Printer driver   You will be asked to provide a driver for the specific printer that you are installing. Make sure you select the correct driver for your model of printer. Most printing problems can be traced to a corrupt or out-of-date printer driver.

NOTE   Some printer drivers can't be installed using the Add Printer Wizard. You must run SETUP or INSTALL from the disk to install the printing software. These programs will not only install the correct printer drivers, they will also set up the printer for use with Windows.

Printer port   Another part of the configuration is to choose which port the printer is hooked to. You can choose from a list of ports that Windows knows about, including parallel (LPT), serial (COM), and infrared (IR) ports. If necessary, you can choose Configure Port to configure any special port settings the printer may require or to set a TCP/IP printing port. Remember that even if you are printing through TCP/IP, if you are creating the print queue locally, the printer is still a local printer.

Printer name   You can choose the printer by name when you select Print from any program. By default, the APW will supply the name of the print driver in this field. You can change it by simply clicking in the field and typing a new name.

Default printer In addition, you can select whether or not you want this printer to be the default that Windows selects when you don't select a specific printer. If you want this printer to be the default, click the button next to Yes. If not, click No. When you've finished changing these settings, click Next.

Managing a Printer Configuration

If you have a printer installed on your Windows computer, there will be times where you need to change the way the printer functions. For this reason, you should know how to manage an existing printer under Windows.

First, most of what you need to configure is centered around the printer icon (in the PRINTERS folder) that represents the printer you want to configure. You can configure most items from the property page of the printer by double-clicking the icon of the printer you want to configure.

If you right-click a printer's icon in the PRINTERS folder and choose Properties, you will see a screen with a number of different options. These options vary, depending on the type of printer it is. Each tab is used to configure different properties. Table 8.10 lists some common tabs and a description of the function of each one.

TABLE 8.10: Printer Properties Tabs and Functions

Tab	Description
General	Displays the printer's name as well as any comments you want to enter to describe the printer's functions (or eccentricities).
Details	Used to configure how Windows communicates with the printer.
Sharing	Used to share the printer on the network to which the machine is connected.

TABLE 8.10: Printer Properties Tabs and Functions *(continued)*

Tab	Description
Paper	Used to configure what kind of paper the printer is using (size-wise) as well as its orientation when printing.
Graphics	Used to configure the resolution of the printer. Lower resolutions use less toner.
Fonts	Displays the installed fonts. Also used to install other fonts.
Device Options	Varies depending on what kind of printer it is. Used to set the device-specific settings for the printer.

There are a number of configurable options you should keep in mind:

Spooling   One of the most important options on this screen is the Spool Settings button. This button allows you to configure whether or not Windows will spool print jobs. If print jobs are spooled, every time you click Print in a program, the job is printed to a spool directory (usually a subdirectory of the C:\WINDOWS\SPOOL directory) by a program called SPOOL32.EXE. Then the job is sent to the printer in the background while you continue to work. If you don't want print jobs to be spooled (it is the default), click the Spool Settings button. You can then choose either Spool Print Jobs or Print Directly To The Printer.

Scheduling   Printers can be scheduled to send documents at only a particular time. This allows you to print from only a particular queue during the day or print only in the evenings, for example.

Priority   The priority of a queue determines which print queue will have first dibs on a particular print device.

Managing Documents

Other printer-management options are found in the Printer item in the System Tray. When you print a document, an icon of a printer will appear in the System Tray. By double-clicking it, you can open it so that you can manage the print jobs. You can see any pending print jobs listed as well as their statistics. Among the options are the following:

- Pause The Printer
- Cancel All Documents
- Use The Printer Offline

Besides these printer options, you can also choose from document-specific options:

- Pause
- Resume
- Restart
- Cancel

Network Printing

Network printing is a lot like local printing except that with network printing, you are introducing a degree of separation between the computer and the printer. That degree of separation is a network. Configuring network printing is very similar to configuring local printing except that you must configure the Windows printer driver to print to the network instead of to a local printer port. Usually, this involves installing network software that comes with the printer; the software will create a virtual printer port that points to the specified network printer.

For the A+ exam, you will not be expected to know everything about connecting network printers (after all, that is what the Network+ exam is for). However, you should know the basic steps involved in using a network printer.

USING A SHARED PRINTER

Accessing shared printers is very similar to accessing shared resources; in both cases, you are accessing a resource that has been shared on the host computer. In both cases, you are also pointing a local resource (in this case, a printer icon) to a network resource (a shared printer).

To set up the printer on your workstation, you simply start the Installation Wizard, just as in a local install. After choosing to install a network printer, you can browse to the printer's location under the name of the machine the printer is managed by. In Windows 2000, you can also search for printers in Active Directory. Once you have found the printer, you will need to name it and install the driver, as with a local printer.

For the test, this is all you really need, as all other work in creating the shared printer, setting any permissions, and managing the configuration is taken care of by a system administrator.

Exam Essentials

Know how Windows Plug and Play works. Understand how the Plug-and-Play process manages hardware, and also know what its limitations are.

Know how to access application setup files on CD or the network and how to start an installation. The network part of this is covered in domain 4.0, but test questions cross domain lines occasionally. Make sure you know how to attach to an installation share, as shown in the networking information.

Know how to install and update hardware device drivers. Practice with Device Manager, and know how to find and add drivers for hardware that is detected but that Windows does not have standard drivers for.

Understand how DOS applications work in Windows 9*x* and Windows NT/2000.   Remember that in 9*x*, DOS apps generally need to be configured. In NT/2000, they generally need to be replaced!

Be able to install and configure printers in Windows and to attach to an existing network printer.   Printer questions are always a major part of a test. Spend some time reviewing and expanding your printer skills before the exam.

Key Terms and Concepts

Application   Software that is added to an operating system to give it enhanced functionality, such as a word processor or a game.

Legacy device   Hardware that is not Plug-and-Play compatible.

Update   A newer version of a piece of software. Upgrades generally have new features and must be purchased, but updates are usually free and are provided to fix problems or improve performance.

API   An application programming interface is software code used to provide an interpreter between an application and the OS.

Port   An interface through which the computer can send or receive information.

Spool   The process by which the printer sends a document to a location on the hard drive (or on a print server). This location then stores the print job until the printer is ready to process it, allowing the application that submitted the job to return to other tasks.

Chapter

9

Domain 3.0 Diagnosing and Troubleshooting

he general theme of the third domain of the A+ Operating System objectives is troubleshooting. Topics range from how to best get information out of users about what problem they are having to how to research or solve some of the more common problems.

Being able to troubleshoot problems—to find out what is wrong with a particular system—is one of the most basic job requirements of a technician. Rarely does a user send a machine in for repair with a note that says, "WIN.COM file is missing." or "The network card driver is corrupt." They just bring in a computer, give a basic description of what is happening ("My computer doesn't work" is a common one), and it's up to you to decipher what is wrong and fix it. You will soon learn, by the way, that grilling the user a bit can often turn up valuable information, and we'll cover how to do that as well.

There are two sections to this domain. The first deals with the particular problem of troubleshooting the boot process, while the second deals with more general areas of customer service and common system errors.

3.1 Recognize and interpret the meaning of common error codes and startup messages from the boot sequence, and identify steps to correct the problems.

- Safe Mode
- No operating system found
- Error in CONFIG.SYS line XX
- Bad or missing COMMAND.COM

- **HIMEM.SYS not loaded**
- **Missing or corrupt HIMEM.SYS**
- **SCSI**
- **Swap file**
- **NT boot issues**
- **Dr. Watson**
- **Failure to start GUI**
- **Windows Protection Error**
- **Event Viewer – Event log is full**
- **A device referenced in SYSTEM.INI, WIN.INI, Registry is not found**

This domain covers some of the more common problems that can appear during startup. We will examine these problems and learn how you can find information about what is causing you trouble.

Critical Information

Normally if there is a problem with Windows, it will become apparent during the startup process. This content area will look at problems that either keep the system from starting or cause the startup to be abnormal.

Safe Mode

When Windows won't start properly, it is probably due to a driver or some piece of software that's not loading correctly. To fix problems of this nature, you should first try to boot Windows in *Safe Mode*. In Safe Mode, Windows loads a minimal set of drivers (including a VGA-only video driver) so that you can disable an offending driver to keep it from loading—and from failing again. To start Windows in Safe Mode, press the F8 key when you see the Starting Windows display during Windows bootup. This brings up a menu that will allow you to start Windows in Safe Mode. Once booted in Safe Mode, you can uninstall any driver you suspect is causing a Windows boot problem or reinstall the driver if you suspect it is corrupted. Upon reboot, the system should go back to normal operation (non-Safe Mode).

TIP A "corrupt" driver is one in which the software files for the driver have been damaged. This can be caused by a disk error, by a virus, or by standard "act of God" problems such as power outages.

Both Windows 9*x* and Windows 2000 offer Safe Mode. Windows NT does not. You can also use the F8 menu in 9*x* or 2000 to select other boot options, such as logging all messages to a log file during boot, booting to a command prompt, or starting Windows in Safe Mode with network support. The Windows 2000 options include those in the list below. Windows 9*x* offers similar options, but with differences based on the version.

Safe Mode Starts Windows 2000 using only basic files and drivers (mouse, except serial mice; monitor; keyboard; mass storage; base video; default system services; and no network connections). Once in Safe Mode, you can restore files that are missing or fix a configuration error.

Safe Mode With Networking Same as Safe Mode, but tries to load networking components as well.

Safe Mode With Command Prompt Similar to Safe Mode, but doesn't load the Windows GUI. Presents the user with a Windows 2000 command-prompt interface.

Enable Boot Logging Logs all boot information to a file called Ntbtlog.txt. This file can be found in the \WINNT directory. You can then check the log for assistance in diagnosing system startup problems.

Enable VGA Mode Starts Windows 2000 using the basic VGA driver, but loads the rest of the system as normal. If you happen to install an incorrect video driver or a video driver corrupts, this allows you to get into the system to fix the problem.

Last Known Good Configuration This option is useful if you have changed a configuration setting in the Registry, which then causes the system to have serious problems. Every time you log into a Windows system, the last step of the logon process is to save a copy of the Registry configuration used to log in, as shown in Figure 9.1. This is then considered the Last Known Good Configuration

(LKGC), which keeps track of Registry entries and software settings. If you have just changed the system configuration and problems occur when you restart, *do not log on.* Shut the machine down, boot into the Last Known Good Configuration, and try a different change. Remember that the LKGC only recovers configuration problems—it will not save you from a corrupt file or a deleted file.

FIGURE 9.1: Windows 2000 Current and Saved Registry Information

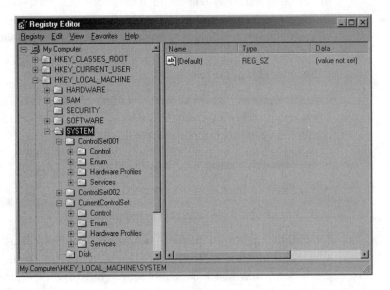

Debugging Mode   A sort of advanced boot logging, Debugging Mode requires that another machine be hooked up to the computer through a serial port. The debug information is then passed to that machine during the boot process.

For the test, know what all of the Safe Mode options are and which problems Safe Mode can (and can't) allow you to correct.

No Operating System Found

Every operating system or operating environment has certain key system files that must be present in order for it to function. If these files are missing or corrupt, the operating system will cease to function properly. Files can be deleted by accident rather easily, so it's important to know what these system files are, where they are located, and how to replace them.

When you boot Windows 9x or Windows NT/2000, the presence of the system files (e.g., HIMEM.SYS, NTLDR, etc.) is checked, and each file is loaded. If you'll remember, the computer's BIOS first checks the hardware of the PC, then looks for a boot sector on one of the disks and loads the operating system found in that boot sector. However, if the computer can't find a boot sector with an operating system installed on any of the disks, it will display an error similar to the following:

```
No operating system found
```

This error means that the computer's BIOS checked all the drives it knew about and couldn't find any disk with a bootable sector. There could be any number of reasons for this error, including:

- An operating system wasn't installed.
- The boot sector has been corrupted.
- The boot files have been corrupted or deleted.

Thankfully, there are a couple of solutions to these problems. First of all, if the file or files are simply missing, just copy them from another machine or from a backup (assuming you have one). The same holds true if you have corrupt files—just delete them and replace them with new copies. Most system files for any of the OSes are identical on all computers running the same version. The exception to this is the Windows NT/2000 BOOT.INI file, which we will examine.

NOTE When deleting and/or replacing system files on a FAT drive, you must use the ATTRIB command to remove the hidden, system, and read-only attributes before you replace these files. Most system files are hidden by the OS to make it less likely that someone will accidentally delete them. They also can be marked with a special System attribute to indicate their importance to the OS.

Bad or Missing COMMAND.COM, HIMEM.SYS Not Loaded, or Missing or Corrupt HIMEM.SYS

These same concepts hold true for other system file-related problems, such as

```
Bad or missing COMMAND.COM
HIMEM.SYS not loaded
Missing or corrupt HIMEM.SYS
```

These errors just mean that the specified files (e.g., COMMAND.COM, HIMEM.SYS) are either not on the drive or have become unusable. Just replace them with fresh copies. The error should go away, and the computer should function properly. If that does not happen, then you may have more serious problems with the hard drives themselves.

Also, remember that if a number of files are missing or damaged, you may find that you get one error, resolve the problem that it points to, and then reboot only to find a different problem. This is actually extremely common in troubleshooting, and all you can do in such a case is deal with each problem until you have the system back in working order. If, for instance, all Startup files for Windows 9*x* are missing, you will receive a "Bad or missing COMMAND.COM" message, as that is the first file Windows 9*x* attempts to load. In Windows NT or 2000, you would get a "Missing NTLDR" error.

WARNING   Remember that the system files for each version of Windows are different. When replacing a file, make certain that you are using a replacement from the correct OS—and the correct version of that OS. If you have applied a patch or a Service Pack to a system, you will need to get the proper files for that Service Pack level.

Error in CONFIG.SYS Line XX or a Device Referenced in SYSTEM.INI, WIN.INI, Registry Is Not Found

Windows 9*x* and Windows NT contain several files that hold configuration data for Windows, such as the Registry, SYSTEM.INI, WIN.INI, and CONFIG.SYS. Because a user can edit these files, the possibility for introduction of invalid configurations is relatively likely. In addition, many software installation programs modify these files when a new program is installed. These files are modified so frequently, in fact, that it is a wonder they aren't corrupted more often.

Some of the more commonly seen errors in Windows that are related to configuration files are listed here:

```
A device referenced in SYSTEM.INI can not be found
A device referenced in WIN.INI can not be found
A device referenced in the Registry can not be found
Error in CONFIG.SYS line XX
```

These errors are basically all of the same type. There is configuration information about all hardware or software on the machine stored in either the Registry or other configuration files. If that information does not properly initialize the software or device that it refers to, the system will report an error. Sometimes this occurs because a device or file has been removed or deleted. The difference is which file the error is contained in. Again, with missing items, the solution is very simple: Just replace the item. In fact, in "Error in CONFIG.SYS line XX," the error message actually tells you which line of the CONFIG.SYS file references the missing information. You can then go directly to that line and begin to troubleshoot.

The process is the same for the Registry except that you must use the Registry Editor (REGEDIT.EXE or REGEDT32.EXE, for Windows 9x and Windows NT, respectively) to search for corrupt or invalid entries. You will learn more about the Registry later in this chapter.

One major difference between this group of errors and the earlier boot errors is that normally the system will start, but it will lack full functionality due to the errors. The good thing about this is that you should be able to use standard Windows configuration tools to fix the problem. With the SYSTEM.INI and WIN.INI files, you will be given information about the problem, and you must search through using your favorite text editor to find the invalid line, as in Figure 9.2. It may be something as hard to find as an additional backslash put in the wrong place or as easy to find as a string of corrupt characters. If the Registry is the problem, you will be able to use the REGEDIT or REGEDT32 tool.

FIGURE 9.2: Editing the SYSTEM.INI file

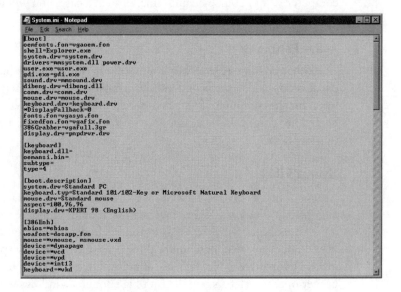

SCSI

When using an IDE or EIDE drive, support for the drive is generally not a problem. With SCSI drives, though, it is possible for the files that initialize and control the SCSI controller to be corrupted or lost, and in such a case the system will not be able to read the drive and the system will not load.

Because each SCSI controller has a specific driver or set of drivers that it requires, if these are not present, you will need to research which type of controller the system uses and then obtain the drivers needed for a particular OS to access that controller.

A+ Complete Exam Notes

Another problem, of course, is general to any hard drive type. Hard drives, whether they are SCSI, IDE, or EIDE, are all fixed. Once installed, they are expected to be permanently attached to the system, and if one is removed, extensive reconfiguration may need to be done on the system. Floppy drives and CD-ROM drives are designed to support removable, interchangeable media, but if the drive that the Windows system files is on is damaged or cannot be accessed, the computer will of course be unusable. In such a case, you will usually need to recover the system from backup.

Active Partitions

One other possible reason why the system may not boot is that the partition on which the boot files reside must be set as the active partition for the computer. If no active partition is found, the system will be unable to boot. In this case, you need to use FDISK to set a partition as active.

Swap File

As mentioned in earlier chapters, Windows uses *swap files* (called *page files* in Windows NT) to increase the amount of usable memory it has by using hard disk space as memory. However, sometimes problems can occur when a computer doesn't have enough disk space to make a proper swap file. Because Windows relies on swap files for proper operation, if a swap file isn't big enough, Windows will slow down and start running out of usable memory. All sorts of memory-related problems can stem from incorrect or too small swap files. Symptoms of swap file problems include an extremely slow system speed and a disk that is constantly being accessed. This condition is known as hard disk *thrashing* and occurs because Windows doesn't have enough memory to contain all the programs that are running, and there isn't enough disk space for a swap file to contain them all. This causes Windows to swap between memory and hard disk.

One solution to this problem is to delete enough unused files so that the swap file can expand and become large enough. This happens automatically, as shown in Figure 9.3. Another is to install a bigger hard drive to allow for more space. It is very possible, however, that neither of these will help, because if you do not have enough actual physical memory (RAM), just increasing the page file won't improve overall performance much. In such cases, the only effective option is to actually add RAM.

FIGURE 9.3: Windows 98 Virtual Memory settings

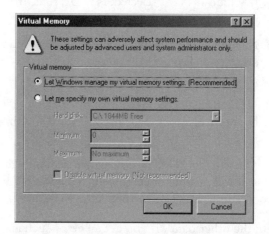

NT Boot Issues

Troubleshooting Windows NT boot issues is another common type of Windows troubleshooting. To understand Windows NT boot issues, you must first understand the NT boot process, which is as follows:

1. The POST routine examines the boot sector and loads the Master Boot Record (MBR).

2. The boot sector is loaded from the active partition.

3. NTLDR is loaded from the boot sector and initialized.

4. NTLDR loads the appropriate minifile drivers for the type of file system on the boot partition (e.g., FAT or NTFS). The minifile driver is a basic version of a file system driver that loads the minimum information necessary.

5. NTLDR reads the BOOT.INI file and looks for the list of operating systems installed on the computer. Windows NT is one of the choices, along with any other operating system that was installed over when Windows NT was installed.

6. A user selects an operating system to boot to.

7. If Windows NT is selected, NTLDR runs NTDETECT.COM to detect new hardware.

8. NTLDR then loads the kernel file (NTOSKRNL.EXE), the hardware abstraction layer (HAL), and the Registry, as well as any device drivers found there.

9. NTLDR finally passes control to NTOSKRNL.EXE. At this point, the boot process is finished, and NTOSKRNL can start loading other files.

As you can see, NTLDR is heavily relied upon during the boot process. If it is missing or corrupted, Windows NT will not be able to boot, and you'll get an error similar to "Can't find NTLDR."

On the other hand, if you get an error such as "NTOSKRNL.EXE missing or corrupt" on bootup, it may be an error in the BOOT.INI file. This is a common occurrence if you have improperly used the multi(0)disk(0)rdisk(0)partition(1)\WINNT="Windows NT Server" syntax entries. If these entries are correct, the NTOSKRNL.EXE file may be corrupt or missing. Boot to a startup disk and replace the file from the setup disks or CD-ROM.

TIP The NT boot process described above is identical to the Windows 2000 boot process.

Dr. Watson

Windows NT 4 includes a special utility known as Dr. Watson. This utility intercepts all error conditions and, instead of presenting the user with a cryptic Windows error, presents the user with information that can be used to troubleshoot the problem. In addition, Dr. Watson logs all errors to log files stored in the `WINDOWS\DRWATSON` directory.

The doctor also makes house calls, as you can run `DRWATSON.EXE` manually, and Windows will go out and take a "snapshot" of the system. If any configuration problems are found, they will be reported on, and the basic health of the system will be reported. Figure 9.4 shows the Dr. Watson screen, with the Diagnosis tab displayed.

FIGURE 9.4: The Dr. Watson application

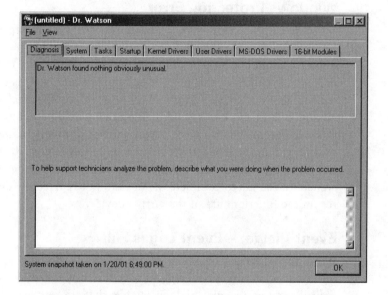

Failure to Start GUI

Occasionally, the GUI of Windows won't appear. The system will hang just before the GUI appears. Or, in the case of Windows NT, the Blue Screen of Death (BSOD)—not a technical term, by the way—will appear. The BSOD is another way of describing the blue-screen error condition that occurs when Windows NT/2000 fails to boot properly or quits unexpectedly. In Windows 9x, instead of a BSOD, you will simply get a black screen (usually with a blinking cursor in the upper-left corner) that indicates there is a problem. Because it is at this stage that the device drivers for the various pieces of hardware are installed, if your Windows GUI fails to start properly, more than likely the problem is related to a misconfigured driver or misconfigured hardware. Try booting Windows in Safe Mode to bypass this problem. Alternatively, some of the files necessary for the GUI may be having problems, and you may need to replace WIN.COM or other system files from the \WINDOWS or \WINNT directory.

Windows Protection Error

A Windows protection error is a condition that usually happens on either startup or shutdown. Protection errors occur because Windows 9x could not load or unload a virtual device driver (VxD) properly. Thankfully, this error usually tells which VxD is experiencing the problem, so you can check to see if the specified VxD is missing or corrupt. If it is, you can replace it with a new copy. Often this error occurs when a piece of software is improperly uninstalled or when the uninstall program does not completely remove Registry or INI file references. In such a case, you need to either remove the references to the file to complete the uninstall or replace the file to regain the functionality of the virtual device.

Event Viewer – Event Log Is Full

Windows keeps track of system information and problems by employing error and informational logging routines. In Windows 9x, this is limited to startup logging and any log files that are kept by particular applications. Every program and process theoretically could have its own logging utility. Similarly, Windows NT/2000 machines could do the same, but Microsoft has come up with a rather slick utility, Event Viewer, which tracks all events on a particular Windows NT/2000 computer through log files. Event Viewer is shown in Figure 9.5. Anyone can view events, but you must be an administrator or a member of the Administrators group to modify or clear Event Viewer.

FIGURE 9.5: Windows 2000 Event Viewer

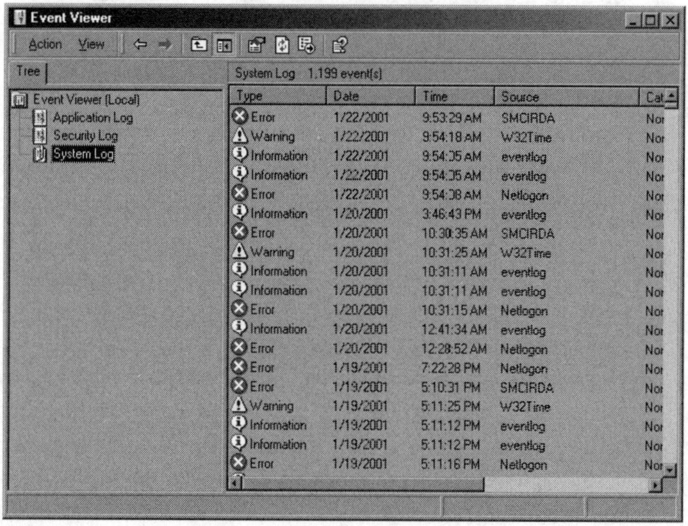

To start Event Viewer, log in as an administrator (or equivalent) and go to Start ➤ Settings ➤ Control Panel ➤ Administrative Tools ➤ Event Viewer. From here you can view the three log files within Event Viewer:

System   This log file displays alerts that pertain to the operation of Windows. System startup information, problems with NT services, and other general health and status events are recorded here.

Application   The Application log file logs server application errors. Any application written to log information about its operation to NT/2000 writes its data here. Examples of this include anti-virus programs and database programs, although not all such programs are designed to use the Application log.

Security   The Security log file logs security events, such as login successes and failures. It also allows administrators to audit the use of files or printers. By default, security logging is turned off, and this log file will be empty unless security auditing has been explicitly enabled.

These log files can give a general indication of a Windows computer's health, and it is important that they be available in case of trouble. There are a couple of possible log problems. One is that the log files will become corrupted. In such a case, you will need to delete the log files and let Windows re-create them. Also, the Event Viewer log files can fill up, and the log will not be able to add new information. There are two solutions to this problem. The first is to simply enable circular logging, which will allow the system to delete old events as new ones are added. In most cases, this works well, but valuable troubleshooting information can be lost. The other solution is to back up and clean out the log files occasionally. This will allow you to keep a record of all events, but it does require more work. To do this, use Event Viewer to save each of the log files, and then choose Clear All Events from the Log menu. This will erase all events in the current log file, allowing you to see new events more easily when they occur. Another option, of course, is to increase the size of the logs, which can also be done through Event Viewer.

Necessary Procedures

Most troubleshooting is done on a case-by-case basis, but nonetheless there are a number of basic steps you should be familiar with. The exercise below is a sort of standard template for PC troubleshooting.

Basic Troubleshooting

1. Read the trouble ticket or work order to see what problem the machine has.

2. If possible, contact the person who reported the problem and ask them the following questions:

   - How long has the problem been occurring?

   - Has the system ever worked correctly?

   - Does the problem occur only when you are using certain programs or only in certain circumstances?

- Did you get any particular error messages?

- Can you replicate the error?

- One other question linked to those above is "Has anything odd happened to the computer lately, or has anything changed on it?" If a new piece of hardware, a driver, or other software was installed about the time the problem began, or if the machine shut down during a power outage, these may be clues.

3. Once you have talked to the user and have determined the symptoms of the problem, check to see if the problem has occurred before. Microsoft and many hardware vendors have support databases that you can search for answers.

4. In conjunction with checking the support sites, you can also check the many log files and error files created by Windows. One of these may have a helpful message.

5. When you start working to fix the error, be careful to try only one solution at a time. If you think that a change to the CONFIG.SYS file or a change to the Registry might solve the problem, do not try both of them at once. By trying one at a time, you will be able to see the effects of each change, know which solution worked, and change the system as little as possible.

6. Once you have found the solution, be sure to record what happened and how you solved the problem, so that if it recurs you will know how to solve it immediately.

Exam Essentials

Know how to identify common startup problems and recover from startup errors.   This includes knowing which files are needed to boot Windows 9*x*, NT, and 2000, as well as what steps should be taken to bring these files back.

Understand how Safe Mode works in Windows 9*x* and 2000. Knowing when to use Safe Mode can help you recover from numerous problems, primarily including driver troubles.

Know which system files can be modified and what they do. These include AUTOEXEC.BAT and CONFIG.SYS, INI files, and the NT/2000 BOOT.INI file. Know how to use a text editor to modify these files.

Know how to deal with Windows error messages. Understand how Dr. Watson works in shutting down and controlling problems and how Event Viewer and other files record information useful for troubleshooting.

Key Terms and Concepts

Troubleshooting The process of determining what is wrong with a machine and then taking steps to solve the problem.

Swap file Space on the hard drive used as extra RAM for the machine.

Dr. Watson A program that intercepts errors and reports on them.

VxD A Windows virtual device driver.

Circular logging A log file option that deletes old information as the log file reaches its capacity, thereby preventing the log from becoming filled.

3.2 Recognize common problems and determine how to resolve them.

- Eliciting problem symptoms from customers
- Having customer reproduce error as part of the diagnostic process
- Identifying recent changes to the computer environment from the user

- **Troubleshooting Windows-specific printing problems**
- **Other common problems**
- **Viruses and virus types**

In domain 3.1, we looked at a number of possible problems with the Windows boot process and some of the files and tools for dealing with these problems. In domain 3.2, this examination continues and expands into other problems.

Critical Information

Many of the errors and repair issues covered by domain 3.2 will not cause a machine to be completely dysfunctional, but rather will affect a particular part of the system, often rendering that part useless. Being able to identify the most common problems and the parts of the system that generally are responsible is crucial for being an effective technician. Oh, and this information also helps a lot on the test!

In a computer system, there are at least four main parts to consider, any of which can potentially cause problems:

- There is a collection of hardware pieces that are integrated into a working system. As you know, the hardware can be quite complex, what with motherboards, hard drives, video cards, etc. This section does not deal with hardware failures, but you should always keep in mind that they are a possible source of trouble.

- There is an operating system that is dependent on the hardware. DOS and Windows operating systems have kernels, internal commands, and external commands that may interact with the hardware in various ways.

- There is an application or a software program that is supposed to do something. Programs such as Microsoft Word and Excel are now bundled with a great many features. If an application is misbehaving, the system will usually function fine as long as you don't use that application.

- There is a computer user, ready to take the computer system to its limits (and beyond). A technician often forgets that the user is a very complex and important part of the puzzle and can indeed be the problem itself.

Effective troubleshooting requires some experience just for the background required to analyze the problem at hand, but there are also some other logical steps that you must remember. Ask yourself the question, "Is there a problem?" Perhaps the issue is as simple as a customer expecting too much from the computer. Then ask yourself, "If there is a problem, is it just one problem?" Later, in the Necessary Procedures area, we'll give you a number of questions to ask when looking into PC problems.

Dealing with Customers

First off, let me open by noting that on the Beta test for the new A+ exam, I was given no questions that dealt with customer service. They still may add some, though, and since customer service and talking to users has three content points in the objectives, you should know this topic!

Talking to the user is an important first step in the troubleshooting process. Your first contact with a computer that has a problem will usually be through the customer, either directly or by way of a work order that contains the user's complaint. Often, the complaint will be something straightforward, such as "There's a disk stuck in the floppy drive." At other times, the problem will be complex and the customer will not have mentioned everything that has been going wrong.

Eliciting Problem Symptoms from Customers

The act of diagnosis starts with the art of customer relations. Go to the customer with an attitude of trust: Believe what the customer is saying. At the same time, go to the customer with an attitude of hidden skepticism, meaning *don't* believe that the customer has told you everything. This attitude of hidden skepticism is not the same as distrust, but just remember that what you hear isn't always the whole story, and customers may inadvertently forget to give some crucial detail.

For example, a customer may complain that his CD-ROM drive doesn't work. What he fails to mention is that it has never worked and that he installed it himself. On examining the machine, you realize that he had mounted it with screws that were too long and that these prevented the tray from ejecting properly.

Having Customer Reproduce Error as Part of the Diagnostic Process

The most important part of this step is to have the customer show you what the problem is. The best method I've seen of doing this is to ask them, "Show me what 'not working' looks like." That way, you see the conditions and methods under which the problem occurs. The problem may be a simple matter of an improper method. The user may be doing an operation incorrectly or doing the process in the wrong order. During this step, you have the opportunity to observe how the problem occurs, so pay attention.

Identifying Recent Changes to the Computer Environment from the User

The user can give you vital information. The most important question is "What changed?" Problems don't usually come out of nowhere. Was a new piece of hardware or software added? Did the user drop some equipment? Was there a power outage or a storm? These are the types of questions that you can ask a user in trying to find out what is different.

If nothing changed, at least outwardly, then what was going on at the time of failure? Can the problem be reproduced? Can the problem be worked around? The point here is to ask as many questions as you need to in order to pinpoint the trouble.

Using the Information

Once the problem or problems have been clearly identified, your next step is to isolate possible causes. If the problem cannot be clearly identified, then further tests will be necessary. A common technique for hardware and software problems alike is to strip the system down to bare-bones basics. In a hardware situation, this could mean removing all interface cards except those absolutely required for the system to operate. In a software situation, this may mean booting up with the CONFIG.SYS and AUTOEXEC.BAT files disabled or disabling elements within Device Manager.

Generally, then, you can gradually rebuild the system toward the point where the trouble started. When you reintroduce a component and the problem reappears, then you know that component is the one causing the problem.

Let me make one last point in this brief introduction to troubleshooting: You should document your work. If the process of elimination or the process of questioning the user goes beyond two or three crucial elements, start writing them down. Nothing is more infuriating than knowing you did something to make the system work but not being able to remember what it was.

Troubleshooting Printing

Printers are one of the most important things to become proficient with, because printer problems are generally "mission-critical" for users. There are a number of things that can go wrong with printers, many of which have nothing to do with software or configuration.

Troubleshooting Windows-Specific Printing Problems

There are a number of different printer-related issues that could possibly cause a PC to require service. Some of the general problem areas include the following:

Printer hardware problems Sometimes you have an actual problem with physical printer hardware—something is broken, a paper jam occurs, etc. This is not something that will be covered in the A+ OS exam, as hardware issues are covered in the Core exam instead.

"Out of" errors   It is sad to say, but these are by far the most common printer problems. Paper, toner, or ink supplies are depleted, and the printer therefore does not produce as hoped. Again, this will not be covered in the A+ OS exam.

Problems with PC or cable hardware   It is also possible that the computer's printer port is malfunctioning or that the printer cable is either disconnected or damaged. In such a case, you will need to either replace or reattach the cable or check out the PC's printer port. Again, though, this is not information for the A+ OS test.

If none of these seems to be the problem, then you need to start looking for OS issues, and it is these issues that *are* covered during the A+ OS exam. Below are a number of issues that may come up.

Incorrect/Incompatible Driver for Print

The print driver is the crucial software for configuring—and therefore for troubleshooting—printer problems. Each printer has a particular set of features and implements them through its own specific driver. Because of this, in order to function properly, a printer must be matched with its proper driver. Incorrect drivers can either be designed for a completely different printer or can simply be outdated software.

If the driver that is installed for a printer is not even close, print jobs sent to the printer normally come out as nothing more than a garbled mess of odd characters. If the driver is close, but not exact, only certain elements—such as color or particular fonts—may be a problem. In either case, the solution is to obtain and install an updated driver, using the Details tab of the printer's Properties page, as shown in Figure 9.6.

FIGURE 9.6: Printer Properties Details showing the New Driver button

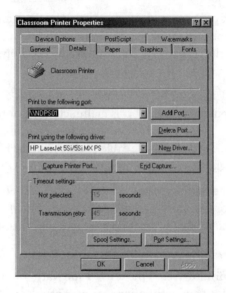

Another common source of printer driver errors is corruption of the driver. If a printer driver does not appear to be properly processing information, and you have verified that the driver is the proper version, you can delete the printer from the Printer Settings window and reinstall it.

A quick way to test the printer functionality is to use the Print Test Page option. This option is presented to you as the last step when setting up a new printer in Windows. Always select this option when you're setting up a new printer so you can test its functionality. To print a test page for a printer that's already set up, look for the option on the Properties menu for the particular printer.

After the test page is sent to the printer, the computer will ask if it printed correctly. For the first few times, you'll probably want to answer No and use the Troubleshooting Wizard that appears, but after you have troubleshot a few printer problems, you may prefer to answer Yes and bypass the Wizard, which is rather simplistic.

Print Spool Is Stalled

One of the most important options on this screen is the Spool Settings button. This button allows you to configure whether or not Windows will spool print jobs. If print jobs are spooled, every time you click Print in a program, the job is printed to a spool directory (usually a subdirectory of the C:\WINDOWS\SPOOL directory) by a program called SPOOL32.EXE. Then the job is sent to the printer in the background while you continue to work. If you don't want print jobs to be spooled (the default), click the Spool Settings button. From the screen shown in Figure 9.7, you can choose either Spool Print Jobs So Program Finishes Printing Faster or Print Directly To The Printer. Choose the appropriate option and click OK. Once you have made changes to a printer, click OK on the Properties page to save them.

FIGURE 9.7: Spool Settings

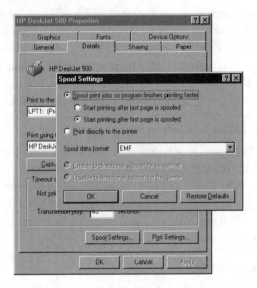

Incorrect Parameter

Each printer driver may have any of a number of additional settings, and depending on how these are configured, any number of problems may appear. For the A+ exam, though, remember that you are not expected to know how to set the particular properties for a particular printer. There are just too many of them! This is the sort of thing that experience will teach you, but that you won't be tested on.

Other Common Problems

This chapter has talked about startup problems, printer problems, and system errors. Now it is time for the "grab bag" of troubleshooting information. These are additional trouble areas that you need to know about for the test.

General Protection Faults

A General Protection Fault (GPF) is probably the most common and most frustrating error. A GPF happens in Windows when a program accesses memory that another program is using or when a program accesses a memory address that doesn't exist. Generally, GPFs are the result of sloppy programming. A simple reboot will usually clear the memory. If GPFs keep occurring, check to see which software is causing them. Then find out if the manufacturer of the software has a patch to prevent it from failing. If not, you may want to consider another software package.

Windows Protection Error

A Windows protection error is a condition that usually happens on either startup or shutdown. Protection errors occur because Windows 9x could not load or unload a virtual device driver properly. Thankfully, this error usually tells which VxD is experiencing the problem, so you can check to see if the specified VxD is missing or corrupt. If it is, you can replace it with a new copy.

Illegal Operation

Occasionally, a program will quit for apparently no reason and present you with a window that says, "This program has performed an illegal operation and will be shut down. If the problem persists, contact the program vendor." An illegal operation error usually means that a program was forced to quit because it did something Windows didn't like. It then displays this error window. The name of the program that has been shut down will appear at the top of the window. Use the Details button to view the details of the error. Details include which module experienced the problem, the memory location being accessed at the time, and the registers and flags of the processor at the time of the error.

Illegal operations can happen due to nothing more than a glitch and often do not reappear. Some illegal operations, however, are chronic, and in this case it is likely that some sort of hardware or software incompatibility (or conflict) is the problem. Also, this is the error that Windows NT/2000 reports when DOS applications try to access hardware directly, which is not allowed on those systems. In such a case, you cannot run these programs on NT/2000, and you'll need to find a Windows 9x machine or buy an NT/2000 version of the software.

Invalid Working Directory

Some Windows programs are extremely processing-intensive. These programs require an area on the hard disk to store their temporary files while they work. This area is commonly known as a *working directory*, and the location of it is usually specified during that program's installation and can be accessed by examining the properties of the app's shortcut icon, as shown in Figure 9.8. If that directory changes after installation, or if the working directory is deleted, Windows will report an error that says something such as "Invalid working directory." The solution is to either reinstall the program with the correct parameters for the working directory or create the directory the program is trying to point to. Some programs use a unique directory as their working directory, while others do not specify any working directory at all and instead just use the system default (normally TEMP). In Windows NT and 2000, you may find that permissions restrictions on the file system cause a user to not have access to the directory an application tries to write temporary information to. Since the permissions of the application are an extension of the permissions of the logged-on user, this can also produce this error.

FIGURE 9.8: A working directory

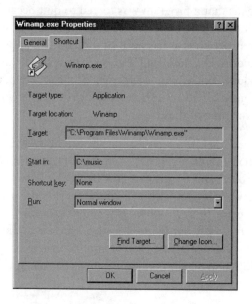

System Lock Up

It is obvious when a system lockup occurs. The system simply stops responding to commands and stops processing completely. System lockups can occur when a critical system file is corrupted or when an application issues an instruction that the OS interprets as a "STOP" error—a dangerous system event. Often lockups occur because two applications have attempted to access the same critical resource simultaneously. While system lockups were common in Windows 3.*x* and happened occasionally in Windows 9*x*, they are rare in Windows NT or 2000. The remedy for a system lockup is to simply reboot, but if the lockups are persistent, it may be that the machine has a serious hardware-related problem or needs to have its software reinstalled to repair corrupt files.

Option (Sound Card, Modem, or Input Device) Will Not Function

When you are using Windows, you are constantly interacting with some piece of hardware. Each piece of hardware has a Windows driver that must be loaded in order for Windows to be able to use it. In addition, the hardware has to be installed and functioning properly. If the device driver is not installed properly or the hardware is misconfigured, the device won't function properly. Common reasons for hardware to not work include:

Hardware is non-functional.   Replace the device.

Hardware is not properly connected to the computer.   Check connections or reseat the device in its slot or port.

Device is not detected by Plug and Play.   This actually can be a symptom of any of a number of problems. First, the connection port the device is using may be disabled. A printer on LPT1: won't be detected if LPT1: is disabled. Also, the device itself may not be Plug-and-Play-compliant. In such a case, you will have to install it by specifying all drivers and resource settings.

Resource conflicts   In newer machines, most devices are PCI, and the PCI architecture allows resource sharing between PCI devices using a "resource pool" idea. Older ISA devices do not have this happy option, and if two devices try to use the same interrupt or I/O address, one or possibly both of them will be unusable. This is probably the most common reason for problems with hardware in older machines.

Be ready for problems like this on the test, where you will be asked how to diagnose problems with Windows and hardware access. Problems installing or configuring new hardware are among the most common reasons for a machine to be sent in for service.

Application Will Not Start or Load

Once you have an application successfully installed, you may run across a problem getting the application to start properly. This problem can come from any number of sources, including an improper installation, software conflict, or system instability. If your application was installed incorrectly, the files required to properly run the program may not be present, and the program can't function without them. If a shared file that's used by other programs is installed, it could be a different version from what should be installed that causes conflicts with other programs. Finally, if one program fails, it can cause memory problems that can destabilize the system and cause other programs to crash. The solution to these problems is to reinstall the offending application, first making sure that all programs are closed.

TIP   One of the primary improvements of the 32-bit architecture is the ability to isolate applications from each other and from the OS. This makes it less likely that the failure of one application will affect the entire system.

Cannot Log On to Network (NIC Not Functioning)

If your computer is hooked to a network (and most computers today are), problems that prevent the PC from accessing the network are frequent. In most cases, the problem can be attributed to the following:

Malfunctioning network interface card   If you have checked everything, and you simply can't get the card to initialize, it may be bad. Replace it, or try it in another machine.

Improperly installed or configured network software   If you do not have the proper combination of driver/protocol/client, then you won't be able to access network resources. For a scenario in which the NIC appears to be not functioning, the problem is usually that the NIC driver is incorrect. It is also possible that the NIC driver has been configured improperly—perhaps it is set to 100Mbps and is on a 10Mbps network. The Advanced tab for the NIC displays any of these settings that are available, as shown in Figure 9.9.

Corrupt network software   As always, the files could simply be bad. Before trying too much else, simply reinstall the drivers for the NIC.

FIGURE   9.9: The Advanced Properties window for a NIC

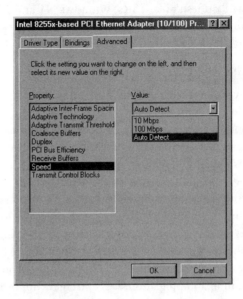

The biggest indicator in Windows that some component of the network software is nonfunctional is that you can't log on to the network or access any network service. You may not even see the Network Neighborhood on the Desktop. To fix this problem, you must first fix the underlying hardware problem (if one exists), then properly install or configure the network software.

TSR (Terminate and Stay Resident) Programs

In the days of DOS, there was no easy way of running a utility program in the background while you ran an application. Because necessity is the mother of invention, programmers came up with Terminate and Stay Resident (TSR) programs. These programs were loaded from the AUTOEXEC.BAT file and stayed resident in memory until called for by some key combination. Unfortunately, while that worked for DOS, Windows 95 had its own method for using background utilities. If any DOS TSR programs are in memory when Windows $9x$ is running, the TSRs can interfere with the proper operation of Windows programs. Before you install Windows $9x$, make sure that any DOS TSRs are disabled in the AUTOEXEC.BAT file. While Windows 9x doesn't like TSRs, Windows NT and 2000 will not run them at all. TSRs have been replaced in NT/2000 by services, which are far more stable and efficient.

Applications Won't Install

We've all experienced this frustration. You are trying to install the coolest new program and, for whatever reason, it just won't install properly. It may give you one of the above-mentioned errors or a cryptic installation error. If a software program won't install and it gives you any previously mentioned errors (e.g., GPF or Illegal Operation), use the solutions for those errors first. If the error that occurs during the install is unique to the application being installed, check the application manufacturer's Web site for an explanation or update. These errors generally occur when you're trying to install over an application that already exists or when you're trying to replace a file that already exists but that another application has in use. When installing an application, it is extremely important that you quit all running programs before installing so that the installer can replace any files it needs to. Also, some programs are written specifically for Windows 98 or Windows NT and will not run on any other OS. Make sure that the hardware and OS you are installing the application on are supported.

Network Connection

If the machine will not attach to the network, but you are certain that the NIC is functional and properly configured, it is very possible that the network resource you are attempting to find is having problems or that the network itself is down. In this case, you should contact the network administrator to see if there are problems. We'll cover other network-related configuration settings in domain 4.0.

Viruses and Virus Types

Most computer problems come in one of two sorts: accidents (hardware goes bad or software corrupts) or self-inflicted wounds (user deletes files or changes something). There is one other option, though. For reasons entirely their own, there are people with strong computer knowledge who use that knowledge to create programs called viruses that can damage your computer software—and potentially even your hardware.

What They Are

A computer *virus* is a program that replicates itself to other computers, usually causing the computers to behave abnormally. Generally speaking, a virus's main function is to reproduce. A virus attaches itself to files on a hard disk and modifies the files. When these files are accessed by a program, the virus can "infect" the program with its own code. The program may then, in turn, replicate the virus code to other files and other programs. In this manner, a virus may infect an entire computer.

There are two real categories of viruses, benign and malicious. The benign viruses don't do much besides replicate themselves and exist. They may cause the occasional problem, but it is usually an unintentional side effect. Malicious viruses, on the other hand, are designed to destroy things.

Sources (Floppy Disks, E-mails, Etc.)

Most viruses and other malicious problems are passed on through opening and using executable files, such as SETUP.EXE. Installing applications acquired off the Internet can also be dangerous to the health of a machine, and the growth of the Internet has made the problem of keeping viruses under wraps far more difficult that it previously was. Download and use only content direct from vendor sites or respected mirror sites, and try to get users to do the same. Also, one of the most common sources of viruses in recent years has been e-mail. Virus authors seem to especially enjoy writing viruses for Microsoft's Outlook software, often using Visual Basic scripts (VBS files) to do their dirty work.

When an infected file is transferred to another computer (via disk or modem download), the process begins on the other computer. Because of the ease and speed of virus transmission in the age of the Internet, viruses can run rampant if left unchecked. For this reason, anti-virus programs are crucial for every computer user's system.

They check files and programs for any program code that shouldn't be there and either eradicate it or prevent the virus from replicating. An anti-virus program is generally run in the background on a computer and examines all the file activity on that computer. When it detects a suspicious activity, it notifies the user of a potential problem and asks them what to do about it. Some anti-virus programs can also make intelligent decisions about what to do as well. The process of installing an anti-virus program on a computer is known as *inoculating* the computer against a virus.

How to Determine Their Presence

Wouldn't it be nice if Microsoft included an anti-virus program with their operating systems? They did, but only with MS-DOS. MS-DOS comes with anti-virus software that lets you detect viruses on your computer as well as clean any infected files. This software is called Microsoft Anti-Virus and has been included with DOS since version 6.0. The same program contains files to allow it to work with Windows.

Although Windows 9x and NT/2000 do not come with anti-virus software, these programs are available from a number of third-party vendors. The better ones can scan for viruses in both files and e-mail and can be updated regularly off the Internet or through product updates. It is recommended that you update any virus software regularly—generally monthly.

Know how to use install, use, and update anti-virus programs, as well as how to check for viruses on a system you suspect is infected. Remember, though, that because these are third-party programs, you will not need to know specifics, just general concepts.

WARNING Because its job is to prevent programs from modifying your system's configuration or files, anti-virus software can cause problems during application installations, and you will generally want to disable any anti-virus software while installing a new application—after scanning the install files for problems, of course!

Driver Signing

This is an option new to Windows 2000. In order to minimize the risks involved with adding third-party software to your Windows 2000 Professional machine, Microsoft has come up with a technique called *driver signing* (see Figure 9.10). Installing new hardware drivers onto the system is a situation in which both viruses and badly written software can threaten your system's health. To minimize the risks of this, you can choose to use only drivers that have been "signed." The signing process is meant to ensure that you are getting drivers that have been checked with Windows 2000 and that those drivers have not been modified maliciously.

FIGURE 9.10: Driver Signing Options

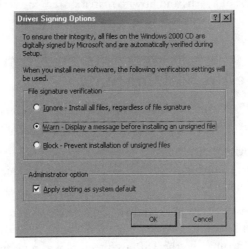

Exam Essentials

Know how to deal with customers.   The ability to talk to—and to listen to—customers is critical to your success as a technician. Learn how to ask questions tactfully. "Why the $%# would you have done something so stupid as that?" is not going to cut it.

Know where to find answers. Understand how Help, FAQs, and other support options can assist you in finding answers.

Know how the printing process works and how to troubleshoot problems. Printing is well represented on the exam, and you will want to be very familiar with how print spooling, print drivers, and printer ports work.

Know how to solve configuration and corruption errors within Windows. For the test, this really means just being familiar with the common error messages and knowing which class of error they represent. There is only so much troubleshooting you can do in a test question, so the problems and answers are generally very straightforward.

Understand viruses and virus protection. Know how to spot the signs of a virus and how to scan a system for viruses. Also know how to install virus software.

Key Terms and Concepts

GPF General Protection Fault. An error caused when a Windows program accesses memory that another program is using.

Working directory The place where an application stores files it creates during the course of its operation. This is the application's "cubicle."

TSR A Terminate and Stay Resident program. These are programs that load into memory but are not actually active unless needed. Unfortunately, the TSR architecture was a perfect place for viruses.

Virus A self-replicating program that "infects" files on a computer. These can be harmless, or they can be extremely destructive.

Innoculation The process of protecting a machine from viruses.

Chapter

10

Domain 4.0 Networks

COMPTIA A+ EXAM OBJECTIVES COVERED IN THIS CHAPTER:

▶ **4.1 Identify the networking capabilities of Windows including procedures for connecting to the network.** *(pages 477 – 502)*

- Protocols
- IPCONFIG.EXE
- WINIPCFG.EXE
- Sharing disk drives
- Sharing print and file services
- Network type and network card
- Installing and configuring browsers
- Configure OS for network connection

▶ **4.2 Identify concepts and capabilities relating to the Internet and basic procedures for setting up a system for Internet access.** *(pages 502 – 522)*

- ISP
- TCP/IP
- IPX/SPX
- NetBEUI
- E-mail
- PING.EXE
- HTML
- HTTP://
- FTP
- Domain names (Web sites)
- Dial up networking
- TRACERT.EXE

n preparing for a career as a computer technician, you may have already done a great deal of work putting together computers, troubleshooting hardware, and installing Windows and various software. If you are like most PC techs, the networking questions will probably be the part of the A+ test you are most concerned about. Many companies draw a distinct line between PC techs and network techs—and for good reason. Both jobs require a high level of knowledge, and it is best to specialize to a degree.

In the modern computing environment, though, it is simply not possible for a tech to ignore networks. In troubleshooting and repairing computers, there are two very broad categories on which your concern with networking should focus:

- Being able to troubleshoot a customer's connections to a LAN or dial-up connection

- Being able to effectively use your local network or the Internet to gain access to needed software and information

The first of these requires that you know how to install and configure networking components and how to set up any shared resources that a particular computer needs to share with the network. The second looks at how you can use that connection to access a shared drive or information on the Internet.

Over the course of this chapter, we will examine the most critical aspects of networking—or more specifically, of *Microsoft* networking, which is what the test covers. This information is actually relatively straightforward, and the A+ networking domain breaks it down into two simple parts: how to get a machine on the network (domain 4.1) and how to set up and use an Internet connection (domain 4.2).

4.1 Identify the networking capabilities of Windows including procedures for connecting to the network.

- **Protocols**
- **IPCONFIG.EXE**
- **WINIPCFG.EXE**
- **Sharing disk drives**
- **Sharing print and file services**
- **Network type and network card**
- **Installing and configuring browsers**
- **Configure OS for network connection**

Domain 4.1 is full of great test possibilities. These pretty much break down into two main questions: "How do you install networking?" and "How do you share out resources on the network?" The installation and use of browsers is an objective here also, but this topic will be covered in domain 4.2, along with other Internet concepts.

Critical Information

In this section, we'll cover all the objectives, but we'll shuffle them around a bit to deal with them in a better order. At the start of each section, we'll list the objectives dealt with in a particular section.

Network Components

The objectives covered in this area include the following:

- Protocols
- Network type and card
- Configuring the OS for a network connection

In order for a machine to communicate with another machine, the most basic criterion is that some sort of network-capable hardware be installed. This can be one of any of a number of things—modem, network interface card (NIC), infrared port, etc. The key point is that the OS itself can't do anything without help from the hardware.

Once you have a network connection device, that device needs to be configured for use by the operating system. This requires the introduction of three software elements—adapter, client, and protocol—and allows for an optional fourth—service—as shown in Figure 10.1. Let's take a brief look at each.

FIGURE 10.1: The Select Network Component Type window

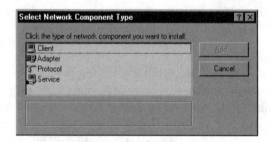

TIP These components can be installed or uninstalled by any user on Windows 9x but only by an administrator or power user on Windows NT/2000. Users without the proper permissions will also be unable to modify network settings or share resources on Windows NT/2000.

Adapter The *adapter* is technically the peripheral hardware that installs into your computer, but in this case, it refers to the software that defines how the computer talks to that hardware. If you do not have the proper adapter software installed, your PC will be unable to talk properly to the NIC and you will be unable to access the network until you change the adapter to one that is compatible with the hardware. It is often best to simply think of an adapter as a network driver, which is what it is. Windows 95 supports a long list of adapters, and Windows 98 supports even more, with additional support for more recent hardware. You can also download adapter drivers from most NIC vendors' Web sites.

Client The *client* is software that allows your machine to talk to servers on the network. Each server vendor uses a different way of designing its network access, though, so if a computer needs to get to both a Novell and a Microsoft network, the computer must have two pieces of client software installed, one for each type of server. Windows 95 supports three network client groups: Microsoft, Novell, and Banyan servers. Windows 98/NT/2000 supports only Microsoft and Novell networks out of the box.

Protocol Once the client service and the adapter are installed, you have cleared a path for communication from your machine to the network servers. The *protocol* is the computer language that you use to facilitate communication between the machines. If you want to talk to someone, you have to speak a common language. Computers are no different. Among the languages available to Windows 98 are NetBEUI, NWLink, and TCP/IP.

Service A *service* is an optional component that gives a bit back to the network that gives it so much. Services add functionality to the network by providing resources or doing tasks for other computers. In Windows 98, services include file and printer sharing for Microsoft or Novell networks.

Installing a Network Interface Card

The first step in readying a machine for use on the network is the installation and configuration of the adapter. In most corporate machines, this takes the form of a network interface card (NIC). There are dozens of companies that produce NICs, and each of these companies has numerous models. Therefore, testing you on the particulars of any one card or company would be extremely unfair, and so any questions on NIC installation and configuration must be relatively general.

Installing a network card is a fairly simple task. The NIC is just an expansion card installed the same way as a video card or a sound card. Below are some things to watch for when installing a NIC that could come up on the test.

- Some older NICs have jumpers to set their IRQ and DMA settings. If this is the case, you will have to know these. Other cards do not have jumpers but are configurable only by using special software available from the manufacturer. In either of these cases, it is very possible that a resource conflict will occur if you are not careful to check and properly modify the resource values.

- If the card is Plug and Play, it should be detected and automatically installed. If it is too new (such as a 1999 model card on a Windows 95 Rev A machine) or if it comes from an unsupported manufacturer, you may have to supply the drivers during installation.

- Each NIC is unique in the way that it communicates with Windows. Even cards from the same company generally cannot share drivers!

- Each OS is unique in the way it communicates with the NIC. Although Windows 95 and 98 can usually share drivers, Windows 2000 cannot use a Windows 98 driver and neither can Windows NT. Because of this, when installing a card you have to make sure that you have the correct driver for a particular card on a particular OS.

Once you have gotten the card into the machine and have turned it back on, one of two things will happen. The first possibility is that the OS will automatically see the new hardware and install it (perhaps asking you for a driver if one is not available in the standard driver database). If this does not happen, then the card was not detected at all. At that point, you will need to run the Add New Hardware Wizard by double-clicking Add New Hardware in Control Panel. This forces the system to go out and do a more intensive search, in an effort to discover any new non-Plug-and-Play components.

If neither of these methods turns up the new NIC, then you have a problem. Generally in this case, there is a hardware conflict that is preventing the board from being seen. Check the settings on the NIC and on the other hardware on the machine, and modify the settings as needed. Go to Device Manager to see whether it is listed, and if so, what the NIC's status is. If Windows is reporting a problem, check to see what information it can give you.

Once you have installed the NIC, you must also hook the card up to the network using a cable supplied by your network administrator. You will need to attach this "patch cable" to the connector on the NIC and to a port in the wall, thus connecting your PC to the rest of the network.

Choosing a Network Type and Client

Once you have the card installed, the next thing that the test may ask about is how to configure it for use on the network. There are two possible meanings of the term "network type" that could concern you. One of these deals with network structure and the other with network technologies.

Network type (structure)   There are two types of networks you need to be aware of: peer-to-peer and server-based. Peer-to-peer networks use the built-in sharing abilities of Windows 9x, NT Workstation, or 2000 Professional to establish a small, decentralized network. Server-based networks center on a server or group of servers running special software such as Novell's NetWare or Microsoft's Windows 2000 Server. These OSes are more expensive, but they provide features unavailable in a peer-to-peer environment. As far as setting up the network connection, both are similar, but you will need to configure the client software differently depending on which option you will be using.

Network type (technologies)   A number of different companies sell networking systems. Among these are Microsoft and Novell, who are the most important network operating system (NOS) vendors for PC networks. If you are using a server-based network, the servers generally handle all security and authentication for the machines on the network. For the test, you will find that only Novell and Microsoft networks will be considered. Support for both is built into all post-95 Microsoft OSes.

The network type (technologies version) that you choose will determine which client software you will need to install. The primary clients included with Windows are:

- Client for Microsoft Networks (9x, NT, and 2000)

- Client for NetWare Networks (9x, NT) or Client Service for NetWare (2000)

Windows 95 included support for Banyan Vines as well, and other server software can be used through additional clients. Only the two above should concern you for now. The choice is actually pretty straightforward. To attach to a NetWare server, you need the NetWare client. To attach to a Microsoft-based resource (on 9x, NT, or 2000), you need the Microsoft client. To find out which to install, simply ask the administrator of the network.

TIP   The Client for Microsoft Networks installs by default when you first install an adapter.

Once you have installed a client, a login screen for that network type appears each time you start the machine. This then allows you to enter a network username and password that will give you access to resources on that type of server.

Choosing a Protocol

Protocols are the languages of networks. In order for two people to communicate, they must speak the same language, and the same is true with computers. There are three protocols you should be familiar with: NWLink, NetBEUI, and TCP/IP.

If you look at the objectives, you will see that they are a bit off once again, as "Protocols" is listed for domain 4.1, but "TCP/IP," "IPX/SPX," and "NetBEUI" are listed under domain 4.2. As 4.2 is ostensibly about Internet concepts, and IPX and NetBEUI are largely out of place there anyhow, I have moved the discussion of them up to this domain.

NWLINK

Developed by IEEE committees 802.2 and 802.3, the IPX/SPX protocol was adopted by Novell as the primary protocol for their NetWare server family. In order to connect Microsoft machines to older NetWare servers, the IPX/SPX protocol—or its Microsoft equivalent, NWLink—had to be used by the client. Now that NetWare is also going to a TCP/IP-based architecture, NWLink is quickly being made obsolete, but it is still installed by default whenever the Client for NetWare Networks or Client Service for NetWare is installed. If the NetWare server uses IP only, you will need to add TCP/IP and remove the unneeded NWLink. If, on the other hand, the network runs on NWLink, setup is very easy. Simply install the protocol through the Network properties, and then set the network number to whatever value the network administrator specifies.

TIP About the only configuration problems possible with NWLink are an incorrect network number or the wrong frame type. The network number is a way of grouping machines logically on a network. Machines with different network numbers cannot see one another. The frame type is best thought of as a protocol dialect for NWLink. For machines running NWLink to communicate, they must both be using the same frame type.

NETBEUI

The NetBEUI protocol is insufficient on so many levels that discussing its faults is too big a job for this chapter. It is an extremely fast protocol for allowing a few computers on a single network to communicate, but due to the fact that it is not routable, it just doesn't scale very well, which doomed it as networks grew and started to interconnect.

The death knell of NetBEUI wasn't a problem because TCP/IP and other protocols were ready to take over. The one thing that has continued to cause confusion and trouble, though, is that NetBEUI was tied to another Microsoft protocol called NetBIOS, which has been far more difficult to replace.

NetBEUI and NetBIOS are obviously similar-looking terms, and unfortunately, there has been a certain amount of confusion surrounding them. Briefly, *NetBEUI* is a transport protocol. It is responsible for how data is transmitted between two computers. It is not routable and is rarely used in modern computing. *NetBIOS* is a name-resolution system. It allows a computer to search for another computer on the network by its Microsoft computer name. It must be operational on every Microsoft-based network up to Windows 2000, or Microsoft OS-based machines will not be able to communicate properly. The NetBIOS naming process can work with NWLink or TCP/IP, so NetBEUI is not required for it to function. You will hear more about how NetBIOS works in the next section.

TCP/IP

Developed in the late 1960s by the Department of Defense, and originally known as the DOD protocol, TCP/IP stands for Transmission Control Protocol/Internet Protocol. TCP and IP are actually just two of the many different protocols that make up the TCP/IP protocol suite. Commonly referred to simply as "IP," this protocol is the standard communication language for the Internet and for Microsoft's Windows 2000 Active Directory. Unix and Macintosh can use IP, as can NetWare and all Windows OSes. In most environments, this is the only protocol you will need.

There are two ways to manage TCP/IP. The manual way involves going to each machine and setting upward of 10 separate values for TCP/IP. This would also be known as the "hard way" of configuring IP. Another possibility is the use of the Dynamic Host Configuration Protocol (DHCP). If your network is using DHCP, all you have to do is install IP and reboot. A special server called a *DHCP server* will then provide your machine with all the values it needs when it starts up again. Machines are given leases to the IP addresses that the server manages and must periodically renew these leases. Manually setting a TCP/IP configuration will be covered in domain 4.2.

If you are wondering what the IP settings for a machine are, there are a number of utilities you can use to find out. The primary options, though, are listed in Table 10.1.

TABLE 10.1: TCP/IP Utilities

Protocol	Function
WINIPCFG	A graphical utility on Windows 9x that allows you to get information about your IP configuration. It also allows you to release a DHCP lease and request a new one.
IPCONFIG	Does the same thing as WINIPCFG but for Windows NT and 2000. IPCONFIG is also different in that it is a command-line utility.
PING	The ping command allows you to test connectivity with another host by just typing **ping** and the name or IP address of the machine you are trying to communicate with—for instance, **ping www.sybex.com** or **ping 192.168.1.250**.
TRACERT	This trace route utility allows you to watch the path that information takes getting from your machine to another one.

Using these utilities is pretty straightforward. You will want to work with each of these—and know what their options are—before you take the test. Remember that both WINIPCFG, shown in Figure 10.2, and IPCONFIG are essentially "read-only" utilities. Their only configuration option is to allow you to release or renew DHCP leases (if you are using DHCP). PING and TRACERT are troubleshooting tools. To modify your network or TCP/IP settings on Windows 9x or NT/2000, you have to use the Network Properties page.

FIGURE 10.2: The Windows IP Configuration Utility

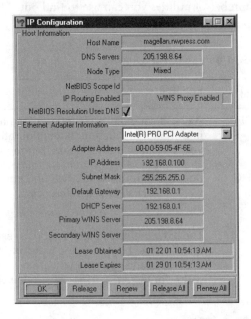

Configuring an OS for Network Connection

Once you have installed and configured the network card and know what type of network you will be connecting to, the rest of the process is relatively simple. Go to the Network Properties page and simply add in the components you need, while removing those that may be installed but are not necessary.

TIP Generally, if you find a client or protocol is installed but not needed, you should remove it, as having extra components installed on the machine can slow down network access time and produce additional network traffic.

Remember that in order for the network connection to be functional, all three pieces—the adapter, the protocol and the client—must be installed and configured properly. This process may include setting the workgroup or domain name for the machine, as well as creating or using a username/password set.

Bindings

One other networking term to remember is *binding*. Binding is the process of attaching a protocol to a network card (or any network component to another). When you install TCP/IP, it is automatically bound to the network card. If a protocol is not bound to a particular adapter, it cannot be used over any connections that use the adapter.

Primary Logon

A Windows 9*x* workstation can support multiple simultaneous network types. For example, a user can log on to both Novell and Microsoft networks, assuming they have both network clients installed and configured correctly. The Primary Network Logon drop-down list determines which network type you will log on to first. If you have not yet installed a network client, this list will give you only one option: Windows Logon.

You should know how to set up these logon options and understand how changes to them affect the machine.

File and Disk Sharing

This should come as no surprise, but the objectives are not actually written very well here. One of the options is "Sharing disk drives." You can't actually just share out an entire drive. Rather, you have to share out each partition separately. Technically, each of these is a drive, but they are logical drives, not disk drives.

While we are on this subject, the other thing to remember is that "file sharing" is also not actually possible. All sharing in Windows is done at the folder (directory) level, so if you want to share C:\PUBLIC\APLUS.txt, you can either share the entire C: drive or you can share the C:\PUBLIC folder. Either will work, but of course sharing just PUBLIC is better from a security standpoint.

It is possible to set up both Windows 9x and Windows 2000 Professional to share files and printers with other users on the network. This sort of networking, in which users share each other's resources, is an example of the peer-to-peer network type discussed earlier, where each computer acts as both a client and a server.

In order to share, the machine must already have a working client configuration. This is a must, because file and printer sharing is possible only if the proper adapter, client, and protocol are already set up. Once they are in place, you simply need to enable file and print sharing and then specify which resources you wish to share.

Simply enabling file and printer sharing does not make any folders or printers available on the network in Windows 9x. You must specifically share any directory or printer that you want to make available on the network. We will look at the issues with both of these steps.

Setting Up File Sharing

The first step in sharing out resources is setting up sharing. On Windows 9x, you do this by clicking the File And Print Sharing button on the Network Properties tab. In 9x, you can choose to enable either file or printer sharing (or both). In Windows 2000, sharing is enabled by default when networking is installed, and this is reflected by the presence of File And Printer Sharing For Microsoft Networks in the Local Area Connection Properties page.

TIP Besides enabling sharing, Windows 2000 also creates a number of default shares: printers, scheduled tasks, and a hidden administrative-only share of the root of each drive. Hidden drives in NT and 2000 are designated by using a $ at the end of the share name. Therefore, the admin share of the C: drive would be C$ and of D: would be D$.

Sharing Files

Any folder can be shared (including the root of the C: drive). When you share a folder, the person you share it with will be able to see not only the folder you've shared but also any folders inside that folder. Therefore, you should be certain that all subfolders under a share are intended to be shared as well. If they are not, move them out of the share path.

Once you have decided what to share, simply right-click the folder that will be the start of the share and choose Sharing from the menu that pops up. This option will bring up the Properties window of that folder with the Sharing tab in front. You can also access the Sharing tab (Figure 10.3) by right-clicking a folder, choosing Properties, and clicking the tab.

FIGURE 10.3: The Sharing tab of the Properties window

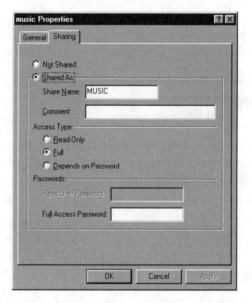

To enable the share, click the Shared As radio button. Two previously grayed-out fields will become visible. The first field is Share Name. The name you enter here will be used to access this folder. It should be something that accurately represents what you are sharing. The second field allows you to enter a description of the share as a comment that will help identify the contents of the share to users. The share name is required, and the comment is optional.

NOTE Remember that if the share name is over eight characters long, many older OSes, such as DOS, will not be able to access it properly. That and other file naming/file recognition issues between Windows long filenames and DOS could easily come up on a test question.

WINDOWS 9*x* SHARE SECURITY

Finally, you may specify the access rights and password(s) for the share. Two different security schemes are available: Share Level and User Level. Share Level security is the default selection.

There are three options for Windows 9*x* access rights when you're using the share-level security scheme. Click the radio button next to the option you want to use:

Read-Only With this option selected, anyone accessing the share will only be able to open and read the files inside the folder and any subfolders. You must specify a password that users can use to access the share in read-only mode.

Full In full access mode, everyone accessing the share has the ability to do anything to the files in the folder as well as any subfolders. This includes being able to delete those files. You must specify a password that the users can use to access this share.

Depends On Password This option is probably the best option of the three. With this option, users can use one password to access the share in read-only mode and a different password to access it in full access mode. You can give everyone the read-only password so that they can view the files and give the full access password only to users who need to modify the files. Note, though, that this option uses only one password for each security level and does not require a username.

WARNING   By default, a new share is a full-control share. This means that anyone on the network can come in and view, modify, or even delete the files in the share. Often this is just a bit too dangerous, and so you will probably want to use a read-only or a depends-on-password security setting.

The second security scheme option, User Level, requires that you have another machine available to provide a user/password database for the Windows 9*x* machine to draw from. As 9*x* does not have a user database, it cannot authenticate users on its own, but it can be configured to authenticate through a Windows NT Workstation, Windows 2000 Professional, or NT/2000/NetWare server.

If you choose User Level security, you will need to manually select the users or groups of users whom you want to have access to the folder and then also set the level of access that you want them to have.

WINDOWS 2000 SECURITY

In Windows 2000, sharing is enabled in exactly the same way as in Windows 9*x*, and shares can be created in much the same way (right-click the folder that will be the start of the share and choose Sharing from the menu that pops up). After that, however, the differences start to become important, and if CompTIA decides to test you on Windows NT/2000 security, they can make things tough. Since security issues are not actually discussed in the objectives, we won't spend much time on them, but you should realize that Windows 2000 can use the NTFS security scheme to allow extremely powerful and flexible file-level security. Depending on the file system you are using, your sharing options include the following:

Share Level   NT/2000 can also use "Share Level" security, but its definition of "Share Level," oddly, is actually far closer to Windows 9*x*'s User Level security. With Share Level security, Windows NT/2000 sets user/password security at the level of the shared folder, exactly as Windows 9*x* does. All files and folders under the share will have the same access permissions through the share. Drives formatted with FAT or FAT32 can use only this level.

File Level If the NT/2000 drive is formatted with NTFS, you have the option of setting files directly on the folder or specific files, rather than simply setting them on the share. This may seem like a small distinction, but it is actually a tremendous difference. Using File Level security, you can ensure that files always have the same level of access for a particular user, regardless of which share they come through. File Level security even protects files if the user logs on to the machine itself, something Share Level protection cannot do.

NOTE There is no equivalent of Windows 9*x*'s Share Level security in Windows NT/2000.

Again, CompTIA has not given any indication that NTFS security will be featured on the test, but it technically does fall under the sharing objective, so they may add a question or two. Just to be safe, a bit of outside study on NTFS wouldn't be a bad idea. A quick overview is available by searching Windows 2000 Help for NTFS and then scanning the articles provided.

Accessing a Shared Resource

You will also need to know how to get to files shared on other machines. To access shared folders and printers, we'll turn to the Network Neighborhood icon. When you double-click this icon, you can browse the network for resources. The icons that look like computers are just that, computers on the network. Note that there isn't a different icon for a Novell server, an NT server, or a Windows 9*x* machine sharing out part of its hard drive. They all look the same.

You can double-click any computer to see the resources that are hosted by that computer. Once you have found the share you require, using a shared folder is just like using any other folder on your computer, with one or two exceptions: First, the folder exists on the network, so you have to be connected to the network to use it. Also, for some programs to work properly, you must map a local drive letter to the network folder.

UNC PATHS AND DRIVE MAPPING

This brings up a distinction you should be familiar with. Windows (and other systems) use a standardized method to reference resources on the network called the *Universal Naming Convention (UNC)*. A UNC path is used to provide an easy and exact reference format. UNC paths come in the form of \\machinename\share\path\, so a directory called JAN2000 underneath a share called REPORTS on a machine called MYPC would be expressed as \\MYPC\REPORTS\JAN2000. Typing this in at a Run prompt will take you directly to that directory (if you have permission to access it).

Although using UNC paths works well in most cases, there is another option for using network shares—drive mapping. Mapping a drive involves associating a UNC path to an alphabetical shortcut. This makes it simpler and faster to access a resource regularly. For instance, mapping \\MYSERVER\REPORTS to R:, a user can then access the JAN2000 directory by simply typing **R:\JAN2000**, rather than having to use the entire path. Also, mapped drives are listed in the Explorer, meaning the user does not have to remember the path to access them. One important distinction here is that the drive letter *cannot* be mapped directly to the \\MYSERVER\REPORTS\JAN2000 directory. Drive mappings go only to the share level, and any further levels must be appended onto the drive letter. To map a drive, you reach the share by browsing to it, and then right-click the share to get to the Map Network Drive option. You must then pick a drive letter (one that is not being used) and click OK to map the drive.

Drive mappings are often done through login (or logon) scripts if the machine is on a network, using the command-line NET utility. These allow the network administrator to set up network resources for users, making them even more convenient to use. To map a drive, you simply need to type **NET USE R: \\MYSERVER\REPORTS**. As mentioned earlier, some programs will work only if they are able to access files using a drive letter. Older DOS programs, for instance, are notorious for this. Most newer programs can use either option without problems.

Now that you can see all the resources the computer is hosting, you can map a drive letter to a resource by right-clicking the folder (REPORTS in this case) and choosing Map Network Drive. This will cause the screen shown in Figure 10.4 to appear. Remember that most Windows applications can use UNC paths and don't need drive mappings, but even some newer applications still require a drive letter.

FIGURE 10.4: The Map Network Drive dialog box

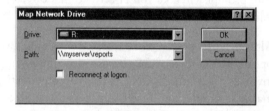

New Sharing Options in Windows 2000

Windows 2000 is very similar to Windows 9*x* when it comes to accessing network resources, but there are just a few modifications:

- Network Neighborhood is renamed My Network Places.

- To search for computers by name, you no longer go to the Find menu (now renamed Search, anyhow). Instead, the Search For Computers and Search For Files Or Folders options have been moved to My Network Places.

Sharing Print Services

Sharing printers is similar to sharing folders. First, you must have the printer correctly set up to print on the machine that will be the print server. Second, print sharing must be enabled in My Network Places.

Once you've done this, right-click a printer in the PRINTERS folder and click Sharing. The Printer Properties page will appear with the Sharing tab selected to allow you to share the printer.

To share the printer, simply click Shared As and specify a name for the share. The name will default to a truncated version of the printer name you gave it when you installed it. The name you give this share (called the *share name*) should be something that everyone will recognize when they see it on the network and that accurately describes the printer. Good names are "Classroom printer" or "3rd floor conference room printer." Note that you can use long names and spaces, as long as DOS or older 16-bit Windows applications do not need the printer.

WARNING   If older apps will be printing, you need to use a share name of eight or fewer characters, with no spaces.

In addition to specifying the name of the printer share, you can also enter a comment that describes the printer accurately. To finish sharing the printer, click OK. Windows will prompt you for the password again, just to verify that you know what it is and that you didn't misspell it. Retype the password in the box that appears and click OK, and the share will be active. The PRINTERS folder now has a hand under it, indicating that it is shared.

Securing a Shared Printer

Finally, you want to know a bit about how to secure a printer so that only authorized users can print to—or modify—the printer. There are three permissions available for printers:

Print   This allows users to submit documents and to manage their own documents. This includes the ability to cancel or pause their print jobs. Users with Print permission cannot modify other people's documents.

Manage Documents   This gives a user rights to print and to manage both their own print jobs and other people's. This is, essentially, a "middle-management" print permission.

Manage Printers   The highest print permission. This gives the user rights to print and to manage all documents, but it also allows them to change the printer's configuration, driver, and other properties.

Connecting to a Shared Printer

Accessing shared printers is very similar to accessing shared resources; in both cases, you are accessing a resource that has been shared on a machine out on the network. In addition, in both cases, you are pointing a local resource (in this case, a printer icon) to a network resource (a shared printer).

POINT AND PRINT

Point and Print allows you to locate a printer in Network Neighborhood and click and drag it to the PRINTERS folder. This then starts the Add Printer Wizard, which will set up the printer icon and set up the right drivers on your machine.

You should be familiar with this and other shortcuts available to you in Windows, not so much because they will be the focus of questions, but because they are a part of the context, for example, "You are installing a printer through Point and Print, and the driver cannot be found..." type of things.

The key to Point and Print is that in order for it to work properly, you have to be able to download the driver to your machine or have it available. Remember that each printer uses its own driver and that each OS needs its own version of the driver. If a printer is installed on a Windows NT Server machine, and a Windows 98 client needs to print to it, you need to have the Windows 98 drivers.

TIP   Windows NT and 2000 both allow administrators to load additional drivers for a printer, so a 2000 print server can store NT and Windows 98 drivers as well as its own 2000 drivers. When a client attaches to the printer, the appropriate driver is then offered to them.

Other than having to find the share out on the network, rather than searching for the printer on the local printer port (LPT), there is little difference between installing a printer and connecting to a shared printer.

Other Printing Options

Besides the above information, you should be aware of these other printing options, which may come up as part of a printing question:

Pooling   Printer pooling is used to allow a single print queue and print driver to be used for a number of printers. This is an excellent way to allow heavily used print queues to provide better printing speed by adding hardware.

Availability   If you have a printer that you don't want to be used at particular times, you can create an availability schedule. During off times, any jobs sent to the printer will simply wait until the printer is available again.

Priority   Changing the priority of a document allows it to move up in a queue and print before other documents, even if those others were submitted first.

Windows 2000 Printing Enhancement

Probably one of the nicest enhancements of the Windows 2000 sharing system is the addition of Internet printing capability. Windows 2000 machines can allow access to shared printers using the format `http://`*machinename/printers* to reach a list of printers on a machine. Once there, printers can be installed directly through Windows Explorer and used through the Printers icon as usual.

Oddly, it doesn't seem that many of the Windows 2000 features are being considered for use on the test. Because of this, the Windows 2000 Internet printing functionality may not be there. Still, it certainly could (should?) be.

Necessary Procedures

As part of your review, you should work on creating and using network resources. Below is an example of how to enable sharing on 9x, as well as a walkthrough on using a network-shared printer. These are by no means the only practice you should do, but they are a good start!

Enabling File and Printer Sharing on Windows 9x

To add file and printer sharing services, perform the following steps:

1. Open the Network program and click the File And Print Sharing button. You will see a screen that will allow you to select which services you want to share.

2. Click the box next to the top option (I Want To Be Able To Give Others Access To My Files) if you want to share files on your machine with someone else on the network. If you want others to be able to print to a printer hooked to your machine, click the box next to the bottom option, I Want To Be Able To Allow Others To Print To My Printer(s). A check mark will appear in the box next to an option when it is enabled. To disable an option, simply click the box again and the check mark will disappear.

3. Once you have enabled file and printer sharing, the service called File And Printer Sharing For Microsoft Networks will appear in the list of installed network components. In addition to specifying what you are going to share, you must specify how security is going to be handled. There are two options: Share-Level Access Control and User-Level Access Control. With share-level control, you supply a username, password, and security settings for each resource that you share. With user-level control, there is a central database of users (usually administrated by the network administrator) that Windows 9x can use to specify security settings for each shared resource. Most of the time, share-level access control is fine. There are only a few cases where user-level control is needed (such as in a network where the administrator has said that

you will do it this way). To specify these settings, choose the Access Control tab in the Network window (Figure 10.5) and choose the appropriate option.

4. Click OK to save all of these new settings.

5. Windows 9*x* will copy some files and ask you to reboot (big surprise, huh?). Reboot your computer to start sharing files and printers.

FIGURE 10.5: Specifying the access control method

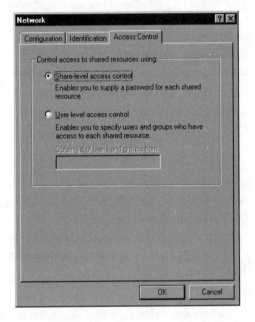

Using a Shared Printer

To use a shared printer, perform the following steps:

1. Browse to the computer that hosts the printer you want to set up, and double-click the computer name so you can see the printer you want to install.

2. Open up the PRINTERS folder under Start ➤ Settings ➤ Printers. Arrange these windows so you can see both at the same time.

3. To start the Add Printer Wizard, drag the printer you want to set up from the list of resources the computer is hosting to the Printers window. As soon as you release the mouse button, the wizard will start.

4. The wizard will ask you a series of questions that will help you to configure the printer. If you are using Windows 9x, the wizard will ask, "Do you print from MS-DOS–based programs?" The reasoning behind this question is similar to the reason we map drive letters: Most older DOS programs (and to a lesser extent, Windows programs) don't understand the UNC path syntax for access to a shared resource. Instead, they understand a name for a local hardware resource (such as LPT1: for the first local parallel port). So, you must point out a local printer port name to the network in a process known as *capturing*. If you need to capture a printer port, answer "Yes" to this question; otherwise, leave it set to the default (No). For our example, click Yes and then click Next to move to the next step of the wizard.

5. If you chose Yes in the preceding step, the next step is to capture the printer port. This screen allows you to capture a printer port so that DOS programs can print to the network printer. Click the Capture Printer Port button to bring up the screen shown in Figure 10.6, which allows you to choose which local port you want to capture. Select a port (generally LPT:1).

6. The next step is to give the printer instance a name. You should give a network printer a name that reflects what kind of printer it is and which machine is hosting it. In this example, the printer is labeled HP LaserJet III (the default name of the driver), but we could have named it Laser on Bob's PC. Enter the name for the printer in the screen that the wizard presents. You also have the choice as to whether or not you want the printer to be the default printer that gets used by all Windows applications.

7. When you have finished the wizard, the new printer will be available in your Printers window.

FIGURE 10.6: Choosing which local port to capture

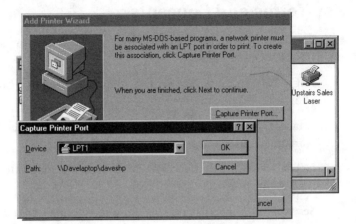

Exam Essentials

Know how to install and configure network components.   This includes Windows 9*x* and 2000, as well as Windows NT, which appears to be prominent on the test, if not in the objectives. Also, know what the available components for each OS are and how they work together.

Understand how to share resources on Windows 9*x* and NT/2000. You should be familiar with how the Share Level and User Lever security schemes work on 9*x* and how Share and File permissions interact on Windows NT/2000.

Be able to access network resources using a Windows client.   Be able to get to network resources using Network Neighborhood (My Network Places in 2000), the Search/Find function, or the NET command.

Know how to create, share, set permissions on, and connect to printers.   This is absolutely critical stuff. Work on it!

Key Terms and Concepts

Protocol   A computer language. Examples of protocols are NetBEUI, IPX/SPX, and TCP/IP.

NIC   Network interface card. A computer peripheral card that allows the PC to communicate with a network.

Adapter   A term used to describe both the NIC itself and the software that is used to communicate with it.

Client   Software that allows a machine to communicate with a particular type of network.

Service   Software that allows a PC to receive and respond to requests from the network.

IPCONFIG and WINIPCFG   Utilities used to display Windows TCP/IP configuration information.

Bindings   The logical connections that allow network components to work with each other.

Sharing   The process of making a resource available for use by other PCs through a network.

4.2 Identify concepts and capabilities relating to the Internet and basic procedures for setting up a system for Internet access.

- ISP
- TCP/IP
- IPX/SPX
- NetBEUI
- E-mail

- **PING.EXE**
- **HTML**
- **HTTP://**
- **FTP**
- **Domain names (Web sites)**
- **Dial-up networking**
- **TRACERT.EXE**

While many of the other content areas branch out widely in their coverage, domain 4.2 is extremely focused. This is, to be quite frank, an Internet-only zone. This does make the presence of NetBEUI and IPX/SPX in the content list extremely suspect, though. While it is technically possible to tunnel these protocols over TCP/IP through a VPN connection, I highly doubt that this is something you need to worry about for the test. In fact, forget I even mentioned it. Both of these are protocols, and as such they belong to and were covered in domain 4.1 under the Protocols heading. We won't go over them again here. TCP/IP was also touched on in 4.1, but it is far more complex than the other protocols and will be reviewed in depth here as it is *the* protocol of the Internet. The installation and use of browsers will also be here, rather than in 4.1, because without covering HTML and HTTP, browsers don't make much sense.

Critical Information

In this section we will look at the following concepts:

- Internet concepts and terminology

- Configuring TCP/IP for Internet connectivity

- Installing and using Internet applications

Internet Concepts and Terminology

There are some common terms and concepts every technician must understand about the Internet. First of all, the Internet is really just a bunch of private networks connected together using public telephone lines. These private networks are the access points to the Internet and are run by companies called Internet Service Providers (ISPs). They will sell you a connection to the Internet for a monthly service charge (kind of like your cable bill or phone bill). Your computer talks to the ISP using public phone lines, or even using new technologies such as cable or wireless.

There probably won't be any "What is an ISP?" questions on the test, as most of the exam centers on practical knowledge rather than vocabulary. Even so, you should be familiar with the following terms.

Browsers

A *browser* is software that will allow you to view Web pages from the Internet. The two browsers with the largest market share are Netscape Navigator and Microsoft Internet Explorer (also known as IE), shown in Figure 10.7. Both work equally well for browsing the Internet. Microsoft includes its browser, IE, with both Windows 98 and Windows 2000, whereas Netscape Navigator, which is free, must be downloaded separately.

Because Internet Explorer is installed by default (and is, according to Microsoft, "integral" to the OS), you don't really need to worry about installing/uninstalling it. However, if you are looking for a newer version of IE, you can go to Microsoft's Web site, `www.microsoft.com/windows/ie`. Netscape Navigator, though, is not installed by default, so to obtain—or upgrade—it, you should go to `www.netscape.com`. Once you are there, select the version you want and specify what type of machine you will be using it on. You can then download and install the software, just like any other application.

FIGURE 10.7: The Internet Explorer browser

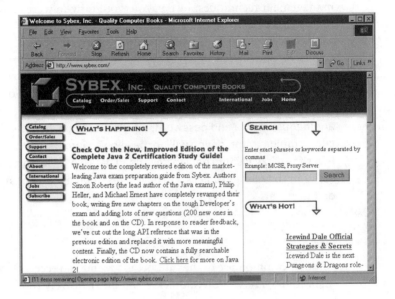

FTP

The File Transfer Protocol (FTP) is available to you either through the command-line FTP client or through your browser. To access the Microsoft FTP site through the command prompt, open a prompt and type **FTP ftp.microsoft.com**. The site will respond with a request for your e-mail address, and you will then be given access. You can use standard DOS navigation commands to move between directories, and you can retrieve or send files using the GET *<filename>* or PUT *<filename>* commands. When you are finished with your session, simply type **QUIT**.

Internet Explorer also supports FTP. To go to Microsoft's Web site, you can simply type in **http://www.microsoft.com,** and you will be taken to a Web page. If you change the first part of the name to **ftp://,** though, the system knows to look for an FTP resource instead. Typing **ftp://ftp.microsoft.com** will also take you to the Microsoft Web site, and you can then use all of the standard Explorer GUI file-management techniques, just as you would if you were connecting to any other network drive.

NOTE Because Microsoft's FTP site is a public site, it allows you to use a special anonymous account that provides access. If you go to a site where that account has been disabled, you will need to provide another username and password, which should be provided by the site's administrator, or you will not be allowed into the site. Also, most FTP sites allow visitors only to download data, so PUT commands generally will be rejected unless you have a real (non-anonymous) account on the server.

E-mail

Another common use of the Internet is to send and receive electronic mail. E-mail allows you to quickly and inexpensively transfer messages to other people. To send and receive e-mail, you need to have only two things: an e-mail account and an e-mail client. A company can provide the account, or it can be associated with your ISP account. Either way, you will have an address that looks like *username@domain.com*.

The last part of this address (after the @) identifies the domain name of the company or ISP that provides you with your e-mail account. The part before the @ is your username. A username must be unique on each domain. Two Bill the Bard users on a single network, for instance, might be billthebard@domain.com and billthebard1@domain.com.

As with other TCP/IP services, e-mail needs to be configured. Nothing in TCP/IP networking ever just works, it seems. Still, Windows provides a service called *Messaging Application Programming Interface* (*MAPI*) to make configuring e-mail easier, and overall, configuring e-mail is relatively straightforward.

Your MAPI settings can be defined in Control Panel's Mail program. Figure 10.8 shows just a few of the many Internet e-mail settings you can define. Among these are the *Post Office Protocol v 3 (POP3)* and *Simple Mail Transport Protocol (SMTP)* server settings, which you will need to be given by an administrator. A POP3 server is a machine on the Internet that accepts and stores Internet e-mail and allows you to retrieve that mail when you are online. An SMTP server is a server that accepts mail you want to send and forwards it to the proper user. In order to send and receive mail, you need both!

FIGURE 10.8: Mail settings windows

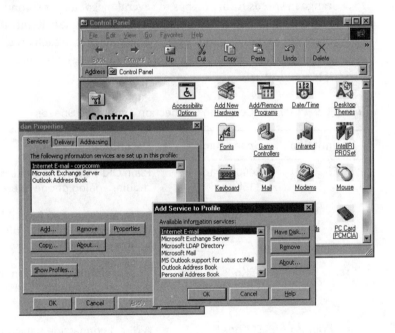

TIP Once you have the settings configured, you will need to simply install an e-mail client or use the built-in client included with Windows 98 and 2000. That client is called Outlook Express, and it's a good basic e-mail application.

For the test, the key with these technologies is to know how they work and be able to see when something is obviously configured badly. Also, dig into the options on the browser a bit (in the Tools ➤ Options menu) and know the commands available on the MS FTP program. There is little to worry about with e-mail, unless it is something with POP3/SMTP or with authentication. Because e-mail is private, e-mail servers require passwords on users' accounts, and many configuration problems are caused by bad usernames or passwords.

Types of Connections

There are several designations and types of public phone lines that range in speeds from 56Kbps to several megabits per second (Mbps) and that your computer might use to talk to an ISP. Remember that these same types of phone lines connect the ISPs to each other to form the Internet. Table 10.2 details a few of the more common connection types and speeds.

TABLE 10.2: Common Connection Types and Speeds

Designation	Speed Range	Description
POTS	2400bps to 115Kbps	Plain Old Telephone System. Your regular analog phone line.
ISDN	64Kbps to 1.554Mbps	Integrated Services Digital Network. Popular for home office Internet connections.
Frame Relay	56Kbps to 1.554Mbps	Cheap, simple connection where you share bandwidth with several other people.
56K Point-to-Point	56Kbps	A direct connection between two points at a guaranteed bandwidth.
T1	1.554Mbps	A direct connection between two points at a guaranteed bandwidth.
T3	44Mbps	A direct connection between two points at a guaranteed bandwidth. Extremely fast.

TABLE 10.2: Common Connection Types and Speeds *(continued)*

Designation	Speed Range	Description
DSL	256Kbps and up	Digital Subscriber Line. Shares existing phone wires with voice service.
ATM	155Mbps	Asynchronous Transfer Mode. Fiber optic ring network. Extremely fast.

The majority of home Internet connections use POTS (Plain Old Telephone System) and a modem. Most ISPs connect with each other using phone lines of T1 speeds (1.554Mbps) or faster. Certain ISPs that make up the backbone of the Internet use technologies like SONET that can get the data moving at gigabit speeds. Chances are you won't be asked many specific questions about these technologies, but they may come up as part of questions.

Connection Protocols

Whichever connection type is used, there must be a plan for how to transmit data across a network's lines. Network connection types also use different protocols to communicate, just as computers do, and because of this we also need to mention these connection protocols. For instance, TCP/IP Internet traffic runs over two different analog connection protocols:

- Serial Line Internet Protocol (SLIP)
- Point-to-Point Protocol (PPP)

Either can get you onto the Internet, but PPP is more commonly used because it is more easily configured; it's also more stable because it includes enhanced error-checking capabilities. Many ISPs now support only PPP for dial-up connections. Other common connection protocols include X.25 and ATM (the name is used for both the network and the connection protocol controlling traffic across it). An analog line is just a normal phone line, which transfers information (such as human voices) using waves rather than using binary electrical signals.

Configuring TCP/IP for Internet Connectivity

Unlike IPX and NetBEUI, both of which are pretty much "Plug-and-Play protocols," there are a number of configuration options with TCP/IP that need to be dealt with in order for machines to communicate properly using it. The following is a brief review of the information you will need to know for the test (and for setting up networked machines).

When reviewing TCP/IP for the test, remember that the protocol is managed by using two independent hierarchical structures. The first is the IP address hierarchy. Each computer that runs TCP/IP must have a unique IP address assigned to it, and that address must fall within a specific range. IP addresses are composed of a set of four numbers, each of which must be from 0 to 255. The IP address can either be automatically assigned to the machine or an administrator can specifically assign it.

Aside from its IP address, a machine will also have a *hostname*, which identifies it on the network. Hostnames are friendly names by which computers can be more easily located, and they are managed using a worldwide naming system called the *Domain Name System (DNS)*. DNS allows a user to type in http://www.yahoo.com and be taken directly to a computer hundreds or thousands of miles away. The same user could have used an IP address such as http://216.115.105.2, but most people find that the domain name (yahoo.com) is far easier to remember!

In setting up TCP/IP communication, there are two settings that are absolutely crucial. Without an IP address and a subnet mask, TCP/IP will not function. You specify these settings in the TCP/IP Properties window, shown in Figure 10.9. A number of other settings may also be needed, depending on what you are planning to access. The settings are listed in Table 10.3, with those settings that are generally needed for Internet access marked by an asterisk (*).

TABLE 10.3: TCP/IP Configuration Settings

Setting	Example	Purpose
IP address*	192.168.1.75	Uniquely identifies the computer on the network.
Subnet mask*	255.255.255.0	Used to determine whether other IP addresses are on the same network or on another network. Sadly, there is no easy explanation for a subnet mask. Suffice it to say that you need it, and it has to be right! The network administrator should give you the subnet mask setting (and all other necessary info).
Default gateway*	192.168.1.1	The address of the router your machine will use to access the outside world.
Host*	coyote	The name by which the machine is referred to in DNS.
Domain	sybex.com	The name of the organization you are in. Similar to a workgroup, but for TCP/IP.
DNS server*	192.168.1.250	The machine that resolves names for the network. This machine will answer a question such as "What IP address does coyote.sybex.com have?" with an answer of "192.168.1.75."
WINS server	192.168.1.250	Serves the same purpose as DNS, but deals with computer names, not hostnames. Answers questions such as "What IP address does coyote have?"

FIGURE 10.9: The TCP/IP Properties window

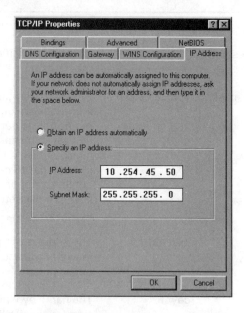

Computer Name Resolution

This topic isn't in the objectives, so you may not see it on the test, but it is incredibly important to understanding how machines communicate on Microsoft networks, so then again you just might. When Microsoft first started producing network-capable operating systems, such as DOS with networking, LAN Manager, and Windows NT 3.1, the Internet was nothing but a group of mainframe computers connecting selected military and university campuses. At that time, it seemed that the thing to do when you created network software was to also create your own proprietary protocol and assume that no one would ever connect to any network but yours. Novell helped develop IPX/SPX, Apple had AppleTalk, and Microsoft, sadly, came up with NetBEUI. While NetBEUI itself didn't last, the NetBIOS name resolution system that debuted with it did and is still in use on Microsoft networks everywhere.

Computer Names and Hostnames

The continuing presence of NetBIOS makes for some interesting confusion in that a Microsoft 9x machine with TCP/IP installed actually has two distinct names. Its NetBIOS computer name is set in the Identification tab of the Network program (Figure 10.10), whereas its hostname is set in the DNS Configuration tab of TCP/IP Properties (Figure 10.11). In the figures, both names are set to coyote, and usually the computer and hostname will be the same because they are set that way by default. If you are having trouble reaching a 9x or NT machine, though, you may want to check this setting.

FIGURE 10.10: The NetBIOS computer name

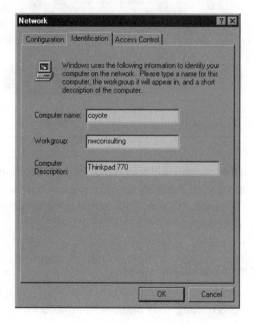

FIGURE 10.11: The TCP/IP hostname

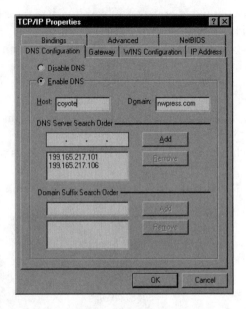

TIP In Windows 2000, Microsoft has finally started to make a break from this nonsense. Computer names and hostnames in 2000 must be the same, and NetBIOS name resolution has largely been replaced with DNS naming resolution (although it is still around for backward compatibility).

SO WHAT IS RESOLUTION?

In order for a computer to talk to another computer, it must be able to access it using an IP address. Computers speak in numbers, not letters! Because of this, the "friendly" names that we use to make computers easy to remember and find must be *resolved* to find out what IP address the machine is using. There are a number of methods of doing this, but WINS servers and DNS servers are the most common. WINS resolves NetBIOS computer names to IP addresses, and DNS does so for hostnames. More on this in a minute.

Another way of resolving names is to use either the LMHOSTS file (computer names) or the HOSTS file (hostnames). These are text files into which you can put entries that specifically tell your machine what the address of another machine is, as in the following line:

    192.168.1.250   NTSERVER

Although these files work fine, they require a lot of maintenance and are not used regularly in modern networking. Even so, they are *great* for tests, so be sure to review these files and how they are used!

Installing and Using Internet Utilities and Applications

The most important distinction when setting up or troubleshooting an Internet connection is to determine what type of connection is being used. The two basic options here are dial-up and network.

If you want to connect your Windows 95 machine to the Internet through the network, the process is pretty simple. Some connections, such as cable or DSL, do not use a modem and so are configured through the use of network cards and standard network clients. Configuring Internet access for DSL is very similar to configuring access on a company network. You simply install TCP/IP, configure it properly, and then follow the instructions in the next section, "Connecting to the Internet." In most corporate networks, this is how Internet access is configured, as there is a server on the network that acts as an Internet access point, and clients use the LAN to access the Web and e-mail.

TIP   DNS, subnet mask, and DHCP issues are common reasons for connectivity problems on LANs.

You will need information from the ISP when configuring these systems. If the machine uses dial-up to access the Internet, you will need to obtain certain configuration information from the ISP. Generally, they will give you a sheet with all the information you need to connect, or in some cases even a disk with a pre-configured connection and browser so all you have to do is install the software and you'll be ready to connect to the Internet. If you have to manage the connection yourself, the steps are as follows:

1. Install a modem in the machine, and configure it with the proper device drivers. Remember to hook up the phone line to the modem!

2. Install TCP/IP (usually DHCP is fine).

3. Install dial-up networking (DUN), if it is not already.

4. Configure a dial-up networking connection to the ISP (see the "Necessary Procedures" section).

At that point, you should be able to test the connection by opening a dial-up session with the ISP and then either using PING or a browser to contact machines on the Internet. You will want to know how to set up such a connection and what problems can arise with modems during the install.

Connecting to the Internet

Connecting to the Internet is simple once you get the connection configured. Simply double-click the connection, enter the password (unless you chose the Save Password button previously), and click Connect. A window will appear that allows you to follow the status of the connection). You should hear the modem dial and then connect. When it connects, the status screen will say "Verifying Username and Password" and then "Connected." Once you are connected, the status screen will go away, and you will see an icon on the Taskbar (the same icon that's on the status screen). At this point, you are connected to your ISP and, through it, to the rest of the world. You can then fire up your favorite Web browser and start surfin'.

TIP If you are configuring the system for someone who just wants to click and go, you can also right-click the Internet Explorer icon on the Desktop and use the Connection tab of the Internet Settings window to configure auto-dial. Set the connection you have created as the default and specify that the system should Always Dial My Default Connection. Any time an application needs to access the Internet, it can simply initiate the DUN connection automatically.

Installing Software for and from the Internet

When users are planning on using the Internet, the following is a list of the software they may need:

- Dial-up networking (Windows component)

- Web browser (Windows component in Windows 98 and higher). Netscape is also common, but it must be installed separately.

- FTP client (included as a command-line tool). Graphical FTP clients can be installed as well.

- E-mail client (included as Outlook Express). Other e-mail clients, of varying functionality, are available from Microsoft and other vendors.

Obtaining and installing these applications is similar to setting up any other application you might need.

Monitoring and Disconnecting from the Internet

To see information (such as speed and quantity) about the data you have transferred during your Internet session, you can double-click the connection icon in the System Tray (the lower-right portion of the screen) to bring up a status window. From this window, you can see the number of bytes sent and received, and you can disconnect from the Internet. You can also disconnect by simply right-clicking the connection icon itself and choosing Disconnect.

Necessary Procedures

Here are a few of the tasks you should be ready for concerning the Internet.

Creating a Windows 9x DUN Connection

To create a new DUN connection, open the Dial-Up Networking folder under Start ➤ Programs ➤ Accessories. This will open a window that shows all the DUN connections that are configured. You must create a new one to connect to the Internet. To do so, double-click the item in this folder called Make New Connection. From this screen, you can give the connection a name. As with other names in Windows 9x, use one that reflects what it is (in this case, a connection to the Internet). This screen will allow you to select which modem you want to use to dial this connection (if you only have one configured in Windows 9x, it will default to that one).

The next step is to enter the phone number of the system you are dialing (Figure 10.12). Simply type in the area code and phone number of your ISP and click Next to continue. When it dials, Windows 9x will automatically determine if it's a long-distance number and either add or omit the 1 plus the area code.

FIGURE 10.12: Entering the ISP's phone number

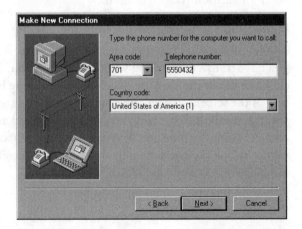

Finally, you are presented with the screen that tells you that you are finished setting up the connection. All you have to do is click the Finish button to finish creating the connection.

Configuring the Properties of a Windows 9*x* DUN Connection

Now that you have a DUN connection, you need to configure the settings specific to your Internet connection. Simply right-click the connection in the Dial-Up Networking folder. From the menu that appears, you can choose to use the connection to connect (the Connect option), or you can choose the Properties option to configure it. Because you aren't ready to connect yet, choose the Properties item from the menu.

You should now see a screen similar to the one in Figure 10.13. From this screen, you can configure the same properties you configured in the Make New Connection Wizard (i.e., telephone number, connection name, and modem). This screen has two more tabs that you can use to configure the other properties (such as protocol settings).

FIGURE 10.13: Properties of the Internet DUN connection

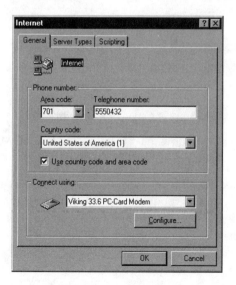

If you click the Server Types tab, you will see the settings for the type of server you are dialing in to. For an Internet connection, this is usually set to PPP: Windows 95, Windows NT 3.5, Internet (unless your ISP instructs you to use another setting). Notice also that there are check boxes for several other settings, including which protocol(s) this dial-up connection will use. TCP/IP must be selected in order for an Internet connection to work. Configure these settings according to your ISP's instructions, and click OK to accept them.

You can also configure DUN parameters in the Connect screen of the Internet connection. To access this area, double-click the connection. In this screen, you enter the username and password that your ISP has assigned you. Also, double-check the phone number you entered to make sure it's correct. Once you've finished configuring the phone number, you're ready to connect to the Internet.

TIP   If you want to save the password so you don't have to type it in every time, click the check box next to Save Password. Be careful, though. If you save your password, anyone can get onto the Internet from your computer (using your username) without having to enter a password.

Installing DUN on Windows 2000

With Windows 2000, wizards are used everywhere, including the creation of a dial-up networking connection:

1. Choose Start ➤ Settings➤ Network And Dial-up Connections.

2. In the window that appears, double-click Make New Connection.

3. If this is the first time you have created a network connection, the Location Information window will appear. You cannot escape this window without entering an area code, so enter it and click OK. You will get another location screen as well. Click OK again, and the Network Connection Wizard will appear.

4. In the Network Connection Wizard, choose Dial Up To The Internet, and the Welcome To The Internet Connection Wizard (ICW) window will appear (Figure 10.14). That makes three nested wizards. A bit extreme, no?

5. In the ICW, you will be led through a long series of choices. Click through and enter the values that apply to your Internet setup. You will be asked what type of device (modem or network) you are using, what number you need to dial, and what your username and password are. At the end, you can even set up your mail account, and the wizard will offer to connect you when you are finished.

FIGURE 10.14: The first screen of the Internet Connection Wizard

6. A new icon will appear in the Network And Dial-Up Connections window showing that your new connection has been added. You can view the status of a connection by double-clicking it or change its settings by right-clicking and selecting Properties.

Exam Essentials

Know how to configure TCP/IP through both DHCP and manual configuration.   Understanding the language of the Internet is the key to understanding the Internet itself. Both for the A+ test and for your work, this is a critical issue.

Understand what functions the Internet is commonly used for, and know about the software used in those functions.   Be able to configure and use e-mail, FTP, and HTTP. This includes knowing about available software and how to install and set options on that software.

Understand how domain names and DNS allow Internet communication.   Know how DNS works and how it interacts with TCP/IP.

Understand how to install and use Windows' dial-up networking. Be able to install dial-up networking and configure a connection to an ISP.

Key Terms and Concepts

ISP   Internet Service Providers are companies that provide access to the Internet.

Browser   Software used to access the World Wide Web, the Internet's graphical interface.

FTP   The File Transfer Protocol is used to transfer data across the Internet.

PPP   The Point-to-Point Protocol is used to allow computers to communicate over analog (standard telephone) lines.

NetBIOS   A naming structure used extensively by Microsoft networking.

Index

ribbon cable
   for floppy drives, 37–38
   for IDE drives, 332
   for SCSI devices, 59, 60, 62, 332
ribbon cartridge, 217
   and print quality, 222–223
RIMM (Rambus Inline Memory Module),
   146
ring topology, 258–259, 259, 261, 286
   specified in IEEE 802.5, 267
RJ-11 connector, 50, 52
RJ-45 connector, 51, 52
rollers
   pickup, inkjet printer, 227
   in laser printers, 201, 201, 203, 207, 209–
      210
      circumferences of, 231–232
      corona, 202, 208, 230
      developing, 207
      exit, 228
      feed, 201, 228
      fusing, 201, 203, 209
      pickup, 228
      pressure, 203, 209
      and print quality, 231
      registration, 201, 201, 207, 208
      worn, 227–228
ROM (read-only memory), 22, 28, 146, 163
root drive, 337, 339
routers, 260, 279, 284–285, 287
routing, 263
RS-232 cable, 48, 68, 274
Run command, 302

S

Safe Mode, 415, 441, 452, 455
   Windows 9x options, 407–408
   Windows 2000 options, 408–409, 442–
      443
Safe Mode Command Prompt Only option,
   408, 442
Safe Mode with Command Prompt option,
   409
Safe Mode with Networking option, 409, 442
safety issues, with PCs, 120–124
sag, power, 118, 131
SAM (Security Accounts Management) data-
   base, 313, 322, 328
SAM key, 322
Scan Disk tool, 347
SCANDISK command, 324, 347, 355
SCANREG command, 324
Scanreg tool, 347, 354

Scheduled Tasks tool, 347, 352
Scheduler service, 352
scripts, 347
SCSI bus, 58
SCSI controllers, 332–333
   IRQ address, 43
   drivers for, 447
   unsupported, 365, 383
SCSI devices, 58
   address (ID number), 59, 63, 64, 332–333
   bootable, 63, 406, 407
   cables, 49, 59, 60–62
      external, 60, 61–63, 62
      internal, 60–61, 61, 62
   configuring, 59, 63–64
   connectors, 59, 60–62
   daisy-chaining, 60, 62
   external, 61–62
   installing, 60–63
   internal, 61, 62
   terminators, 59, 61–63, 64, 65
SCSI drives, 332–333, 356
   reformatting, 88
   troubleshooting, 447–448
SCSI implementations, 59–60, 64
SDRAM (Synchronous DRAM), 145, 162
Seagate Power Quest Drive Image, 74
Search submenu, 301
SEC (Single Edge Connector), 138
secret self-test, 236
security
   for file shares, 490–492, 498–499, 499,
      501
   for printer shares, 495–496
   in Windows 9x, 313, 320–321
   in Windows 2000, 380, 381–382
Security Accounts Management (SAM) database, 313, 322, 328
SECURITY key, 322
Security log file, 453
self tests, laser printer, 235–236, 239
serial cable, 274
Serial Line Internet Protocol (SLIP), 509
serial ports, 17, 17, 49
   connectors, 49–50
   enabling/disabling, 190
   for modems, 68
serial printers, 211
servers, 246–247, 248–249, 251
   application, 246
   Compaq, 174
   dedicated, 249–250
   DHCP, 484
   DNS, 511

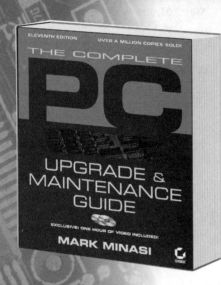